MYTHS and FACTS

A GUIDE TO THE
Arab-Israeli Conflict

By *Mitchell G. Bard*

American-**I**sraeli **C**ooperative **E**nterprise (AICE)

2810 Blaine Dr.
Chevy Chase, MD 20815

http://www.JewishVirtualLibrary.org

ISBN 0-9712945-1-8

Printed in the United States of America

American Israeli Cooperative Enterprise (AICE)
2810 Blaine Dr.
Chevy Chase, MD 20815
Tel. 301-565-3918
Fax. 301-587-9056
Email. mgbard@aol.com
http://www.JewishVirtualLibrary.org

Other studies available from AICE *(all are now available on our web site)***:**

■ **Partners for Change:** How U.S.-Israel Cooperation Can Benefit America

■ **Learning Together:** Israeli Innovations In Education That Could Benefit Americans

■ **Breakthrough Dividend:** Israeli Innovations In Biotechnology That Could Benefit Americans

■ **Experience Counts:** Innovative Programs For The Elderly In Israel That Can Benefit Americans

■ **Building Bridges:** Lessons For America From Novel Israeli Approaches To Promote Coexistence

■ **Good Medicine:** Israeli Innovations In Health Care That Could Benefit Americans

■ **Rewriting History in Textbooks**

Book Logo Design, Cover concept, Typography, Map Illustration
Graphic design and Production: *Danakama / Nick Moscovitz / NYC*

Table of Contents

TABLES

MAPS

Preface

In 1957, Si Kenen started a newsletter — *Near East Report* — to inform the public about events relating to the Middle East. Much of what he published in *NER* was current, but he also recognized the need to educate readers about the Arab-Israeli conflict and to debunk myths perpetrated by those who wished to rewrite history to suit their own purposes. Toward this end, *NER* began to publish special surveys of pertinent issues. Gradually these analyses grew to book length and were published as *Myths and Facts*.

Myths about the Middle East did not originate in the 1950's, nor have they ceased to be promulgated. The tumultuous events in the region seem to be consistently accompanied by all new distortions of the facts about the Arab-Israeli conflict. With Near East Research's permission, and by popular demand, AICE produced an updated version of this classic text online. This version has the advantage of being hyperlinked to the vast resources available in our Jewish Virtual Library and is constantly updated as new events occur.

The response to our online version was overwhelming, and people began to ask for hard copies of the text; consequently, we published this book for quick, easy reference. This is the second edition, which includes events since the tragedy of September 11. And when new issues arise, check Myths and Facts Online for the latest facts:

http://www.JewishVirtualLibrary.org

Readers familiar with the publication often note that it has gotten much larger over the years. Well, if Israel's detractors would stop propagating new myths at such a prodigious rate, it would not be necessary to respond with so many new facts. To keep the size of this edition from growing unmanageable, we have chosen to omit the texts of Israel's peace treaties with Egypt and Jordan and the agreements signed between Israel and the Palestinians. This is not because we believe they are any less important, but because the documents are available in the Jewish Virtual Library for anyone who wishes to consult them.

I would like to acknowledge the contributions of the distinguished group of past editors: Sheila Segal, Wolf Blitzer, Alan Tigay, Moshe Decter, M.J. Rosenberg, Jeff Rubin, Eric Rozenman, Lenny Davis and Joel Himelfarb. I would also like to thank Rafi Danziger, Rebecca Weiner, Isaac Wolf, David Shyovitz, Alden Oreck, Elihai Braun and Sarah Szymkowicz for their invaluable assistance in preparing this edition.

AICE is especially grateful for the financial sponsorship of the Ben and Esther Rosenbloom Foundation and the Everett Foundation.

AICE also wants to acknowledge Eli Hertz for his past work on behalf of the organization, and for being the principal sponsor of our first edition of this book.

"Truth," Lord Acton said, "is the only merit that gives dignity and worth to history." The following pages lay out the truth about the Arab-Israeli conflict. It is the best weapon we have against the purveyors of falsehood.

Mitchell G. Bard
November 2002

1. Israel's Roots

MYTH

"The Jews have no claim to the land they call Israel."

FACT

A common misperception is that all the Jews were forced into the Diaspora by the Romans after the destruction of the Second Temple in Jerusalem in the year 70 C.E.* and then, 1,800 years later, suddenly returned to Palestine demanding their country back. In reality, the Jewish people have maintained ties to their historic homeland for more than 3,700 years.

The Jewish people base their claim to the Land of Israel on at least four premises: 1) the Jewish people settled and developed the land; 2) the international community granted political sovereignty in Palestine to the Jewish people; 3) the territory was captured in defensive wars and 4) God promised the land to the patriarch Abraham.

Even after the destruction of the Second Temple in Jerusalem and the beginning of the exile, Jewish life in the Land of Israel continued and often flourished. Large communities were reestablished in Jerusalem and Tiberias by the ninth century. In the 11th century, Jewish communities grew in Rafah, Gaza, Ashkelon, Jaffa and Caesarea.

> *"Nobody does Israel any service by proclaiming its 'right to exist.' Israel's right to exist, like that of the United States, Saudi Arabia and 152 other states, is axiomatic and unreserved. Israel's legitimacy is not suspended in midair awaiting acknowledgement.... There is certainly no other state, big or small, young or old, that would consider mere recognition of its 'right to exist' a favor, or a negotiable concession."*
>
> **— Abba Eban**[1]

The Crusaders massacred many Jews during the 12th century, but the community rebounded in the next two centuries as large numbers of rabbis and Jewish pilgrims immigrated to Jerusalem and the Galilee. Prominent rabbis established communities in Safed, Jerusalem and elsewhere during the next 300 years. By the early 19th century — years before the birth of the modern Zionist movement — more than 10,000 Jews lived throughout what is today Israel.[2] The 78 years of nation-building, beginning in 1870, culminated in the reestablishment of the Jewish State.

Israel's international "birth certificate" was validated by Jewish statehood in the Land of Israel in Biblical times; uninterrupted Jewish presence from the time of Joshua onward; the Balfour Declaration of 1917; the League of Nations Mandate, which incorporated the Balfour Declaration; the United Nations partition resolution of 1947; Israel's admission to the UN in 1949; the recognition of Israel by most other states; and, most of all, the society created by Israel's people in decades of thriving, dynamic national existence.

MYTH

"Palestine was always an Arab country."

FACT

The term "Palestine" is believed to be derived from the Philistines, an Aegean people who, in the 12th Century B.C.E.*, settled along the Mediterranean coastal plain of what are now Israel and the Gaza Strip. In the second century C.E., after crushing the last Jewish revolt, the Romans first applied the name Palaestina to Judea (the southern portion of what is now called the West Bank) in an attempt to minimize Jewish identification with the Land of Israel. The Arabic word *"Filastin"* is derived from this Latin name.[3]

The Hebrews entered the Land of Israel about 1300 B.C.E., living under a tribal confederation until being united under the first monarch, King Saul. The second king, David, established Jerusalem as the capital around 1000 B.C.E. David's son, Solomon built the Temple soon thereafter and consolidated the military, administrative and religious functions of the kingdom. The nation was divided under Solomon's son, with the northern kingdom (Israel) lasting until 722 B.C.E., when the Assyrians destroyed it, and the southern kingdom (Judah) surviving until the Babylonian conquest in 586 B.C.E. The Jewish people enjoyed brief periods of sovereignty afterward before most Jews were finally driven from their homeland in 135 C.E.

Jewish independence in the Land of Israel lasted for more than 400 years. This is much longer than Americans have enjoyed independence in what has become known as the United States.[4] In fact, if not for foreign conquerors, Israel would be 3,000 years old today.

Palestine was never an exclusively Arab country, although Arabic gradually became the language of most the population after the Muslim invasions of the seventh century. No independent Arab or Palestinian state ever existed in Palestine. When the distinguished Arab-American historian, Princeton University Prof. Philip Hitti, testified against partition before the Anglo-American

---

* We use B.C.E. (Before the Common Era) and C.E. (Common Era), because they are neutral terms for the periods traditionally labeled B.C. (Before Christ) and A.D. (Anno Domini – "Year of the Lord").

Committee in 1946, he said: "There is no such thing as 'Palestine' in history, absolutely not."[5]

Prior to partition, Palestinian Arabs did not view themselves as having a separate identity. When the First Congress of Muslim-Christian Associations met in Jerusalem in February 1919 to choose Palestinian representatives for the Paris Peace Conference, the following resolution was adopted:

> We consider Palestine as part of Arab Syria, as it has never been separated from it at any time. We are connected with it by national, religious, linguistic, natural, economic and geographical bonds.[6]

In 1937, a local Arab leader, Auni Bey Abdul-Hadi, told the Peel Commission, which ultimately suggested the partition of Palestine: "There is no such country [as Palestine]! 'Palestine' is a term the Zionists invented! There is no Palestine in the Bible. Our country was for centuries part of Syria."[7]

The representative of the Arab Higher Committee to the United Nations submitted a statement to the General Assembly in May 1947 that said "Palestine was part of the Province of Syria" and that, "politically, the Arabs of Palestine were not independent in the sense of forming a separate political entity." A few years later, Ahmed Shuqeiri, later the chairman of the PLO, told the Security Council: "It is common knowledge that Palestine is nothing but southern Syria."[8]

Palestinian Arab nationalism is largely a post-World War I phenomenon that did not become a significant political movement until after the 1967 Six-Day War and Israel's capture of the West Bank.

MYTH

"The Palestinians are descendants of the Canaanites and were in Palestine long before the Jews."

FACT

Palestinian claims to be related to the Canaanites are a recent phenomenon and contrary to historical evidence. The Canaanites disappeared from the face of the earth three millennia ago, and no one knows if any of their descendants survived or, if they did, who they would be.

Sherif Hussein, the guardian of the Islamic Holy Places in Arabia, said the Palestinians' ancestors had only been in the area for 1,000 years.[9]

Even the Palestinians themselves have acknowledged their association with the region came long after the Jews. In testimony before the Anglo-American Committee in 1946, for example, they claimed a connection to Palestine of more than 1,000 years, dating back no further than the conquest of Muhammad's followers in the 7th century.[10] And that claim is also dubious. Over the last 2,000 years, there have been massive invasions that killed off most of the local people (e.g., the Crusades), migrations, the plague, and other manmade or natural disasters. The entire local population was replaced many times over. During the British mandate alone, more than 100,000 Arabs emigrated from neighboring countries and are today considered Palestinians.

By contrast, no serious historian questions the more than 3,000-year-old Jewish connection to the Land of Israel, or the modern Jewish people's relation to the ancient Hebrews.

MYTH

"The Balfour Declaration did not give Jews a right to a homeland in Palestine."

FACT

In 1917, Britain issued the Balfour Declaration:

> His Majesty's Government views with favor the establishment in Palestine of a national home for the Jewish people, and will use their best endeavors to facilitate the achievement of this object, it being clearly understood that nothing shall be done which may prejudice the civil and religious rights of existing non-Jewish communities in Palestine or the rights and political status enjoyed by Jews in any other country.

The Mandate for Palestine included the Balfour Declaration. It specifically referred to "the historical connections of the Jewish people with Palestine" and to the moral validity of "reconstituting their National Home in that country." The term "reconstituting" shows recognition of the fact that Palestine had been the Jews' home. Furthermore, the British were instructed to "use their best endeavors to facilitate" Jewish immigration, to encourage settlement on the land and to "secure" the Jewish National Home. The word "Arab" does not appear in the Mandatory award.[11]

The Mandate was formalized by the 52 governments at the League of Nations on July 24, 1922.

MYTH

"The 'traditional position' of the Arabs in Palestine was jeopardized by Jewish settlement."

FACT

For many centuries, Palestine was a sparsely populated, poorly cultivated and widely-neglected expanse of eroded hills, sandy deserts and malarial marshes. As late as 1880, the American consul in Jerusalem reported the area was continuing its historic decline. "The population and wealth of Palestine has not increased during the last forty years," he said.[12]

The Report of the Palestine Royal Commission quotes an account of the Maritime Plain in 1913:

> The road leading from Gaza to the north was only a summer track suitable for transport by camels and carts...no orange groves, orchards or vineyards were to be seen until one reached [the Jewish village of] Yabna [Yavne].... The western part, towards the sea, was almost a desert....The villages in this area were few and thinly populated. Many ruins of villages were scattered over the area, as owing to the prevalence of malaria, many villages were deserted by their inhabitants.[13]

Lewis French, the British Director of Development wrote of Palestine:

> We found it inhabited by fellahin who lived in mud hovels and suffered severely from the prevalent malaria....Large areas...were uncultivated....The fellahin, if not themselves cattle thieves, were always ready to harbor these and other criminals. The individual plots...changed hands annually. There was little public security, and the fellahin's lot was an alternation of pillage and blackmail by their neighbors, the Bedouin.[14]

Surprisingly, many people who were not sympathetic to the Zionist cause believed the Jews would improve the condition of Palestinian Arabs. For example, Dawood Barakat, editor of the Egyptian paper *Al-Ahram*, wrote:

> "It is absolutely necessary that an entente be made between the Zionists and Arabs, because the war of words can only do evil. The Zionists are necessary for the country: The money which they will bring, their knowledge and intelligence, and the industriousness which characterizes them will contribute without doubt to the regeneration of the country."[15]

Even a leading Arab nationalist believed the return of the Jews to their homeland would help resuscitate the country. According to Sherif Hussein, the guardian of the Islamic Holy Places in Arabia:

> The resources of the country are still virgin soil and will be developed by the Jewish immigrants. One of the most amazing things until recent times was that the Palestinian used to leave his country, wandering over the high seas in every direction. His native soil could not retain a hold on him, though his ancestors had lived on it for 1000 years. At the same time we have seen the Jews from foreign countries streaming to Palestine from Russia, Germany, Austria, Spain, America. The cause of causes could

not escape those who had a gift of deeper insight. They knew that the country was for its original sons *(abna'ihilasliyin),* for all their differences, a sacred and beloved homeland. The return of these exiles *(jaliya)* to their homeland will prove materially and spiritually [to be] an experimental school for their brethren who are with them in the fields, factories, trades and in all things connected with toil and labor.[16]

As Hussein foresaw, the regeneration of Palestine, and the growth of its population, came only after Jews returned in massive numbers.

> *Mark Twain, who visited Palestine in 1867, described it as: "...[a] desolate country whose soil is rich enough, but is given over wholly to weeds-a silent mournful expanse....A desolation is here that not even imagination can grace with the pomp of life and action....We never saw a human being on the whole route....There was hardly a tree or a shrub anywhere. Even the olive and the cactus, those fast friends of the worthless soil, had almost deserted the country."*[17]

MYTH

"Zionism is racism."

FACT

In 1975, the UN General Assembly adopted a resolution slandering Zionism by equating it with racism. In his spirited response to the resolution, Israel's Ambassador to the UN, Chaim Herzog noted the irony of the timing, the vote coming exactly 37 years after *Kristallnacht.*

Zionism is the national liberation movement of the Jewish people, which holds that Jews, like any other nation, are entitled to a homeland.

History has demonstrated the need to ensure Jewish security through a national homeland. Zionism recognizes that Jewishness is defined by shared origin, religion, culture and history. The realization of the Zionist dream is exemplified by more than five million Jews, from more than 100 countries, who are Israeli citizens.

Israel's Law of Return grants automatic citizenship to Jews, but non-Jews are also eligible to become citizens under naturalization procedures similar to those in other countries. Approximately 1,000,000 Muslim and Christian Arabs, Druze, Baha'is, Circassians and other ethnic groups also are represented in Israel's population. The presence in Israel of thousands of dark-skinned Jews from Ethiopia, Yemen and India is the best refutation of the calumny against Zionism. In a series of historic airlifts, labeled Moses (1984), Joshua (1985) and Solomon (1991), Israel rescued almost 42,000 members of the ancient Ethiopian Jewish community.

Zionism does not discriminate against anyone. Israel's open and democratic character, and its scrupulous protection of the religious and political rights of Christians and Muslims, rebut the charge of exclusivity. Moreover, anyone — Jew or non-Jew, Israeli, American, or Saudi, black, white, yellow or purple — can be a Zionist.

> *Writing after "Operation Moses" was revealed, William Safire noted: "...For the first time in history, thousands of black people are being brought to a country not in chains but in dignity, not as slaves but as citizens."*[18]

By contrast, the Arab states define citizenship strictly by native parentage. It is almost impossible to become a naturalized citizen in many Arab states, especially Algeria, Saudi Arabia and Kuwait. Several Arab nations have laws that facilitate the naturalization of foreign Arabs, with the specific exception of Palestinians. Jordan, on the other hand, instituted its own "law of return" in 1954, according citizenship to all former residents of Palestine, except for Jews.[19]

To single out Jewish self-determination for condemnation is itself a form of racism. When approached by a student at Harvard in 1968 who attacked Zionism, Martin Luther King responded: "When people criticize Zionists, they mean Jews. You're talking anti-Semitism."[20]

The 1975 UN resolution was part of the Soviet-Arab Cold War anti-Israel campaign. Almost all the former non-Arab supporters of the resolution have apologized and changed their positions. When the General Assembly voted to repeal the resolution in 1991, only some Arab and Muslim states, as well as Cuba, North Korea and Vietnam were opposed.

MYTH
"The delegates of the UN World Conference Against Racism agreed that Zionism is racism."

FACT
In 2001, Arab nations again were seeking to delegitimize Israel by trying to equate Zionism with racism at the UN World Conference Against Racism in Durban, South Africa. The United States joined Israel in boycotting the conference when it became clear that rather than focus on the evils of racism,

anti-Semitism and xenophobia that were supposed to be the subject of the event, the conference had turned into a forum for bashing Israel.

The United States withdrew its delegation: "to send a signal to the freedom loving nations of the world that we will not stand by, if the world tries to describe Zionism as racism. That is as wrong as wrong can be." White House Press Secretary Ari Fleischer added that "the President is proud to stand by Israel and by the Jewish community and send a signal that no group around the world will meet with international acceptance and respect if its purpose is to equate Zionism with racism."[21]

MYTH

*"The Zionists could have chosen
another country besides Palestine."*

FACT

In the late 19th century, the rise of religious and racist anti-Semitism led to a resurgence of pogroms in Russia and Eastern Europe, shattering promises of equality and tolerance. This stimulated Jewish immigration to Palestine from Europe.

Simultaneously, a wave of Jews immigrated to Palestine from Yemen, Morocco, Iraq and Turkey. These Jews were unaware of Theodor Herzl's political Zionism or of European pogroms. They were motivated by the centuries-old dream of the "Return to Zion" and a fear of intolerance. Upon hearing that the gates of Palestine were open, they braved the hardships of travel and went to the Land of Israel.

The Zionist ideal of a return to Israel has profound religious roots. Many Jewish prayers speak of Jerusalem, Zion and the Land of Israel. The injunction not to forget Jerusalem, the site of the Temple, is a major tenet of Judaism. The Hebrew language, the Torah, laws in the Talmud, the Jewish calendar and Jewish holidays and festivals all originated in Israel and revolve around its seasons and conditions. Jews pray toward Jerusalem and recite the words "next year in Jerusalem" every Passover. Jewish religion, culture and history make clear that it is only in the land of Israel that the Jewish commonwealth can be built.

In 1897, Jewish leaders formally organized the Zionist political movement, calling for the restoration of the Jewish national home in Palestine, where Jews could find sanctuary and self-determination, and work for the renascence of their civilization and culture.

MYTH

"Herzl himself proposed Uganda as the Jewish state as an alternative to Palestine."

FACT

Theodor Herzl sought support from the great powers for the creation of a Jewish homeland. He turned to Great Britain, and met with Joseph Chamberlain, the British colonial secretary and others. The British agreed, in principle, to Jewish settlement in East Africa.

At the Sixth Zionist Congress at Basle on August 26, 1903, Herzl proposed the British Uganda Program as a temporary emergency refuge for Jews in Russia in immediate danger. While Herzl made it clear that this program would not affect the ultimate aim of Zionism, a Jewish entity in the Land of Israel, the proposal aroused a storm at the Congress and nearly led to a split in the Zionist movement. The Uganda Program, which never had much support, was formally rejected by the Zionist movement at the Seventh Zionist Congress in 1905.

MYTH

"All Arabs opposed the Balfour Declaration, seeing it as a betrayal of their rights."

FACT

Emir Faisal, son of Sherif Hussein, the leader of the Arab revolt against the Turks, signed an agreement with Chaim Weizmann and other Zionist leaders during the 1919 Paris Peace Conference. It acknowledged the "racial kinship and ancient bonds existing between the Arabs and the Jewish people" and concluded that "the surest means of working out the consummation of their national aspirations is through the closest possible collaboration in the development of the Arab states and Palestine." Furthermore, the agreement looked to the fulfillment of the Balfour Declaration and called for all necessary measures "...to encourage and stimulate immigration of Jews into Palestine on a large scale, and as quickly as possible to settle Jewish immigrants upon the land through closer settlement and intensive cultivation of the soil."[22]

Faisal had conditioned his acceptance of the Balfour Declaration on the fulfillment of British wartime promises of independence to the Arabs. These were not kept.

Critics dismiss the Weizmann-Faisal agreement because it was never enacted; however, the fact that the leader of the Arab nationalist movement and the Zionist movement could reach an understanding is significant because it demonstrated that Jewish and Arab aspirations were not necessarily mutually exclusive.

MYTH

"The Zionists made no effort to compromise with the Arabs."

FACT

In 1913, the Zionist leadership recognized the desirability of reaching an agreement with the Arabs. Sami Hochberg, owner of the newspaper, *Le-Jeune-Turc,* informally represented the Zionists in a meeting with the Cairo-based Decentralization Party and the anti-Ottoman Beirut Reform Society and was able to reach an agreement. This "entente verbale" led to the adoption of a resolution assuring Jews equal rights under a decentralized government. Hochberg also secured an invitation to the First Arab Congress held in Paris in June 1913.

The Arab Congress proved to be surprisingly receptive to Zionist aspirations. Hochberg was encouraged by the Congress's favorable response to the entente verbale. Abd-ul-Hamid Yahrawi, the President of the Congress, summed up the attitude of the delegates:

> All of us, both Muslims and Christians, have the best of feelings toward the Jews. When we spoke in our resolutions about the rights and obligations of the Syrians, this covered the Jews as well. Because they are our brothers in race *and we regard them as Syrians who were forced to leave the country at one time but whose hearts always beat together with ours,* we are certain that our Jewish brothers the world over will know how to help us so that our common interests may succeed and our common country will develop both materially and morally (author's emphasis).[23]

The entente verbale Hochberg negotiated was rendered ineffectual by wartime developments. The outspoken Arab opposition to the Balfour Declaration convinced the Zionist leadership of the need to make a more concerted effort to reach an understanding with the Arabs.

Chaim Weizmann considered the task important enough to lead a Zionist Commission to Palestine to explain the movement's aims to the Arabs. Weizmann went first to Cairo in March 1918 and met with Said Shukeir, Dr. Faris Nimr and Suleiman Bey Nassif (Syrian Arab nationalists who had been chosen by the British as representatives). He stressed the desire to live in harmony with the Arabs in a British Palestine.

Weizmann's diplomacy was successful. Nassif said "there was room in Palestine for another million inhabitants without affecting the position of those already there."[24] Dr. Nimr disseminated information through his Cairo newspaper to dispel the Arab public's misconceptions about Zionist aims.[25]

In 1921, Winston Churchill tried to arrange a meeting between Palestinians and Zionists. On November 29, 1921, the two sides met, but no progress was made because the Arabs insisted that the Balfour Declaration be abrogated.[26]

Weizmann led a group of Zionists that met with Syrian nationalist Riad al-Sulh in 1921. The Zionists agreed to support Arab nationalist aspirations and Sulh said he was willing to recognize the Jewish National Home. The talks resumed a year later and raised hopes for an agreement. In May 1923, however, Sulh's efforts to convince Palestinian Arab leaders that Zionism was an accomplished fact were rejected.[27]

Over the next 25 years, Zionist leaders inside and outside Palestine would try repeatedly to negotiate with the Arabs. Similarly, Israeli leaders since 1948 have sought peace treaties with the Arab states, but Egypt and Jordan are the only nations that have signed them.

MYTH

"The Zionists were colonialist tools of Western imperialism."

FACT

"Colonialism means living by exploiting others," Yehoshofat Harkabi has written. "But what could be further from colonialism than the idealism of city-dwelling Jews who strive to become farmers and laborers and to live by their own work?"[28]

Moreover, as British historian Paul Johnson noted, Zionists were hardly tools of imperialists given the powers' general opposition to their cause. "Everywhere in the West, the foreign offices, defense ministries and big business were against the Zionists."[29]

> *"Our settlers do not come here as do the colonists from the Occident to have natives do their work for them; they themselves set their shoulders to the plow and they spend their strength and their blood to make the land fruitful. But it is not only for ourselves that we desire its fertility. The Jewish farmers have begun to teach their brothers, the Arab farmers, to cultivate the land more intensively; we desire to teach them further: together with them we want to cultivate the land -- to 'serve' it, as the Hebrew has it. The more fertile this soil becomes, the more space there will be for us and for them. We have no desire to dispossess them: we want to live with them. We do not want to dominate them: we want to serve with them....."*
>
> **— Martin Buber**[30]

Emir Faisal also saw the Zionist movement as a companion to the Arab nationalist movement, fighting against imperialism, as he explained in a letter to Harvard law professor and future Supreme Court Justice Felix Frankfurter on March 3, 1919, one day after Chaim Weizmann presented the Zionist case to the Paris conference. Faisal wrote:

> The Arabs, especially the educated among us, look with deepest sympathy on the Zionist movement....We will wish the Jews a hearty welcome home....We are working together for a reformed and revised Near East and our two movements complete one another. *The Jewish movement is nationalist and not imperialist.* And there is room in Syria for us both. Indeed, I think that neither can be a real success without the other (emphasis added).[31]

MYTH

"The British promised the Arabs independence in Palestine in the Hussein-MacMahon Correspondence."

FACT

The central figure in the Arab nationalist movement at the time of World War I was Hussein ibn 'Ali, who was appointed by the Turkish Committee of Union and Progress to the position of Sherif of Mecca in 1908. As Sherif, Hussein was responsible for the custody of Islam's shrines in the Hejaz and, consequently, was recognized as one of the Muslims' spiritual leaders.

In July 1915, Hussein sent a letter to Sir Henry MacMahon, the High Commissioner for Egypt, informing him of the terms for Arab participation in the war against the Turks.

The letters between Hussein and MacMahon that followed outlined the areas that Britain was prepared to cede to the Arabs. The Hussein-MacMahon correspondence conspicuously fails to mention Palestine. The British argued the omission had been intentional, thereby justifying their refusal to grant the Arabs independence in Palestine after the war.[32] MacMahon explained:

> I feel it my duty to state, and I do so definitely and emphatically, that it was not intended by me in giving this pledge to King Hussein to include Palestine in the area in which Arab independence was promised. I also had every reason to believe at the time that the fact that Palestine was not included in my pledge was well understood by King Hussein.[33]

Nevertheless, the Arabs held then, as now, that the letters constituted a promise of independence for the Arabs.

Notes

[1]   *New York Times,* (November 18, 1981).

[2]   Dan Bahat, ed. *Twenty Centuries of Jewish Life in the Holy Land,* (Jerusalem: The Israel Economist, 1976), pp. 61-63.

[3]   Yehoshua Porath, *The Emergence of the Palestinian-Arab National Movement, 1918-1929,*

(London: Frank Cass, 1974), p. 4.

4 Max Dimont, *Jews, God and History,* (NY: Signet, 1962), pp. 49-53.

5 *Jerusalem Post,* (November 2, 1991).

6 Yehoshua Porath, *Palestinian Arab National Movement: From Riots to Rebellion: 1929-1939,* vol. 2, (London: Frank Cass and Co., Ltd., 1977), pp. 81-82.

7 *Jerusalem Post,* (November 2, 1991).

8 Avner Yaniv, PLO, (Jerusalem: Israel Universities Study Group of Middle Eastern Affairs, August 1974), p. 5.

9 *Al-Qibla,* (March 23, 1918), quoted in Samuel Katz, *Battleground-Fact and Fantasy in Palestine,* (NY: Bantam Books, 1977), p. 128.

10 British Government, *Report of the Anglo-American Committee of Enquiry,* 1946, Part VI, (April 20, 1946).

11 Howard Sachar, *A History of Israel: From the Rise of Zionism to Our Time,* (NY: Alfred A. Knopf, 1979), p. 129.

12 Halpern, p. 108.

13 Palestine Royal Commission Report, p. 233.

14 Palestine Royal Commission Report, pp. 259-260.

15 Neville Mandel, "Attempts at an Arab-Zionist Entente: 1913-1914," *Middle Eastern Studies,* (April 1965), p. 243.

16 *Al-Qibla,* (March 23, 1918), quoted in Samuel Katz, *Battleground-Fact and Fantasy in Palestine,* (NY: Bantam Books, 1977), p. 128.

17 Mark Twain, *The Innocents Abroad,* (London, 1881).

18 *New York Times,* (January 7, 1985).

19 Jordanian Nationality Law, Article 3(3) of Law No. 6 of 1954, Official Gazette, No. 1171, February 16, 1954.

20 Seymour Martin Lipset, "The Socialism of Fools-The Left, the Jews and Israel," *Encounter,* (December 1969), p. 24.

21 White House briefing regarding U.S. threat to boycott the UN Conference on racism, (July 27, 2001).

22 Chaim Weizmann, *Trial and Error,* (NY: Schocken Books, 1966), pp. 246-247; Howard Sachar, *A History of Israel: From the Rise of Zionism to Our Time,* (NY: Alfred A. Knopf, 1979), p. 121.

23 Aharon Cohen, *Israel and the Arab World,* (NY: Funk and Wagnalls, 1970), p. 97.

24 Jon Kimche, *There Could Have Been Peace: The Untold Story of Why We Failed With Palestine and Again With Israel,* (England: Dial Press, 1973), pp. 136-137.

25 Aharon Cohen, *Israel and the Arab World,* (NY: Funk and Wagnalls, 1970), p. 71-73.

26 Yehoshua Porath, *The Emergence of the Palestinian-Arab National Movement, 1918-1929,* (London: Frank Cass, 1974), pp. 65-67.

27 Yehoshua Porath, *The Emergence of the Palestinian-Arab National Movement, 1918-1929,* (London: Frank Cass, 1974), pp. 112-114.

28 Yehoshofat Harkabi, *Palestinians And Israel,* (Jerusalem: Keter, 1974), p. 6.

29 Paul Johnson, *Modern Times: The World from the Twenties to the Nineties,* (NY: Harper & Row, 1983), p. 485.

30 From an open letter from Martin Buber to Mahatma Gandhi in 1939, quoted in Arthur Hertzberg, *The Zionist Idea,* (PA: Jewish Publications Society, 1997), p. 464.

31 Samuel Katz, *Battleground-Fact and Fantasy in Palestine,* (NY: Bantam Books, 1977), p. 55.

32 George Kirk, *A Short History of the Middle East,* (NY: Frederick Praeger Publishers, 1964), p. 314.

33 *London Times,* (July 23, 1937).

2. The Mandatory Period

MYTH

"The British helped the Jews displace the native Arab population of Palestine."

FACT

Herbert Samuel, a British Jew who served as the first High Commissioner of Palestine, placed restrictions on Jewish immigration "in the 'interests of the present population' and the ' absorptive capacity' of the country."[1] The influx of Jewish settlers was said to be forcing the Arab *fellahin* (native peasants) from their land. This was at a time when less than a million people lived in an area that now supports more than nine million.

The British actually limited the absorptive capacity of Palestine by partitioning the country.

In 1921, Colonial Secretary Winston Churchill severed nearly four-fifths of Palestine-some 35,000 square miles-to create a brand new Arab entity, Transjordan. As a consolation prize for the Hejaz and Arabia (which are both now Saudi Arabia) going to the Saud family, Churchill rewarded Sherif Hussein's son Abdullah for his contribution to the war against Turkey by installing him as Transjordan's emir.

The British went further and placed restrictions on Jewish land purchases in what remained of Palestine, contradicting the provision of the Mandate (Article 6) stating that "the Administration of Palestine...shall encourage, in cooperation with the Jewish Agency...close settlement by Jews on the land, including State lands and waste lands not acquired for public purposes." By 1949, the British had allotted 87,500 acres of the 187,500 acres of cultivable land to Arabs and only 4,250 acres to Jews.[2]

Ultimately, the British admitted the argument about the absorptive capacity of the country was specious. The Peel Commission said: "The heavy immigration in the years 1933-36 would seem to show that the Jews have been able to enlarge the absorptive capacity of the country for Jews."[3]

MYTH

"The British allowed Jews to flood Palestine while Arab immigration was tightly controlled."

FACT

The British response to Jewish immigration set a precedent of appeasing the Arabs, which was followed for the duration of the Mandate. The British placed restrictions on Jewish immigration while allowing Arabs to enter the

Map 1 Great Britain's Division of the Mandated Area
1921-1923

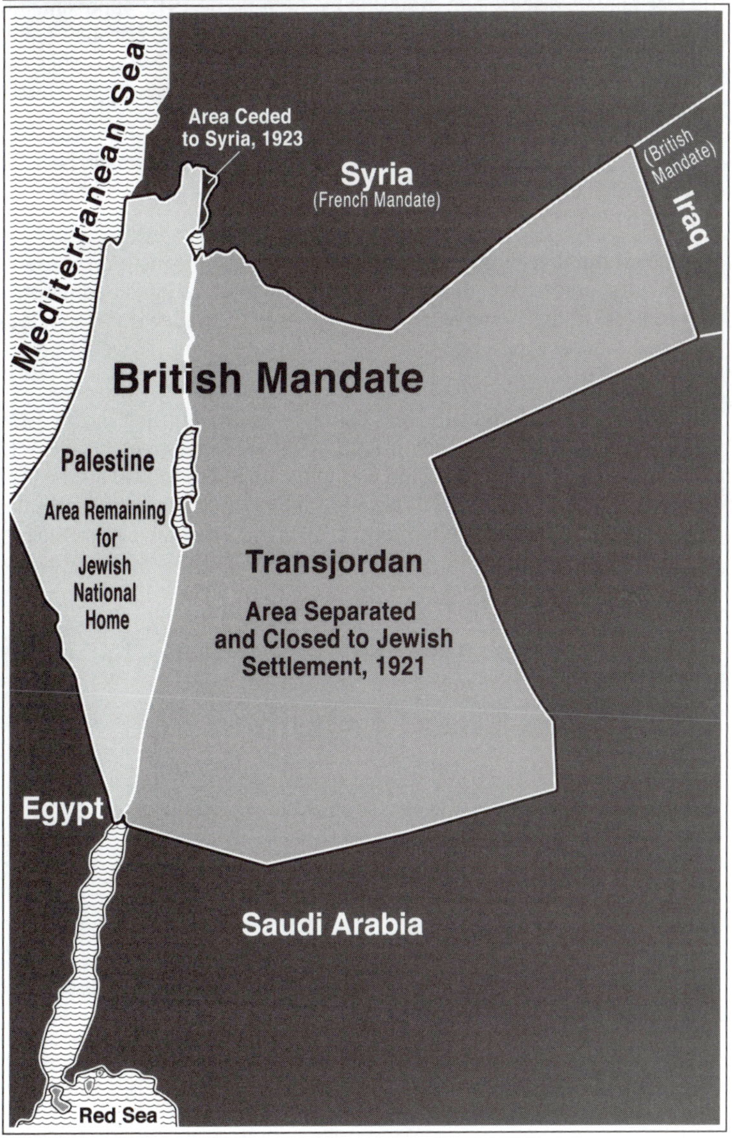

Mediterranean Sea

Area Ceded
to Syria, 1923

Syria
(French Mandate)

(British
Mandate)

Iraq

British Mandate

Palestine

Area Remaining
for
Jewish
National
Home

Transjordan

**Area Separated
and Closed to Jewish
Settlement, 1921**

Egypt

Saudi Arabia

Red Sea

country freely. Apparently, London did not feel that a flood of Arab immigrants would affect the country's absorptive capacity.

During World War I, the Jewish population in Palestine declined because of the war, famine, disease and expulsion by the Turks. In 1915, approximately 83,000 Jews lived in Palestine among 590,000 Muslim and Christian Arabs. According to the 1922 census, the Jewish population was 84,000, while the Arabs numbered 643,000.[4] Thus, the Arab population grew exponentially while that of the Jews stagnated.

In the mid-1920s, Jewish immigration to Palestine increased primarily because of anti-Jewish economic legislation in Poland and Washington's imposition of restrictive quotas.[5]

The record number of immigrants in 1935 (see table) was a response to the growing persecution of Jews in Nazi Germany. The British administration considered this number too large, however, so the Jewish Agency was informed that less than one-third of the quota it asked for would be approved in 1936.[6]

The British gave in further to Arab demands by announcing in the 1939 White Paper that an independent Arab state would be created within 10 years, and that Jewish immigration was to be limited to 75,000 for the next five years, after which it was to cease altogether. It also forbade land sales to Jews in 95 percent of the territory of Palestine. The Arabs, nevertheless, rejected the proposal.

Jewish Immigrants to Palestine[7]

Year	Number	Year	Number
1919	1,806	1931	4,075
1920	8,223	1932	12,533
1921	8,294	1933	37,337
1922	8,685	1934	45,267
1923	8,175	1935	66,472
1924	13,892	1936	29,595
1925	34,386	1937	10,629
1926	13,855	1938	14,675
1927	3,034	1939	31,195
1928	2,178	1940	10,643
1929	5,249	1941	4,592
1930	4,944		

By contrast, throughout the Mandatory period, Arab immigration was unrestricted. In 1930, the Hope Simpson Commission, sent from London to investigate the 1929 Arab riots, said the British practice of ignoring the uncontrolled illegal Arab immigration from Egypt, Transjordan and Syria had the effect of displacing the prospective Jewish immigrants.[8]

The British Governor of the Sinai from 1922-36 observed: "This illegal immigration was not only going on from the Sinai, but also from Transjordan and Syria, and it is very difficult to make a case out for the misery of the Arabs if at the same time their compatriots from adjoining states could not be kept from going in to share that misery."[9]

The Peel Commission reported in 1937 that the "shortfall of land is...due less to the amount of land acquired by Jews than to the increase in the Arab population."[10]

MYTH

"The British changed their policy after World War II to allow the survivors of the Holocaust to settle in Palestine."

FACT

The gates of Palestine remained closed for the duration of the war, stranding hundreds of thousands of Jews in Europe, many of whom became victims of Hitler's "Final Solution." After the war, the British refused to allow the survivors of the Nazi nightmare to find sanctuary in Palestine. On June 6, 1946, President Truman urged the British government to relieve the suffering of the Jews confined to displaced persons camps in Europe by immediately accepting 100,000 Jewish immigrants. Britain's Foreign Minister, Ernest Bevin, replied sarcastically that the United States wanted displaced Jews to immigrate to Palestine "because they did not want too many of them in New York."[11]

Some Jews were able to reach Palestine, many by way of dilapidated ships that members of the Jewish resistance organizations used to smuggle them in. Between August 1945 and the establishment of the State of Israel in May 1948, 65 illegal immigrant ships, carrying 69,878 people, arrived from European shores. In August 1946, however, the British began to intern those they caught in camps in Cyprus. Approximately 50,000 people were detained in the camps, 28,000 of whom were still imprisoned when Israel declared independence.[12]

MYTH

"As the Jewish population in Palestine grew, the plight of the Palestinian Arabs worsened."

FACT

The Jewish population increased by 470,000 between World War I and World War II, while the non-Jewish population rose by 588,000.[13] In fact, the permanent Arab population increased 120 percent between 1922 and 1947.[14] This rapid growth was a result of several factors. One was immigration from neighboring states — constituting 37 percent of the total immigration to pre-state Israel — by Arabs who wanted to take advantage of the higher standard of living the Jews had made possible.[15] The Arab population also grew because of the improved living conditions created by the Jews as they drained malarial swamps and brought improved sanitation and health care to the region. Thus, for example, the Muslim infant mortality rate fell from 201 per thousand in 1925 to 94 per thousand in 1945 and life expectancy rose from 37 years in 1926 to 49 in 1943.[16]

The Arab population increased the most in cities where large Jewish populations had created new economic opportunities. From 1922-1947, the non-Jewish population increased 290 percent in Haifa, 131 percent in Jerusalem and 158 percent in Jaffa. The growth in Arab towns was more modest: 42 percent in Nablus, 78 percent in Jenin and 37 percent in Bethlehem.[17]

MYTH
"Jews stole Arab land."

FACT

Despite the growth in their population, the Arabs continued to assert they were being displaced. The truth is that from the beginning of World War I, part of Palestine's land was owned by absentee landlords who lived in Cairo, Damascus and Beirut. About 80 percent of the Palestinian Arabs were debt-ridden peasants, semi-nomads and Bedouins.[18]

Jews actually went out of their way to avoid purchasing land in areas where Arabs might be displaced. They sought land that was largely uncultivated, swampy, cheap and, most important, without tenants. In 1920, Labor Zionist leader David Ben-Gurion expressed his concern about the Arab fellahin, whom he viewed as "the most important asset of the native population." Ben-Gurion said "under no circumstances must we touch land belonging to fellahs or worked by them." He advocated helping liberate them from their oppressors. "Only if a fellah leaves his place of settlement," Ben-Gurion added, "should we offer to buy his land, at an appropriate price."[19]

It was only after the Jews had bought all of the available uncultivated land that they began to purchase cultivated land. Many Arabs were willing to sell because of the migration to coastal towns and because they needed money to invest in the citrus industry.[20]

When John Hope Simpson arrived in Palestine in May 1930, he observed: "They [Jews] paid high prices for the land, and in addition they paid to certain of the occupants of those lands a considerable amount of money which they were not legally bound to pay."[21]

In 1931, Lewis French conducted a survey of landlessness and eventually offered new plots to any Arabs who had been "dispossessed." British officials received more than 3,000 applications, of which 80 percent were ruled invalid by the Government's legal adviser because the applicants were not landless Arabs. This left only about 600 landless Arabs, 100 of whom accepted the Government land offer.[22]

In April 1936, a new outbreak of Arab attacks on Jews was instigated by a Syrian guerrilla named Fawzi al-Qawukji, the commander of the Arab Liberation Army. By November, when the British finally sent a new commission headed by Lord Peel to investigate, 89 Jews had been killed and more than 300 wounded.[23]

The Peel Commission's report found that Arab complaints about Jewish land acquisition were baseless. It pointed out that "much of the land now carrying orange groves was sand dunes or swamp and uncultivated when it was purchased....there was at the time of the earlier sales little evidence that the owners possessed either the resources or training needed to develop the land."[24] Moreover, the Commission found the shortage was "due less to the amount of land acquired by Jews than to the increase in the Arab population." The report concluded that the presence of Jews in Palestine, along with the work of the British Administration, had resulted in higher wages, an improved standard of living and ample employment opportunities.[25]

In his memoirs, Transjordan's King Abdullah wrote:

> It is made quite clear to all, both by the map drawn up by the Simpson Commission and by another compiled by the Peel Commission, that the Arabs are as prodigal in selling their land as they are in useless wailing and weeping (emphasis in the original).[26]

Even at the height of the Arab revolt in 1938, the British High Commissioner to Palestine believed the Arab landowners were complaining about sales to Jews to drive up prices for lands they wished to sell. Many Arab landowners had been so terrorized by Arab rebels they decided to leave Palestine and sell their property to the Jews.[27]

The Jews were paying exorbitant prices to wealthy landowners for small tracts of arid land. "In 1944, Jews paid between $1,000 and $1,100 per acre in Palestine, mostly for arid or semiarid land; in the same year, rich black soil in Iowa was selling for about $110 per acre."[28]

By 1947, Jewish holdings in Palestine amounted to about 463,000 acres. Approximately 45,000 of these acres were acquired from the Mandatory Government; 30,000 were bought from various churches and 387,500 were purchased from Arabs. Analyses of land purchases from 1880 to 1948 show that 73 percent of Jewish plots were purchased from large landowners, not poor *fellahin*.[29] Those who sold land included the mayors of Gaza, Jerusalem and Jaffa. As'ad el-Shuqeiri, a Muslim religious scholar and father of

PLO chairman Ahmed Shuqeiri, took Jewish money for his land. Even King Abdullah leased land to the Jews. In fact, many leaders of the Arab nationalist movement, including members of the Muslim Supreme Council, sold land to Jews.[30]

MYTH

"The British helped the Palestinians to live peacefully with the Jews."

FACT

In 1921, Haj Amin el-Husseini first began to organize *fedayeen* ("one who sacrifices himself") to terrorize Jews. Haj Amin hoped to duplicate the success of Kemal Atatürk in Turkey by driving the Jews out of Palestine just as Kemal had driven the invading Greeks from his country.[31] Arab radicals were able to gain influence because the British Administration was unwilling to take effective action against them until they finally revolted against British rule.

Colonel Richard Meinertzhagen, former head of British military intelligence in Cairo, and later Chief Political Officer for Palestine and Syria, wrote in his diary that British officials "incline towards the exclusion of Zionism in Palestine." In fact, the British encouraged the Palestinians to attack the Jews. According to Meinertzhagen, Col. Waters Taylor (financial adviser to the Military Administration in Palestine 1919-23) met with Haj Amin a few days before Easter, in 1920, and told him "he had a great opportunity at Easter to show the world...that Zionism was unpopular not only with the Palestine Administration but in Whitehall and if disturbances of sufficient violence occurred in Jerusalem at Easter, both General Bols [Chief Administrator in Palestine, 1919-20] and General Allenby [Commander of Egyptian Force, 1917-19, then High Commissioner of Egypt] would advocate the abandonment of the Jewish Home. Waters-Taylor explained that freedom could only be attained through violence."[32]

Haj Amin took the Colonel's advice and instigated a riot. The British withdrew their troops and the Jewish police from Jerusalem, allowing the Arab mob to attack Jews and loot their shops. Because of Haj Amin's overt role in instigating the pogrom, the British decided to arrest him. Haj Amin escaped, however, and was sentenced to 10 years imprisonment in absentia.

A year later, some British Arabists convinced High Commissioner Herbert Samuel to pardon Haj Amin and to appoint him Mufti. By contrast, Vladimir Jabotinsky and several of his followers, who had formed a Jewish defense organization during the unrest, were sentenced to 15 years' imprisonment.[33]

Samuel met with Haj Amin on April 11, 1921, and was assured "that the influences of his family and himself would be devoted to tranquility." Three weeks later, riots in Jaffa and elsewhere left 43 Jews dead.[34]

Haj Amin consolidated his power and took control of all Muslim religious funds in Palestine. He used his authority to gain control over the mosques, the schools and the courts. No Arab could reach an influential position without being loyal to the Mufti. His power was so absolute "no Muslim in Palestine could be born or die without being beholden to Haj Amin."[35] The Mufti's henchmen also insured he would have no opposition by systematically killing Palestinians from rival clans who were discussing cooperation with the Jews.

As the spokesman for Palestinian Arabs, Haj Amin did not ask that Britain grant them independence. On the contrary, in a letter to Churchill in 1921, he demanded that Palestine be reunited with Syria and Transjordan.[36]

The Arabs found rioting to be an effective political tool because of the lax British attitude and response toward violence against Jews. In handling each riot, the British did everything in their power to prevent Jews from protecting themselves, but made little or no effort to prevent the Arabs from attacking them. After each outbreak, a British commission of inquiry would try to establish the cause of the violence. The conclusion was always the same: the Arabs were afraid of being displaced by Jews. To stop the rioting, the commissions would recommend that restrictions be placed on Jewish immigration. Thus, the Arabs came to recognize that they could always stop the influx of Jews by staging a riot.

This cycle began after a series of riots in May 1921. After failing to protect the Jewish community from Arab mobs, the British appointed the Haycraft Commission to investigate the cause of the violence. Although the panel concluded the Arabs had been the aggressors, it rationalized the cause of the attack: "The fundamental cause of the riots was a feeling among the Arabs of discontent with, and hostility to, the Jews, due to political and economic causes, and connected with Jewish immigration, and with their conception of Zionist policy...."[37] One consequence of the violence was the institution of a temporary ban on Jewish immigration.

The Arab fear of being "displaced" or "dominated" was used as an excuse for their merciless attacks on peaceful Jewish settlers. Note, too, that these riots were not inspired by nationalistic fervor — nationalists would have rebelled against their British overlords — they were motivated by racial strife and misunderstanding.

In 1929, Arab provocateurs succeeded in convincing the masses that the Jews had designs on the Temple Mount (a tactic that would be repeated on numerous occasions, the most recent of which was in 2000 after the visit of Ariel Sharon). A Jewish religious observance at the Western Wall, which forms a part of the Temple Mount, served as a catalyst for rioting by Arabs against Jews, which spilled out of Jerusalem into other villages and towns, including Safed and Hebron.

Again, the British Administration made no effort to prevent the violence and, after it began, the British did nothing to protect the Jewish population. After six days of mayhem, the British finally brought troops in to quell the disturbance. By this time, virtually the entire Jewish population of Hebron had fled or been killed. In all, 133 Jews were killed and 399 wounded in the pogroms.[38]

After the riots were over, the British ordered an investigation, which resulted in the Passfield White Paper. It said the "immigration, land purchase and settlement policies of the Zionist Organization were already, or were likely to become, prejudicial to Arab interests. It understood the Mandatory's obligation to the non-Jewish community to mean that Palestine's resources must be primarily reserved for the growing Arab economy...."[39] This, of course, meant it was necessary to place restrictions not only on Jewish immigration but on land purchases.

MYTH
"The Mufti was not anti-Semitic."

FACT
In 1941, Haj Amin al-Husseini fled to Germany and met with Adolf Hitler, Heinrich Himmler, Joachim Von Ribbentrop and other Nazi leaders. He wanted to persuade them to extend the Nazis' anti-Jewish program to the Arab world.

The Mufti sent Hitler 15 drafts of declarations he wanted Germany and Italy to make concerning the Middle East. One called on the two countries to declare the illegality of the Jewish home in Palestine. Furthermore, "they accord to Palestine and to other Arab countries the right to solve the problem of the Jewish elements in Palestine and other Arab countries, in accordance with the interest of the Arabs and, by the same method, that the question is now being settled in the Axis countries."[40]

In November 1941, the Mufti met with Hitler, who told him the Jews were his foremost enemy. The Nazi dictator rebuffed the Mufti's requests for a declaration in support of the Arabs, however, telling him the time was not right. The Mufti offered Hitler his "thanks for the sympathy which he had always shown for the Arab and especially Palestinian cause, and to which he had given clear expression in his public speeches....The Arabs were Germany's natural friends because they had the same enemies as had Germany, namely....the Jews...." Hitler replied:

Germany stood for uncompromising war against the Jews. That naturally included active opposition to the Jewish national home in Palestine....Germany would furnish positive and practical aid to the Arabs involved in the same struggle....Germany's objective [is]...solely the destruction of the Jewish element residing in the Arab sphere....In that hour the Mufti would be the most authoritative spokesman for the Arab world. The Mufti thanked Hitler profusely.[41]

In 1945, Yugoslavia sought to indict the Mufti as a war criminal for his role in recruiting 20,000 Muslim volunteers for the SS, who participated in the killing of Jews in Croatia and Hungary. He escaped from French detention in 1946, however, and continued his fight against the Jews from Cairo and later Beirut. He died in 1974.

MYTH

"The Irgun bombed the King David Hotel as part of a terror campaign against civilians."

FACT

The King David Hotel was the site of the British military command and the British Criminal Investigation Division. The Irgun chose it as a target after British troops invaded the Jewish Agency June 29, 1946, and confiscated large quantities of documents. At about the same time, more than 2,500 Jews from all over Palestine were placed under arrest. The information about Jewish Agency operations, including intelligence activities in Arab countries, was taken to the King David Hotel.

A week later, news of a massacre of 40 Jews in a pogrom in Poland reminded the Jews of Palestine how Britain's restrictive immigration policy had condemned thousands to death.

Irgun leader Menachem Begin stressed his desire to avoid civilian casualties and said three telephone calls were placed, one to the hotel, another to the French Consulate, and a third to the *Palestine Post*, warning that explosives in the King David Hotel would soon be detonated.

On July 22, 1946, the calls were made. The call into the hotel was apparently received and ignored. Begin quotes one British official who supposedly refused to evacuate the building, saying: "We don't take orders from the Jews."[42] As a result, when the bombs exploded, the casualty toll was high: a total of 91 killed and 45 injured. Among the casualties were 15 Jews. Few people in the hotel proper were injured by the blast.[43]

In contrast to Arab attacks against Jews, which were widely hailed by Arab leaders as heroic actions, the Jewish National Council denounced the bombing of the King David.[44]

For decades the British denied they had been warned. In 1979, however, a member of the British Parliament introduced evidence that the Irgun had indeed issued the warning. He offered the testimony of a British officer who heard other officers in the King David Hotel bar joking about a Zionist threat to the headquarters. The officer who overheard the conversation immediately left the hotel and survived.[45]

Notes

[1] Aharon Cohen, *Israel and the Arab World*, (NY: Funk and Wagnalls, 1970), p. 172; Howard Sachar, *A History of Israel: From the Rise of Zionism to Our Time*, (NY: Alfred A. Knopf, 1979), p. 146.

[2] Moshe Auman, "Land Ownership in Palestine 1880-1948," in Michael Curtis, et al., *The Palestinians*, (NJ: Transaction Books, 1975), p. 25.

[3] *Palestine Royal Commission Report* (the Peel Report), (London: 1937), p. 300.[Henceforth Palestine Royal Commission Report].

[4] Arieh Avneri, *The Claim of Dispossession*, (Tel Aviv: Hidekel Press, 1984), p. 28; Yehoshua Porath, *The Emergence of the Palestinian-Arab National Movement*, 1918-1929, (London: Frank Cass, 1974), pp. 17-18.

[5] Porath (1974), p. 18.

[6] Cohen, p. 53.

[7] Yehoshua Porath, *Palestinian Arab National Movement: From Riots to Rebellion: 1929-1939*, vol. 2, (London: Frank Cass and Co., Ltd., 1977), pp. 17-18, 39.

[8] John Hope Simpson, *Palestine: Report on Immigration, Land Settlement and Development*, (London, 1930), p. 126.

[9] *Palestine Royal Commission Report*, p. 291.

[10] *Palestine Royal Commission Report*, p. 242.

[11] George Lenczowski, *American Presidents and the Middle East*, (NC: Duke University Press, 1990), p. 23.

[12] Cohen p. 174.

[13] Dov Friedlander and Calvin Goldscheider, *The Population of Israel*, (NY: Columbia Press, 1979), p. 30.

[14] Avneri, p. 254.

[15] Curtis, p. 38.

[16] Avneri, p. 264; Cohen p. 60.

[17] Avneri, pp. 254-55.

[18] Moshe Aumann, *Land Ownership in Palestine 1880-1948*, (Jerusalem: Academic Committee on the Middle East, 1976), p. 5.

[19] Shabtai Teveth, *Ben-Gurion and the Palestinian Arabs: From Peace to War*, (London: Oxford University Press, 1985), p. 32.

[20] Porath, pp. 80, 84.

[21] Hope Simpson Report, p. 51.

[22] Avneri, pp. 149-158; Cohen, p. 37; based on the Report on Agricultural Development and Land Settlement in Palestine by Lewis French, (December 1931, Supplementary; Report, April 1932) and material submitted to the Palestine Royal Commission.

[23] Netanel Lorch, *One Long War*, (Jerusalem: Keter, 1976), p. 27; Sachar, p. 201.

[24] Palestine Royal Commission Report (1937), p. 242.

[25] Palestine Royal Commission (1937), pp. 241-242.

[26] King Abdallah, *My Memoirs Completed*, (London, Longman Group, Ltd., 1978), pp. 88-89.

[27] Porath (77), pp. 86-87.

[28] Aumann, p. 13.

[29] Abraham Granott, *The Land System in Palestine*, (London, Eyre and Spottiswoode, 1952), p. 278.

[30] Avneri, pp. 179-180, 224-225, 232-234; Porath (77), pp. 72-73.

[31] Jon Kimche, *There Could Have Been Peace: The Untold Story of Why We Failed With Palestine and Again With Israel*, (England: Dial Press, 1973), p. 189.

[32] Richard Meinertzhagen, *Middle East Diary 1917-1956*, (London: The Cresset Press, 1959), pp. 49, 82, 97.

[33] Samuel Katz, *Battleground-Fact and Fantasy in Palestine*, (NY: Bantam Books, 1977), pp. 63-65; Howard Sachar, *A History of Israel: From the Rise of Zionism to Our Time*, (NY: Alfred A. Knopf, 1979), p. 97.

[34] Paul Johnson, *Modern Times: The World from the Twenties to the Nineties*, (NY: Harper & Row, 1983), p. 438.

[35] Larry Collins and Dominique Lapierre, *O Jerusalem!*, (NY: Simon and Schuster, 1972), p. 52.

[36] Kimche, p. 211.

[37] Ben Halpern, *The Idea of a Jewish State*, (MA: Harvard University Press, 1969), p. 323.

[38] Sachar, p. 174.

[39] Halpern, p. 201.

[40] "Grand Mufti Plotted To Do Away With All Jews In Mideast," *Response*, (Fall 1991), pp. 2-3.

[41] Record of the Conversation Between the Fuhrer and the Grand Mufti of Jerusalem on November 28, 1941, in the Presence of Reich Foreign Minister and Minister Grobba in Berlin, *Documents on German Foreign Policy, 1918-1945*, Series D, Vol. XIII, London, 1964, p. 881ff in Walter Lacquer and Barry Rubin, *The Israel-Arab Reader,* (NY: Penguin Books, 2001), pp. 51-55.

[42] Menachem Begin, *The Revolt*, (NY: Nash Publishing, 1977), p. 224.

[43] J. Bowyer Bell, *Terror Out Of Zion,* (NY: St. Martin's Press), p. 172.

[44] Anne Sinai and I. Robert Sinai, *Israel and the Arabs: Prelude to the Jewish State*, (NY: Facts on File, 1972), p. 83.

[45] Benjamin Netanyahu, ed., *"International Terrorism: Challenge And Response,"* Proceedings of the Jerusalem Conference on International Terrorism, July 2-5, 1979, (Jerusalem: The Jonathan Institute, 1980), p. 4.

3. Partition

MYTH

"The United Nations unjustly partitioned Palestine."

FACT

As World War II ended, the magnitude of the Holocaust became known. This accelerated demands for a resolution to the question of Palestine so the survivors of Hitler's "Final Solution" might find sanctuary in a homeland of their own.

The British tried to work out an agreement acceptable to both Arabs and Jews, but their insistence on the former's approval guaranteed failure because the Arabs would not make any concessions. They subsequently turned the issue over to the UN in February 1947.

The UN established a Special Commission on Palestine (UNSCOP) to devise a solution. Delegates from 11 nations went to the area and found what had long been apparent: The conflicting national aspirations of Jews and Arabs could not be reconciled.

The contrasting attitudes of the two groups "could not fail to give the impression that the Jews were imbued with the sense of right and were prepared to plead their case before any unbiased tribunal, while the Arabs felt unsure of the justice of their cause, or were afraid to bow to the judgment of the nations."[1]

Although most of the Commission's members acknowledged the need to find a compromise solution, it was difficult for them to envision one given the parties' intractability. At a meeting with a group of Arabs in Beirut, the Czechoslovakian member of the Commission told his audience: "I have listened to your demands and it seems to me that in your view the compromise is: We want our demands met completely, the rest can be divided among those left."[2]

When they returned, the delegates of seven nations — Canada, Czechoslovakia, Guatemala, The Netherlands, Peru, Sweden and Uruguay — recommended the establishment of two separate states, Jewish and Arab, to be joined by economic union, with Jerusalem an internationalized enclave. Three nations — India, Iran and Yugoslavia — recommended a unitary state with Arab and Jewish provinces. Australia abstained.

The Jews of Palestine were not satisfied with the small territory allotted to them by the Commission, nor were they happy that Jerusalem was severed from the Jewish State; nevertheless, they welcomed the compromise. The Arabs rejected the UNSCOP's recommendations.

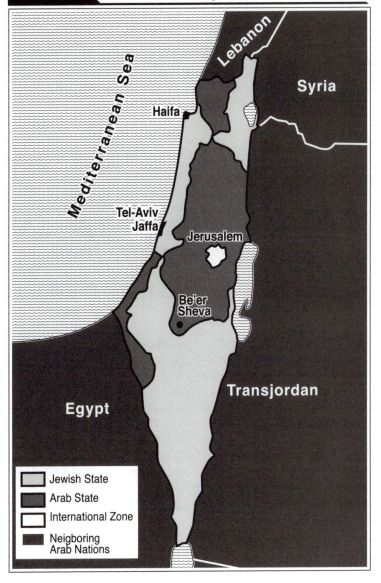

Map 2 The Partition Plan - 1947
UN General Assembly Resolution 181

Lebanon

Syria

Mediterranean Sea

Haifa

Tel-Aviv
Jaffa

Jerusalem

Be'er
Sheva

Transjordan

Egypt

- Jewish State
- Arab State
- International Zone
- Neigboring
  Arab Nations

The *ad hoc* committee of the UN General Assembly rejected the Arab demand for a unitary Arab state. The majority recommendation for partition was subsequently adopted 33-13 with 10 abstentions on November 29, 1947.[3]

> "It is hard to see how the Arab world, still less the Arabs of Palestine, will suffer from what is mere recognition of accomplished fact — the presence in Palestine of a compact, well organized, and virtually autonomous Jewish community."
>
> — **London Times** editorial[4]

MYTH
"The partition plan gave the Jews most of the land, and all of the cultivable area."

FACT
The partition plan took on a checkerboard appearance largely because Jewish towns and villages were spread throughout Palestine. This did not complicate the plan as much as the fact that the high living standards in Jewish cities and towns had attracted large Arab populations, which insured that any partition would result in a Jewish state that included a substantial Arab population. Recognizing the need to allow for additional Jewish settlement, the majority proposal allotted the Jews land in the northern part of the country, Galilee, and the large, arid Negev desert in the south. The remainder was to form the Arab state.

These boundaries were based solely on demographics. The borders of the Jewish State were arranged with no consideration of security; hence, the new state's frontiers were virtually indefensible.

Further complicating the situation was the UN majority's insistence that Jerusalem remain apart from both states and be administered as an international zone. This arrangement left more than 100,000 Jews in Jerusalem isolated from their country and circumscribed by the Arab state.

Critics claim the UN gave the Jews fertile land while the Arabs were allotted hilly, arid land. This is untrue. Approximately 60 percent of the Jewish state was to be the arid desert in the Negev.

The Arabs constituted a majority of the population in Palestine as a whole — 1.2 million Arabs versus 600,000 Jews. The Jews never had a chance of reaching a majority in the country given the restrictive immigration policy of the British. By contrast, the Arabs were free to come — and thousands did — to take advantage of the rapid development stimulated by Zionist settlement. Still, the *Jews were a majority in the area allotted to them by the resolution* and in Jerusalem.

In addition to roughly 600,000 Jews, 350,000 Arabs resided in the Jewish state created by partition. Approximately 92,000 Arabs lived in Tiberias, Safed, Haifa and Bet Shean, and another 40,000 were Bedouins, most of whom were living in the desert. The remainder of the Arab population was spread throughout the Jewish state and occupied most of the agricultural land.[5]

According to British statistics, more than 70% of the land in what would become Israel was not owned by Arab farmers, it belonged to the mandatory government. Those lands reverted to Israeli control after the departure of the British. Nearly 9% of the land was owned by Jews and about 3% by Arabs who became citizens of Israel. That means only about 18% belonged to Arabs who left the country before and after the Arab invasion of Israel.[6]

MYTH

"Israel usurped all of Palestine in 1948."

FACT

Nearly 80 percent of what was the historic land of Palestine and the Jewish National Home, as defined by the League of Nations, was severed by the British in 1922 and allocated to what became Transjordan. Jewish settlement there was barred. The UN partitioned the remaining 20 percent of Palestine into two states. With Jordan's annexation of the West Bank in 1950, Arabs controlled approximately 80 percent of the territory of the Mandate, while the Jewish State held a bare 17.5 percent (Gaza, occupied by Egypt, was the remainder).

MYTH

"The Palestinian Arabs were never offered a state and therefore have been denied the right to self-determination."

FACT

The Peel Commission in 1937 concluded the only logical solution to resolving the contradictory aspirations of the Jews and Arabs was to partition Palestine into separate Jewish and Arab states. The Arabs rejected the plan because it forced them to accept the creation of a Jewish state, and required some Palestinians to live under "Jewish domination." The Zionists opposed the Peel Plan's boundaries because they would have been confined to little more than a ghetto of 1,900 out of the 10,310 square miles remaining in Palestine. Nevertheless, the Zionists decided to negotiate with the British, while the Arabs refused to consider any compromises.

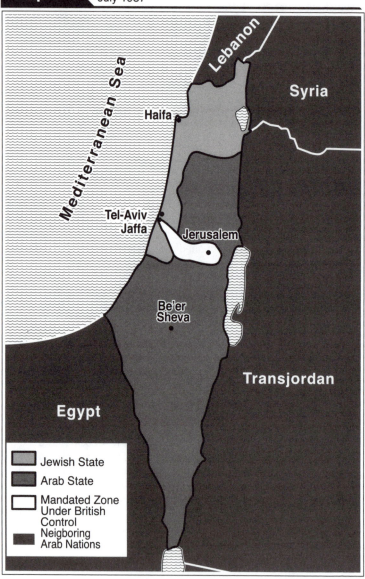

Map 3 Peel Commission Partition Plan
July 1937

Legend:
- Jewish State
- Arab State
- Mandated Zone Under British Control
- Neigboring Arab Nations

Mediterranean Sea

Lebanon

Syria

Haifa

Tel-Aviv Jaffa

Jerusalem

Be'er Sheva

Transjordan

Egypt

Again, in 1939, the British White Paper called for the establishment of an Arab state in Palestine within 10 years, and for limiting Jewish immigration to no more than 75,000 over the following five years. Afterward, no one would be allowed in without the consent of the Arab population. Though the Arabs had been granted a concession on Jewish immigration, and been offered independence – the goal of Arab nationalists – they repudiated the White Paper.

With partition, the Palestinians were given a state and the opportunity for self-determination. This too was rejected.

MYTH

"The Arabs were prepared to compromise to avoid bloodshed."

FACT

As the partition vote approached, it became clear little hope existed for a political solution to a problem that transcended politics: the Arabs' unwillingness to accept a Jewish state in Palestine and the refusal of the Zionists to settle for anything less. The implacability of the Arabs was evident when Jewish Agency representatives David Horowitz and Abba Eban made a last-ditch effort to reach a compromise in a meeting with Arab League Secretary Azzam Pasha on September 16, 1947. Pasha told them bluntly:

> The Arab world is not in a compromising mood. It's likely, Mr. Horowitz, that your plan is rational and logical, but the fate of nations is not decided by rational logic. Nations never concede; they fight. You won't get anything by peaceful means or compromise. You can, perhaps, get something, but only by the force of your arms. We shall try to defeat you. I am not sure we'll succeed, but we'll try. We were able to drive out the Crusaders, but on the other hand we lost Spain and Persia. It may be that we shall lose Palestine. But it's too late to talk of peaceful solutions.[7]

Notes

[1] Aharon Cohen, *Israel and the Arab World*, (Boston: Beacon Press, 1976), pp. 369-370.

[2] Cohen, p. 212.

[3] **Voting in favor of partition:** Australia, Belgium, Bolivia, Brazil, Byelorussian SSR, Canada, Costa Rica, Czechoslovakia, Denmark, Dominican Republic, Ecuador, France, Guatemala, Haiti, Iceland, Liberia, Luxembourg, Netherlands, New Zealand, Nicaragua, Norway, Panama, Paraguay, Peru, Philippines, Poland, Sweden, Ukrainian SSR, Union of South Africa, USSR, USA, Uruguay, Venezuela. **Voting against partition:** Afghanistan, Cuba, Egypt, Greece, India, Iran, Iraq, Lebanon, Pakistan, Saudi Arabia, Syria, Turkey and Yemen. **Abstained:** Argentina, Chile, China, Columbia, El Salvador, Ethiopia, Honduras, Mexico, UK and Yugoslavia
Yearbook of the United Nations, 1947-48, (NY: United Nations, 1949), pp. 246-47.

[4] *London Times*, (December 1, 1947).

[5] Cohen, p. 238.

[6] Moshe Aumann, *"Land Ownership in Palestine, 1880-1948,"* in Michael Curtis, et al., *The Palestinians*, (NJ: Transaction Books, 1975), p. 29, quoting p. 257 of the Government of Palestine, *Survey of Palestine*.

[7] David Horowitz, *State in the Making*, (NY: Alfred A. Knopf, 1953), p. 233.

4. The War of 1948

MYTH

"The Jews started the first war with the Arabs."

FACT

The chairman of the Arab Higher Committee said the Arabs would "fight for every inch of their country."[1] Two days later, the holy men of Al-Azhar University in Cairo called on the Muslim world to proclaim *jihad* (holy war) against the Jews.[2] Jamal Husseini, the Arab Higher Committee's spokesman, had told the UN prior to the partition vote the Arabs would drench "the soil of our beloved country with the last drop of our blood..."[3]

Husseini's prediction began to come true almost immediately after the UN approved the partition resolution on November 29, 1947. The Arabs declared a protest strike and instigated riots that claimed the lives of 62 Jews and 32 Arabs. Violence continued to escalate through the end of the year.[4]

The first large-scale assaults began on January 9, 1948, when approximately 1,000 Arabs attacked Jewish communities in northern Palestine. By February, the British said so many Arabs had infiltrated they lacked the forces to run them back.[5] In fact, the British turned over bases and arms to Arab irregulars and the Arab Legion.

In the first phase of the war, lasting from November 29, 1947, until April 1, 1948, the Palestinian Arabs took the offensive, with help from volunteers from neighboring countries. The Jews suffered severe casualties and passage along most of their major roadways was disrupted.

On April 26, 1948, Transjordan's King Abdullah said:

> [A]ll our efforts to find a peaceful solution to the Palestine problem have failed. The only way left for us is war. I will have the pleasure and honor to save Palestine.[6]

On May 4, 1948, the Arab Legion attacked Kfar Etzion. The defenders drove them back, but the Legion returned a week later. After two days, the ill-equipped and outnumbered settlers were overwhelmed. Many defenders were massacred after they had surrendered.[7] This was prior to the invasion by the regular Arab armies that followed Israel's declaration of independence.

The UN blamed the Arabs for the violence. The UN Palestine Commission was never permitted by the Arabs or British to go to Palestine to implement the resolution. On February 16, 1948, the Commission reported to the Security Council:

Powerful Arab interests, both inside and outside Palestine, are defying the resolution of the General Assembly and are engaged in a deliberate effort to alter by force the settlement envisaged therein.[8]

The Arabs were blunt in taking responsibility for starting the war. Jamal Husseini told the Security Council on April 16, 1948:

The representative of the Jewish Agency told us yesterday that they were not the attackers, that the Arabs had begun the fighting. We did not deny this. We told the whole world that we were going to fight.[9]

The British commander of Jordan's Arab Legion, John Bagot Glubb admitted:

Early in January, the first detachments of the Arab Liberation Army began to infiltrate into Palestine from Syria. Some came through Jordan and even through Amman . . . They were in reality to strike the first blow in the ruin of the Arabs of Palestine.[10]

Despite the disadvantages in numbers, organization and weapons, the Jews began to take the initiative in the weeks from April 1 until the declaration of independence on May 14. The Haganah captured several major towns including Tiberias and Haifa, and temporarily opened the road to Jerusalem.

The partition resolution was never suspended or rescinded. Thus, Israel, the Jewish State in Palestine, was born on May 14, as the British finally left the country. Five Arab armies (Egypt, Syria, Transjordan, Lebanon and Iraq) immediately invaded Israel. Their intentions were declared by Azzam Pasha, Secretary-General of the Arab League: "This will be a war of extermination and a momentous massacre which will be spoken of like the Mongolian massacres and the Crusades."[11]

MYTH

"The Bernadotte Plan was a viable alternative to partition."

FACT

During the summer of 1948, Count Folke Bernadotte was sent by the UN to Palestine to mediate a truce and try to negotiate a settlement. Bernadotte's plan called for the Jewish State to relinquish the Negev and Jerusalem to Transjordan and to receive the western Galilee. This was similar to the boundaries that had been proposed prior to the partition vote, and had been rejected by all sides. Now, the proposal was being offered after the Arabs had gone to war to prevent partition and a Jewish state had been declared. The Jews and Arabs both rejected the plan.

Ironically, Bernadotte found little enthusiasm among the Arabs for independence. He wrote in his diary:

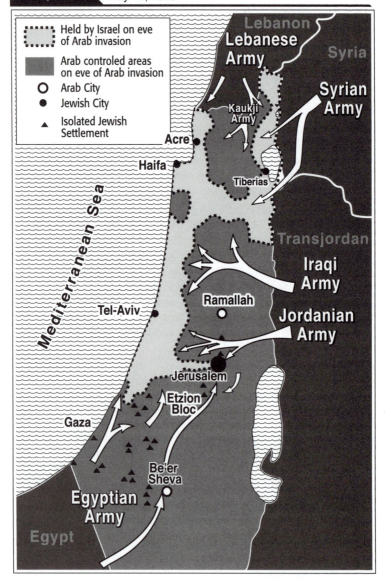

Map 4

The Arab Invasion
May 15, 1948

Held by Israel on eve
of Arab invasion

Arab controled areas
on eve of Arab invasion

○ Arab City

● Jewish City

▲ Isolated Jewish
Settlement

Lebanon

Lebanese
Army

Syria

Syrian
Army

Kaukji
Army

Acre

Haifa

Tiberias

Mediterranean Sea

Transjordan

Iraqi
Army

Ramallah

Tel-Aviv

Jordanian
Army

Jerusalem

Etzion
Bloc

Gaza

Be'er
Sheva

Egyptian
Army

Egypt

> The Palestinian Arabs had at present no will of their own. Neither have they ever developed any specifically Palestinian nationalism. The demand for a separate Arab state in Palestine is consequently relatively weak. It would seem as though in existing circumstances most of the Palestinian Arabs would be quite content to be incorporated in Transjordan.[12]

The failure of the Bernadotte scheme came as the Jews began to have greater success in repelling the invading Arab forces and expanding control over territory outside the partition boundaries.

MYTH

"The United States was the only nation that criticized the Arab attack on Israel."

FACT

The United States, the Soviet Union and most other states recognized Israel soon after it declared independence on May 14, 1948, and immediately indicted the Arabs for their aggression. The United States urged a resolution charging the Arabs with breach of the peace.

Soviet delegate Andrei Gromyko told the Security Council, May 29, 1948:

> This is not the first time that the Arab states, which organized the invasion of Palestine, have ignored a decision of the Security Council or of the General Assembly. The USSR delegation deems it essential that the council should state its opinion more clearly and more firmly with regard to this attitude of the Arab states toward decisions of the Security Council.[13]

On July 15, the Security Council threatened to cite the Arab governments for aggression under the UN Charter. By this time, the Israel Defense Forces had succeeded in stopping the Arab offensive and the initial phase of the fighting ended.

MYTH

"The West's support of Israel allowed the Jews to conquer Palestine."

FACT

The Jews won their war of independence with minimal help from the West. In fact, they won despite efforts to undermine their military strength.

Although the United States vigorously supported the partition resolution, the State Department did not want to provide the Jews with the means to defend themselves. "Otherwise," Undersecretary of State Robert Lovett argued, "the

Arabs might use arms of U.S. origin against Jews, or Jews might use them against Arabs."[14] Consequently, on December 5, 1947, the U.S. imposed an arms embargo on the region.

Many in the State Department saw the embargo as yet another means of obstructing partition. President Truman nevertheless went along with it hoping it would be a means of averting bloodshed. This was naive given Britain's rejection of Lovett's request to suspend weapons shipments to the Arabs and subsequent agreements to provide additional arms to Iraq and Transjordan.[15]

The Arabs had no difficulty obtaining all the arms they needed. In fact, Jordan's Arab Legion was armed and trained by the British, and led by a British officer. At the end of 1948 and beginning of 1949, British RAF planes flew with Egyptian squadrons over the Israel-Egypt border. On January 7, 1949, Israeli planes shot down four of the British aircraft.[16]

The Jews, on the other hand, were forced to smuggle weapons, principally from Czechoslovakia. When Israel declared its independence in May 1948, the army did not have a single cannon or tank. Its air force consisted of nine obsolete planes. Although the Haganah had 60,000 trained fighters, only 18,900 were fully mobilized, armed and prepared for war.[17] On the eve of the war, chief of operations Yigael Yadin told David Ben-Gurion: "The best we can tell you is that we have a 50-50 chance."[18]

The Arab war to destroy Israel failed. Indeed, because of their aggression, the Arabs wound up with less territory than they would have had if they had accepted partition.

The cost to Israel, however, was enormous. "Many of its most productive fields lay gutted and mined. Its citrus groves, for decades the basis of the Yishuv's [Jewish community] economy, were largely destroyed."[19] Military expenditures totaled approximately $500 million. Worse yet, 6,373 Israelis were killed, nearly one percent of the Jewish population of 650,000.

Had the West enforced the partition resolution or given the Jews the capacity to defend themselves, many lives might have been saved.

The Arab countries signed armistice agreements with Israel in 1949, starting with Egypt (Feb. 24), followed by Lebanon (March 23), Jordan (April 3) and Syria (July 20). Iraq was the only country that did not sign an agreement with Israel, choosing instead to withdraw its troops and hand over its sector to Jordan's Arab Legion. None of the Arab states would negotiate a peace agreement.

Map 5   Armistice Lines
1949

Mediterranean Sea

Lebanon

Syria

Haifa

Samaria

Tel-Aviv
Yafo

Jerusalem

Judea

Transjordan

Gaza

Be'er
Sheva

Egypt

Eilat

Under Jordanian Rule
Under Egyptian Rule

MYTH

"The Arab economic boycott of Israel
was imposed after the 1948 war."

FACT

The Arab boycott was formally declared by the newly formed Arab League Council on December 2, 1945: "Jewish products and manufactured goods shall be considered undesirable to the Arab countries." All Arab "institutions, organizations, merchants, commission agents and individuals" were called upon "to refuse to deal in, distribute, or consume Zionist products or manufactured goods."[20] As is evident in this declaration, the terms "Jewish" and "Zionist" were used synonymously. Thus, even before the establishment of Israel, the Arab states had declared an economic boycott against the Jews of Palestine.

The boycott, as it evolved after 1948, is divided into three components. The primary boycott prohibits direct trade between Israel and the Arab nations. The secondary boycott is directed at companies that do business with Israel. The tertiary boycott involves the blacklisting of firms that trade with other companies that do business with Israel.[21]

The objective of the boycott has been to isolate Israel from its neighbors and the international community, and deny it trade that might be used to augment its military and economic strength. While undoubtedly isolating Israel and separating the Jewish State from its most natural markets, the boycott failed to undermine Israel's economy to the degree intended.

In 1977, Congress prohibited U.S. companies from cooperating with the Arab boycott. When President Carter signed the law, he said the "issue goes to the very heart of free trade among nations" and that it was designed to "end the divisive effects on American life of foreign boycotts aimed at Jewish members of our society."[22]

The Arab League threatened to take a decisive stand against the new law, which was regarded as part of "a campaign of hysterical laws and bills . . . which Israel and world Zionism are trying not only to enforce on the U.S.; but also in some countries of Western Europe."

Contrary to claims that the bill would lead to a drastic reduction in American trade with the Arab world, imports and exports increased substantially. Broader diplomatic and cultural relations also improved. Nevertheless, certain U.S. companies were blacklisted for their relations with Israel.

On September 30, 1994, the six Gulf Cooperation Council states announced they would no longer support the secondary boycott barring trade with companies doing business with Israel. At a meeting in Taba, Egypt, February 7-8, 1995, Egyptian, American, Jordanian and Palestinian trade leaders signed a joint document — the Taba Declaration — supporting "all efforts to end the boycott of Israel."

Since the signing of peace agreements between Israel and the PLO and Jordan, the boycott has gradually crumbled. The Arab League was forced to cancel several boycott meetings called by the Syrian hosts because of opposition from countries like Kuwait, Morocco and Tunisia. The primary boycott — prohibiting direct relations between Arab countries and Israel — cracked when nations such as Qatar, Oman and Morocco negotiated deals with Israel. Furthermore, few countries outside the Middle East comply with the boycott. Still, the boycott remains technically in force, and several countries, most notably Saudi Arabia (which, for example, bans products bearing the Star of David), continue to enforce it.[23]

Notes

[1] *New York Times*, (December 1, 1947).

[2] *Facts on File* 1948, p. 48.

[3] J.C. Hurewitz, *The Struggle For Palestine*, (NY: Shocken Books, 1976), p. 308.

[4] *Facts on File Yearbook*, (NY: Facts on File, Inc., 1948), p. 231.

[5] *Facts on File* 1947, p. 231.

[6] Howard Sachar, *A History of Israel: From the Rise of Zionism to Our Time*, (NY: Alfred A. Knopf, 1979), p. 322.

[7] Netanel Lorch, *One Long War*, (Jerusalem: Keter Books, 1976), p. 47; Ralph Patai, ed., *Encyclopedia of Zionism and Israel*, (NY: McGraw Hill, 1971), pp. 307-308.

[8] Security Council Official Records, Special Supplement, (1948), p. 20.

[9] Security Council Official Records, S/Agenda/58, (April 16, 1948), p. 19.

[10] John Bagot Glubb, *A Soldier with the Arabs*, (London: Staughton and Hodder, 1957), p. 79.

[11] Isi Leibler, *The Case For Israel*, (Australia: The Globe Press, 1972), p. 15.

[12] Folke Bernadotte, *To Jerusalem*, (London: Hodder and Stoughton, 1951), p. 113.

[13] Security Council Official Records, SA/Agenda/77, (May 29, 1948), p. 2.

[14] Foreign Relations of the United States 1947, (DC: GPO, 1948), p. 1249. [Henceforth FRUS].

[15] Mitchell Bard, *The Water's Edge And Beyond*, (NJ: Transaction Books, 1991), pp. 171-175; FRUS, pp. 537-39; Robert Silverberg, *If I Forget Thee O Jerusalem: American Jews and the State of Israel*, (NY: William Morrow and Co., Inc., 1970), pp. 366, 370; Shlomo Slonim, "The 1948 American Embargo on Arms to Palestine," *Political Science Quarterly*, (Fall 1979), p. 500.

[16] Sachar, p. 345.

[17] Larry Collins and Dominique Lapierre, *O Jerusalem!*, (NY: Simon and Schuster, 1972), p. 352.

[18] Golda Meir, *My Life*, (NY: Dell, 1975), pp. 213, 222, 224.

[19] Sachar, p. 452.

[20] Terence Prittie and Walter Nelson, *The Economic War Against The Jews*, (London: Corgi Books, 1977), p. 1; Dan Chill, The Arab Boycott of Israel, (NY: Praeger, 1976), p. 1.

[21] Prittie and Nelson, pp. 47-48; Sol Stern, "On and Off the Arabs' List," *The New Republic*, (March 27, 1976), p. 9; Kennan Teslik, *Congress, the Executive Branch and Special Interests*, (CT: Greenwood Press, 1982), p. 11.

[22] Bard, pp. 91-115.

[23] *Jerusalem Post*, (June 5, 2002).

5. The Road to Suez

MYTH

"Arab governments were prepared to accept Israel after the 1948 war."

FACT

In the fall of 1948, the UN Security Council called on Israel and the Arab states to negotiate armistice agreements. Thanks to UN mediator Ralph Bunche's insistence on direct bilateral talks between Israel and each Arab state, armistice agreements between Israel and Egypt, Jordan, Lebanon and Syria were concluded by the summer of 1949. Iraq, which had also fought against Israel, refused to follow suit.

Meanwhile, on December 11, 1948, the General Assembly adopted a resolution calling on the parties to negotiate peace and creating a Palestine Conciliation Commission (PCC), which consisted of the United States, France and Turkey. All Arab delegations voted against it.

After 1949, the Arabs insisted that Israel accept the borders in the 1947 partition resolution and repatriate the Palestinian refugees before they would negotiate an end to the war they had initiated. This was a novel approach that they would use after subsequent defeats: the doctrine of the limited-liability war. Under this theory, aggressors may reject a compromise settlement and gamble on war to win everything in the comfortable knowledge that, even if they fail, they may insist on reinstating the status quo ante.

MYTH

"Israel's military strike in 1956 was unprovoked."

FACT

Egypt had maintained its state of belligerency with Israel after the armistice agreement was signed. The first manifestation of this was the closing of the Suez Canal to Israeli shipping. On August 9, 1949, the UN Mixed Armistice Commission upheld Israel's complaint that Egypt was illegally blocking the canal. UN negotiator Ralph Bunche declared: "There should be free movement for legitimate shipping and no vestiges of the wartime blockade should be allowed to remain, as they are inconsistent with both the letter and the spirit of the armistice agreements."[1]

On September 1, 1951, the Security Council ordered Egypt to open the Canal to Israeli shipping. Egypt refused to comply.

The Egyptian Foreign Minister, Muhammad Salah al-Din, said early in 1954:

The Arab people will not be embarrassed to declare: We shall not be satisfied except by the final obliteration of Israel from the map of the Middle East.[2]

In 1955, Egyptian President Gamal Abdel Nasser began to import arms from the Soviet Bloc to build his arsenal for the confrontation with Israel. In the short-term, however, he employed a new tactic to prosecute Egypt's war with Israel. He announced it on August 31, 1955:

Egypt has decided to dispatch her heroes, the disciples of Pharaoh and the sons of Islam and they will cleanse the land of Palestine....There will be no peace on Israel's border because we demand vengeance, and vengeance is Israel's death.[3]

These "heroes" were Arab terrorists, or *fedayeen*, trained and equipped by Egyptian Intelligence to engage in hostile action on the border, and to infiltrate Israel to commit acts of sabotage and murder. The *fedayeen* operated mainly from bases in Jordan, so that Jordan would bear the brunt of Israel's retaliation, which inevitably followed. The terrorist attacks violated the armistice agreement provision that prohibited the initiation of hostilities by paramilitary forces; nevertheless, it was Israel that was condemned by the UN Security Council for its counterattacks.

The escalation continued with the Egyptian blockade of Israel's shipping lane in the Straits of Tiran, and Nasser's nationalization of the Suez Canal in July 1956. On October 14, Nasser made clear his intent:

I am not solely fighting against Israel itself. My task is to deliver the Arab world from destruction through Israel's intrigue, which has its roots abroad. Our hatred is very strong. There is no sense in talking about peace with Israel. There is not even the smallest place for negotiations.[4]

Less than two weeks later, on October 25, Egypt signed a tripartite agreement with Syria and Jordan placing Nasser in command of all three armies.

The continued blockade of the Suez Canal and Gulf of Aqaba to Israeli shipping, combined with the increased *fedayeen* attacks and the bellicosity of recent Arab statements, prompted Israel, with the backing of Britain and France, to attack Egypt on October 29, 1956. The Israeli attack on Egypt was successful, with Israeli forces capturing the Gaza Strip, much of the Sinai and Sharm al-Sheikh. A total of 231 soldiers died in the fighting.

Israeli Ambassador to the UN Abba Eban explained the provocations to the Security Council on October 30:

During the six years during which this belligerency has operated in violation of the Armistice Agreement there have occurred 1,843 cases of armed robbery and theft, 1,339 cases of armed clashes with Egyptian armed forces, 435 cases of incursion from Egyptian

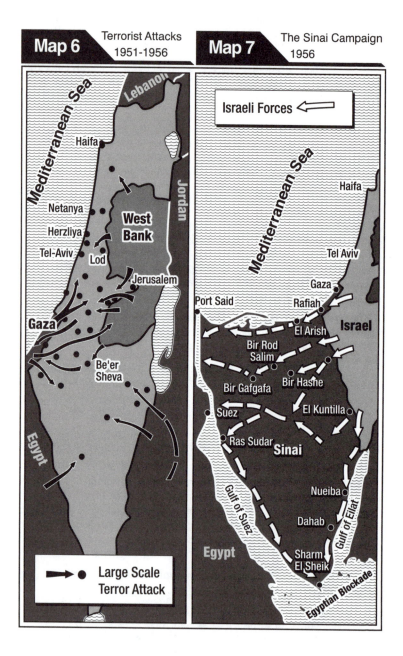

Map 6 — Terrorist Attacks 1951-1956

Map 7 — The Sinai Campaign 1956

Israeli Forces

Large Scale Terror Attack

controlled territory, 172 cases of sabotage perpetrated by Egyptian military units and *fedayeen* in Israel. As a result of these actions of Egyptian hostility within Israel, 364 Israelis were wounded and 101 killed. In 1956 alone, as a result of this aspect of Egyptian aggression, 28 Israelis were killed and 127 wounded.[5]

One reason these raids were so intolerable for Israel was that the country had chosen to create a relatively small standing army and to rely primarily on reserves in the event of war. This meant that Israel had a small force to fight in an emergency, that threats provoking the mobilization of reserves could virtually paralyze the country, and that an enemy's initial thrust would have to be withstood long enough to complete the mobilization.

MYTH

"Israel had no reason to attack Egypt; it went to war to advance the imperialist interests of France and Great Britain."

FACT

Eisenhower had successfully persuaded the British and French not to attack Egypt after Nasser nationalized the Suez Canal in July 1956. When the agreement on the Canal's use proved reliable over the succeeding weeks, it became increasingly difficult to justify military action. Still, the French and British desperately wanted to put Nasser in his place and recapture their strategic asset.

The French had grown increasingly close to the new Israeli government, politically, diplomatically and militarily. In fact over the next two decades, the French would be Israel's principal arms supplier. The British attitude toward Israel had hardly changed from the mandatory period. Residual bitterness over the nearly three decade long battle fought with the Zionists, combined with the ongoing alliance with Jordan, discouraged any shift in policy.

The French concluded, however, that they could use Israel's fear of Egyptian aggression, and the continuing blockade, as a pretext for their own strike against Nasser. The British couldn't pass up the chance to join in.

The three nations subsequently agreed on a plan whereby Israel would land paratroopers near the Canal and send its armor across the Sinai desert. The British and French would then call for both sides to withdraw from the canal zone, fully expecting the Egyptians to refuse. At that point, British and French troops would be deployed to "protect" the canal.

From Israel's perspective, the continued blockade of the Suez Canal and Gulf of Aqaba, combined with the increased *fedayeen* attacks, and the bellicosity of recent Arab statements, made the situation intolerable. Rather than continue to fight a war of attrition with the terrorists and wait for Nasser and his allies to build their forces up sufficiently to wage a new war, Israeli Prime Minister

Ben-Gurion decided to launch a preemptive strike. The backing of the British and French, he thought, would give him cover against the opposition of the United States. He was wrong.[6]

MYTH
"The United States' blind support for Israel was apparent during the Suez War."

FACT

President Dwight Eisenhower was upset by the fact that Israel, France and Great Britain had secretly planned the campaign to evict Egypt from the Suez Canal. Israel's failure to inform the United States of its intentions, combined with ignoring American entreaties not to go to war, sparked tensions between the countries. The United States subsequently joined the Soviet Union (ironically, just after the Soviets invaded Hungary) in a campaign to force Israel to withdraw. This included a threat to discontinue all U.S. assistance, UN sanctions and expulsion from the UN.

U.S. pressure resulted in an Israeli withdrawal from the areas it conquered without obtaining any concessions from the Egyptians. This sowed the seeds of the 1967 war.

One reason Israel did give in to Eisenhower was the assurance he gave to Prime Minister David Ben-Gurion. Before evacuating Sharm al-Sheikh, the strategic point guarding the Straits of Tiran, Israel elicited a promise that the United States would maintain the freedom of navigation in the waterway.[7] In addition, Washington sponsored a UN resolution creating the United Nations Emergency Force (UNEF) to supervise the territories vacated by the Israeli forces.

The war temporarily ended the activities of the *fedayeen*; however, they were renewed a few years later by a loosely knit group of terrorist organizations that became know as the Palestine Liberation Organization (PLO).

Notes

1   Eliezer Ereli, "The Bat Galim Case Before the Security Council," *Middle Eastern Affairs,* (April 1955), pp. 108-9.

2   *Al-Misri,* (April 12, 1954).

3   *Middle Eastern Affairs,* (December 1956), p. 461.

4   *Middle Eastern Affairs,* (December 1956), p. 460.

5   *Security Council Official Record*s, S/3706, (October 30, 1956), p. 14.

6   Mitchell Bard, *The Complete Idiot's Guide to Middle East Conflict.* (NY: Alpha Books, 1999), pp. 208-209.

7   Janice Gross Stein and Raymond Tanter, *Rational Decision Making: Israel's Security Choices,* (OH: Ohio State University, 1976), p. 163.

6. The 1967 Six-Day War

MYTH

*"Arab governments were prepared
to accept Israel after the Suez War."*

FACT

Israel consistently expressed a desire to negotiate with its neighbors. In an address to the UN General Assembly on October 10, 1960, Foreign Minister Golda Meir challenged Arab leaders to meet with Prime Minister David Ben-Gurion to negotiate a peace settlement. Nasser answered on October 15, saying that Israel was trying to deceive the world, and reiterating that his country would never recognize the Jewish State.[1]

The Arabs were equally adamant in their refusal to negotiate a separate settlement for the refugees. As Nasser told the United Arab Republic National Assembly March 26, 1964:

> Israel and the imperialism around us, which confront us, are two separate things. There have been attempts to separate them, in order to break up the problems and present them in an imaginary light as if the problem of Israel is the problem of the refugees, by the solution of which the problem of Palestine will also be solved and no residue of the problem will remain. The danger of Israel lies in the very existence of Israel as it is in the present and in what she represents.[2]

Meanwhile, Syria used the Golan Heights, which tower 3,000 feet above the Galilee, to shell Israeli farms and villages. Syria's attacks grew more frequent in 1965 and 1966, while Nasser's rhetoric became increasingly bellicose: "We shall not enter Palestine with its soil covered in sand," he said on March 8, 1965. "We shall enter it with its soil saturated in blood."[3]

Again, a few months later, Nasser expressed the Arabs' aspiration: "...the full restoration of the rights of the Palestinian people. In other words, we aim at the destruction of the State of Israel. The immediate aim: perfection of Arab military might. The national aim: the eradication of Israel."[4]

MYTH

"Israel's military strike in 1967 was unprovoked."

FACT

A combination of bellicose Arab rhetoric, threatening behavior and, ultimately, an act of war left Israel no choice but preemptive action. To do this successfully,

Map 8

The Golan Heights Prior to the 1967 War.
Distances and Elevations

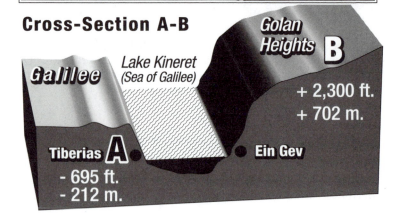

Israel needed the element of surprise. Had it waited for an Arab invasion, Israel would have been at a potentially catastrophic disadvantage.

While Nasser continued to make speeches threatening war, Arab terrorist attacks grew more frequent. In 1965, 35 raids were conducted against Israel. In 1966, the number increased to 41. In just the first four months of 1967, 37 attacks were launched.[5]

Meanwhile, Syria's attacks on Israeli kibbutzim from the Golan Heights provoked a retaliatory strike on April 7, 1967, during which Israeli planes shot down six Syrian MiGs. Shortly thereafter, the Soviet Union — which had been providing military and economic aid to both Syria and Egypt — gave Damascus information alleging a massive Israeli military buildup in preparation for an attack. Despite Israeli denials, Syria decided to invoke its defense treaty with Egypt.

On May 15, Israel's Independence Day, Egyptian troops began moving into the Sinai and massing near the Israeli border. By May 18, Syrian troops were prepared for battle along the Golan Heights.

Nasser ordered the UN Emergency Force, stationed in the Sinai since 1956, to withdraw on May 16. Without bringing the matter to the attention of the General Assembly, as his predecessor had promised, Secretary-General U Thant complied with the demand. After the withdrawal of the UNEF, the Voice of the Arabs proclaimed (May 18, 1967):

> As of today, there no longer exists an international emergency force to protect Israel. We shall exercise patience no more. We shall not complain any more to the UN about Israel. The sole method we shall apply against Israel is total war, which will result in the extermination of Zionist existence.[6]

An enthusiastic echo was heard May 20 from Syrian Defense Minister Hafez Assad:

> Our forces are now entirely ready not only to repulse the aggression, but to initiate the act of liberation itself, and to explode the Zionist presence in the Arab homeland. The Syrian army, with its finger on the trigger, is united....I, as a military man, believe that the time has come to enter into a battle of annihilation.[7]

On May 22, Egypt closed the Straits of Tiran to all Israeli shipping and all ships bound for Eilat. This blockade cut off Israel's only supply route with Asia and stopped the flow of oil from its main supplier, Iran. The following day, President Johnson expressed the belief that the blockade was illegal and unsuccessfully tried to organize an international flotilla to test it.

Nasser challenged Israel to fight almost daily. "Our basic objective will be the destruction of Israel. The Arab people want to fight," he said on May 27.[8] The following day, he added: "We will not accept any...coexistence with

Map 9

Israel Before June 1967

Israel...Today the issue is not the establishment of peace between the Arab states and Israel....The war with Israel is in effect since 1948."[9]

King Hussein of Jordan signed a defense pact with Egypt on May 30. Nasser then announced:

> The armies of Egypt, Jordan, Syria and Lebanon are poised on the borders of Israel...to face the challenge, while standing behind us are the armies of Iraq, Algeria, Kuwait, Sudan and the whole Arab nation. This act will astound the world. Today they will know that the Arabs are arranged for battle, the critical hour has arrived. We have reached the stage of serious action and not declarations.[10]

President Abdur Rahman Aref of Iraq joined in the war of words: "The existence of Israel is an error which must be rectified. This is our opportunity to wipe out the ignominy which has been with us since 1948. Our goal is clear -- to wipe Israel off the map."[11] On June 4, Iraq joined the military alliance with Egypt, Jordan and Syria.

The Arab rhetoric was matched by the mobilization of Arab forces. Approximately 250,000 troops (nearly half in Sinai), more than 2,000 tanks and 700 aircraft ringed Israel.[12]

By this time, Israeli forces had been on alert for three weeks. The country could not remain fully mobilized indefinitely, nor could it allow its sea lane through the Gulf of Aqaba to be interdicted. Israel's best option was to strike first. On June 5, the order was given to attack Egypt.

MYTH
"Nasser had the right to close the Straits of Tiran to Israeli shipping."

FACT

In 1956, the United States gave Israel assurances that it recognized the Jewish State's right of access to the Straits of Tiran. In 1957, at the UN, 17 maritime powers declared that Israel had a right to transit the Strait. Moreover, the blockade violated the Convention on the Territorial Sea and Contiguous Zone, which was adopted by the UN Conference on the Law of the Sea on April 27, 1958.[13]

The closure of the Strait of Tiran was the *casus belli* in 1967. Israel's attack was a reaction to this Egyptian first strike. President Johnson acknowledged as much after the war (June 19, 1967):

> If a single act of folly was more responsible for this explosion than any other it was the arbitrary and dangerous announced decision that the Strait of Tiran would be closed. The right of innocent maritime passage must be preserved for all nations.[14]

MYTH

"The United States helped Israel defeat the Arabs in six days."

FACT

The United States tried to prevent the war through negotiations, but it could not persuade Nasser or the other Arab states to cease their belligerent statements and actions. Still, right before the war, Johnson warned: "Israel will not be alone unless it decides to go alone."[15] Then, when the war began, the State Department announced: "Our position is neutral in thought, word and deed."[16]

Moreover, while the Arabs were falsely accusing the United States of airlifting supplies to Israel, Johnson imposed an arms embargo on the region (France, Israel's other main arms supplier, also embargoed arms to Israel).

By contrast, the Soviets were supplying massive amounts of arms to the Arabs. Simultaneously, the armies of Kuwait, Algeria, Saudi Arabia and Iraq were contributing troops and arms to the Egyptian, Syrian and Jordanian fronts.[17]

MYTH

"Israel attacked Jordan to capture Jerusalem."

FACT

Prime Minister Levi Eshkol sent a message to King Hussein saying Israel would not attack Jordan unless he initiated hostilities. When Jordanian radar picked up a cluster of planes flying from Egypt to Israel, and the Egyptians convinced Hussein the planes were theirs, he then ordered the shelling of West Jerusalem. It turned out the planes were Israel's, and were returning from destroying the Egyptian air force on the ground. Meanwhile, Syrian and Iraqi troops attacked Israel's northern frontier.

Had Jordan not attacked, the status of Jerusalem would not have changed during the course of the war. Once the city came under fire, however, Israel needed to defend it, and, in doing so, took the opportunity to unify its capital once and for all.

MYTH

"Israel did not have to shoot first."

FACT

After just six days of fighting, Israeli forces broke through the enemy lines and were in a position to march on Cairo, Damascus and Amman. A cease-fire was invoked on June 10. The victory came at a very high cost. In storming the Golan Heights, Israel suffered 115 dead — roughly the number of Americans

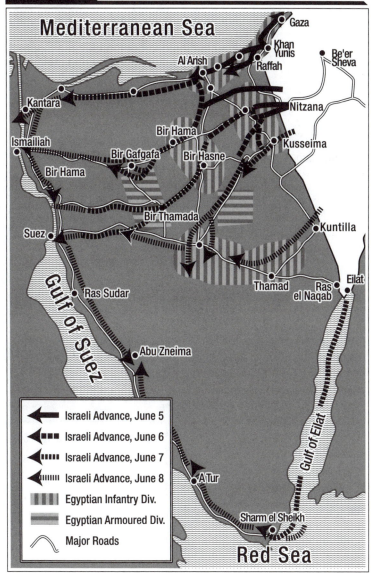

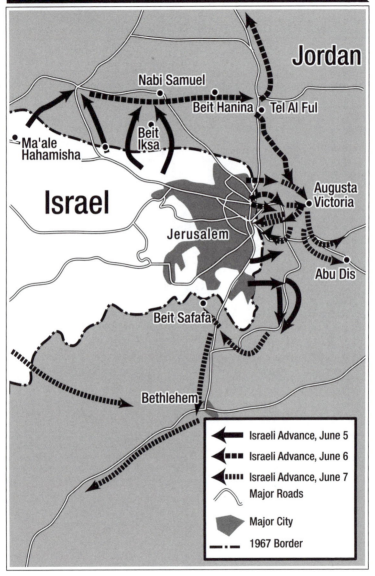

Map 11 The Battle for Jerusalem
June 5-7, 1967

Jordan

Nabi Samuel

Beit Hanina • Tel Al Ful

Ma'ale
Hahamisha

Beit
Iksa

Israel

Augusta
Victoria

Jerusalem

Abu Dis

Beit Safafa

Bethlehem

Israeli Advance, June 5
Israeli Advance, June 6
Israeli Advance, June 7
Major Roads
Major City
1967 Border

killed during Operation Desert Storm. Altogether, Israel lost twice as many men — 777 dead and 2,586 wounded — in proportion to her total population as the U.S. lost in eight years of fighting in Vietnam.[18] Also, despite the incredible success of the air campaign, the Israeli Air Force lost 46 of its 200 fighters.[19] Had Israel waited for the Arabs to strike first, as it did in 1973, and not taken preemptive action, the cost would certainly have been much higher and victory could not have been assured.

MYTH

"Israel viewed the territories it captured as conquered lands that were now part of Israel and had no intention of negotiating over their return."

FACT

By the end of the war, Israel had captured enough territory to more than triple the size of the area it controlled, from 8,000 to 26,000 square miles. The victory enabled Israel to unify Jerusalem. Israeli forces had also captured the Sinai, the Golan Heights, the Gaza Strip and the West Bank.

Israel's leaders fully expected to negotiate a peace agreement with their neighbors that would involve some territorial compromise. Almost immediately after the war, Israel's leaders expressed their willingness to negotiate a return of at least some of the territories. Israel subsequently returned all of the Sinai to Egypt, territory claimed by Jordan was returned to the Hashemite Kingdom, and nearly all of the Gaza Strip and more than 40 percent of the West Bank was given to the Palestinians to establish the Palestinian Authority.

To date, approximately 93 percent of the territories won in the defensive war have been given by Israel to its Arab neighbors in the course of negotiations. This demonstrates Israel's willingness to trade land for peace.

MYTH

"Israel expelled peaceful Arab villagers from the West Bank and prevented them from returning after the war."

FACT

After Jordan launched its attack on June 5, approximately 325,000 Palestinians living in the West Bank fled.[20] These were Jordanian citizens who moved from one part of what they considered their country to another, primarily to avoid being caught in the cross fire of a war.

A Palestinian refugee who was an administrator in a UNRWA camp in Jericho said Arab politicians had spread rumors in the camp. "They said all the young people would be killed. People heard on the radio that this is not the end, only the beginning, so they think maybe it will be a long war and they want to be in Jordan."[21]

Map 12 Cease-Fire Lines After the Six-Day War
1967

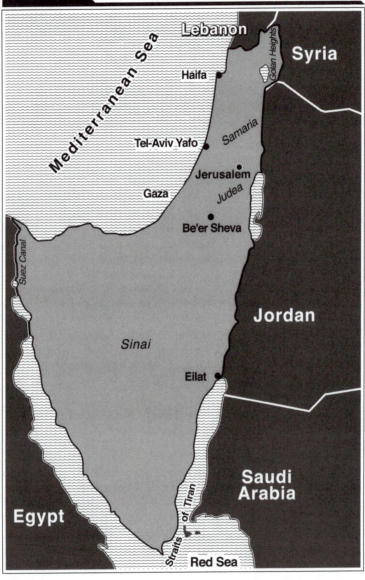

Some Palestinians who left preferred to live in an Arab state rather than under Israeli military rule. Members of various PLO factions fled to avoid capture by the Israelis. Nils-Göran Gussing, the person appointed by the UN Secretary-General to investigate the situation, found that many Arabs also feared they would no longer be able to receive money from family members working abroad.[22]

Israeli forces ordered a handful of Palestinians to move for "strategic and security reasons." In some cases, they were allowed to return in a few days, in others Israel offered to help them resettle elsewhere.[23]

Israel now ruled more than three-quarters of a million Palestinians — most of whom were hostile to the government. Nevertheless, more than 9,000 Palestinian families were reunited in 1967. Ultimately, more than 60,000 Palestinians were allowed to return.[24]

MYTH

"Israel imposed unreasonable restrictions on the Palestinians in the West Bank, Gaza Strip and East Jerusalem."

FACT

After the 1967 war, Israel chose not to annex the West Bank or Gaza Strip and instituted a military administration instead. This was necessary as an interim step until negotiations could resolve the future of the territories. This was by no means an ideal situation for the inhabitants, but the Israeli authorities tried to minimize the impact on the population. Don Peretz, a frequent writer on the situation of Arabs in Israel and a sharp critic of the Israeli government, visited the West Bank shortly after the Israeli troops had taken over. He found they were trying to restore normal life and prevent any incidents that might encourage the Arabs to leave their homes.[25]

Except for the requirement that school texts in the territories be purged of anti-Israel and anti-Semitic language, the authorities tried not to interfere with the inhabitants. They did provide economic assistance; for example, Palestinians in the Gaza Strip were moved from camps to new homes. This stimulated protests from Egypt, which had done nothing for the refugees when it controlled the area.

Arabs were given freedom of movement. They were allowed to travel to and from Jordan. In 1972, elections were held in the West Bank. Women and non-landowners, unable to participate under Jordanian rule, were now permitted to vote.

East Jerusalem Arabs were given the option of retaining Jordanian citizenship or acquiring Israeli citizenship. They were recognized as residents of united Jerusalem and given the right to vote and run for the city council. Also, Islamic holy places were put in the care of a Muslim Council. Despite the Temple Mount's significance in Jewish history, Jews were barred from conducting prayers there.

> *After the Six-Day War ended, President Johnson announced his view of what was required next to end the conflict:*
>
> *"Certainly, troops must be withdrawn; but there must also be recognized rights of national life, progress in solving the refugee problem, freedom of innocent maritime passage, limitation of the arms race and respect for political independence and territorial integrity."[26]*

MYTH

"During the 1967 War, Israel deliberately attacked the USS Liberty."

FACT

The Israeli attack on the *USS Liberty* was a grievous error, largely attributable to the fact that it occurred in the midst of the confusion of a full-scale war in 1967. Ten official United States investigations and three official Israeli inquiries have all conclusively established the attack was a tragic mistake.

On June 8, 1967, the fourth day of the Six-Day War, the Israeli high command received reports that Israeli troops in El Arish were being fired upon from the sea, presumably by an Egyptian vessel, as they had a day before. The United States had announced that it had no naval forces within hundreds of miles of the battle front on the floor of the United Nations a few days earlier; however, the *USS Liberty*, an American intelligence ship assigned to monitor the fighting, arrived in the area, 14 miles off the Sinai coast, as a result of a series of United States communication failures, whereby messages directing the ship not to approach within 100 miles were not received by the *Liberty*. The Israelis mistakenly thought this was the ship doing the shelling and war planes and torpedo boats attacked, killing 34 members of the *Liberty's* crew and wounding 171.

Numerous mistakes were made by both the United States and Israel. For example, the *Liberty* was first reported — incorrectly, as it turned out — to be cruising at 30 knots (it was later recalculated to be 28 knots). Under Israeli (and U.S.) naval doctrine at the time, a ship proceeding at that speed was presumed to be a warship. The sea was calm and the U.S. Navy Court of Inquiry found that the *Liberty's* flag was very likely drooped and not discernible; moreover, members of the crew, including the Captain, Commander William McGonagle, testified that the flag was knocked down after the first or second assault.

According to Israeli Chief of Staff Yitzhak Rabin's memoirs, there were standing orders to attack any unidentified vessel near the shore.[27] The day fighting began, Israel had asked that American ships be removed from its coast or that it be notified of the precise location of U.S. vessels.[28] The Sixth Fleet was moved because President Johnson feared being drawn into a confrontation with the Soviet Union. He also ordered that no aircraft be sent near Sinai.

A CIA report on the incident issued June 13, 1967, also found that an overzealous pilot could mistake the *Liberty* for an Egyptian ship, the *El Quseir*. After the air raid, Israeli torpedo boats identified the *Liberty* as an Egyptian naval vessel. When the *Liberty* began shooting at the Israelis, they responded with the torpedo attack, which killed 28 of the sailors.

Initially, the Israelis were terrified that they had attacked a Soviet ship and might have provoked the Soviets to join the fighting.[29] Once the Israelis were sure what had happened, they reported the incident to the U.S. Embassy in Tel Aviv and offered to provide a helicopter for the Americans to fly out to the ship and any help they required to evacuate the injured and salvage the ship. The offer was accepted and a U.S. naval attaché was flown to the *Liberty*.

Many of the survivors of the *Liberty* remain bitter, and are convinced the attack was deliberate. In 1991, columnists Rowland Evans and Robert Novak trumpeted their discovery of an American who said he had been in the Israeli war room when the decision was made to knowingly attack the American ship.[30] In fact, that individual, Seth Mintz, wrote a letter to the *Washington Post* on November 9, 1991, in which he said he was misquoted by Evans and Novak and that the attack, was, in fact, a "case of mistaken identity." Moreover, the man who Mintz originally said had been with him, a Gen. Benni Matti, does not exist.

Also, contrary to claims that an Israeli pilot identified the ship as American on a radio tape, no one has ever produced this tape. In fact, the only tape in existence is the official Israeli Air Force tape, which clearly established that no such identification of the ship was made by the Israeli pilots prior to the attack. It also indicates that once the pilots became concerned about the identity of the ship, by virtue of reading its hull number, they terminated the attack. The tapes do not contain any statement suggesting the pilots saw a U.S. flag before the attack.[31]

None of Israel's accusers can explain why Israel would deliberately attack an American ship at a time when the United States was Israel's only friend and supporter in the world. Confusion in a long line of communications, which occurred in a tense atmosphere on both the American and Israeli sides (five messages from the Joint Chiefs of Staff for the ship to remain at least 25 miles — the last four said 100 miles — off the Egyptian coast arrived after the attack was over) is a more probable explanation.

Accidents caused by "friendly fire" are common in wartime. In 1988, the U.S. Navy mistakenly downed an Iranian passenger plane, killing 290 civilians. During the Gulf War, 35 of the 148 Americans who died in battle were killed by "friendly fire." In April 1994, two U.S. Black Hawk helicopters with large U.S. flags painted on each side were shot down by U.S. Air Force F-15s on a clear day in the "no fly" zone of Iraq, killing 26 people. In April 2002, an American F-16 dropped a bomb that killed four Canadian soldiers in Afghanistan. In fact, the day before the *Liberty* was attacked, Israeli pilots accidentally bombed one of their own armored columns.[32]

Retired Admiral, Shlomo Erell, who was Chief of the Navy in Israel in June 1967, told the Associated Press (June 5, 1977): "No one would ever have dreamt that an American ship would be there. Even the United States didn't know where its ship was. We were advised by the proper authorities that there was no American ship within 100 miles."

Secretary of Defense Robert McNamara told Congress on July 26, 1967: "It was the conclusion of the investigatory body, headed by an admiral of the Navy in whom we have great confidence, that the attack was not intentional."

In 1987, McNamara repeated his belief that the attack was a mistake, telling a caller on the "Larry King Show" that he had seen nothing in the 20 years since to change his mind that there had been no "cover-up."[33]

Israel apologized for the tragedy and paid nearly $13 million in humanitarian reparations to the United States and to the families of the victims in amounts established by the U.S. State Department. The matter was officially closed between the two governments by an exchange of diplomatic notes on December 17, 1987.

Notes

1 *Encyclopedia Americana Annual* 1961, (NY: Americana Corporation, 1961), p. 387.

2 Yehoshafat Harkabi, *Arab Attitudes To Israel,* (Jerusalem: Keter Publishing House, 1972), p. 27.

3 Howard Sachar, *A History of Israel: From the Rise of Zionism to Our Time,* (NY: Alfred A. Knopf, 1979), p. 616.

4 Samuel Katz, *Battleground-Fact and Fantasy in Palestine,* (NY: Bantam Books, 1985), pp. 10-11, 185.

5 Netanel Lorch, *One Long War,* (Jerusalem: Keter, 1976), p. 110.

6 Isi Leibler, *The Case For Israel,* (Australia: The Globe Press, 1972), p. 60.

7 Ibid.

8 Leibler, p. 60.

9 Leibler, p. 18.

10 Leibler, p. 60.

11 Leibler, p. 18.

12 Chaim Herzog, *The Arab-Israeli Wars,* (NY: Random House, 1982), p. 149.

13 *United Nations Conference on the Law of the Sea,* (Geneva: UN Publications 1958), pp. 132-134.

14 Yehuda Lukacs, *Documents on the Israeli-Palestinian Conflict 1967-1983,* (NY: Cambridge University Press, 1984), pp. 17-18; Abba Eban, *Abba Eban,* (NY: Random House, 1977), p. 358.

[15] Lyndon B. Johnson, *The Vantage Point: Perspectives of the Presidency* 1963-1969, (NY: Holt, Rinehart and Winston, 1971), p. 293.

[16] AP, (June 5, 1967).

[17] Sachar, p. 629.

[18] Katz, p. 3.

[19] *Jerusalem Post*, (April 23, 1999).

[20] *Encyclopedia Americana Annual* 1968, p. 366.

[21] George Gruen, *"The Refugees of Arab-Israeli Conflict,"* (NY: American Jewish Committee, March 1969), p. 5.

[22] Gruen, p. 5.

[23] Gruen, p. 4.

[24] *Encyclopedia Americana Annual* 1968, p. 366.

[25] Don Peretz, *"Israel's New Dilemma," Middle East Journal*, (Winter 1968), pp. 45-46.

[26] Lyndon B. Johnson, *Public Papers of the President*, (DC: GPO 1968), p. 683.

[27] Yitzhak Rabin, *The Rabin Memoirs*, (CA: University of California Press, 1996), pp. 108-109.

[28] *Rabin*, pp. 110.

[29] Dan Kurzman, *Soldier of Peace: The Life of Yitzhak Rabin*, (NY: HarperCollins, 1998), pp. 224-227; Rabin, pp. 108-109.

[30] *Washington Post*, (November 6, 1991).

[31] Hirsh Goodman, *"Messrs. Errors and No Facts,"* Jerusalem Report, (November 21, 1991).

[32] Hirsh Goodman and Ze'ev Schiff, "The Attack on the *Liberty," Atlantic Monthly,* (September 1984).

[33] *"The Larry King Show"* (radio), (February 5, 1987).

7. Between the Wars

MYTH

"After the 1967 war, Israel refused to negotiate a settlement with the Arabs."

FACT

After its victory in the Six-Day War, Israel hoped the Arab states would enter peace negotiations. Israel signaled to the Arab states its willingness to relinquish virtually all the territories it acquired in exchange for peace. As Moshe Dayan put it, Jerusalem was waiting only for a telephone call from Arab leaders to start negotiations.[1]

But these hopes were dashed in August 1967 when Arab leaders meeting in Khartoum adopted a formula of three noes: "no peace with Israel, no negotiations with Israel, no recognition of Israel."[2]

As former Israeli President Chaim Herzog wrote: "Israel's belief that the war had come to an end and that peace would now reign along the borders was soon dispelled. Three weeks after the conclusion of hostilities, the first major incident occurred on the Suez Canal."[3]

MYTH

"According to Security Council Resolution 242, Israel's acquisition of territory through the 1967 war is 'inadmissible.'"

FACT

On November 22, 1967, the UN Security Council unanimously adopted Resolution 242, establishing the principles that were to guide the negotiations for an Arab-Israeli peace settlement. This resolution was a tortuously negotiated compromise between competing proposals.

The first point addressed by the resolution is the "inadmissibility of the acquisition of territory by war." Some people take this to mean that Israel is required to withdraw from all the territories it captured. On the contrary, the reference clearly applies only to an offensive war. If not, the resolution would provide an incentive for aggression. If one country attacks another, and the defender repels the attack and acquires territory in the process, the former interpretation would require the defender to return all the land it took. Thus, aggressors would have little to lose because they would be insured against the main consequence of defeat.

The ultimate goal of 242, as expressed in paragraph 3, is the achievement of a "peaceful and accepted settlement." This means a negotiated agreement based on the resolution's principles rather than one imposed upon the parties.

This is also the implication of Resolution 338, according to Arthur Goldberg, the American ambassador who led the delegation to the UN in 1967.[4] That resolution, adopted after the 1973 war, called for negotiations between the parties to start immediately and concurrently with the cease-fire.

> *"This is the first war in history which has ended with the victors suing for peace and the vanquished calling for unconditional surrender."*
> — **Abba Eban**[5]

MYTH
"Resolution 242 requires Israel to return to its pre-1967 boundaries."

FACT

The most controversial clause in Resolution 242 is the call for the "Withdrawal of Israeli armed forces from territories occupied in the recent conflict." This is linked to the second unambiguous clause calling for "termination of all claims or states of belligerency" and the recognition that "every State in the area" has the "right to live in peace within secure and recognized boundaries free from threats or acts of force."

The resolution does not make Israeli withdrawal a prerequisite for Arab action. Moreover, it does not specify how much territory Israel is required to give up. The Security Council did not say Israel must withdraw from "all the" territories occupied after the Six-Day War. This was quite deliberate. The Soviet delegate wanted the inclusion of those words and said that their exclusion meant "that part of these territories can remain in Israeli hands." The Arab states pushed for the word "all" to be included, but this was rejected. They nevertheless asserted that they would read the resolution as if it included the word "all." The British Ambassador who drafted the approved resolution, Lord Caradon, declared after the vote: "It is only the resolution that will bind us, and we regard its wording as clear."[6]

This literal interpretation, without the implied "all," was repeatedly declared to be the correct one by those involved in drafting the resolution. On October 29, 1969, for example, the British Foreign Secretary told the House of Commons the withdrawal envisaged by the resolution would not be from "all the territories."[7] When asked to explain the British position later, Lord Caradon said: "It would have been wrong to demand that Israel return to its positions of June 4, 1967, because those positions were undesirable and artificial."[8]

Similarly, Ambassador Arthur Goldberg explained: "The notable omissions — which were not accidental — in regard to withdrawal are the words 'the' or 'all' and 'the June 5, 1967 lines'....the resolution speaks of withdrawal from occupied territories without defining the extent of withdrawal."[9]

The resolutions clearly call on the Arab states to make peace with Israel. The principal condition is that Israel withdraw from "territories occupied" in 1967. Since Israel withdrew from approximately 93 percent of the territories when it gave up the Sinai and portions of the Gaza Strip and West Bank, it has already partially, if not wholly, fulfilled its obligation under 242.

The Arab states also objected to the call for "secure and recognized boundaries" because they feared this implied negotiations with Israel. The Arab League explicitly ruled this out at Khartoum in August 1967, when it proclaimed the three "noes." Goldberg explained that this phrase was specifically included because the parties were expected to make "territorial adjustments in their peace settlement encompassing less than a complete withdrawal of Israeli forces from occupied territories, inasmuch as Israel's prior frontiers had proved to be notably insecure."

The question, then, is whether Israel has to give up any additional territory. Now that peace agreements have been signed with Egypt and Jordan, and Israel has withdrawn to the international border with Lebanon, the only remaining territorial disputes are with the Palestinians (who are not even mentioned in 242) and Syria.

The dispute with Syria is over the Golan Heights. Israeli Prime Minister Yitzhak Rabin expressed a willingness to negotiate a compromise in exchange for peace; however, then-President Hafez Assad refused to consider even a limited peace treaty unless Israel first agreed to a complete withdrawal. Under 242, Israel has no obligation to withdraw from any part of the Golan in the absence of a peace accord with Syria.

It is also important to realize that other Arab states -- such as Saudi Arabia, Iraq and Libya -- that continue to maintain a state of war with Israel, or have refused to grant Israel diplomatic recognition, have no territorial disputes with Israel. They have nevertheless conditioned their relations (at least rhetorically) on an Israeli withdrawal to the pre-1967 borders.

Although ignored by most analysts, Resolution 242 does have other provisions. One requirement is that freedom of navigation be guaranteed. This clause was included because a principal cause of the 1967 war was Egypt's blockade of the Strait of Tiran.

MYTH

"Resolution 242 recognizes a Palestinian right to self-determination."

FACT

The Palestinians are not mentioned anywhere in Resolution 242. They are only alluded to in the second clause of the second article of 242, which calls for "a just settlement of the refugee problem." Nowhere does it require that Palestinians be given any political rights or territory.

MYTH

"The Arab states and the PLO accepted Resolution 242 whereas Israel rejected it."

FACT

The Arab states have traditionally said they accepted 242 as defined by them, that is, as requiring Israel's total, unconditional withdrawal from the occupied territories.

In a statement to the General Assembly October 15, 1968, the PLO, rejecting Resolution 242, said "the implementation of said resolution will lead to the loss of every hope for the establishment of peace and security in Palestine and the Middle East region."

By contrast, Ambassador Abba Eban expressed Israel's position to the Security Council on May 1, 1968: "My government has indicated its acceptance of the Security Council resolution for the promotion of agreement on the establishment of a just and lasting peace. I am also authorized to reaffirm that we are willing to seek agreement with each Arab State on all matters included in that resolution."

It took nearly a quarter century, but the PLO finally agreed that Resolutions 242 and 338 should be the basis for negotiations with Israel when it signed the Declaration of Principles in September 1993.

MYTH

"The Palestinians were willing to negotiate a settlement after the Six-Day War."

FACT

The Arab League created the Palestine Liberation Organization (PLO) in Cairo in 1964 as a weapon against Israel. Until the Six-Day War, the PLO engaged in terrorist attacks that contributed to the momentum toward conflict. Neither the PLO nor any other Palestinian groups campaigned for Jordan or Egypt to create an independent Palestinian state in the West Bank and Gaza. The focus of Palestinian activism was on the destruction of Israel.

After the Arab states were defeated in 1967, the Palestinians did not alter their basic objective. With one million Arabs coming under Israeli rule, some Palestinians believed the prospect for waging a popular war of liberation had grown. Toward that end, Yasser Arafat instigated a campaign of terror from the West Bank. During September-December 1967, 61 attacks were launched, most against civilian targets such as factories, movie theaters and private homes.[10]

Israeli security forces gradually became more effective in thwarting terrorist plans inside Israel and the territories. Consequently, the PLO began to pursue a different strategy — attacking Jews and Israeli targets abroad. In early 1968, the first of many aircraft was hijacked by Palestinian terrorists.

Notes

[1] Walter Lacquer, *The Road to War*, (London: Weidenfeld and Nicolson, 1968), p. 297.

[2] Yehuda Lukacs, *Documents on the Israeli-Palestinian Conflict 1967-1983*, (NY: Cambridge University Press, 1984), p. 213.

[3] Chaim Herzog, *The Arab-Israeli Wars*, (NY: Random House, 1982), p. 195.

[4] *Jerusalem Post*, (May 28, 1984).

[5] Abba Eban, *Abba Eban*, (NY: Random House, 1977), p. 446.

[6] Prosper Weil, "Territorial Settlement in the Resolution of November 22, 1967," in John Moore, ed., *The Arab-Israeli Conflict*, (NJ: Princeton University Press, 1974), p. 321.

[7] Eban, p. 452.

[8] *Beirut Daily Star*, (June 12, 1974).

[9] Speech to AIPAC Policy Conference, (May 8, 1973).

[10] Netanel Lorch, *One Long War*, (Jerusalem: Keter, 1976), pp. 139-146.

8. The War of Attrition, 1967-1970

MYTH

"Israel was responsible for the War of Attrition."

FACT

Egypt's President Gamal Nasser thought that because most of Israel's army consisted of reserves, it could not withstand a lengthy war of attrition. He believed Israel would be unable to endure the economic burden, and the constant casualties would undermine Israeli morale. To pursue this strategy of slowly weakening Israel, Nasser ordered attacks on Israel that were calibrated so that they would not provoke an all-out Israeli war in response.

As early as July 1, 1967, Egypt began shelling Israeli positions near the Suez Canal. On October 21, 1967, Egypt sank the Israeli destroyer *Eilat*, killing 47. A few months later, Egyptian artillery began to shell Israeli positions along the Suez Canal and ambush Israeli military patrols. This bloody War of Attrition, as it became known, lasted three years. The Israeli death toll between June 15, 1967, and August 8, 1970 (when a cease-fire was declared), was 1,424 soldiers and more than 100 civilians. Another 2,000 soldiers and 700 civilians were wounded.[1]

MYTH

"Egypt terminated the War of Attrition, and sought to reach some accommodation with Israel, only to have Jerusalem spurn these initiatives."

FACT

In the summer of 1970, the United States persuaded Israel and Egypt to accept a cease-fire. This cease-fire was designed to lead to negotiations under UN auspices. Israel declared that it would accept the principle of withdrawal from territories it had captured.

But on August 7, the Soviets and Egyptians deployed sophisticated ground-to-air SAM-2 and SAM-3 missiles in the restricted 32-mile-deep zone along the west bank of the Suez Canal. This was a clear violation of the cease-fire agreement, which barred the introduction or construction of any military installations in this area.

Time magazine observed that U.S. reconnaissance "showed that the 36 SAM-2 missiles sneaked into the cease-fire zone constitute only the first line of the most massive anti-aircraft system ever created."[2]

Defense Department satellite photos demonstrated conclusively that 63 SAM-2 sites were installed in a 78-mile band between the cities of Ismailia and Suez. Three years later, these missiles provided air coverage for Egypt's surprise attack against Israel.[3]

Despite the Egyptian violations, the UN-sponsored talks resumed — additional evidence that Israel was anxious to make progress toward peace. The talks were swiftly short-circuited, however, by UN Special Envoy Gunnar Jarring, when he accepted the Egyptian interpretation of Resolution 242 and called for Israel's total withdrawal to the pre-June 5, 1967, demarcation lines.

On that basis, Egypt expressed its willingness "to enter into a peace agreement with Israel" in a February 20, 1971, letter to Jarring. But this seeming moderation masked an unchanging Egyptian irredentism and unwillingness to accept a real peace, as shown by the letter's sweeping reservations and preconditions.

The crucial sentences about a "peace agreement with Israel" were neither published nor broadcast in Egypt. Moreover, Egypt refused to enter direct talks with the Jewish State. Israel attempted to at least transform the struggling Jarring mission into indirect talks by addressing all letters not to Jarring, but to the Egyptian government. Egypt refused to accept them.

Just after the letter to Jarring, Anwar Sadat, Egypt's new president, addressed the Palestine National Council (PNC) meeting in Cairo. He promised support to the PLO "until victory" and declared that Egypt would not accept Resolution 242.[4]

Five days after Sadat suggested he was ready to make peace with Israel, Mohammed Heikal, a Sadat confidant and editor of the semi-official *Al-Ahram*, wrote:

> Arab policy at this stage has but two objectives. The first, the elimination of the traces of the 1967 aggression through an Israeli withdrawal from all the territories it occupied that year. The second objective is the elimination of the traces of the 1948 aggression, by the means of the elimination of the State of Israel itself. This is, however, as yet an abstract, undefined objective, and some of us have erred in commencing the latter step before the former.[5]

MYTH

"Egypt repeatedly expressed a willingness to begin peace negotiations with Israel from 1971 to 1973. Israel's rejection of these initiatives led to the Yom Kippur War."

FACT

With the collapse of the Jarring mission, the United States undertook a new initiative. It proposed an Israeli-Egyptian interim agreement, calling for the

Jewish State's partial withdrawal from the Suez Canal and the opening of that waterway.

Israel was willing to enter negotiations without preconditions, but Sadat demanded that Israel agree, as part of an interim agreement, to withdraw ultimately to the old 1967 lines. In effect, Sadat was seeking an advance guarantee of the outcome of "negotiations." This was unacceptable to Israel and suggested that Sadat was not genuinely interested in peace.

Notes

[1] Some historians consider the starting date of the War of Attrition in 1968 or 1969. We are using Chaim Herzog's time frame. Chaim Herzog, *The Arab-Israeli Wars*, (NY: Vintage Books, 1984), pp. 195-221; Nadav Safran, *Israel The Embattled Ally*, (MA: Harvard University Press, 1981), p. 266.

[2] *Time*, (September 14, 1970).

[3] John Pimlott, *The Middle East Conflicts From 1945 to the Present*, (NY: Crescent Books, 1983), p. 99.

[4] Radio Cairo, (February 27, 1971).

[5] *Al-Ahram*, (February 25, 1971).

9. The 1973 Yom Kippur War

MYTH

"Israel was responsible for the 1973 war."

FACT

On October 6, 1973 — Yom Kippur, the holiest day in the Jewish calendar — Egypt and Syria opened a coordinated surprise attack against Israel. The equivalent of the total forces of NATO in Europe were mobilized on Israel's borders.[1] On the Golan Heights, approximately 180 Israeli tanks faced an onslaught of 1,400 Syrian tanks. Along the Suez Canal, fewer than 500 Israeli defenders were attacked by 80,000 Egyptians.

Thrown onto the defensive during the first two days of fighting, Israel mobilized its reserves and eventually repulsed the invaders and carried the war deep into Syria and Egypt. The Arab states were swiftly resupplied by sea and air from the Soviet Union, which rejected U.S. efforts to work toward an immediate cease-fire. As a result, the United States belatedly began its own airlift to Israel. Two weeks later, Egypt was saved from a disastrous defeat by the UN Security Council, which had failed to act while the tide was in the Arabs' favor.

The Soviet Union showed no interest in initiating peacemaking efforts while it looked like the Arabs might win. The same was true for UN Secretary-General Kurt Waldheim.

On October 22, the Security Council adopted Resolution 338 calling for "all parties to the present fighting to cease all firing and terminate all military activity immediately." The vote came on the day that Israeli forces cut off and isolated the Egyptian Third Army and were in a position to destroy it.[2]

Despite the Israel Defense Forces' ultimate success on the battlefield, the war was considered a diplomatic and military failure. A total of 2,688 Israeli soldiers were killed.

MYTH

"Egyptian President Anwar Sadat had agreed to U.S. peace proposals and did not seek war."

FACT

In 1971, Egyptian President Anwar Sadat raised the possibility of signing an agreement with Israel, provided that all the occupied territories were returned by the Israelis. No progress toward peace was made, however, so the following year, Sadat said war was inevitable and he was prepared to sacrifice one million soldiers in the showdown with Israel.[3] His threat did not materialize that year.

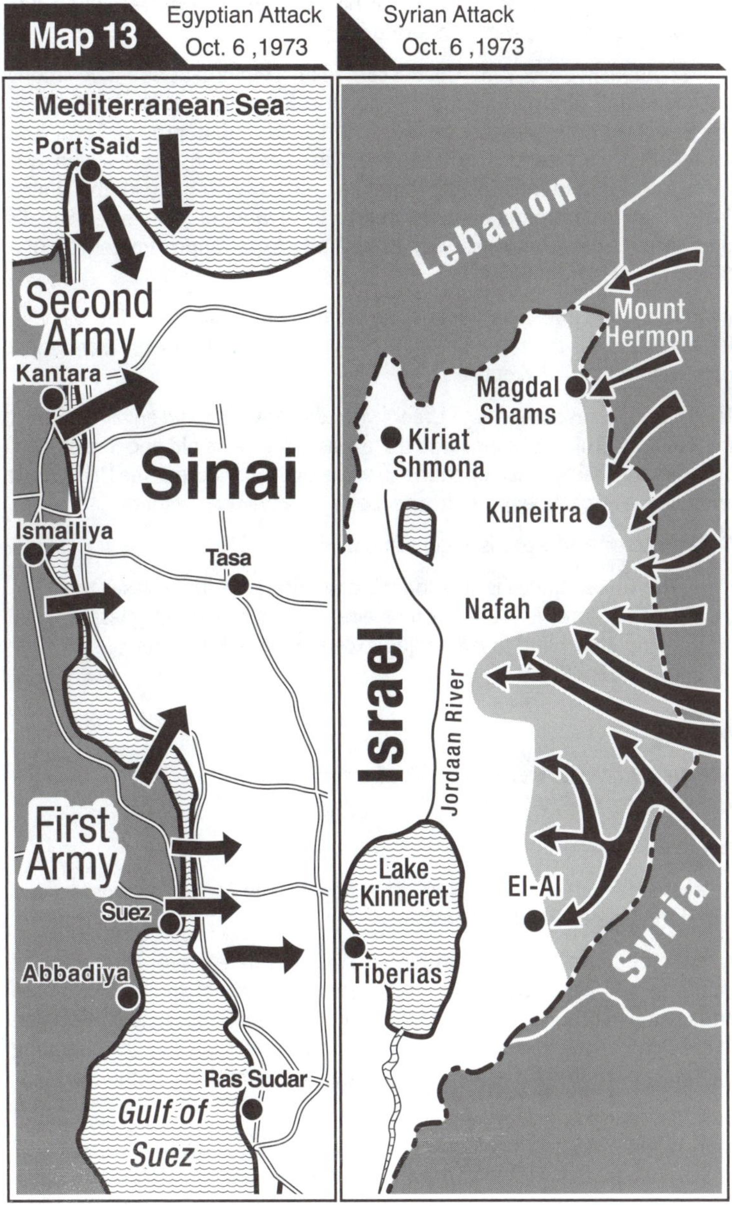

Map 13 | Egyptian Attack Oct. 6, 1973 | Syrian Attack Oct. 6, 1973

Mediterranean Sea
Port Said
Second Army
Kantara
Sinai
Ismailiya
Tasa
First Army
Suez
Abbadiya
Ras Sudar
Gulf of Suez

Lebanon
Mount Hermon
Magdal Shams
Kiriat Shmona
Kuneitra
Nafah
Israel
Jordaan River
Lake Kinneret
Tiberias
El-Al
Syria

Throughout 1972, and for much of 1973, Sadat threatened war unless the United States forced Israel to accept his interpretation of Resolution 242 – total Israeli withdrawal from territories taken in 1967.

Simultaneously, the Egyptian leader carried on a diplomatic offensive among European and African states to win support for his cause. He appealed to the Soviets to bring pressure on the United States and to provide Egypt with more offensive weapons to cross the Suez Canal. The Soviet Union was more interested in maintaining the appearance of détente with the United States than in confrontation in the Middle East; therefore, it rejected Sadat's demands. Sadat's response was to abruptly expel approximately 20,000 Soviet advisers from Egypt.

In an April 1973 interview, Sadat again warned he would renew the war with Israel.[4] But it was the same threat he had made in 1971 and 1972, and most observers remained skeptical.

The United States agreed with Israel's view that Egypt should engage in direct negotiations. The U.S.-sponsored truce was three years old and Secretary of State Henry Kissinger had opened a new dialogue for peace at the UN. Almost everyone was confident the prospect of a new war was remote.

Sadat reacted acidly to Kissinger's initiative:

> The United States is still under Zionist pressure. The glasses the United States is wearing on its eyes are entirely Zionist glasses, completely blind to everything except what Israel wants. We do not accept this.[5]

MYTH

"Egypt and Syria were the only Arab states involved in the 1973 war."

FACT

At least nine Arab states, including four non-Middle Eastern nations, actively aided the Egyptian-Syrian war effort.

A few months before the Yom Kippur War, Iraq transferred a squadron of Hunter jets to Egypt. During the war, an Iraqi division of some 18,000 men and several hundred tanks was deployed in the central Golan and participated in the October 16 attack against Israeli positions.[6] Iraqi MiGs began operating over the Golan Heights as early as October 8, the third day of the war.

Besides serving as financial underwriters, Saudi Arabia and Kuwait committed men to battle. A Saudi brigade of approximately 3,000 troops was dispatched to Syria, where it participated in fighting along the approaches to Damascus. Also, violating Paris's ban on the transfer of French-made weapons, Libya sent Mirage fighters to Egypt (from 1971-1973, Libyan President Muammar

Qaddafi gave Cairo more than $1 billion in aid to rearm Egypt and to pay the Soviets for weapons delivered).[7]

> *"All countries should wage war against the Zionists, who are there to destroy all human organizations and to destroy civilization and the work which good people are trying to do."*
>
> **— King Faisal of Saudi Arabia** [8]

Other North African countries responded to Arab and Soviet calls to aid the front-line states. Algeria sent three aircraft squadrons of fighters and bombers, an armored brigade and 150 tanks. Approximately 1,000-2,000 Tunisian soldiers were positioned in the Nile Delta. The Sudan stationed 3,500 troops in southern Egypt, and Morocco sent three brigades to the front lines, including 2,500 men to Syria.

Lebanese radar units were used by Syrian air defense forces. Lebanon also allowed Palestinian terrorists to shell Israeli civilian settlements from its territory. Palestinians fought on the Southern Front with the Egyptians and Kuwaitis.[9]

The least enthusiastic participant in the October fighting was probably Jordan's King Hussein, who apparently had been kept uninformed of Egyptian and Syrian war plans. But Hussein did send two of his best units — the 40th and 60th Armored Brigades — to Syria. This force took positions in the southern sector, defending the main Amman-Damascus route and attacking Israeli positions along the Kuneitra-Sassa road on October 16. Three Jordanian artillery batteries also participated in the assault, carried out by nearly 100 tanks.[10]

> *Syrian Minister of Defense Mustafa Tlas told the Syrian National Assembly in December 1973 of the following example of "supreme valor" by Syrian troops:*
>
> *"There is the outstanding case of a recruit from Aleppo who murdered 28 Jewish soldiers all by himself, slaughtering them like sheep. All of his comrades in arms witnessed this. He butchered three of them with an ax and decapitated them....He struggled face to face with one of them and throwing down his ax managed to break his neck and devour his flesh in front of his comrades. This is a special case. Need I single it out to award him the Medal of the Republic. I will grant this medal to any soldier who succeeds in killing 28 Jews, and I will cover him with appreciation and honor his bravery."[11]*

MYTH

"Israel mistreated Arab soldiers captured during the 1973 war."

FACT

Numerous observers reported that Israel's treatment of captured Arab soldiers was above reproach. Hugh Baker, a representative of Amnesty International, declared: "They are being treated well...and they seem to be getting the best medical treatment possible."[12]

Soon after his release, Syrian Col. Atnon El-Kodar complained of maltreatment by Israeli doctors, charging that they unnecessarily amputated his leg. An American reporter, Ed deFontaine, who had met Kodar in an Israeli hospital, felt the colonel must "have had a very short memory about what was done to save his life....He told me that he owed his life to [his] doctor."[13]

By contrast, Israeli soldiers captured by Syrian and Egyptian troops *were* mistreated. Upon their surrender, dozens of Israeli POWs were murdered, others were tortured in violation of the Geneva Prisoner of War Convention.

According to a report submitted to the International Red Cross by the Israeli Government on December 8, 1973, Israeli troops discovered bodies of Israeli soldiers on the Golan Heights whose hands and legs had been bound and whose eyes had been gouged. They had been executed at close range.

On the Egyptian front, according to a report submitted to the Red Cross on December 9, 1973, Israeli soldiers fared no better. Surrendering soldiers were beaten, subjected to whippings, sexual attacks, burning and starvation — and many were executed.

After the war, Syria refused for months to provide lists of POWs to Israel, the Red Cross or U.S. Secretary of State Henry Kissinger.

The *London Sunday Times* reported that Syrian officers had turned Israeli prisoners over to Soviet military interrogation teams. "The interrogators...have employed medical and other techniques to break the resistance of the Israelis," the *Times* said.[14]

MYTH

"Israeli troops deliberately destroyed the entire town
of Kuneitra prior to their withdrawal from the area
in June 1974."

FACT

Kuneitra, a small town just north of the Israeli-Syrian border, was not destroyed by Israel after the war. The town was severely damaged in both the 1967 and 1973 conflicts. In the Yom Kippur War, it was shelled and captured by Syrian troops, retaken by Israelis, and then defended against intense Syrian counterattacks. Tanks roamed through the town, between and through buildings. Kuneitra also suffered damage from 81 days of artillery duels that preceded the disengagement.

Kuneitra's strategic position near the Israeli border proved suitable for the location of Syrian army facilities, including command and control centers for the entire front-line area. Syria concentrated at least half its army in this region, of which Kuneitra was the capital. Military installations, barracks, support centers, fuel and ammunition dumps were constructed. As a result, the sources of livelihood of the inhabitants changed from primitive peasant agriculture to service in the army.

Long before Israel's alleged destruction of the town, the *London Times* reported that Kuneitra, which once "had about 17,000 residents plus a Syrian army garrison...is in ruins and deserted after seven years of war and dereliction. It looks like a wild west town struck by an earthquake....Nearly every building is heavily damaged and scores have collapsed...."[15]

Notes

[1]   Chaim Herzog, *The Arab-Israeli Wars*, (NY: Random House, 1982), p. 230.

[2]   Herzog, p. 280.

[3]   Howard Sachar, *A History of Israel: From the Rise of Zionism to Our Time*, (NY: Alfred A. Knopf, 1979), p. 747.

[4]   *Newsweek*, (April 9, 1973).

[5]   Radio Cairo, (September 28, 1973).

[6]   Trevor Dupuy, *Elusive Victory: The Arab-Israeli Wars, 1947-1974*, (NY: Harper & Row, 1978), p. 462.

[7]   Dupuy, p. 376; Herzog, p. 278; Nadav Safran, *Israel The Embattled Ally*, (MA: Harvard University Press, 1981), p. 499.

[8]   *Beirut Daily Star*, (November 17, 1972).

[9]   Herzog, p. 278, 285, 293; Dupuy, 534.

[10]   Herzog, p. 300.

[11]   Official Gazette of Syria, (July 11, 1974).

[12]   *Jerusalem Post*, (January 4, 1974).

[13]   Group W Radio, (June 11, 1974).

[14]   *London Times*, (May 19, 1974).

[15]   *London Times*, (May 5, 1974).

10. Boundaries

MYTH

"The creation of Israel in 1948 changed political and border arrangements between independent states that had existed for centuries."

FACT

The boundaries of Middle East countries were arbitrarily fixed by the Western powers after Turkey was defeated in World War I and the French and British mandates were set up. The areas allotted to Israel under the UN partition plan had all been under the control of the Ottomans, who had ruled Palestine from 1517 until 1917.

When Turkey was defeated in World War I, the French took over the area now known as Lebanon and Syria. The British assumed control of Palestine and Iraq. In 1926, the borders were redrawn and Lebanon was separated from Syria.

Britain installed the Emir Faisal, who had been deposed by the French in Syria, as ruler of the new kingdom of Iraq. In 1922, the British created the emirate of Transjordan, which incorporated all of Palestine east of the Jordan River. This was done so that the Emir Abdullah, whose family had been defeated in tribal warfare in the Arabian peninsula, would have a Kingdom to rule. None of the countries that border Israel became independent until this century. Many other Arab nations became independent after Israel.[1]

MYTH

"Israel has been an expansionist state since its creation."

FACT

Israel's boundaries were determined by the United Nations when it adopted the partition resolution in 1947. In a series of defensive wars, Israel captured additional territory. On numerous occasions, Israel has withdrawn from these areas.

As part of the 1974 disengagement agreement, Israel returned territories captured in the 1967 and 1973 wars to Syria.

Under the terms of the 1979 Israeli-Egyptian peace treaty, Israel withdrew from the Sinai peninsula for the third time. It had already withdrawn from large parts of the desert area it captured in its War of Independence. After capturing the entire Sinai in the 1956 Suez conflict, Israel relinquished the peninsula to Egypt a year later.

In September 1983, Israel withdrew from large areas of Lebanon to positions south of the Awali River. In 1985, it completed its withdrawal from Lebanon, except for a narrow security zone just north of the Israeli border. That too was abandoned, unilaterally, in 2000.

After signing peace agreements with the Palestinians, and a treaty with Jordan, Israel agreed to withdraw from most of the territory in the West Bank captured from Jordan in 1967. A small area was returned to Jordan, and more than 40 percent was ceded to the Palestinian Authority. The agreement with the Palestinians also involved Israel's withdrawal in 1994 from most of the Gaza Strip, which had been captured from Egypt in 1973.

To date, Israel has withdrawn from more than 40 percent of the West Bank and approximately 80 of the Gaza Strip, and Israeli Prime Minister Ehud Barak offered to return 95 percent of the West Bank and 100 percent of the Gaza Strip in a final settlement. In addition, Prime Minister Yitzhak Rabin and his successors offered to withdraw from virtually all of the Golan Heights in exchange for peace with Syria.

Negotiations continue regarding the final disposition of the remaining disputed territories in Israel's possession. Israel's willingness to make territorial concessions in exchange for security proves its goal is peace, not expansion.

MYTH

"Israel has long sought to conquer Arab lands stretching from the Nile to the Euphrates. There is even a map hanging in the Knesset documenting this."

FACT

This theme is frequently used by Israel's enemies, and is routinely repeated throughout the Arab and Islamic worlds.

In Iran, a map purporting to show Israel's "dream" boundaries — an empire including Saudi Arabia, Iraq, Kuwait, and parts of Turkey and Iran — was included in a 1985 reprint of the *Protocols of the Elders of Zion*, the notorious Czarist forgery.

At a May 25, 1990, press conference in Geneva, Yasser Arafat claimed Israel's 10-Agora coin depicts a map of an enlarged Israel, which included all of Jordan and Lebanon, as well as large portions of Iraq, Syria, Saudi Arabia and Egypt.

In fact, the Agora is patterned after an ancient Jewish coin issued at the time of King Mattathias of the Hasmonean dynasty. The modern Israeli version depicts the shape of the original coin, which had eroded during the ensuing 2,000 years. It is this deformed shape of an ancient coin that Arafat asserted represents a secret "map" of an expansionist Israel.

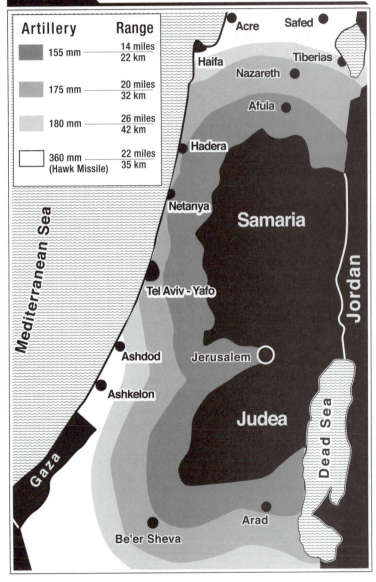

Map 14

Missile and Artillery Ranges From West Bank Positions

Artillery	Range
155 mm	14 miles / 22 km
175 mm	20 miles / 32 km
180 mm	26 miles / 42 km
360 mm (Hawk Missile)	22 miles / 35 km

Mediterranean Sea

Acre

Safed

Haifa

Tiberias

Nazareth

Afula

Hadera

Netanya

Samaria

Tel Aviv - Yafo

Jordan

Ashdod

Jerusalem

Ashkelon

Judea

Dead Sea

Gaza

Arad

Be'er Sheva

Syrian Defense Minister Mustafa Tlas has said that an inscription, "The Land of Israel, from the Euphrates to the Nile," is chiseled over the entrance to the Knesset.[2] Others have claimed a map inside the Knesset shows these borders.

No such inscription or map exists. But many in the Arab world have persuaded themselves it is true. Arabs who have toured the parliament and not seen the map sometimes claim it was removed in anticipation of their visit.[3]

Of course, the best evidence against this myth is the history of Israeli withdrawal from territory captured in 1948, 1956, 1967, 1973 and 1982.

MYTH

"The West Bank is part of Jordan."

FACT

The West Bank was never legally part of Jordan. Under the UN's 1947 partition plan — which the Jews accepted and the Arabs rejected — it was to have been part of an independent Arab state in western Palestine. But the Jordanian army invaded and occupied it during the 1948 war. In 1950, Jordan annexed the West Bank.

Only two governments — Great Britain and Pakistan — formally recognized the Jordanian takeover. The rest of the world, including the United States, never did.

MYTH

"Israel seized the Golan Heights in a war of aggression."

FACT

Between 1948 and 1967, Syria controlled the Golan Heights and used it as a military stronghold from which its troops randomly sniped at Israeli civilians in the Hula Valley below, forcing children living on kibbutzim to sleep in bomb shelters. In addition, many roads in northern Israel could be crossed only after being cleared by mine-detection vehicles. In late 1966, a youth was blown to pieces by a mine while playing football near the Lebanon border. In some cases, attacks were carried out by Yasser Arafat's Fatah, which Syria allowed to operate from its territory.[4]

Israel repeatedly, and unsuccessfully, protested the Syrian bombardments to the UN Mixed Armistice Commission, which was charged with enforcing the cease-fire. For example, Israel went to the UN in October 1966 to demand a halt to the Fatah attacks. The response from Damascus was defiant. "It is not our duty to stop them, but to encourage and strengthen them," the Syrian ambassador responded.[5]

Map 15 The Golan Heights Ridge Line

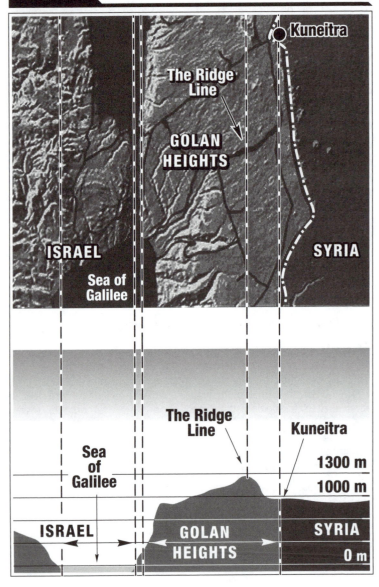

Nothing was done to stop Syria's aggression. A mild Security Council resolution expressing "regret" for such incidents was vetoed by the Soviet Union. Meanwhile, Israel was condemned by the UN when it retaliated. "As far as the Security Council was officially concerned," historian Netanel Lorch wrote, "there was an open season for killing Israelis on their own territory."[6]

After the Six-Day War began, the Syrian air force attempted to bomb oil refineries in Haifa. While Israel was fighting in the Sinai and West Bank, Syrian artillery bombarded Israeli forces in the eastern Galilee, and armored units fired on villages in the Hula Valley below the Golan Heights.

On June 9, 1967, Israel moved against Syrian forces on the Golan. By late afternoon, June 10, Israel was in complete control of the plateau. Israel's seizure of the strategic heights occurred only after 19 years of provocation from Syria, and after unsuccessful efforts to get the international community to act against the aggressors.

MYTH

"The Golan has no strategic significance for Israel."

FACT

It is true that Syria — deterred by an IDF presence within artillery range of Damascus — has kept the Golan quiet since 1974. But during this time, Syria has provided a haven and supported numerous terrorist groups that attack Israel from Lebanon and other countries. These include the Democratic Front for the Liberation of Palestine (DFLP), the Popular Front for the Liberation of Palestine (PFLP), Hizballah and the Popular Front for the Liberation of Palestine-General Command (PFLP-GC). In addition, Syria still deploys hundreds of thousands of troops — as much as 75 percent of its army — on the Israeli front near the Heights.

From the western Golan, it is only about 60 miles — without major terrain obstacles — to Haifa and Acre, Israel's industrial heartland. The Golan — rising from 400 to 1700 feet in the western section bordering on pre-1967 Israel — overlooks the Hula Valley, Israel's richest agricultural area. In the hands of a friendly neighbor, the escarpment has little military importance. If controlled by a hostile country, however, the Golan has the potential to again become a strategic nightmare for Israel.

Before the Six-Day War, when Israeli agricultural settlements in the Galilee came under fire from the Golan, Israel's options for countering the Syrian attacks were constrained by the geography of the Heights. "Counterbattery fires were limited by the lack of observation from the Hula Valley; air attacks were degraded by well-dug-in Syrian positions with strong overhead cover, and a ground attack against the positions...would require major forces with the attendant risks of heavy casualties and severe political repercussions," U.S. Army Col. (Ret.) Irving Heymont observed.[7]

When Israel eventually took these risks and stormed the Syrian positions in 1967, it suffered 115 dead — roughly the number of Americans killed during Operation Desert Storm.

As the peace process faltered in the late 1990's, Syria began to renew threats of war with Israel and to make threatening troop movements. Some Israeli analysts have warned of the possibility of a lightning strike by Syrian forces aimed at retaking the Golan. The Israeli Defense Forces have countered the Syrian moves, however, and — to this point — preserved the peace.

For Israel, relinquishing the Golan to a hostile Syria without adequate security arrangements could jeopardize its early-warning system against surprise attack. Israel has built radar systems on Mt. Hermon, the highest point in the region. If Israel withdrew from the Golan and had to relocate these facilities to the lowlands of the Galilee, they would lose much of their strategic effectiveness.

MYTH

"Israel has refused to offer any compromises on the Golan Heights while Syria has been willing to trade peace for land."

FACT

Under Hafez Assad, Syria's position was consistent: Israel must completely withdraw from the entire Golan Heights before he would entertain any discussion of what Syria might do in return. He never expressed any willingness to make peace with Israel if he received the entire Golan or any part of it.

Israel has been equally adamant that it would not give up any territory without knowing what Syria was prepared to concede. Israel's willingness to trade some or all of the Golan is dependent on Syria's agreement to normalize relations and to sign an agreement that would bring about an end to the state of war Syria says exists between them.

The topographical concerns associated with withdrawing from the Golan Heights could be offset by demilitarization, but Israel needs to have a defensible border from which the nation can be defended with minimum losses. The deeper the demilitarization, and the better the early warning, the more flexible Israel can be regarding that border.

In addition to military security, Israelis seek the normalization of relations between the two countries. At a minimum, ties with Syria should be on a par with those Israel has with Egypt; ideally, they would be closer to the type of peace Israel enjoys with Jordan. This means going beyond a bare minimum of an exchange of ambassadors and flight links and creating an environment whereby Israelis and Syrians will feel comfortable visiting each other's country, engaging in trade and other types of cooperation typical of friendly nations.

In the meantime, substantial opposition exists within Israel to withdrawing from the Golan Heights. The expectation of many is that public opinion will shift if and when the Syrians sign an agreement and take measures, such as reigning in Hizballah attacks on Israel from southern Lebanon, that demonstrate a genuine interest in peace. And public opinion will determine whether a treaty is concluded because of a law adopted during Prime Minister Netanyahu's term that requires any agreement to be approved in a national referendum.

President Hafez Assad died in June 2000 and there have not been any negotiations since, as Assad's son and successor, Bashar, has moved to consolidate his power in Syria. Rhetorically, Bashar has not indicated any shift in Syria's position on the Golan. Absent dramatic changes in Syria's government and its attitude toward Israel; however, the Jewish State's security will depend on its retention of military control over the Golan Heights.

> *"From a strictly military point of view, Israel would require the retention of some captured territory in order to provide militarily defensible borders."*
>
> **—Memorandum for the Secretary of Defense**
> from the Joint Chiefs of Staff, June 29, 1967

MYTH

"Israel illegally annexed the Golan Heights in 1981, contravening international law and UN Resolution 242."

FACT

On December 14, 1981, the Knesset voted to annex the Golan Heights. The statute extended Israeli civilian law and administration to the residents of the Golan, replacing the military authority that had ruled the area since 1967. The law does not foreclose the option of negotiations on a final settlement of the status of the territory.

Following the Knesset's approval of the law, Professor Julius Stone of Hastings College of the Law wrote: "There is no rule of international law which requires a lawful military occupant, in this situation, to wait forever before [making] control and government of the territory permanent....Many international lawyers have wondered, indeed, at the patience which led Israel to wait as long as she did."[8]

Relative Size of the Golan Heights

Map 16

Turkey

Mediterranean Sea

Syria
71,054 sq. mi.

The Golan
Heights
459 sq. mi.

Iraq

Israel – 8,479 sq. mi.

Jordan

Saudi Arabia

MYTH

"Israel can withdraw from the West Bank with little more difficulty than was the case in Sinai."

FACT

Several pages of Israel's peace treaty with Egypt are devoted to security arrangements. For example, Article III of the treaty's annex concerns the areas where reconnaissance flights are permitted, and Article V allows the establishment of early-warning systems in specific zones.

The security guarantees, which were required to give Israel the confidence to withdraw, were only possible because the Sinai was demilitarized. They provide Israel a large buffer zone of more than 100 miles. Today, the Egyptian border is 60 miles from Tel Aviv and 70 from Jerusalem, the nearest major Israeli cities. The Sinai remains sparsely populated desert, with a population of less than 250,000.

The situation in the territories is entirely different. More than two million Arabs live in the West Bank, many in crowded cities and refugee camps. Most of them are located close to Israeli cities such as Tel Aviv and Jerusalem. It is important for Israel that the West Bank not fall into the hands of hostile neighbors. The infiltration in recent years of terrorists from the Palestinian Authority who have committed horrific acts, such as suicide bombings, illustrate the danger.

Despite the danger, Israel has withdrawn from more than 40 percent of the West Bank since Oslo, and offered to give up 95 percent of it in return for a final settlement with the Palestinians. Israel will not, and cannot, however, go back to the pre-1967 borders as demanded by the Palestinians and the Arab states.

The agreements Israel has signed with the Palestinians, and the treaty with Jordan, contain many specific provisions designed to minimize the security risks to Israel. The violence of the "al-Aksa intifada," however, has shown that the Palestinians are not prepared to fulfill their signed commitments to prevent terrorism and incitement.

> *"It is impossible to defend Jerusalem unless you hold the high ground....An aircraft that takes off from an airport in Amman is going to be over Jerusalem in two-and-a-half minutes, so it's utterly impossible for me to defend the whole country unless I hold that land."*
>
> **—Lieutenant General (Ret.) Thomas Kelly, director of operations for the Joint Chiefs of Staff during the Gulf War**[9]

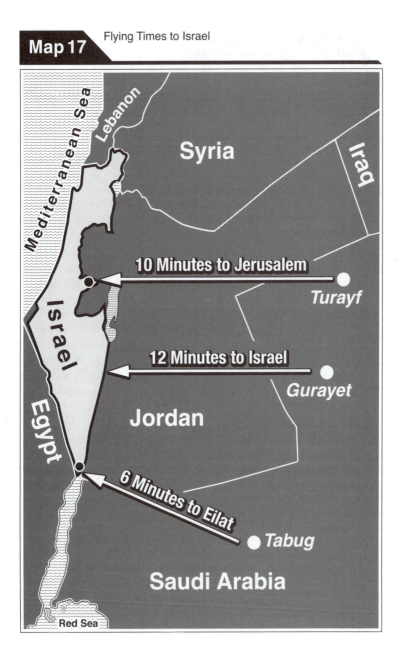

Map 17 Flying Times to Israel

Mediterranean Sea

Lebanon

Syria

Iraq

10 Minutes to Jerusalem

Turayf

Israel

12 Minutes to Israel

Gurayet

Egypt

Jordan

6 Minutes to Eilat

Tabug

Saudi Arabia

Red Sea

MYTH

"The Gulf War proves that Israel's demands for defensible borders are unrealistic in an era of ballistic missiles and long-range bombers capable of crossing vast amounts of territory in minutes."

FACT

History shows that aerial attacks have never defeated a nation. Countries are only conquered by troops occupying land. The most recent example of this was Iraq's invasion of Kuwait, in which the latter nation was overrun and occupied in a matter of hours. Though the multinational force bombed Iraq for close to six weeks, Kuwait was not liberated until the Allied troops marched into that country in the war's final days. Defensible borders are those that would prevent or impede such a ground assault.

Israel's return to its pre-1967 borders, which the Arab states want to reimpose, would sorely tempt potential aggressors to launch attacks on the Jewish State — as they did routinely before 1967. Israel would lose the extensive system of early-warning radars it has set up in the hills of Judea and Samaria. Were a hostile neighbor then to seize control of these mountains, its army could split Israel in two: From there, it is only about 15 miles — without any major geographic obstacles — to the Mediterranean.

At their narrowest point, these 1967 lines are within 9 miles of the Israeli coast, 11 miles from Tel Aviv, 10 from Beersheba, 21 from Haifa and one foot from Jerusalem.

In 1989, the Jaffee Center for Strategic Studies, an Israeli think tank considered dovish, wrote:

> The introduction of surface-to-surface missiles into the arena sometimes gives rise to the question of whether the concepts of strategic depth and security arrangements remain meaningful in this new era. The answer is an unequivocal yes. Early-warning stations and the deployment of surface-to-air missile batteries can provide the time needed to sound an air-raid alert, and warn the population to take shelter from a missile attack. They might even allow enemy missiles to be intercepted in mid-flight.

The study concluded: "As long as such missiles are armed with conventional warheads, they may cause painful losses and damage, but they cannot decide the outcome of a war."[10]

In a report to the Secretary of Defense in 1967, the U.S. Joint Chiefs of Staff wrote that, at a minimum, "Israel would need a defense line generally along the Bardala-Tuba-Nablus-Bira-Jerusalem axis, and then to the northern part

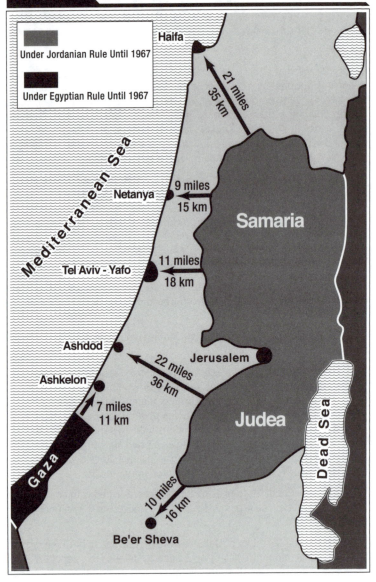

Map 18 — Distances Between Israeli Population Centers and Pre-1967 Armistice Lines

Under Jordanian Rule Until 1967

Under Egyptian Rule Until 1967

Haifa

21 miles
35 km

Mediterranean Sea

Samaria

Netanya
9 miles
15 km

Tel Aviv - Yafo
11 miles
18 km

Ashdod

Jerusalem
22 miles
36 km

Ashkelon
7 miles
11 km

Judea

Dead Sea

Gaza

10 miles
16 km

Be'er Sheva

of the Dead Sea. This line would widen the narrow portion of Israel and provide additional terrain for the defense of Tel Aviv."

The report also provides support for a united Jerusalem under Israeli control. To defend Jerusalem, the Joint Chiefs concluded, Israel would need to have its border "positioned to the east of the city."[11]

> *"For a Texan, a first visit to Israel is an eye-opener. At the narrowest point, it's only 8 miles from the Mediterranean to the old Armistice line: That's less than from the top to the bottom of Dallas-Ft. Worth Airport. The whole of pre-1967 Israel is only about six times the size of the King Ranch near Corpus Christi."*
>
> **— President George W. Bush**[12]

MYTH
"Israel 'occupies' the West Bank."

FACT

In politics words matter and, unfortunately, the misuse of words applying to the Arab-Israeli conflict has shaped perceptions to Israel's disadvantage. As in the case of the term "West Bank," the word "occupation" has been hijacked by those who wish to paint Israel in the harshest possible light. It also gives apologists a way to try to explain away terrorism as "resistance to occupation," as if the women and children killed by suicide bombers in buses, pizzerias and shopping malls were responsible for the plight of the Arabs. Given the negative connotation of an "occupier," it is not surprising that Arab spokespersons use the word, or some variations, as many times as possible when interviewed by the press. The more accurate description of the territories in Judea and Samaria is "disputed" territories.

In fact, most other disputed territories around the world are not referred to as being occupied by the party that controls them. This is true, for example, of the hotly contested region of Kashmir.[13]

Occupation typically refers to foreign control of an area that was under the previous sovereignty of another state. In the case of the West Bank, there was no legitimate sovereign because the territory had been illegally occupied by Jordan from 1948 to 1967. The Palestinians never demanded an end to Jordanian occupation and the creation of a Palestinian state.

It is also important to distinguish the acquisition of territory in a war of conquest as opposed to a war of self-defense. A nation that attacks another and then retains the territory it conquers is an occupier. One that gains territory in the course of defending itself is not in the same category. And this is the situation with Israel, which specifically told King Hussein that if Jordan stayed out of the 1967 war, Israel would not fight against him. Hussein ignored the warning and attacked Israel. While fending off the assault, and driving out the invading Jordanian troops, Israel came to control the West Bank.

By rejecting Arab demands that Israel be required to withdraw from all the territories won in 1967, the UN Security Council in Resolution 242 acknowledged that Israel was entitled to claim at least part of these lands for new defensible borders.

Since Oslo, the case for tagging Israel as an occupying power has been further weakened by the fact that Israel transferred virtually all civilian authority to the Palestinian Authority. Israel retained the power to control its own external security and that of its citizens, but 98 percent of the Palestinian population in the West Bank and Gaza came under the PA's authority. The extent to which Israel has been forced to maintain a military presence in the territories has been governed by the Palestinians' unwillingness to end violence against Israel. The best way to end the dispute over the territories is for the Palestinians to fulfill their obligations under the Oslo agreements, reform the Palestinian Authority, stop the terror and negotiate a final settlement.

Notes

1 Egypt didn't achieve independence until 1922; Lebanon, 1946; Jordan, 1946; and Syria, 1946. Many of the Gulf states became independent after Israel: Kuwait, 1961; Bahrain, 1970; the United Arab Emirates, 1971; and Qatar, 1971.

2 Al-Jazira, (January 17, 1982).

3 Washington Jewish Week, (July 6, 1989).

4 Netanel Lorch, One Long War, (Jerusalem: Keter, 1976), pp. 106-110.

5 Anne Sinai and Allen Pollack, The Syrian Arab Republic, (NY: American Academic Association for Peace in the Middle East, 1976), p. 117.

6 Lorch, p. 111.

7 Sinai and Pollack, pp. 130-31.

8 Near East Report, (January 29, 1982).

9 Jerusalem Post, (November 7, 1991).

10 Israel's Options for Peace, (Tel Aviv: The Jaffee Center for Strategic Studies, 1989), pp. 171-72.

11 Memorandum for the Secretary of Defense, June 29, 1967, cited in Michael Widlanski, Can Israel Survive a Palestinian State?, (Jerusalem: Institute for Advanced Strategic and Political Studies, 1990), p. 148.

12 Speech to the American Jewish Committee, (May 3, 2001).

13 U.S. Department of State, Consular Information Sheet: India, (February 22, 2002).

11. Israel and Lebanon

MYTH

"Israel cannot claim that its 1982 invasion of Lebanon, launched against an ill-equipped PLO, was a defensive war."

FACT

By June 1982, when the IDF went into Lebanon, the PLO had made life in northern Israel intolerable, by its repeated shelling of Israeli towns.

A force of some 15-18,000 PLO members was encamped in scores of locations in Lebanon. About 5,000-6,000 were foreign mercenaries, coming from such countries as Libya, Iraq, India, Sri Lanka, Chad and Mozambique.[1] Israel discovered enough light arms and other weapons in Lebanon to equip five brigades.[2] The PLO had an arsenal that included mortars, Katyusha rockets, and an extensive anti-aircraft network. The PLO also brought hundreds of T-34 tanks into the area.[3] Syria, which permitted Lebanon to become a haven for the PLO and other terrorist groups, brought surface-to-air missiles into that country, creating yet another danger for Israel.

Israeli strikes and commando raids had been unable to stem the growth of this PLO army. Israel was not prepared to wait for more deadly attacks to be launched against its civilian population before acting against the terrorists.

MYTH

"The PLO posed no real threat to Israel. When Israel attacked, the PLO had been observing a year-long cease-fire agreement."

FACT

The PLO had repeatedly violated the July 1981 cease-fire agreement. In the ensuing 11 months, the PLO staged 270 terrorist actions in Israel, the West Bank and Gaza, and along the Lebanese and Jordanian borders. Twenty-nine Israelis died, and more than 300 were injured in the attacks.[4] The situation in the Galilee became intolerable as the frequency of attacks forced thousands of residents to flee their homes or to spend large amounts of time in bomb shelters. During this period, Israel launched retaliatory raids against PLO bases in Lebanon.

After Israel launched one such assault on June 4-5, 1982, the PLO responded with a massive artillery and mortar attack on the Israeli population of the Galilee. On June 6, the IDF moved into Lebanon to drive out the terrorists.

Former Secretary of State Henry Kissinger defended the Israeli operation: "No sovereign state can tolerate indefinitely the buildup along its borders of a military force dedicated to its destruction and implementing its objectives by periodic shellings and raids."[5]

"On Lebanon, it is clear that we and Israel both seek an end to the violence there, and a sovereign, independent Lebanon," President Reagan said June 21, 1982. "We agree that Israel must not be subjected to violence from the north."

MYTH
"The PLO treated the Lebanese with dignity and respect."

FACT

For Arab residents of south Lebanon, PLO rule was a nightmare. After the PLO was expelled from Jordan by King Hussein in 1970, many of its cadres went to Lebanon. The PLO seized whole areas of the country, where it brutalized the population and usurped Lebanese government authority.

On October 14, 1976, Lebanese Ambassador Edward Ghorra told the UN General Assembly the PLO was bringing ruin upon his country: "Palestinian elements belonging to various...organizations resorted to kidnapping Lebanese — and sometimes foreigners — holding them prisoner, questioning them, torturing them and sometimes killing them."[6]

Columnists Rowland Evans and Robert Novak, not known for being sympathetic toward Israel, talked to a doctor whose farm had been taken over without compensation by the PLO, and turned into a military depot. "You ask how do we like the Israelis," he said. "Compared to the hell we have had in Lebanon, the Israelis are brothers."[7] Other Lebanese — Christian and Muslim alike — gave similar accounts.

Countless Lebanese told harrowing tales of rape, mutilation and murders committed by PLO forces. The PLO "killed people and threw their corpses in the courtyards. Some of them were mutilated and their limbs were cut off. We did not go out for fear that we might end up like them," said two Arab women from Sidon. "We did not dare go to the beach, because they molested us, weapons in hand." The women spoke of an incident, which occurred shortly before the Israeli invasion, in which PLO men raped and murdered a woman, dumping her body near a famous statue. A picture of the victim's mangled corpse had been printed in a local newspaper.[8]

Dr. Khalil Torbey, a distinguished Lebanese surgeon, told an American journalist that he was "frequently called in the middle of the night to attend victims of PLO torture. I treated men whose testicles had been cut off in torture sessions. The victims, more often than not, were...Muslims. I saw men — live men — dragged through the streets by fast-moving cars to which they were tied by their feet."[9]

New York Times correspondent David Shipler visited Damour, a Christian village near Beirut, which had been occupied by the PLO since 1976, when

Palestinians and Lebanese leftists sacked the city and massacred hundreds of its inhabitants. The PLO, Shipler wrote, had turned the town into a military base, "using its churches as strongholds and armories."[10]

When the IDF drove the PLO out of Damour in June 1982, Prime Minister Menachem Begin announced that the town's Christian residents could come home and rebuild. Returning villagers found their former homes littered with spray-painted Palestinian nationalist slogans, Fatah literature and posters of Yasser Arafat. They told Shipler how happy they were that Israel had liberated them.[11]

MYTH

"The PLO was willing to leave Beirut in the summer of 1982 to save the civilian population from further attack, but Israel made this impossible."

FACT

For more than a month, the PLO proved itself intransigent, trying to extract a political victory from its military defeat. Arafat declared his willingness "in principle" to leave Beirut, then refused to go to any other country. Throughout the siege, the PLO hid behind innocent civilians, calculating that if Israel were to attack, it would be internationally condemned. That is precisely what happened.

By mid-June, Israeli troops had surrounded 6,000-9,000 terrorists who had taken up positions amid the civilian population of West Beirut. To prevent civilian casualties, Israel agreed to a ceasefire to enable an American diplomat, Ambassador Philip Habib, to mediate a peaceful PLO withdrawal from Lebanon. As a gesture of flexibility, Israel agreed to permit PLO forces to leave Beirut with their personal weapons.[12] But the PLO continued to make new demands.

For weeks, the PLO talked about withdrawal, while attaching conditions that made it impossible. The PLO adopted a strategy of controlled violations of the cease-fire, with the purpose of inflicting casualties on Israel and provoking Israeli retaliation sufficient to get the IDF blamed for disrupting the negotiations and harming civilians.

"The Israelis bombed buildings, innocent looking on the outside, where their intelligence told them that PLO offices were hidden," wrote Middle East analyst Joshua Muravchik. "Their intelligence also told them of the huge network of underground PLO storage facilities for arms and munitions that was later uncovered by the Lebanese Army. No doubt the Israelis dropped some bombs hoping to penetrate those facilities and detonate the dumps. The PLO had both artillery and anti-aircraft [equipment] truck mounted. These would fire at the Israelis and then move."[13] The Israelis would fire back and sometimes miss, inadvertently hitting civilian targets.

In numerous instances, the media mistakenly reported that Israel was hitting civilian targets in areas where no military ones were nearby. On one night in July, Israeli shells hit seven embassies in Beirut. NBC aired a report that appeared to lend credence to PLO claims it had no military positions in the area. Israel, Muravchik noted, "soon released reconnaissance photos showing the embassy area honeycombed with tanks, mortars, heavy machine guns and anti-aircraft positions."[14]

MYTH

"Israel was responsible for the massacre of thousands of innocent Palestinian refugees at Sabra and Shatila."

FACT

The Lebanese Christian Phalangist militia was responsible for the massacres that occurred at the two Beirut-area refugee camps on September 16-17, 1982. Israeli troops allowed the Phalangists to enter Sabra and Shatila to root out terrorist cells believed located there. It had been estimated that there may have been up to 200 armed men in the camps working out of the countless bunkers built by the PLO over the years, and stocked with generous reserves of ammunition.[15]

When Israeli soldiers ordered the Phalangists out, they found hundreds dead (estimates range from 460 according to the Lebanese police, to 700-800 calculated by Israeli intelligence). The dead, according to the Lebanese account, included 35 women and children. The rest were men: Palestinians, Lebanese, Pakistanis, Iranians, Syrians and Algerians. The killings were perpetrated to avenge the murders of Lebanese President Bashir Gemayel and 25 of his followers, killed in a bomb attack earlier that week.[16]

Israel had allowed the Phalange to enter the camps as part of a plan to transfer authority to the Lebanese, and accepted responsibility for that decision. The Kahan Commission of Inquiry, formed by the Israeli government in response to public outrage and grief, found that Israel was indirectly responsible for not anticipating the possibility of Phalangist violence. Israel instituted the panel's recommendations, including the dismissal of Defense Minister Ariel Sharon and Gen. Raful Eitan, the Army Chief of Staff.

The Kahan Commission, declared former Secretary of State Henry Kissinger, was "a great tribute to Israeli democracy....There are very few governments in the world that one can imagine making such a public investigation of such a difficult and shameful episode."[17]

Recently, efforts have been made in Belgium to try Sharon for his role in what happened in Lebanon. The appellate court there, however, threw out the case.[18] The European campaign appears designed to smear Israel in general, and Sharon in particular, and is particularly odious given that Israel's own democratic judicial institutions already dealt with this tragedy.

Ironically, while 300,000 Israelis demonstrated in Israel to protest the killings, little or no reaction occurred in the Arab world. Outside the Middle East, a major international outcry against Israel erupted over the massacres. The Phalangists, who perpetrated the crime, were spared the brunt of the condemnations for it.

By contrast, few voices were raised in May 1985, when Muslim militiamen attacked the Shatila and Burj-el Barajneh Palestinian refugee camps. According to UN officials, 635 were killed and 2,500 wounded. During a two-year battle between the Syrian-backed Shiite Amal militia and the PLO, more than 2,000 people, including many civilians, were reportedly killed. No outcry was directed at the PLO or the Syrians and their allies over the slaughter. International reaction was also muted in October 1990 when Syrian forces overran Christian-controlled areas of Lebanon. In the eight-hour clash, 700 Christians were killed — the worst single battle of Lebanon's Civil War.[19] These killings came on top of an estimated 95,000 deaths that had occurred during the civil war in Lebanon from 1975-1982.[20]

MYTH
"Israel's 1978 and 1982 invasions of Lebanon proved Israel's aggressive intentions."

FACT
Israel has long sought a peaceful northern border. But Lebanon's position as a haven for terrorist groups has made this impossible. In March 1978, PLO terrorists infiltrated Israel. After murdering an American tourist walking near an Israeli beach, they hijacked a civilian bus. When Israeli troops intercepted the bus, the terrorists opened fire. A total of 34 hostages died in the attack. In response, Israeli forces crossed into Lebanon and overran terrorist bases in the southern part of that country, pushing the terrorists away from the border. The IDF withdrew after two months, allowing UN forces to enter. But UN troops were unable to prevent terrorists from reinfiltrating the region and introducing new, more dangerous arms. It was this buildup that led to Israel's 1982 invasion.

Jerusalem repeatedly stressed that Israel did not covet a single inch of Lebanese territory. Israel's 1985 withdrawal from Lebanon confirmed that. The small 1,000-man Israeli force, deployed in a strip of territory extending eight miles into south Lebanon, protected towns and villages in northern Israel from attack. Israel also repeatedly said it would completely withdraw from Lebanon in return for a stable security situation on its northern border.

Israel pulled all its troops out of southern Lebanon on May 24, 2000, ending a 22-year military presence there. The Israeli withdrawal was conducted in coordination with the UN, and according to the UN, constituted Israeli fulfillment of its obligations under Security Council Resolution 425 (1978).

Israel hoped the Lebanese government would subsequently deploy its army along the southern border to disarm terrorists and maintain order, but this has not occurred, despite criticism from the United States, the UN and Israel.[21] "From a point northward, "said Lebanese Defense Minister Khalil Hrawi, "we make the rules, and from a certain point on in the south, there is no presence of the armed forces, and the Hizballah coordinates their actions with themselves."[22] Thus, Hizballah continues to enjoy free reign and threaten Israel's northern border.

MYTH

"Israel still has not satisfied the UN's requirements to withdraw completely from Lebanon because of its illegal occupation of Shebaa Farms."

FACT

Despite the UN ruling that Israel completed its withdrawal from southern Lebanon,[23] Hizballah and the Lebanese government insist that Israel still holds Lebanese territory in eastern Mount Dov, a 100-square-mile, largely uninhabited patch called Shebaa Farms. This claim provides Hizballah with a pretext to continue its activities against Israel. Thus, after kidnapping three Israeli soldiers in that area, it announced that they were captured on Lebanese soil.

Israel, which has built a series of observation posts on strategic hilltops in the area, maintains that the land was captured from Syria; nevertheless, the Syrians have supported Hizballah's claim. According to the *Washington Post*, the controversy benefits each of the Arab parties. "For Syria, it means Hizballah can still be used to keep the Israelis off balance; for Lebanon, it provides a way to apply pressure over issues, like the return of Lebanese prisoners still held in Israeli jails. For Hizballah, it is a reason to keep its militia armed and active, providing a ready new goal for a resistance movement that otherwise had nothing left to resist."[24]

MYTH

"Israel launched an unprovoked attack on UN peacekeeping forces in Lebanon."

FACT

In April 1995, the IDF mounted "Operation Grapes of Wrath" to halt Hizballah's bombardment of Israel's northern frontier. During the operation, Israeli artillery mistakenly hit a UN base in Kafr Kana, killing nearly 100 civilians. Afterward, a Joint Monitoring Machinery, including American, French, Syrian and Lebanese representatives, was created to prohibit unprovoked attacks on civilian populations and the use of civilians as shields for terrorist activities.

MYTH

"Syria has been a force for stability and good in Lebanon. It has always respected Lebanon's sovereignty and independence."

FACT

Damascus has a long and bloody history of intervention in Lebanon, and has made no secret of its hope to make its weaker neighbor part of Syria. Since the creation of contemporary Lebanon in 1920, "most Syrians have never accepted modern Lebanon as a sovereign and independent state."[25] The outbreak of the Lebanese Civil War in 1975 gave Damascus the opportunity to act on its belief that Lebanon and Syria are one.

In 1976, Syria intervened in the Lebanese civil war on behalf of Lebanese Christians. By 1978, Damascus had switched sides, and was supporting a leftist coalition of Palestinians, Druze and Muslims against the Christians. Eventually, Syrian troops occupied two-thirds of Lebanon. Syria's deployment of surface-to-air missile batteries in Lebanon, and its policy of allowing the PLO and other terrorist groups to attack Israel from there, helped trigger the 1982 Lebanon War.[26]

During the first week of Israel's "Operation Peace for Galilee," in June 1982, Syrian troops engaged in battles with Israeli forces. The Israelis destroyed or damaged 18 of the 19 Syrian missile batteries and, in one day, shot down 29 Syrian MiG fighters without the loss of a single plane. Syria and Israel carefully avoided confrontations for the remainder of the war.

Nevertheless, Syria found other ways to hurt Israel. In 1982, Syrian agents murdered President-elect Bashir Gemayel, who wanted peace with Israel. Two years later, Syria forced President Amin Gemayel, Bashir's brother, to renege on a peace treaty he signed with Israel a year earlier.[27]

Syria's activities were aimed not only at Israel, but also at the West. In April 1983, Hizballah terrorists, operating from Syrian-controlled territory, bombed the U.S. embassy in Beirut, killing 49 and wounding 120. Six months later, Hizballah terrorists drove two trucks carrying explosives into the U.S. Marine and French military barracks near Beirut, killing 241 Americans and 56 French soldiers.

In 1985, Hizballah operatives began kidnapping Westerners off the streets of Beirut and other Lebanese cities. From the beginning, it was clear the Syrians and their Iranian collaborators could order the release of the Western hostages at any time. For example, when a Frenchman was kidnapped in August 1991, the Syrians demanded that he be freed. Within days, he was.

Map 19 Israel's Border with Lebanon
(in 2000)

Lebanon

Mediterranean Sea

Former Security Zone

Sidon

Metula

Kiryat
Shmona

Zarit

Shlomi

Dolev

Golan Heights

Syria

Acre

Sea of
Galilee

Haifa

Israel

Jordan

Samaria

Most of the hostages were held in the Bekaa Valley or the suburbs of Beirut. Both areas were controlled by Syria.

From 1985-88, Amal Shiite militiamen, closely aligned with Syria, killed hundreds of Palestinian civilians in attacks on refugee camps.

In October 1990, with the West's attention focused on Kuwait, Syrian troops stormed the Beirut stronghold of Christian insurgent Gen. Michel Aoun. Besides battle deaths, approximately 700 people were massacred.[28] With that blitzkrieg, Damascus wiped out the only remaining threat to its hegemony in Lebanon.

On May 22, 1991, Lebanese President Elias Hrawi traveled to Damascus to sign a "Treaty of Brotherhood, Cooperation and Coordination" with Syrian President Hafez Assad. The agreement states that Syria will ensure Lebanon's "sovereignty and independence," even though Damascus is being allowed to keep its occupation army in that country.

A hint of Syria's real intentions came from Defense Minister Mustafa Tlas several weeks before the treaty's signing. Tlas predicted that unity would be achieved between the two countries "soon, or at least in our generation."[29] Since signing the treaty, Syria has kept a tight grip on Lebanon, and ruthlessly suppressed all challenges to its domination.

MYTH

"Syria has done everything possible to prevent terrorists in Lebanon from threatening regional peace."

FACT

Hizballah receives financial support and arms from Iran, usually via Damascus. Hizballah — which had initially confined itself to launching Katyusha rocket attacks on northern Israel and ambushing Israeli troops in the security zone — has in recent years stepped up its attacks on Israeli civilians.

The Syrian-backed Lebanese Army has yet to take action against Hizballah, or other terrorist organizations, such as the Popular Front for the Liberation of Palestine (PFLP), Popular Front for the Liberation of Palestine-General Command (PFLP-GC) or Democratic Front for the Liberation of Palestine (DFLP), which have bases in the Syrian-controlled Bekaa Valley in eastern Lebanon.

In fact, Syria has given its unqualified support for these organizations. Syria uses these terrorists as surrogates to maintain a level of violence against Israel and put pressure on the Israelis to negotiate over the Golan Heights. Asked about his support for terrorist organizations like Hizballah, Hafez Assad responded that they were really "patriots and militants who fight for the liberty and independence of their country...such people cannot be called terrorists."[30]

MYTH

"Syria intervened in Lebanon only because it was asked to do so by the Arab League."

FACT

Syria moved troops into Lebanon before receiving the Arab League's approval. Damascus intervened in April 1976 after Lebanese Druze warlord Kemal Jumblatt refused Syrian President Hafez Assad's demand for a cease-fire in the war. Jumblatt's refusal to stop his forces' attacks upon Lebanese Christians gave Assad the pretext he needed to intervene.

In June 1976, the Arab League Secretariat convened a meeting at which Syria, Libya, Saudi Arabia and the Sudan agreed to send troops to "enforce peace." Assad sent more Syrian troops into the country, while the others sent only token forces.[31] The Arab League's "endorsement," in short, constituted nothing more than the recognition of a *fait accompli*.

MYTH

"The Syrians and Lebanese have treated captured Israeli soldiers well and allowed the Red Cross to visit them."

FACT

Lebanon and Syria have routinely mistreated Israeli soldiers they have captured. It is difficult for Israel to obtain any information about its soldiers and the Lebanese and Syrians usually have denied permission for the Red Cross to visit the POWs. In addition, even the bodies of Israelis who have been killed are often held hostage in an effort to use them as bargaining chips. For example, in September 1991, Israel released nearly 100 Lebanese Shiite prisoners in exchange for the remains of four Israeli soldiers killed in Lebanon.

Pilot Ron Arad crashed in 1986 and was captured by Shiite terrorists. Israel has offered to release hundreds of Lebanese prisoners in exchange for information about Arad, but Hizballah has refused to cooperate and Arad has been considered an MIA ever since.

On October 7, 2000, three Israeli soldiers — Sgt. Adi Avitan, Staff Sgt. Benyamin Avraham and Staff Sgt. Omar Sawaid — were abducted by Hizballah. They were captured while patrolling the southern (Israeli) side of the Israeli-Lebanese border. On October 16, Hizballah Secretary General announced that his organization was holding an Israeli citizen, Elhanan Tenenboim, who was believed to have been kidnapped while on a private business trip to Europe.

The four Israelis were held incommunicado by Hizballah. The captors denied the International Committee of the Red Cross and other parties permission to visit them. On November 1, 2001, based on new intelligence, Israeli army rabbi Israel Weiss pronounced the soldiers dead. Their remains have yet to be recovered. Tenenboim is still being held hostage.

Notes

[1] Jillian Becker, *The PLO*, (London: Weidenfeld and Nicolson, 1984), pp. 202, 279.

[2] *Jerusalem Post*, (June 28, 1982).

[3] Raphael Israeli. Ed., *PLO in Lebanon*, (London: Weidenfeld and Nicolson, 1983), p. 7.

[4] Becker, p. 205.

[5] *Washington Post,* (June 16, 1982).

[6] Interview with Israel Television, (July 23, 1982).

[7] *Washington Post*, (June 25, 1982).

[8] *Los Angeles Herald-Examiner,* (July 13, 1982), cited in Becker, p. 153.

[9] *New York Times*, (June 21, 1982).

[10] *New York Times*, (June 21, 1982).

[11] *New York Times,* (July 14, 1982).

[12] *Washington Post*, (June 25, 1982).

[13] *New York Times*, (July 3, 1982).

[14] Joshua Muravchik, *"Misreporting Lebanon," Policy Review*, (Winter 1983), p. 60.

[15] Muravchik, p. 60.

[16] Zeev Schiff and Ehud Yaari, *Israel's Lebanon War,* (NY: Simon and Schuster, 1984), p. 70.

[17] *New York Times,* (October 19, 1990).

[18] Radio Free Europe/Radio Free Liberty, (June 26, 2002).

[19] *Washington Post*, (January 30, 2001).

[20] Schiff and Yaari, p. 257.

[21] "Security Council Endorses Secretary-General's Conclusion on Israeli Withdrawal from Lebanon as of 16 June," UN Press Release, (June 18, 2000).

[22] *Washington Post*, (January 30, 2001).

[23] *Washington Post*, (January 30, 2001).

[24] Daniel Pipes, *Damascus Courts The West*, (DC: The Washington Institute for Near East Policy, 1991), p. 26.

[25] Becker, pp. 204-205.

[26] Patrick Seale, *Asad*, (Berkeley: University of California Press, 1988), p. 417.

[27] Pipes, p. 27.

[28] U.S. State Department Report on Human Rights Practices for 1999; *International Narcotics Control Strategy Report*, 1999.

[29] *Al-Hayat*, (May 9, 1991).

[30] *Al-Baath,* (February 18, 1992); *Washington Post, (*July 31, 1991).

[31] Becker, p. 131.

12. The Gulf War

MYTH

"The Gulf War was fought for Israel."

FACT

Prior to President George Bush's announcement of Operation Desert Storm, critics of Israel were claiming the Jewish State and its supporters were pushing Washington to start a war with Iraq to eliminate it as a military threat. President Bush made the U.S. position clear, however, in his speech on August 2, 1990, saying that the United States has "longstanding vital interests" in the Persian Gulf. Moreover, Iraq's "naked aggression" violated the UN charter. The President expressed concern for other small nations in the area as well as American citizens living or working in the region. "I view a fundamental responsibility of my Presidency [as being] to protect American citizens."[1]

Over the course of the Gulf crisis, the President and other top Administration officials made clear that U.S. interests — primarily oil supplies — were threatened by the Iraqi invasion of Kuwait.

Most Americans agreed with the President's decision to go to war. For example, the *Washington Post*/ABC News Poll on January 16, 1991, found that 76 percent of Americans approved of the U.S. going to war with Iraq and 22 percent disapproved.[2]

It is true that Israel viewed Iraq as a serious threat to its security given its leadership of the rejectionist camp. Israeli concerns proved justified after the war began and Iraq fired 39 Scud missiles at its civilian population centers.

Israel has never asked American troops to fight its battles. Although Israeli forces were prepared to participate in the Gulf War, they did not because the United States asked them not to. Even after the provocation of the Scud missile attacks, Israel assented to U.S. appeals not to respond.

MYTH

"Israel's low profile in the Gulf War proves it has no strategic value to the United States."

FACT

Israel was never expected to play a major role in hostilities in the Gulf. American officials knew the Arabs would not allow Israel to help defend them; they also knew U.S. troops would have to intervene because the Gulf states could not protect themselves.

Israel's posture reflected a deliberate political decision in response to American requests. Nevertheless, it did aid the United States' successful campaign to roll back Iraq's aggression. For example:

■ The IDF was the sole military force in the region that could successfully challenge the Iraqi army. That fact, which Saddam Hussein understood, was a deterrent to further Iraqi aggression.

■ By warning that it would take military measures if any Iraqi troops entered Jordan, Israel, in effect, guaranteed its neighbor's territorial integrity against Iraqi aggression.

■ The United States benefited from the use of Israeli-made Have Nap air-launched missiles on its B-52 bombers. The Navy, meanwhile, used Israeli Pioneer pilotless drones for reconnaissance in the Gulf.

■ Israel provided mine plows that were used to clear paths for allied forces through Iraqi minefields.

■ Mobile bridges flown directly from Israel to Saudi Arabia were employed by the U.S. Marine Corps.

■ Israeli recommendations, based upon system performance observations, led to several software changes that made the Patriot a more capable missile defense system.

■ Israel Aircraft Industries developed conformal fuel tanks that enhanced the range of F-15 aircraft. These were used in the Gulf.

■ General Dynamics, a U.S. military contractor, has implemented a variety of Israeli modifications to improve the worldwide F-16 aircraft fleet, including structural enhancements, software changes, increased capability landing gear, radio improvements and avionic modifications.

■ An Israeli-produced targeting system was used to increase the Cobra helicopter's night-fighting capabilities.

■ Israel manufactured the canister for the highly successful Tomahawk missile.

■ Night-vision goggles used by U.S. forces were supplied by Israel.

■ A low-altitude warning system produced and developed in Israel was utilized on Blackhawk helicopters.

■ Israel provided other equipment to U.S. forces including flack vests, gas masks and sandbags.

■ Israel offered the United States the use of military and hospital facilities. U.S. ships utilized Haifa port shipyard maintenance and support on their way to the Gulf.

■ Israel destroyed Iraq's nuclear reactor in 1981. Consequently, U.S. troops did not face a nuclear-armed Iraq.

■ Even in its low-profile mode, Israeli cooperation was extremely valuable: Israel's military intelligence had focused on Iraq much more carefully over the years than had the U.S. intelligence community. Thus, the Israelis were able to provide Washington with detailed tactical intelligence on Iraqi military activities. Defense Secretary Richard Cheney said, for example, that the U.S. utilized Israeli information about western Iraq in its search for Scud missile launchers.[3]

MYTH

"Israel benefited from the Gulf War without paying any price."

FACT

It is true that Israel benefited from the destruction of Iraq's military capability by the United States-led coalition, but the cost was enormous. Even before hostilities broke out, Israel had to revise its defense budget to maintain its forces at a heightened state of alert. The Iraqi missile attacks justified Israel's prudence in keeping its air force flying round the clock. The war required the defense budget to be increased by more than $500 million. Another $100 million boost was needed for civil defense.

The damage caused by the 39 Iraqi Scud missiles that landed in Tel Aviv and Haifa was extensive. Approximately 3,300 apartments and other buildings were affected in the greater Tel Aviv area. Some 1,150 people who were evacuated had to be housed at a dozen hotels at a cost of $20,000 per night.

Beyond the direct costs of military preparedness and damage to property, the Israeli economy was also hurt by the inability of many Israelis to work under the emergency conditions. The economy functioned at no more than 75 percent of normal capacity during the war, resulting in a net loss to the country of $3.2 billion.[4]

The biggest cost was in human lives. A total of 74 people died as a consequence of Scud attacks. Two died in direct hits, four from suffocation in gas masks and the rest from heart attacks.[5]

A UN committee dealing with reparation claims against Iraq dating to the 1991 Gulf War approved more than $31 million to be paid to Israeli businesses and individuals. The 1999 decision stemmed from a 1992 Security Council decision calling on Iraq to compensate victims of the Gulf War.[6] In 2001, the United Nations Compensation Commission awarded $74 million to Israel for the costs it incurred from Iraqi Scud missile attacks during the Gulf War. The Commission rejected most of the $1 billion that Israel had requested.[7]

MYTH

"Israel did nothing to protect Palestinians from Scud attacks."

FACT

The *Los Angeles Times* recognized Israel's dilemma in allocating gas masks for its population:

Gas-mask distribution throughout Israel was calculated according to estimates — based in part on Saddam Hussein's own prewar threats — of where the threat to the population was greatest. First call was given to the Tel Aviv-Haifa coastal area, with its heavy and largely Jewish population density, as well as to Jerusalem, the second-largest city. Smaller urban areas were next given priority, followed by rural areas in Israel proper and finally the occupied territories. Experience has shown the soundness of this ranking. It is Israel's citizens who are most at threat from Iraq's outlawed weapons, not the Palestinians in the West Bank, who are Saddam's partisans.[8]

The vast majority of Palestinians made no secret of their support for Iraq, and many were seen on their rooftops cheering as Scuds rained on Israeli population centers.[9] Because of their support for Saddam Hussein, and the Iraqi dictator's professed concern for the Palestinians, Israel did not believe it was likely the territories would come under attack.

The Israeli courts subsequently ordered the military to distribute gas masks to all the residents of the territories. This was being done, though the war ended before all Palestinians had received them. No Palestinians were injured in any Scud attacks.

MYTH

"Iraq was never a threat to Israel."

FACT

Since coming to power, Iraqi President Saddam Hussein had been a leader of the rejectionist Arab states and one of the most belligerent foes of Israel. On April 2, 1990, Saddam's rhetoric became more threatening: "I swear to God we will let our fire eat half of Israel if it tries to wage anything against Iraq." Saddam said his nation's chemical weapons capability was matched only by that of the United States and the Soviet Union, and that he would annihilate anyone who threatened Iraq with an atomic bomb by the "double chemical."[10]

Several days later, Saddam said that war with Israel would not end until all Israeli-held territory was restored to Arab hands. He added that Iraq could launch chemical weapons at Israel from several different sites.[11] The Iraqi leader also made the alarming disclosure that his commanders had the freedom to launch attacks against Israel without consulting the high command if Israel attacked Iraq. The head of the Iraqi Air Force subsequently said he had orders to strike Israel if the Jewish State launched a raid against Iraq *or any other Arab country*.[12]

On June 18, 1990, Saddam told an Islamic Conference meeting in Baghdad: "We will strike at [the Israelis] with all the arms in our possession if they attack

Iraq or the Arabs." He declared "Palestine has been stolen," and exhorted the Arab world to "recover the usurped rights in Palestine and free Jerusalem from Zionist captivity."[13]

Saddam's threat came in the wake of revelations that Britain and the United States foiled an attempt to smuggle American-made "krytron" nuclear triggers to Iraq.[14] Britain's MI6 intelligence service prepared a secret assessment three years earlier that Hussein had ordered an all-out effort to develop nuclear weapons.[15] After Saddam used chemical weapons against his own Kurdish population in Halabja in 1988, few people doubted his willingness to use nuclear weapons against Jews in Israel if he had the opportunity.

Israeli fears were further raised by reports in the Arabic press, beginning in January 1990, that Jordan and Iraq had formed "joint military battalions" drawn from the various ground, air and naval units. "These battalions will serve as emergency forces to confront any foreign challenge or threat to either of the two countries," one newspaper said.[16] In addition, the two countries were said to have formed a joint air squadron.[17] This was to be the first step toward a unified Arab corps, Jordanian columnist Mu'nis al-Razzaz disclosed. "If we do not hurry up and start forming a unified military Arab force, we will not be able to confront the Zionist ambitions supported by U.S. aid," he said.[18] Given the history of Arab alliances forming as a prelude to planning an attack, Israel found these developments worrisome.

In April 1990, British customs officers found tubes about to be loaded onto an Iraqi-chartered ship that were believed to be part of a giant cannon that would enable Baghdad to lob nuclear or chemical missiles into Israel or Iran.[19] Iraq denied it was building a "supergun," but, after the war, it was learned that Iraq had built such a weapon.[20]

Iraq emerged from its war with Iran with one of the largest and best-equipped military forces in the world. In fact, Iraq had one million battle-tested troops, more than 700 combat aircraft, 6,000 tanks, ballistic missiles and chemical weapons. Although the U.S. and its allies won a quick victory, the magnitude of Hussein's arsenal only became clear after the war when UN investigators found evidence of a vast program to build chemical and nuclear weapons.[21]

Iraq also served as a base for several terrorist groups that menaced Israel, including the PLO and Abu Nidal's Fatah Revolutionary Council.

After the Iraqi invasion of Kuwait, Saddam Hussein consistently threatened to strike Israel if his country was attacked. If the U.S. moves against Iraq, he said in December 1990, "then Tel Aviv will receive the next attack, whether or not Israel takes part."[22] At a press conference, following his January 9, 1991, meeting with Secretary of State James Baker, Iraqi Foreign Minister Tariq Aziz was asked if the war starts, would Iraq attack Israel. He replied bluntly: "Yes. Absolutely, yes."[23]

Ultimately, Saddam carried out his threat.

MYTH

*"Saddam Hussein was never interested
in acquiring nuclear weapons."*

FACT

In 1981, Israel became convinced Iraq was approaching the capability to produce a nuclear weapon. To preempt the building of a weapon they believed would undoubtedly be directed against them, the Israelis launched their surprise attack destroying the Osirak nuclear complex. At the time, Israel was widely criticized. On June 19, the UN Security Council unanimously condemned the raid. Critics minimized the importance of Iraq's nuclear program, claiming that because Baghdad had signed the Nuclear Non-Proliferation Treaty and permitted its facilities to be inspected, Israeli fears were baseless.

It was not until after Iraq invaded Kuwait that U.S. officials began to acknowledge publicly that Baghdad was developing nuclear weapons and that it was far closer to reaching its goal than previously thought. Again, many critics argued the Administration was only seeking a justification for a war with Iraq.

Months later, after allied forces had announced the destruction of Iraq's nuclear facilities, UN inspectors found Saddam's program to develop weapons was far more extensive than even the Israelis believed. Analysts had thought Iraq was incapable of enriching uranium for bombs, but Saddam's researchers used several methods (including one thought to be obsolete) that were believed to have made it possible for Iraq to build at least one bomb.

MYTH

"The PLO was neutral in the Gulf War."

FACT

The PLO, Libya and Iraq were the only members who opposed an Arab League resolution calling for an Iraqi withdrawal from Kuwait. The intifada leadership sent a cable of congratulations to Saddam Hussein, describing the invasion of Kuwait as the first step toward the "liberation of Palestine."[24]

PLO leader Yasser Arafat played a critical role in sabotaging an Arab summit meeting that was to have been convened in Saudi Arabia to deal with the invasion. According to the *New York Times*, Arafat "diverted attention from the planned summit and helped capsize it" by showing up in Egypt with a "peace plan" devised by Libyan dictator Muammar Qaddafi.[25]

According to an eyewitness account by *Al-Ahram* editor Ibrahim Nafei, Arafat worked hard to "water down" any anti-Iraq resolution at the August 1990 Arab League meeting in Cairo. Arafat "moved from delegation to delegation, hand in hand with Tariq Aziz, the Iraqi Foreign Minister, who was openly threatening some Gulf and other Arab delegates that Iraq would turn them upside down," Nafei wrote.[26]

In Amman, Jordan, a PLO official warned that Palestinian fighters had arrived in Yemen. "We expect them to take suicidal operations against the American troops in Saudi Arabia if the Americans move against Iraq," he declared. "There are more than 50,000 Palestinian fighters" in both Kuwait and Iraq, he said, who "will defend the interests of Iraq."[27] Abul Abbas, a member of the PLO Executive Committee, threatened that "any American target will become vulnerable" should the United States attack Iraq.[28]

In Jenin, on August 12, 1,000 Palestinians marched, shouting: "Saddam, you hero, attack Israel with chemical weapons."[29]

According to some sources, the PLO played an active role in facilitating Iraq's conquest of Kuwait. The logistical planning for the Iraqi invasion was at least partially based on intelligence supplied by PLO officials and supporters based in Kuwait. One Arab diplomat was quoted in the *London Independent* as saying that on arrival in Kuwait, Iraqi officials "went straight to their homes, picked them up and ordered them to go to work." The Iraqi Embassy had compiled its own list of key Kuwaiti personnel, said the diplomat, "but who helped them? Who were the skilled technicians who worked alongside the Kuwaitis and knew all this information?" he asked. "The Palestinians."[30]

> *"Leaders of Israel's peace movement expressed their disgust for the PLO's actions. One would need a gas mask to overcome the "toxic, repulsive stench" of the PLO's attitude toward Saddam Hussein, Yossi Sarid said.[31] Another activist, Yaron London, wrote in an open letter to the Palestinians in the territories: "This week you proved to me for many years I was a great fool. When you ask once again for my support for your 'legitimate rights,' you will discover that your shouts of encouragement to Saddam have clogged my ears."[32]*

When the U.S. began massing troops in Saudi Arabia, Arafat called this a "new crusade" that "forebodes the gravest dangers and disasters for our Arab and Islamic nation." He also made clear his position on the conflict: "We can only be in the trench hostile to Zionism and its imperialist allies who are today mobilizing their tanks, planes, and all their advanced and sophisticated war machine against our Arab nation."[33]

Once the war began, the PLO Executive Committee reaffirmed its support for Iraq: "The Palestinian people stand firmly by Iraq's side." The following day, Arafat sent a message to Saddam hailing Iraq's struggle against "American dictatorship" and describing Iraq as "the defender of the Arab nation, of Muslims and of free men everywhere."[34]

Arafat's enthusiasm for Hussein was undaunted by the outcome of the war. "I would like to take this opportunity to renew to your excellency the great pride that we take in the ties of fraternity and common destiny binding us," he said in November 1991. "Let us work together until we achieve victory and regain liberated Jerusalem."[35]

MYTH

"The Gulf War demonstrated why Arab states need more U.S. weapons."

FACT

Iraq had one of the largest and most powerful armies in the world prior to its invasion of Kuwait. None of the Gulf states could have challenged the Iraqis without direct U.S. intervention. Kuwait is a tiny nation, which had received $5 billion worth of arms and yet never had any chance to stop Iraq.

Similarly, the United States has sold Saudi Arabia more than $40 billion worth of arms and military services in the last decade, yet, it too, could not have prevented an Iraqi invasion. It was this realization that ultimately led King Fahd to allow U.S. troops to be based in his country. No amount of military hardware could compensate for the small size of the standing armies in these states.

Moreover, the rapidity with which Iraq overran Kuwait was a reminder that U.S. weapons could easily fall into hostile hands. For example, Iraq captured 150 U.S.-made HAWK antiaircraft missiles and some armored vehicles from Kuwait.

MYTH

"Iraq ceased to be a threat to Israel after the Gulf War."

FACT

Iraq does not share a border with Israel, but since 1948 it has been one of Israel's staunchest enemies. Iraq made Israel a prime target for attack during the Gulf War. While much of Iraq's arsenal of unconventional weaponry has been destroyed, Iraq still remains a long-term threat to Israel's security. Recent revelations that Iraq had biological warheads of anthrax and botulism toxin ready for use in 1990, and was close to completing its program to acquire a nuclear capability, underscore how close Israel and the Allied coalition came to disaster. Much of Baghdad's germ warfare arsenal remains unaccounted for.

Saddam is still clearly bent on rearming Iraq. Much of Iraq's chemical arsenal, nuclear facilities, and hundreds of mobile ballistic missiles survived the conflict intact and Iraq continues to resist UN efforts to destroy them. Although Iraq was forced to destroy many of its remaining Scud missiles, it is believed a large number may remain hidden. In addition, once sanctions are lifted, Baghdad could reproduce a nuclear device within three to five years and restockpile its deadly chemical agents in less than two years.

UN weapons inspectors were forced out of Iraq in 1998 and, two years later, Iraq launched a series of short-range ballistic missiles in tests to perfect a new system that could be used to build missiles with longer-range capabilities.[36]

The military complexes and missile research centers where the missile, dubbed the al-Samoud, is under development were heavily bombed in December 1998 by allied aircraft during Operation Desert Fox. The Pentagon, at the time, believed that Saddam Hussein's new missile activity was put out of commission for at least a year or two. In fact, the first launching of the missile came only six months later.

In January 2001, an Iraqi defector told the London *Sunday Telegraph* that Iraq had acquired two fully operational nuclear bombs and was working to construct more. This claim has been discounted, but numerous studies have reported that Saddam Hussein is anywhere from a few months to a few years away from the production of nuclear weapons and that the principal obstacle has been acquiring the necessary fissile material.[37] No one questions Hussein's desire to acquire weapons of mass destruction.

Meanwhile, despite Iraq's agreement to comply with UN Resolution 687, which prohibits it from allowing any terrorist organizations to operate in its territory, Baghdad still maintains contact with, and provides sanctuary to, several groups and individuals involved in terrorism. Hussein has also publicly promised to pay $25,000 to the families of Palestinian terrorists.

Notes

1   *Washington Post*, (August 3, 1990).
2   *Washington Post*, (January 17, 1991).
3   UPI, (March 8, 1991).
4   *Near East Report*, (February 4, 1991).
5   *Jerusalem Post*, (January 17, 1992).
6   Jewish Telegraphic Agency, (April 14, 1999).
7   Jewish Telegraphic Agency, (June 21, 2001).
8   *Los Angeles Times*, (January 28, 1991).
9   *New York Post*, (February 4, 1991).
10 Reuters, (April 2, 1990).
11 Reuters, (April 18, 1990).
12 UPI, (April 22, 1990).
13 Baghdad Domestic Service, (June 18, 1990).

14 *Washington Post,* (March 29, 1990).

15 *Washington Times,* (April 3, 1990).

16 *Al-Ittihad,* (January 26, 1990).

17 Radio Monte Carlo, (February 17, 1990).

18 *Al-Dustur,* (February, 18, 1990).

19 Reuters, (April 17, 1990).

20 *Washington Post,* (August 14, 1991).

21 *Washington Post,* (August 8, 1991).

22 Reuters, (December 26, 1990).

23 Transcript of January 9, 1991, press conference.

24 *Mideast Mirror,* (August 6, 1990).

25 *New York Times,* (August 5, 1990).

26 *Al-Ahram,* (August 12, 1990).

27 UPI, (August 10, 1990).

28 Reuters, (September 4, 1990).

29 Associated Press, (August 12, 1990).

30 *Jerusalem Post,* (August 8, 1990).

31 *Ha'aretz,* (August 17, 1990).

32 *Yediot Aharonot,* (August 1990).

33 *Sawt al-Sha'b,* (September 4, 1990).

34 Agence France-Presse, (February 26, 1991).

35 Baghdad Republic of Iraq Radio Network, (November 16, 1991).

36 *New York Times,* (July 1, 2000).

37 *Jerusalem Post,* (January 29, 2001).

13. The United Nations

MYTH

"The United Nations has long played a constructive role in Middle East affairs. Its record of fairness and balance makes it an ideal forum for settling the Arab-Israeli dispute."

FACT

Starting in the mid-1970s, an Arab-Soviet-Third World bloc joined to form what amounted to a pro-Palestinian lobby at the United Nations. This was particularly true in the General Assembly where these countries—nearly all dictatorships or autocracies—frequently voted together to pass resolutions attacking Israel and supporting the PLO.

In 1974, for example, the General Assembly invited Yasser Arafat to address it. Arafat did so, a holster attached to his hip. In his speech, Arafat spoke of carrying a gun and an olive branch (he left his gun outside before entering the hall). A year later, at the instigation of the Arab states and the Soviet Bloc, the Assembly approved Resolution 3379, which slandered Zionism by branding it a form of racism.

U.S. Ambassador Daniel Moynihan called the resolution an "obscene act." Israeli Ambassador Chaim Herzog told his fellow delegates the resolution was "based on hatred, falsehood and arrogance." Hitler, he declared, would have felt at home listening to the UN debate on the measure.[1]

On December 16, 1991, the General Assembly voted 111-25 (with 13 abstentions and 17 delegations absent or not voting) to repeal Resolution 3379. No Arab country voted for repeal. The PLO denounced the vote and the U.S. role.

As Herzog noted, the organization developed an "Alice-In-Wonderland" perspective on Israel. "In the UN building...[Alice] would only have to wear a Star of David in order to hear the imperious 'Off with her head' at every turn." Herzog noted that the PLO had cited a 1974 UN resolution condemning Israel as justification for setting off a bomb in Jerusalem.[2]

Bloc voting also made possible the establishment of the pro-PLO "Committee on the Inalienable Rights of the Palestinian People" in 1975. The panel became, in effect, part of the PLO propaganda apparatus, issuing stamps, organizing meetings, preparing films and draft resolutions in support of Palestinian "rights."

In 1976, the committee recommended "full implementation of the inalienable rights of the Palestinian people, including their return to the Israeli part of Palestine." It also recommended that November 29 — the day the UN voted to partition Palestine in 1947 — be declared an "International Day of

Solidarity with the Palestinian People." Since then, it has been observed at the UN with anti-Israel speeches, films and exhibits. Over the objections of the United States, a special unit on Palestine was established as part of the UN Secretariat.

Israel is the object of more investigative committees, special representatives and rapporteurs than any other state in the UN system. The special representative of the Director-General of UNESCO visited Israel 51 times during 27 years of activity. A "Special Mission" has been sent by the Director-General of the ILO to Israel and the territories every year for the past 17 years.

The Commission on Human Rights routinely adopts disproportionate resolutions concerning Israel. Of all condemnations of this agency, 26 percent refer to Israel alone, while rogue states such as Syria and Libya are never criticized.[3]

The U.S. has reacted forcefully to efforts to politicize the UN. In 1977, the U.S. withdrew from the International Labor Organization for two years because of its anti-Israel stance. In 1984, the U.S. left UNESCO, in part because of its bias against the Jewish State (in September 2002, the U.S. said it would return). From 1982-89, the Arab states sought to deny Israel a seat in the General Assembly or put special conditions on Israel's participation. Only a determined U.S. lobbying campaign prevented them from succeeding. In 2001, the U.S. joined Israel in boycotting the UN World Conference Against Racism when it became clear that it had become little more than an Israel-bashing festival.

While the Arab-Israeli peace process that was launched in Madrid in 1991 is structured on the basis of direct negotiations between the parties, the UN constantly undercuts this principle. The Oslo Agreements are predicated on the idea of bilateral talks to resolve differences between Israelis and Palestinians. The General Assembly routinely adopts resolutions, however, that attempt to impose solutions on critical issues such as Jerusalem, the Golan Heights and settlements. Ironically, UN Security Council Resolutions 242 and 338 proposed the bilateral negotiations that are consistently undermined by the General Assembly resolutions.

Thus, the record to date indicates the UN has not played a useful role in resolving the Arab-Israeli conflict.

MYTH
"The Palestinians have been denied a voice at the UN."

FACT
Besides the support the Palestinians have received from the Arab and Islamic world, and most other UN members, the Palestinians have been afforded special treatment at the UN since 1975. That year the General Assembly

awarded permanent representative status to the PLO, which opened an office in midtown Manhattan.

In 1988, the PLO's status was upgraded when the General Assembly designated the PLO as "Palestine." Ten years later, the General Assembly voted to give the Palestinians a unique status as a non-voting member of the 185 member Assembly. The vote in favor was overwhelming, 124 in favor and 4 against with 10 abstentions. The countries opposing the resolution were Israel, the United States, Micronesia and the Marshall Islands.

Palestinian representatives can now raise the issue of the peace process in the General Assembly, cosponsor draft resolutions on Middle East peace and have the right of reply. They still do not have voting power and cannot put forward candidates for UN committees such as the Security Council. The Arabs had originally sought greater powers, including the right to sit with other independent states and to sponsor resolutions. They compromised after the Europeans told the Arabs that they would only support the resolution if the most controversial political items were removed. Still, their status gives the Palestinians procedural privileges that exceed those of other groups with UN observer status such as Switzerland or the Vatican.

MYTH

"Israel enjoys the same rights as any other member of the United Nations."

FACT

A breakthrough in Israel's fifty-year exclusion from UN bodies occurred on May 30, 2000, when Israel accepted an invitation to become a temporary member of the Western European and Others (WEOG) regional group. While only temporary, this historic step could finally end the UN's discrimination against Israel and open the door to Israeli participation in the Security Council.

Israel has been the only UN member excluded from a regional group. Geographically, it belongs in the Asian Group; however, the Arab states have barred its membership. Without membership in a regional group, Israel cannot sit on the Security Council or other key UN bodies.

The WEOG is the only regional group which is not purely geographical, but rather geopolitical, namely a group of states that share a Western-Democratic common denominator. WEOG comprises 27 members: all the West European states; and the "others" — Australia, Canada, New Zealand and the United States.

Israel's membership in the WEOG is severely limited. Every four years Israel will have to reapply for membership, since its status is only temporary. Israel was not allowed to present candidacies for open seats in any UN body for two years and is not able to compete for major UN bodies, such as the Economic and Social Council, for a longer period. Also, for the first two years, Israeli representatives were not allowed to run for positions on the UN Council.

Besides these restrictions, Israel is only allowed to participate in WEOG activities in the New York office of the UN. Israel is excluded from WEOG discussion and consultations at the UN offices in Geneva, Nairobi, Rome and Vienna; therefore, Israel cannot participate in UN talks on human rights, racism and a number of other issues handled in these offices.

In the future, Israel still hopes to gain membership in the Asian group.

MYTH

"The United Nations and its affiliate institutions are critical of Israeli policies, but never attack Jews or engage in anti-Semitic rhetoric."

FACT

The UN has condemned virtually every conceivable form of racism. It has established programs to combat racism and its multiple facets — including xenophobia — but had consistently refused to do the same against anti-Semitism. It was only on November 24, 1998, more than 50 years after the UN's founding, that the word "anti-Semitism" was first mentioned in a UN resolution, appearing near the end of GA Res. A/53/623, "Elimination of Racism and Racial Discrimination."[4]

Since the early 1970s, the UN itself has become permeated with anti-Semitic and anti-Zionist sentiment. The following examples illustrate how ugly the atmosphere has become:

- "Is it not the Jews who are exploiting the American people and trying to debase them?"— Libyan UN Representative Ali Treiki.[5]

- "The Talmud says that if a Jew does not drink every year the blood of a non-Jewish man, he will be damned for eternity." —Saudi Arabian delegate Marouf al-Dawalibi before the 1984 UN Human Rights Commission conference on religious tolerance.[6] A similar remark was made by the Syrian Ambassador at a 1991 meeting, who insisted Jews killed Christian children to use their blood to make matzos.[7]

- On March 11, 1997, the Palestinian representative to the UN Human Rights Commission claimed the Israeli government had injected 300 Palestinian children with the HIV virus. Despite the efforts of Israel, the United States and others, this blood libel remains on the UN record.[8]

MYTH

"The 1991 repeal of the resolution libeling Zionism proves that the UN is no longer biased against Israel."

FACT

The vote did not signal an end to the UN's bias against Israel. The same month the General Assembly approved four new one-sided resolutions on the Middle East. On December 9, 1991, Israel's handling of the intifada was condemned by a vote of 150-2. On the 11th, it voted 104-2 for a resolution calling for a UN-sponsored peace conference that would include the PLO and voted 142-2 to condemn Israeli behavior toward Palestinians in the territories. On December 16 — the very day it repealed the Zionism measure — the UN voted 152-1, with the U.S. abstaining, to call on Israel to rescind a Knesset resolution declaring Jerusalem its capital, to demand Israel's withdrawal from "occupied territories," including Jerusalem and to denounce Israeli administration of the Golan Heights. Another resolution expressed support for Palestinian self-determination and the right of return for Palestinian refugees.

The repeal vote was marred by the fact that 13 of the 19 Arab countries — including those engaged in negotiations with Israel — Syria, Lebanon and Jordan — voted to retain the resolution, as did Saudi Arabia. Six, including Egypt — which lobbied against repeal — were absent.

The Arabs "voted once again to impugn the very birthright of the Jewish State," the *New York Times* noted. "That even now most Arab states cling to a demeaning and vicious doctrine mars an otherwise belated triumph for sense and conscience."[9]

MYTH

"Even if the General Assembly is biased, the Security Council has always been balanced in its treatment of the Middle East."

FACT

A careful analysis of the Security Council's actions on the Middle East shows it has been little better than the General Assembly in its treatment of Israel.

Candidates for the Security Council are proposed by regional blocs. In the Middle East, this means the Arab League and its allies are usually included. Israel, which joined the UN in 1949, has never been elected to the Security Council whereas at least 16 Arab League members have. Syria, a nation on the U.S. list of countries that sponsor terrorism, began a two-year term as a member of the Security Council in 2002 and served as president of the body in June 2002.

Debates on Israel abound, and the Security Council has repeatedly condemned the Jewish State, but not once has it adopted a resolution critical of the PLO or of Arab attacks on Israel. Emergency special sessions of the General Assembly are rare. No such session has ever been convened with respect to the Chinese occupation of Tibet, the Indonesian occupation of East Timor, the Syrian occupation of Lebanon, the slaughters in Rwanda, the disappearances in Zaire or the horrors of Bosnia. For nearly two decades, these sessions have been called primarily to condemn Israel.

MYTH
"The United States has always supported Israel at the UN and can be counted upon to veto any resolutions that are critical."

FACT
Many people believe the United States can always be relied upon to support Israel with its veto in the UN Security Council. The historical record, however, shows that the U.S. has often opposed Israel in the Council.

In 1990, for example, Washington voted for a Security Council resolution condemning Israel's handling of the Temple Mount riot earlier that month. While singling out "the acts of violence committed by Israeli security forces," the resolution omitted mention of the Arab violence that preceded it.

In December 1990, the U.S. went along with condemning Israel for expelling four leaders of Hamas, an Islamic terrorist group. The deportations came in response to numerous crimes committed by Hamas against Arabs and Jews, the most recent of which had been the murders of three Israeli civilians in a Jaffa factory several days earlier. The resolution did not say a word about Hamas and its crimes. It described Jerusalem as "occupied" territory, declared that Palestinians needed to be "protected" from Israel and called on contracting parties of the Geneva Convention to ensure Israel's compliance. It was the first time the Security Council invoked the Convention against a member country.

In January 1992, the U.S. supported a one-sided resolution condemning Israel for expelling 12 Palestinians, members of terrorist groups that were responsible for perpetrating violence against Arab and Jew alike. The resolution, which described Jerusalem as "occupied" territory, made no mention of the events that triggered the expulsions – the murders of four Jewish civilians by Palestinian radicals since October.

In 1996, the U.S. went along with a Saudi-inspired condemnation of Israel for opening a tunnel in "the vicinity" of the al-Aksa mosque. In fact, the tunnel, which allows visitors to see the length of the western wall of the Temple Mount, is nowhere near the mosque. Israel was blamed for reacting to violent attacks by Palestinians who protested the opening of the tunnel.

The United States did not cast its first veto until 1972, on a Syrian-Lebanese complaint against Israel. From 1967-72, the U.S. supported or abstained on 24 resolutions, most critical of Israel. From 1973-2000, the Security Council adopted approximately 100 resolutions on the Middle East, again, most critical of Israel. The U.S. vetoed a total of 35 resolutions and, hence, supported the Council's criticism of Israel by its vote of support, or by abstaining, roughly two-thirds of the time.[10]

In July 2002 the United States shifted its policy and announced that it would veto any Security Council resolution on the Middle East that did not condemn Palestinian terror and name Hamas, Islamic Jihad and the Al-Aksa Martyrs Brigade as the groups responsible for the attacks. The U.S. also said that resolutions must note that any Israeli withdrawal is linked to the security situation, and that both parties must be called upon to pursue a negotiated settlement.[11] The Arabs can still get around the United States by taking issues to the General Assembly, where nonbinding resolutions pass by majority vote, and support for almost any anti-Israel resolution is assured.

> *"The UN has the image of a world organization based on universal principles of justice and equality. In reality, when the chips are down, it is nothing other than the executive committee of the Third World dictatorships."*
>
> **— former UN Ambassador Jeane Kirkpatrick.**[12]

MYTH

"America's Arab allies routinely support U.S. positions at the UN."

FACT

In 2001, Saudi Arabia and Kuwait each voted with the United States on only two resolutions considered important. The other Arab countries, including Jordan and Egypt, did not vote with the United States on a single issue. The year before, the Arab states voted against the United States on more than 70 percent of the important votes. By contrast, Israel has consistently been America's top UN ally. Israel voted with the U.S. 100 percent of the time in 2001, outpacing the support levels of major U.S. allies such as Great Britain, France and Canada.[13]

MYTH

"Israel's failure to implement UN resolutions is a violation of international law."

FACT

UN resolutions are documents issued by political bodies and need to be interpreted in light of the constitution of those bodies. They represent the political viewpoints of those who support them rather than embodying any particular legal rules or principles. Resolutions can have moral and political force when they are perceived as expressing the agreed view of the international community, or the views of leading, powerful and respected nations.

The UN Charter (Articles 10 and 14) specifically empowers the General Assembly to make only nonbinding "recommendations." Assembly resolutions are only considered binding in relation to budgetary and internal procedural matters.

The legality of Security Council resolutions is more ambiguous. It is not clear if all Security Council resolutions are binding or only those adopted under Chapter 7 of the Charter.[14] Under Article 25 of the Charter, UN member states are obligated to carry out "decisions of the Security Council in accordance with the present Charter," but it is unclear which kinds of resolutions are covered by the term "decisions." Regardless, it would be difficult to show that Israel has violated any Security Council resolutions on their wording, and the council has never sanctioned Israel for noncompliance.

Notes

1   Chaim Herzog, *Who Stands Accused?,* (NY: Random House, 1978), pp. 4-5.

2   Herzog, p. 130.

3   Israel's Mission to the UN.

4   "Israel and the UN — An Uneasy Relationship," Israel's Mission to the UN.

5   Speech before the UN, December 8, 1983, quoted in Harris Schoenberg, *Mandate For Terror: The United Nations and the PLO,* (NY: Shapolsky, 1989), p. 296.

6   Speech to UN seminar on religious tolerance and freedom, delivered December 5, 1984, quoted in Anti-Defamation League, News, (February 7, 1985).

7   Morris Abram, "Israel Under Attack: Anti-Semitism in the United Nations," *The Earth Times,* (December 16-31, 1997).

8   Ibid.

9   *New York Times,* (December 17, 1991).

10 U.S. State Department.

11 *Washington Post,* (July 26, 2002).

12 *Jerusalem Post,* (September 5, 2001).

13 Voting Practices at the United Nations - 2001, U.S. State Department.

14 Bruno Simma, ed., *The Charter of the United Nations: A Commentary,* (NY: Oxford University Press, 1994), pp. 237-241; 407-418.

14. The Refugees

MYTH

"One million Palestinians were expelled by Israel from 1947-49."

FACT

The Palestinians left their homes in 1947-49 for a variety of reasons. Thousands of wealthy Arabs left in anticipation of a war, thousands more responded to Arab leaders' calls to get out of the way of the advancing armies, a handful were expelled, but most simply fled to avoid being caught in the cross fire of a battle.

Many Arabs claim that 800,000 to 1,000,000 Palestinians became refugees in 1947-49. The last census was taken by the British in 1945. It found approximately 1.2 million permanent Arab residents in *all* of Palestine. A 1949 Government of Israel census counted 160,000 Arabs living in the country after the war. In 1947, a total of 809,100 Arabs lived in the same area.[1] This meant no more than 650,000 Palestinian Arabs could have become refugees. Reports by the UN Mediator on Palestine arrived at an even lower figure — 472,000, and reported that only about 360,000 Arab refugees required aid.[2]

Although much is heard about the plight of the Palestinian refugees, little is said about the Jews who fled from Arab states. Their situation had long been precarious. During the 1947 UN debates, Arab leaders threatened them. For example, Egypt's delegate told the General Assembly: "The lives of one million Jews in Muslim countries would be jeopardized by partition."[3]

The number of Jews fleeing Arab countries in the years following Israel's independence was nearly double the number of Arabs leaving Palestine. Many Jews were allowed to take little more than the shirts on their backs. These refugees had no desire to be repatriated. Little is heard about them because they did not remain refugees for long. Of the 820,000 Jewish refugees between 1948 and 1972, 586,000 were resettled in Israel at great expense, and without any offer of compensation from the Arab governments who confiscated their possessions.[4] Israel has consequently maintained that any agreement to compensate the Palestinian refugees must also include Arab compensation for Jewish refugees. To this day, the Arab states have refused to pay any compensation to the hundreds of thousands of Jews who were forced to abandon their property before fleeing those countries.

The contrast between the reception of Jewish and Palestinian refugees is even starker when one considers the difference in cultural and geographic dislocation experienced by the two groups. Most Jewish refugees traveled hundreds — and some traveled thousands — of miles to a tiny country whose inhabitants spoke a different language. Most Arab refugees never left Palestine at all; they traveled a few miles to the other side of the truce line, remaining inside the vast Arab nation that they were part of linguistically, culturally and ethnically.

Map 20
Jewish Refugees from Arab States
1948-1972

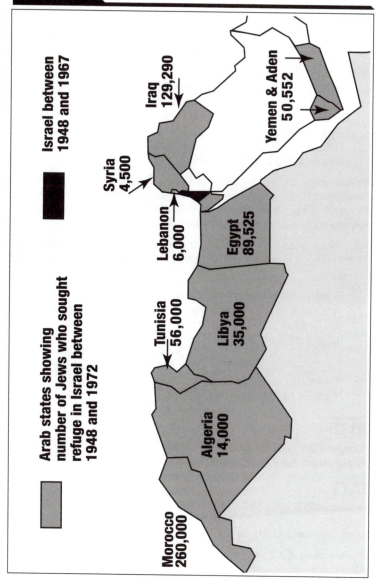

Arab states showing
number of Jews who sought
refuge in Israel between
1948 and 1972

Israel between
1948 and 1967

Morocco
260,000

Algeria
14,000

Tunisia
56,000

Libya
35,000

Egypt
89,525

Lebanon
6,000

Syria
4,500

Iraq
129,290

Yemen & Aden
50,552

MYTH

"The Jews made clear from the outset they had no intention of living peacefully with their Arab neighbors."

FACT

In numerous instances, Jewish leaders urged the Arabs to remain in Palestine and become citizens of Israel. The Assembly of Palestine Jewry issued this appeal on October 2, 1947:

> We will do everything in our power to maintain peace, and establish a cooperation gainful to both [Jews and Arabs]. It is now, here and now, from Jerusalem itself, that a call must go out to the Arab nations to join forces with Jewry and the destined Jewish State and work shoulder to shoulder for our common good, for the peace and progress of sovereign equals.[5]

On November 30, the day after the UN partition vote, the Jewish Agency announced: "The main theme behind the spontaneous celebrations we are witnessing today is our community's desire to seek peace and its determination to achieve fruitful cooperation with the Arabs...."[6]

Israel's Proclamation of Independence, issued May 14, 1948, also invited the Palestinians to remain in their homes and become equal citizens in the new state:

> In the midst of wanton aggression, we yet call upon the Arab inhabitants of the State of Israel to preserve the ways of peace and play their part in the development of the State, on the basis of full and equal citizenship and due representation in all its bodies and institutions....We extend our hand in peace and neighborliness to all the neighboring states and their peoples, and invite them to cooperate with the independent Jewish nation for the common good of all.

MYTH

*"The Jews created the refugee problem
by expelling the Palestinians."*

FACT

Had the Arabs accepted the 1947 UN resolution, not a single Palestinian would have become a refugee. An independent Arab state would now exist beside Israel. The responsibility for the refugee problem rests with the Arabs.

The beginning of the Arab exodus can be traced to the weeks immediately following the announcement of the UN partition resolution. The first to leave were roughly 30,000 wealthy Arabs who anticipated the upcoming war and fled to neighboring Arab countries to await its end. Less affluent Arabs from the mixed cities of Palestine moved to all-Arab towns to stay with relatives or friends.[7] By the end of January 1948, the exodus was so alarming the Palestine Arab Higher Committee asked neighboring Arab countries to refuse visas to these refugees and to seal their borders against them.[8]

On January 30, 1948, the Jaffa newspaper, *Ash Sha'ab*, reported: "The first of our fifth-column consists of those who abandon their houses and businesses and go to live elsewhere....At the first signs of trouble they take to their heels to escape sharing the burden of struggle."[9]

Another Jaffa paper, *As Sarih* (March 30, 1948) excoriated Arab villagers near Tel Aviv for "bringing down disgrace on us all by 'abandoning the villages.'"[10]

Meanwhile, a leader of the Arab National Committee in Haifa, Hajj Nimer el-Khatib, said Arab soldiers in Jaffa were mistreating the residents. "They robbed individuals and homes. Life was of little value, and the honor of women was defiled. This state of affairs led many [Arab] residents to leave the city under the protection of British tanks."[11]

John Bagot Glubb, the commander of Jordan's Arab Legion, said: "Villages were frequently abandoned even before they were threatened by the progress of war."[12]

Contemporary press reports of major battles in which large numbers of Arabs fled conspicuously fail to mention any forcible expulsion by the Jewish forces. The Arabs are usually described as "fleeing" or "evacuating" their homes. While Zionists are accused of "expelling and dispossessing" the Arab inhabitants of such towns as Tiberias and Haifa, the truth is much different. Both of those cities were within the boundaries of the Jewish State under the UN partition scheme and both were fought for by Jews and Arabs alike.

Jewish forces seized Tiberias on April 19, 1948, and the entire Arab population of 6,000 was evacuated under British military supervision. The Jewish Community Council issued a statement afterward: "We did not dispossess them; they themselves chose this course....Let no citizen touch their property."[13]

In early April, an estimated 25,000 Arabs left the Haifa area following an offensive by the irregular forces led by Fawzi al-Qawukji, and rumors that Arab air forces would soon bomb the Jewish areas around Mt. Carmel.[14] On April 23, the Haganah captured Haifa. A British police report from Haifa, dated April 26, explained that "every effort is being made by the Jews to persuade the Arab populace to stay and carry on with their normal lives, to get their shops and businesses open and to be assured that their lives and interests will be safe."[15] In fact, David Ben-Gurion had sent Golda Meir to Haifa to try to persuade the Arabs to stay, but she was unable to convince them because of their fear of being judged traitors to the Arab cause.[16] By the end of the battle, more than 50,000 Palestinians had left.

In Tiberias and Haifa, the Haganah issued orders that none of the Arabs' possessions should be touched, and warned that anyone who violated the orders would be severely punished. Despite these efforts, all but about 5,000 or 6,000 Arabs evacuated Haifa, many leaving with the assistance of British military transports.

> *"Tens of thousands of Arab men, women and children fled toward the eastern outskirts of the city in cars, trucks, carts, and afoot in a desperate attempt to reach Arab territory until the Jews captured Rushmiya Bridge toward Samaria and Northern Palestine and cut them off. Thousands rushed every available craft, even rowboats, along the waterfront, to escape by sea toward Acre."*
>
> **— New York Times, (April 23, 1948)**

Syria's UN delegate, Faris el-Khouri, interrupted the UN debate on Palestine to describe the seizure of Haifa as a "massacre" and said this action was "further evidence that the 'Zionist program' is to annihilate Arabs within the Jewish state if partition is effected."[17]

The following day, however, the British representative at the UN, Sir Alexander Cadogan, told the delegates that the fighting in Haifa had been provoked by the continuous attacks by Arabs against Jews a few days before and that reports of massacres and deportations were erroneous.[18]

The same day (April 23, 1948), Jamal Husseini, the chairman of the Palestine Higher Committee, told the UN Security Council that instead of accepting the Haganah's truce offer, the Arabs "preferred to abandon their homes, their belongings, and everything they possessed in the world and leave the town."[19]

The U.S. Consul-General in Haifa, Aubrey Lippincott, wrote on April 22, 1948, for example, that "local mufti-dominated Arab leaders" were urging "all Arabs to leave the city, and large numbers did so."[20]

An army order issued July 6, 1948, made clear that Arab towns and villages were not to be demolished or burned, and that Arab inhabitants were not to be expelled from their homes.[21]

The Haganah did employ psychological warfare to encourage the Arabs to abandon a few villages. Yigal Allon, the commander of the *Palmach* (the "shock force of the Haganah"), said he had Jews talk to the Arabs in neighboring villages and tell them a large Jewish force was in Galilee with the intention of burning all the Arab villages in the Lake Hula region. The Arabs were told to leave while they still had time and, according to Allon, they did exactly that.[22]

In the most dramatic example, in the Ramle-Lod area, Israeli troops seeking to protect their flanks and relieve the pressure on besieged Jerusalem, forced a portion of the Arab population to go to an area a few miles away that was occupied by the Arab Legion. "The two towns had served as bases for Arab irregular units, which had frequently attacked Jewish convoys and nearby settlements, effectively barring the main road to Jerusalem to Jewish traffic."[23]

As was clear from the descriptions of what took place in the cities with the largest Arab populations, these cases were clearly the exceptions, accounting for only a small fraction of the Palestinian refugees.

MYTH

"The Arab invasion had little impact on the Palestinian Arabs."

FACT

Once the invasion began in May 1948, most Arabs remaining in Palestine left for neighboring countries. Surprisingly, rather than acting as a strategically valuable "fifth-column" that would fight the Jews from within the country, the Palestinians chose to flee to the safety of the other Arab states, still confident of being able to return. A leading Palestinian nationalist of the time, Musa Alami, revealed the attitude of the fleeing Arabs:

> The Arabs of Palestine left their homes, were scattered, and lost everything. But there remained one solid hope: The Arab armies were on the eve of their entry into Palestine to save the country and return things to their normal course, punish the aggressor, and throw oppressive Zionism with its dreams and dangers into the sea. On May 14, 1948, crowds of Arabs stood by the roads leading to the frontiers of Palestine, enthusiastically welcoming the advancing armies. Days and weeks passed, sufficient to accomplish the sacred mission, but the Arab armies did not save the country. They did nothing but let slip from their hands Acre, Sarafand, Lydda, Ramleh, Nazareth, most of the south and the rest of the north. Then hope fled.[24]

As the fighting spread into areas that had previously remained quiet, the Arabs began to see the possibility of defeat. As the possibility turned into reality, the flight of the Arabs increased — more than 300,000 departed after May 15 — leaving approximately 160,000 Arabs in the State of Israel.[25]

Although most of the Arabs had left by November 1948, there were still those who chose to leave even after hostilities ceased. An interesting case was the evacuation of 3,000 Arabs from Faluja, a village between Tel Aviv and Beersheba:

> Observers feel that with proper counsel after the Israeli-Egyptian armistice, the Arab population might have advantageously

remained. They state that the Israeli Government had given guarantees of security of person and property. However, no effort was made by Egypt, Transjordan or even the United Nations Palestine Conciliation Commission to advise the Faluja Arabs one way or the other.[26]

MYTH

"Arab leaders never encouraged the Palestinians to flee."

FACT

A plethora of evidence exists demonstrating that Palestinians were encouraged to leave their homes to make way for the invading Arab armies.

The *Economist*, a frequent critic of the Zionists, reported on October 2, 1948: "Of the 62,000 Arabs who formerly lived in Haifa not more than 5,000 or 6,000 remained. Various factors influenced their decision to seek safety in flight. There is but little doubt that the most potent of the factors were the announcements made over the air by the Higher Arab Executive, urging the Arabs to quit....It was clearly intimated that those Arabs who remained in Haifa and accepted Jewish protection would be regarded as renegades."

Time's report of the battle for Haifa (May 3, 1948) was similar: "The mass evacuation, prompted partly by fear, partly by orders of Arab leaders, left the Arab quarter of Haifa a ghost city....By withdrawing Arab workers their leaders hoped to paralyze Haifa."

Benny Morris, the historian who documented instances where Palestinians were expelled, also found that Arab leaders encouraged their brethren to leave. The Arab National Committee in Jerusalem, following the March 8, 1948, instructions of the Arab Higher Committee, ordered women, children and the elderly in various parts of Jerusalem to leave their homes: "Any opposition to this order...is an obstacle to the holy war...and will hamper the operations of the fighters in these districts."[27]

Morris also said that in early May units of the Arab Legion reportedly ordered the evacuation of all women and children from the town of Beisan. The Arab Liberation Army was also reported to have ordered the evacuation of another village south of Haifa. The departure of the women and children, Morris says, "tended to sap the morale of the menfolk who were left behind to guard the homes and fields, contributing ultimately to the final evacuation of villages. Such two-tier evacuation — women and children first, the men following weeks later — occurred in Qumiya in the Jezreel Valley, among the Awarna bedouin in Haifa Bay and in various other places."

Who gave such orders? Leaders like Iraqi Prime Minister Nuri Said, who declared: "We will smash the country with our guns and obliterate every place the Jews seek shelter in. The Arabs should conduct their wives and children to safe areas until the fighting has died down."[28]

The Secretary of the Arab League Office in London, Edward Atiyah, wrote in his book, *The Arabs*: "This wholesale exodus was due partly to the belief of the Arabs, encouraged by the boastings of an unrealistic Arabic press and the irresponsible utterances of some of the Arab leaders that it could be only a matter of weeks before the Jews were defeated by the armies of the Arab States and the Palestinian Arabs enabled to reenter and retake possession of their country."[29]

> *"The [refugee] problem was a direct consequence of the war that the Palestinians – and... surrounding Arab states – had launched."*
>
> **– Israeli historian Benny Morris**[30]

In his memoirs, Haled al Azm, the Syrian Prime Minister in 1948-49, also admitted the Arab role in persuading the refugees to leave:

> Since 1948 we have been demanding the return of the refugees to their homes. But we ourselves are the ones who encouraged them to leave. Only a few months separated our call to them to leave and our appeal to the United Nations to resolve on their return.[31]

"The refugees were confident their absence would not last long, and that they would return within a week or two," Monsignor George Hakim, a Greek Orthodox Catholic Bishop of Galilee told the Beirut newspaper, *Sada al-Janub* (August 16, 1948). "Their leaders had promised them that the Arab Armies would crush the 'Zionist gangs' very quickly and that there was no need for panic or fear of a long exile."

On April 3, 1949, the Near East Broadcasting Station (Cyprus) said: "It must not be forgotten that the Arab Higher Committee encouraged the refugees' flight from their homes in Jaffa, Haifa and Jerusalem."[32]

"The Arab States encouraged the Palestine Arabs to leave their homes temporarily in order to be out of the way of the Arab invasion armies," according to the Jordanian newspaper *Filastin* (February 19, 1949).

One refugee quoted in the Jordan newspaper, *Ad Difaa* (September 6, 1954), said: "The Arab government told us: Get out so that we can get in. So we got out, but they did not get in."

"The Secretary-General of the Arab League, Azzam Pasha, assured the Arab peoples that the occupation of Palestine and Tel Aviv would be as simple as a military promenade," said Habib Issa in the New York Lebanese paper,

Al Hoda (June 8, 1951). "He pointed out that they were already on the frontiers and that all the millions the Jews had spent on land and economic development would be easy booty, for it would be a simple matter to throw Jews into the Mediterranean....Brotherly advice was given to the Arabs of Palestine to leave their land, homes and property and to stay temporarily in neighboring fraternal states, lest the guns of the invading Arab armies mow them down."

The Arabs' fear was naturally exacerbated by fabricated stories of Jewish atrocities following the attack on Deir Yassin. The native population lacked leaders who could calm them; their spokesmen, such as the Arab Higher Committee, were operating from the safety of neighboring states and did more to arouse their fears than to pacify them. Local military leaders were of little or no comfort. In one instance the commander of Arab troops in Safed went to Damascus. The following day, his troops withdrew from the town. When the residents realized they were defenseless, they fled in panic.[33]

According to Dr. Walid al-Qamhawi, a former member of the Executive Committee of the PLO, "it was collective fear, moral disintegration and chaos in every field that exiled the Arabs of Tiberias, Haifa and dozens of towns and villages."[34]

As panic spread throughout Palestine, the early trickle of refugees became a flood, numbering more than 200,000 by the time the provisional government declared the independence of the State of Israel.

Even Jordan's King Abdullah, writing in his memoirs, blamed Palestinian leaders for the refugee problem:

> The tragedy of the Palestinians was that most of their leaders had paralyzed them with false and unsubstantiated promises that they were not alone; that 80 million Arabs and 400 million Muslims would instantly and miraculously come to their rescue.[35]

> *"The Arab armies entered Palestine to protect the Palestinians from the Zionist tyranny but, instead, they abandoned them, forced them to emigrate and to leave their homeland, and threw them into prisons similar to the ghettos in which the Jews used to live."*
>
> **— PLO spokesman Mahmud Abbas ("Abu Mazen")**[36]

MYTH

"The Palestinian Arabs had to flee to avoid being massacred as were the peaceful villagers in Deir Yassin."

FACT

The United Nations resolved that Jerusalem would be an international city apart from the Arab and Jewish states demarcated in the partition resolution. The 150,000 Jewish inhabitants were under constant military pressure; the 2,500 Jews living in the Old City were victims of an Arab blockade that lasted five months before they were forced to surrender on May 29, 1948. Prior to the surrender, and throughout the siege on Jerusalem, Jewish convoys tried to reach the city to alleviate the food shortage, which, by April, had become critical.

Meanwhile, the Arab forces, which had engaged in sporadic and unorganized ambushes since December 1947, began to make an organized attempt to cut off the highway linking Tel Aviv with Jerusalem — the city's only supply route. The Arabs controlled several strategic vantage points, which overlooked the highway and enabled them to fire on the convoys trying to reach the beleaguered city with supplies. Deir Yassin was situated on a hill, about 2,600 feet high, which commanded a wide view of the vicinity and was located less than a mile from the suburbs of Jerusalem. The population was 750.[37]

On April 6, Operation Nachshon was launched to open the road to Jerusalem. The village of Deir Yassin was included on the list of Arab villages to be occupied as part of the operation.

The Irgun decided to attack Deir Yassin on April 9, while the Haganah was still engaged in the battle for Kastel. This was the first major Irgun attack against the Arabs. Previously, the Irgun and Lehi had concentrated their attacks against the British.

According to Irgun leader Menachem Begin, the assault was carried out by 100 members of that organization; other authors say it was as many as 132 men from both groups. Begin stated that a small open truck fitted with a loudspeaker was driven to the entrance of the village before the attack and broadcast a warning to civilians to evacuate the area, which many did.[38] Most writers say the warning was never issued because the truck with the loudspeaker rolled into a ditch before it could broadcast the warning.[39] One of the fighters said, the ditch was filled in and the truck continued on to the village. "One of us called out on the loudspeaker in Arabic, telling the inhabitants to put down their weapons and flee. I don't know if they heard, and I know these appeals had no effect."[40]

Contrary to revisionist histories that the town was filled with peaceful innocents, residents and foreign troops opened fire on the attackers. One fighter described his experience:

> My unit stormed and passed the first row of houses. I was among the first to enter the village. There were a few other guys with me, each encouraging the other to advance. At the top of the street I saw a man in khaki clothing running ahead. I thought he was one of ours. I ran after him and told him, "advance to that house." Suddenly he turned around, aimed his rifle and shot. He was an Iraqi soldier. I was hit in the foot.[41]

The battle was ferocious and took several hours. The Irgun suffered 41 casualties, including four dead.

Surprisingly, after the "massacre," the Irgun escorted a representative of the Red Cross through the town and held a press conference. The *New York Times'* subsequent description of the battle was essentially the same as Begin's. The *Times* said more than 200 Arabs were killed, 40 captured and 70 women and children were released. No hint of a massacre appeared in the report.

"Paradoxically, the Jews say about 250 out of 400 village inhabitants [were killed], while Arab survivors say only 110 of 1,000."[42] A study by Bir Zeit University, based on discussions with each family from the village, arrived at a figure of 107 Arab civilians dead and 12 wounded, in addition to 13 "fighters," evidence that the number of dead was smaller than claimed and that the village did have troops based there.[43] Other Arab sources have subsequently suggested the number may have been even lower.[44]

In fact, the attackers left open an escape corridor from the village and more than 200 residents left unharmed. For example, at 9:30 A.M., about five hours after the fighting started, the Lehi evacuated 40 old men, women and children on trucks and took them to a base in Sheikh Bader. Later, the Arabs were taken to East Jerusalem. Seeing the Arabs in the hands of Jews also helped raise the morale of the people of Jerusalem who were despondent from the setbacks in the fighting to that point.[45] Another source says 70 women and children were taken away and turned over to the British.[46] If the intent was to massacre the inhabitants, no one would have been evacuated.

After the remaining Arabs feigned surrender and then fired on the Jewish troops, some Jews killed Arab soldiers and civilians indiscriminately. None of the sources specify how many women and children were killed (the *Times* report said it was about half the victims; their original casualty figure came from the Irgun source), but there were some among the casualties.

At least some of the women who were killed became targets because of men who tried to disguise themselves as women. The Irgun commander reported, for example, that the attackers "found men dressed as women and therefore they began to shoot at women who did not hasten to go down to the place designated for gathering the prisoners."[47] Another story was told by a member of the Haganah who overheard a group of Arabs from Deir Yassin who said "the Jews found out that Arab warriors had disguised themselves as women. The Jews searched the women too. One of the people being checked realized he had been caught, took out a pistol and shot the Jewish commander. His friends, crazed with anger, shot in all directions and killed the Arabs in the area."[48]

Contrary to claims from Arab propagandists at the time and some since, no evidence has ever been produced that any women were raped. On the contrary, every villager ever interviewed has denied these allegations. Like many of the claims, this was a deliberate propaganda ploy, but one that backfired. Hazam Nusseibi, who worked for the Palestine Broadcasting Service in 1948, admitted being told by Hussein Khalidi, a Palestinian Arab leader, to fabricate the atrocity claims. Abu Mahmud, a Deir Yassin resident in 1948 told Khalidi "there was no rape," but Khalidi replied, "We have to say this, so the Arab armies will come to liberate Palestine from the Jews." Nusseibeh told the BBC 50 years later, "This was our biggest mistake. We did not realize how our people would react. As soon as they heard that women had been raped at Deir Yassin, Palestinians fled in terror."[49]

The Jewish Agency, upon learning of the attack, immediately expressed its "horror and disgust." It also sent a letter expressing the Agency's shock and disapproval to Transjordan's King Abdullah.

The Arab Higher Committee hoped exaggerated reports about a "massacre" at Deir Yassin would shock the population of the Arab countries into bringing pressure on their governments to intervene in Palestine. Instead, the immediate impact was to stimulate a new Palestinian exodus.

Just four days after the reports from Deir Yassin were published, an Arab force ambushed a Jewish convoy on the way to Hadassah Hospital, killing 77 Jews, including doctors, nurses, patients, and the director of the hospital. Another 23 people were injured. This *massacre* attracted little attention and is never mentioned by those who are quick to bring up Deir Yassin. Moreover, despite attacks such as this against the Jewish community in Palestine, in which more than 500 Jews were killed in the first four months after the partition decision alone, Jews did not flee.

The Palestinians knew, despite their rhetoric to the contrary, the Jews were not trying to annihilate them; otherwise, they would not have been allowed to evacuate Tiberias, Haifa or any of the other towns captured by the Jews. Moreover, the Palestinians could find sanctuary in nearby states. The Jews, however, had no place to run had they wanted to. They were willing to fight to the death for their country. It came to that for many, because the Arabs *were* interested in annihilating the Jews, as Secretary-General of the Arab League Azzam Pasha made clear in an interview with the BBC on the eve of the war (May 15, 1948): "The Arabs intend to conduct a war of extermination and momentous massacre which will be spoken of like the Mongolian massacres and the Crusades."

References to Deir Yassin have remained a staple of anti-Israel propaganda for decades because the incident was unique.

MYTH

"Israel refused to allow Palestinians to return to their homes so Jews could steal their property."

FACT

Israel could not simply agree to allow all Palestinians to return, but consistently sought a solution to the refugee problem. Israel's position was expressed by David Ben-Gurion (August 1, 1948):

> When the Arab states are ready to conclude a peace treaty with Israel this question will come up for constructive solution as part of the general settlement, and with due regard to our counter-claims in respect of the destruction of Jewish life and property, the long-term interest of the Jewish and Arab populations, the stability of the State of Israel and the durability of the basis of peace between it and its neighbors, the actual position and fate of the Jewish communities in the Arab countries, the responsibilities of the Arab governments for their war of aggression and their liability for reparation, will all be relevant in the question whether, to what extent, and under what conditions, the former Arab residents of the territory of Israel should be allowed to return.[50]

The Israeli government was not indifferent to the plight of the refugees; an ordinance was passed creating a Custodian of Abandoned Property "to prevent unlawful occupation of empty houses and business premises, to administer ownerless property, and also to secure tilling of deserted fields, and save the crops...."[51]

The implied danger of repatriation did not prevent Israel from allowing some refugees to return and offering to take back a substantial number as a condition for signing a peace treaty. In 1949, Israel offered to allow families that had been separated during the war to return, to release refugee accounts frozen in Israeli banks (eventually released in 1953), to pay compensation for abandoned lands and to repatriate 100,000 refugees.[52]

The Arabs rejected all the Israeli compromises. They were unwilling to take any action that might be construed as recognition of Israel. They made repatriation a precondition for negotiations, something Israel rejected. The result was the confinement of the refugees in camps.

Despite the position taken by the Arab states, Israel did release the Arab refugees' blocked bank accounts, which totaled more than $10 million, paid thousands of claimants cash compensation and granted thousands of acres as alternative holdings.

MYTH

"UN resolutions call for Israel to repatriate all Palestinian refugees."

FACT

The United Nations took up the refugee issue and adopted Resolution 194 on December 11, 1948. This called upon the Arab states and Israel to resolve all outstanding issues through negotiations either directly, or with the help of the Palestine Conciliation Commission established by this resolution. Furthermore, Point 11 resolves:

> that refugees wishing to return to their homes *and live at peace* with their neighbors should be permitted to do so at the earliest practicable date, and that compensation should be paid for property of those choosing not to return and for loss of or damage to property which under principles of international law or in equity should be made good by Governments or authorities responsible. Instructs the Conciliation Commission to facilitate the repatriation, *resettlement* and economic and social rehabilitation of refugees and payment of compensation... (emphasis added).

The emphasized words demonstrate that the UN recognized that Israel could not be expected to repatriate a hostile population that might endanger its security. The solution to the problem, like all previous refugee problems, would require at least some Palestinians to be resettled in Arab lands. Furthermore, the resolution uses the word "should" instead of "shall," which, in legal terms, is not mandatory language.

The resolution met most of Israel's concerns regarding the refugees, whom they regarded as a potential fifth-column if allowed to return unconditionally. The Israelis considered the settlement of the refugee issue a negotiable part of an overall peace settlement. As President Chaim Weizmann explained: "We are anxious to help such resettlement provided that real peace is established and the Arab states do their part of the job. The solution of the Arab problem can be achieved only through an all-around Middle East development scheme, toward which the United Nations, the Arab states and Israel will make their respective contributions."[53]

At the time the Israelis did not expect the refugees to be a major issue; they thought the Arab states would resettle the majority and some compromise on the remainder could be worked out in the context of an overall settlement. The Arabs were no more willing to compromise in 1949, however, than they had been in 1947. In fact, they unanimously rejected the UN resolution.

The UN discussions on refugees had begun in the summer of 1948, before Israel had completed its military victory; consequently, the Arabs still believed they could win the war and allow the refugees to return triumphant. The

Arab position was expressed by Emile Ghoury, the Secretary of the Arab Higher Committee:

> It is inconceivable that the refugees should be sent back to their homes while they are occupied by the Jews, as the latter would hold them as hostages and maltreat them. The very proposal is an evasion of responsibility by those responsible. It will serve as a first step towards Arab recognition of the State of Israel and partition.[54]

The Arabs demanded that the United Nations assert the "right" of the Palestinians to return to their homes, and were unwilling to accept anything less until after their defeat had become obvious. The Arabs then reinterpreted Resolution 194 as granting the refugees the absolute right of repatriation and have demanded that Israel accept this interpretation ever since. Regardless of the interpretation, 194, like other General Assembly resolutions, is not legally binding.

> *"The Palestinian demand for the 'right of return' is totally unrealistic and would have to be solved by means of financial compensation and resettlement in Arab countries."*
>
> **— Egyptian President Hosni Mubarak[55]**

MYTH

"Israel blocked negotiations by the Palestine Conciliation Commission."

FACT

Early in 1949, the Palestine Conciliation Commission (PCC) opened negotiations at Lausanne. The Arabs insisted that Israel yield the territory won in the 1948 fighting and agree to repatriation. The Israelis told the commission the solution of the refugee problem depended on the conclusion of peace.

Israel did make a substantial repatriation offer during these negotiations. The government said it would accept 100,000 refugees in a general settlement of the problem. Israel hoped that each Arab state would make a similar commitment. This offer was rejected.

On April 1, 1950, the Arab League adopted a resolution forbidding its members from negotiating with Israel.

The PCC made another effort to bring the parties together in 1951, but finally gave up. It reported:

The Arab Governments...are not prepared fully to implement paragraph 5 of the said resolution, which calls for the final settlement of all questions outstanding between them and Israel. The Arab Governments in their contacts with the Commission have evinced no readiness to arrive at such a peace settlement with the Government of Israel.[56]

MYTH

"Palestinians who wanted to return to their homes posed no danger to Israeli security."

FACT

When plans for setting up a state were made in early 1948, Jewish leaders in Palestine expected the new nation to include a significant Arab population. From the Israeli perspective, the refugees had been given an opportunity to stay in their homes and be a part of the new state. Approximately 160,000 Arabs had chosen to do so. To repatriate those who had fled would be, in the words of Foreign Minister Moshe Sharett, "suicidal folly."[57]

In the Arab world, the refugees were viewed as a potential fifth-column within Israel. As one Lebanese paper wrote:

The return of the refugees should create a large Arab majority that would serve as the most effective means of reviving the Arab character of Palestine, while forming a powerful fifth-column for the day of revenge and reckoning.[58]

The Arabs believed the return of the refugees would virtually guarantee the destruction of Israel, a sentiment expressed by Egyptian Foreign Minister Muhammad Salah al-Din:

It is well-known and understood that the Arabs, in demanding the return of the refugees to Palestine, mean their return as masters of the Homeland and not as slaves. With a greater clarity, they mean the liquidation of the State of Israel.[59]

The plight of the refugees remained unchanged after the Suez War. In fact, even the rhetoric stayed the same. In 1957, the Refugee Conference at Homs, Syria, passed a resolution stating:

Any discussion aimed at a solution of the Palestine problem which will not be based on ensuring the refugees' right to annihilate Israel will be regarded as a desecration of the Arab people and an act of treason.[60]

A parallel can be drawn to the time of the American Revolution, during which many colonists who were loyal to England fled to Canada. The British wanted he newly formed republic to allow the loyalists to return to claim their property. Benjamin Franklin rejected this suggestion in a letter to Richard Oswald, the British negotiator, dated November 26, 1782:

Your ministers require that we should receive again into our bosom those who have been our bitterest enemies and restore their properties who have destroyed ours: and this while the wounds they have given us are still bleeding![61]

MYTH

"The Palestinian refugees were ignored by an uncaring world."

FACT

The General Assembly subsequently voted, on November 19, 1948, to establish the United Nations Relief For Palestinian Refugees (UNRPR) to dispense aid to the refugees. The UNRPR was replaced by the United Nations Relief and Works Agency (UNWRA) on December 8, 1949, and given a budget of $50 million.

UNWRA was designed to continue the relief program initiated by the UNRPR, substitute public works for direct relief and promote economic development. The proponents of the plan envisioned that direct relief would be almost completely replaced by public works, with the remaining assistance provided by the Arab governments.

UNRWA had little chance of success, however, because it sought to solve a political problem using an economic approach. By the mid-1950s, it was evident neither the refugees nor the Arab states were prepared to cooperate on the large-scale development projects originally foreseen by the Agency as a means of alleviating the Palestinians' situation. The Arab governments, and the refugees themselves, were unwilling to contribute to any plan that could be interpreted as fostering resettlement. They preferred to cling to their interpretation of Resolution 194, which they believed would eventually result in repatriation.

Table 2 - Palestinian Refugees Registered By UNRWA [62]

Field of Operations	Official Camps	Registered Refugees	Registered Refugees in Camps
Jordan	10	1,639,718	287,951
Lebanon	12	382,973	214,728
Syria	10	391,651	109,466
West Bank	19	607,770	163,139
Gaza Strip	8	852,626	460,031
Agency total	59	3,874,738	1,235,315

MYTH

"The Arab states have provided most of the funds for helping the Palestinian refugees."

FACT

While Jewish refugees from Arab countries received no international assistance, Palestinians received millions of dollars through UNRWA. Initially, the United States contributed $25 million and Israel nearly $3 million. The total Arab pledges amounted to approximately $600,000. For the first 20 years, the United States provided more than two-thirds of the funds, while the Arab states continued to contribute a tiny fraction. Israel donated more funds to UNRWA than most Arab states. The Saudis did not match Israel's contribution until 1973; Kuwait and Libya, not until 1980. As recently as 1994, Israel gave more to UNRWA than all Arab countries except Saudi Arabia, Kuwait and Morocco.

The United States is still by far the organization's largest contributor, donating nearly $90 million in 2000, approximately 31 percent of the organization's $293 million in receipts. Meanwhile, for all their rhetorical support for the Palestinians, the Arab states contributed only 2 percent of the UNRWA budget. Israel and the other host countries make their contributions in kind rather than cash and Israel has dramatically reduced its assistance since transferring responsibility of the territories to the Palestinian Authority.[63]

MYTH

"The Arab states have always welcomed the Palestinians and done their best to resettle them."

FACT

Jordan was the only Arab country to welcome the Palestinians and grant them citizenship (to this day Jordan is the only Arab country where Palestinians *as a group* can become citizens). King Abdullah considered the Palestinian Arabs and Jordanians one people. By 1950, he annexed the West Bank and forbade the use of the term Palestine in official documents.[64]

Although demographic figures indicated ample room for settlement existed in Syria, Damascus refused to consider accepting any refugees, except those who might refuse repatriation. Syria also declined to resettle 85,000 refugees in 1952-54, though it had been offered international funds to pay for the project. Iraq was also expected to accept a large number of refugees, but proved unwilling. Lebanon insisted it had no room for the Palestinians. In 1950, the UN tried to resettle 150,000 refugees from Gaza in Libya, but was rebuffed by Egypt.

After the 1948 war, Egypt controlled the Gaza Strip and its more than 200,000 inhabitants, but refused to allow the Palestinians into Egypt or permit them to move elsewhere. Egypt's handling of Palestinians in Gaza was so bad Saudi Arabian radio compared Nasser' regime in Gaza to Hitler's rule in occupied Europe in World War II.[65]

In 1952, the UNWRA set up a fund of $200 million to provide homes and jobs for the refugees, but it went untouched.

> "The Arab States do not want to solve the refugee problem. They want to keep it as an open sore, as an affront to the United Nations and as a weapon against Israel. Arab leaders don't give a damn whether the refugees live or die."
>
> **— former director of UNRWA, Ralph Garroway, in August 1958[66]**

Little has changed in succeeding years. Arab governments have frequently offered jobs, housing, land and other benefits to Arabs and non-Arabs, *excluding* Palestinians. For example, Saudi Arabia chose not to use unemployed Palestinian refugees to alleviate its labor shortage in the late 1970's and early 1980's. Instead, thousands of South Koreans and other Asians were recruited to fill jobs.

The situation grew even worse in the wake of the Gulf War. Kuwait, which employed large numbers of Palestinians but denied them citizenship, expelled more than 300,000 of them. "If people pose a security threat, as a sovereign country we have the right to exclude anyone we don't want," said Kuwaiti Ambassador to the United States, Saud Nasir Al-Sabah.[67]

Today, Palestine refugees in Lebanon do not have social and civil rights, and have very limited access to public health or educational facilities. The majority relies entirely on UNRWA as the sole provider of education, health and relief and social services. Considered foreigners, Palestine refugees are prohibited by law from working in more than 70 trades and professions.[68]

The Palestinian refugees held the UN responsible for ameliorating their condition; nevertheless, many Palestinians were unhappy with the treatment they were receiving from their Arab brethren. Some, like Palestinian nationalist leader Musa Alami were incredulous: "It is shameful that the Arab governments should prevent the Arab refugees from working in their countries and shut the doors in their faces and imprison them in camps."[69] Most refugees, however, focused their discontentment on "the Zionists," whom they blamed for their predicament rather than the vanquished Arab armies.

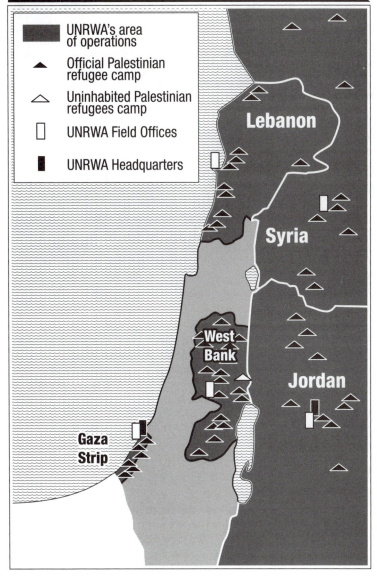

Map 21 — UNRWA Refugee Camps (in 2000)

- UNRWA's area of operations
- Official Palestinian refugee camp
- Uninhabited Palestinian refugees camp
- UNRWA Field Offices
- UNRWA Headquarters

Lebanon

Syria

West Bank

Jordan

Gaza Strip

MYTH

"Millions of Palestinians are confined to squalid refugee camps."

FACT

By the middle of 2001, the number of Palestinian refugees on UNRWA rolls had risen to 3.9 million, five or six times the number that left Palestine in 1948. One-third of the registered Palestine refugees, about 1.2 million, live in 59 recognized refugee camps in Jordan, Lebanon, Syria, the West Bank and Gaza Strip. The other two-thirds of the registered refugees live in and around the cities and towns of the host countries, and in the West Bank and the Gaza Strip, often in the environs of official camps.[70]

MYTH

"Israel forced the Palestinian refugees to stay in camps in the Gaza Strip."

FACT

During the years that Israel controlled the Gaza Strip, a consistent effort was made to get the Palestinians into permanent housing. The Palestinians opposed the idea because the frustrated and bitter inhabitants of the camps provided the various terrorist factions with their manpower. Moreover, the Arab states routinely pushed for the adoption of UN resolutions demanding that Israel desist from the removal of Palestinian refugees from camps in Gaza and the West Bank. They preferred to keep the Palestinians as symbols of Israeli "oppression."

Now the camps are in the hands of the Palestinian Authority (PA), but little is being done to improve the lot of the Palestinians living in them. Journalist Netty Gross visited Gaza and asked an official why the camps there hadn't been dismantled. She was told the Palestinian Authority had made a "political decision" not to do anything for the more than 400,000 Palestinians living in the camps until the final-status talks with Israel took place.[71] To this day, the PA has not used a dime of the billions of dollars in foreign aid it has received to build permanent housing for the refugees.

MYTH

"Refugees have always been repatriated, only the Palestinians have been barred from returning to their homes."

FACT

Despite Arab intransigence, no one expected the refugee problem to persist. John Blandford Jr., the Director of UNRWA, wrote in his report on November 29, 1951, that he expected the Arab governments to assume responsibility for relief by July 1952. Moreover, Blandford stressed the need to end relief operations: "Sustained relief operations inevitably contain the germ of human deterioration."[72]

In fact, the Palestinians are the only displaced persons to have become wards of the international community.

Israel's agreement to pay compensation to the Palestinians who fled during 1948 can be contrasted with the treatment of the 12.5 million Germans in Poland and Czechoslovakia, who were expelled after World War II and allowed to take only those possessions they could carry. They received no compensation for confiscated property. World War II's effects on Poland's boundaries and population were considered "accomplished facts" that could not be reversed after the war.

Another country seriously affected by the war was Finland, which was forced to give up almost one-eighth of its land and absorb more than 400,000 refugees (11 percent of the nation's population) from the Soviet Union. Unlike Israel, these were the *losers* of the war. There was no aid for their resettlement.

Perhaps an even better analogy can be seen in Turkey's integration of 150,000 Turkish refugees from Bulgaria in 1950. The difference between the Turks' handling of their refugees and the Arab states. treatment of the Palestinians was the attitude of the respective governments.

> Turkey has had a bigger refugee problem than either Syria or Lebanon and almost as big as Egypt has....But you seldom hear about them because the Turks have done such a good job of resettling them....The big difference is in spirit. The Turks, reluctant as they were to take on the burden, accepted it as a responsibility and set to work to clean it up as fast as possible.[73]

Had the Arab states wanted to alleviate the refugees' suffering, they could easily have adopted an attitude similar to Turkey's.

Another massive population transfer resulted from the partition of India and Pakistan in 1947. The eight *million* Hindus who fled Pakistan and the six *million* Muslims who left India were afraid of becoming a minority in their respective countries. Like the Palestinians, these people wanted to avoid being caught in the middle of the violence that engulfed their nations. In contrast to the Arab-Israeli conflict, however, the exchange of populations was considered the best solution to the problem of communal relations within the two states. Despite the enormous number of refugees and the relative poverty of the two nations involved, no special international relief organizations were established to aid them in resettlement.

MYTH

"Had the Palestinian refugees been repatriated, the Arab-Israeli conflict could have ended."

FACT

Israel consistently sought a solution to the refugee problem, but could not simply agree to allow all Palestinians to return.

No nation, regardless of past rights and wrongs, could contemplate taking in a fifth-column of such a size. And fifth-column it would be — people nurtured for 20 years [in 1967] in hatred of and totally dedicated to its destruction. The readmission of the refugees would be the equivalent to the admission to the U.S. of nearly 70,000,000 sworn enemies of the nation.[74]

The Arabs, meanwhile, adamantly refused to negotiate a separate agreement. The crux of the issue was the Arab states' unwillingness to accept Israel's existence. This was exemplified by Egyptian President Nasser's belligerent acts toward the Jewish State, which had nothing to do with the Palestinians. He was only interested in the refugees to the extent that they could contribute to his ultimate objective. As he told an interviewer on September 1, 1961: "If refugees return to Israel, Israel will cease to exist."[75]

MYTH

"Israel expelled more Palestinians in 1967."

FACT

After ignoring Israeli warnings to stay out of the war, King Hussein launched an attack on Jerusalem, Israel's capital. UNRWA estimated that during the fighting 175,000 of its registrants fled for a second time and approximately 350,000 fled for the first time. About 200,000 moved to Jordan, 115,000 to Syria and approximately 35,000 left Sinai for Egypt. Most of the Arabs who left came from the West Bank.

Israel allowed some West Bank Arabs to return. In 1967, more than 9,000 families were reunited and, by 1971, Israel had readmitted 40,000 refugees. By contrast, in July 1968, Jordan prohibited people intending to remain in the East Bank from emigrating from the West Bank and Gaza.[76]

When the Security Council empowered U Thant to send a representative to inquire into the welfare of civilians in the wake of the war, he instructed the mission to investigate the treatment of Jewish minorities in Arab countries, as well as Arabs in Israeli-occupied territory. Syria, Iraq and Egypt refused to permit the UN representative to carry out his investigation.[77]

MYTH

"UNRWA is purely a humanitarian organization
that bears no responsibility for the terror and incitement
that originates in the refugee camps."

FACT

The chief of the UNRWA Public Information Office, Paul McCann, asserted that "UNRWA is scrupulous about protecting its installations against misuse by any person or group. Only once, in Lebanon in 1982, has there been credible evidence of such misuse by Palestinians, and it was promptly dealt with."[78]

The fact is the refugee camps have long been nests of terrorism, but the evidence was not publicized until after Israel's Operation Defensive Shield in early 2002. The UNRWA-administered camps in the West Bank were found to have small-arms factories, explosives laboratories, arms caches and large numbers of suicide bombers and other terrorists using the refugees as shields.

UNRWA's failure to report on these activities or to prevent them violate the UN's own conventions. Security Council resolutions oblige UNRWA representatives to take "appropriate steps to help create a secure environment" in all "situations where refugees [are]...vulnerable to infiltration by armed elements." With regard to Africa, UN Secretary-General Kofi Annan, said refugee camps should "be kept free of any military presence or equipment, including arms and ammunition."[79] The same rule applies to the disputed territories.

Schools under UNRWA's jurisdiction are also problematic. UNRWA takes credit for assisting the development of the Palestinian curricula, which, among other things, does not show Israel on any maps. The schools are also filled with posters and shrines to suicide bombers. In 1998, the State Department requested that UNRWA investigate allegations that Palestinian Authority curricular materials contained anti-Semitic references. One book taught that "Treachery and disloyalty are character traits of the Jews," but UNRWA said this was not offensive because it described actual "historical events." The State Department ultimately reported to Congress that "UNRWA's review did reveal instances of anti-Semitic characterizations and content" in the PA textbooks.[80]

Notes

[1] Arieh Avneri, *The Claim of Dispossession,* (NJ: Transaction Books, 1984), p. 272; Kedar, Benjamin. *The Changing Land Between the Jordan and the Sea,* (Israel: Yad Izhak Ben-Zvi Press, 1999), p. 206; Paul Johnson, *A History of the Jews,* (NY: Harper & Row, 1987), p. 529.

[2] "Progress Report of the United Nations Mediator on Palestine," Submitted to the Secretary-General for Transmission to the Members of the United Nations, General Assembly Official Records: Third Session, Supplement No.11 (A\648), Paris, 1948, p. 47 and Supplement No. 11A (A\689, and A\689\Add.1, p. 5; "Conclusions From Progress Report of the United Nations Mediator on Palestine," (September 16, 1948), U.N. doc. A/648 (part one, p. 29; part two, p. 23 and part three, p. 11), (September 18, 1948).

[3] *New York Times,* (November 25, 1947).

[4] Avneri, p. 276.

[5] David Ben-Gurion, *Rebirth and Destiny of Israel,* (NY: Philosophical Library, 1954), p. 220.

[6] Isi Liebler, *The Case For Israel,* (Australia: The Globe Press, 1972), p. 43.

[7] Joseph Schechtman, *The Refugee in the World,* (NY: A.S. Barnes and Co., 1963), p. 184.

[8] I.F. Stone, *This is Israel,* (NY: Boni and Gaer, 1948), p. 27.

[9] *Ash Sha'ab,* (January 30, 1948).

[10] *As Sarih,* (March 30, 1948).

[11] Avneri, p. 270.

[12] *London Daily Mail,* (August 12, 1948).

13 *New York Times*, (April 23, 1948).

14 Howard Sachar, *A History of Israel: From the Rise of Zionism to Our Time*, (NY: Alfred A. Knopf, 1979), p. 332; Avneri, p. 270.

15 Secret memo dated April 26, 1948, from the Superintendent of Police, regarding the general situation in Haifa. See also his April 29 memo.

16 Golda Meir, *My Life*, (NY: Dell, 1975), pp. 267-268.

17 *New York Times*, (April 23, 1948).

18 *London Times*, (April 24, 1948).

19 Schechtman, p. 190.

20 *Foreign Relations of the U.S. 1948*, Vol. V, (DC: GPO, 1976), p. 838.

21 Tom Segev, *1949: The First Israelis*, (NY: The Free Press, 1986), pp. 27-28.

22 Yigal Allon in *Sefer ha-Palmach*, quoted in Larry Collins and Dominique Lapierre, *O Jerusalem!*, (NY: Simon and Schuster, 1972), p. 337; Yigal Allon, *My Father's House*, (NY: W.W Norton and Company, Inc., 1976), p. 192.

23 Benny Morris, "Operation Dani and the Palestinian Exodus from Lydda and Ramle in 1948," *Middle East Journal*, (Winter 1986), pp. 82-83.

24 *Middle East Journal*, (October 1949).

25 Terence Prittie, "Middle East Refugees," in Michael Curtis, et *al.*, *The Palestinians*, (NJ: Transaction Books, 1975), p. 52.

26 *New York Times*, (March 4, 1949).

27 *Middle Eastern Studies*, (January 1986).

28 Myron Kaufman, *The Coming Destruction of Israel*, (NY: The American Library Inc., 1970), pp. 26-27.

29 Edward Atiyah, *The Arabs*, (London: Penguin Books, 1955), p. 183.

30 *The Guardian*, (February, 21, 2002).

31 *The Memoirs of Haled al Azm*, (Beirut, 1973), Part 1, pp. 386-387.

32 Samuel Katz, *Battleground-Fact and Fantasy in Palestine*, (NY: Bantam Books, 1985), p. 15.

33 *King Abdallah, My Memoirs Completed*, (London: Longman Group, Ltd., 1978), p. xvi. [Abdullah generally, but spelled Abdallah in his memoir].

34 Schechtman, p. 186.

35 Yehoshofat Harkabi, *Arab Attitudes To Israel*, (Jerusalem: Israel Universities Press, 1972), p. 364.

36 *Falastin a-Thaura*, (March 1976).

37 "*Dayr Yasin*," Bir Zeit University.

38 Dan Kurzman, *Genesis 1948*, (OH: New American Library, Inc., 1970), p. 141.

39 Menachem Begin, *The Revolt*, (NY: Nash Publishing, 1977), pp. xx-xxi, 162-163.

40 See, for example, Amos Perlmutter, *The Life and Times of Menachem Begin*, (NY: Doubleday, 1987), p. 214; J. Bowyer Bell, *Terror Out Of Zion*, (NY: St. Martin's Press, 1977), p. 292-96; Kurzman, p. 142.

41 Uri Milstein, *History of Israel's War of Independence*, Vol. IV, (Lanham: University Press of America. 1999), p. 262.

42 Milstein, p. 262.

43 Sharif Kanaana and Nihad Zitawi, "Deir Yassin," Monograph No. 4, Destroyed Palestinian Villages Documentation Project, (Bir Zeit: Documentation Center of Bir Zeit University, 1987), p. 55.

44 Sharif Kanaana, "Reinterpreting Deir Yassin," Bir Zeit University, (April 1998).

45 Milstein, p. 267

46 Rami Nashashibi, "Dayr Yasin," Bir Zeit University, (June 1996).

47 Yehoshua Gorodenchik testimony at Jabotinsky Archives.

48 Milstein, p. 276.

49 "*Israel and the Arabs: The 50 Year Conflict*," BBC.

[50] Sachar, p. 335.

[51] Schechtman, p. 268.

[52] Prittie in Curtis, pp. 66-67.

[53] *New York Times*, (July 17, 1949).

[54] *Telegraph* (Beirut), (August 6, 1948), quoted in Schechtman, p. 210-211.

[55] *Jerusalem Post*, (January 26, 1989).

[56] Palestine Conciliation Commission Report Supplement 18 to the Official Records of the Sixth Session of the Assembly (A/1985), quoted in Pablo Azcarate, *Mission in Palestine 1948-1952*, (DC: Middle East Institute, 1966), p. 177.

[57] Moshe Sharett, "Israel's Position and Problems," *Middle Eastern Affairs*, (May 1952), p. 136.

[58] Lebanese newspaper, *Al Said*, (April 6, 1950), quoted in Prittie in Curtis, p. 69.

[59] *Al-Misri*, (October 11, 1949).

[60] *Beirut al Massa*, (July 15, 1957).

[61] *The Writings of Benjamin Franklin*, (NY: The Macmillan Company, 1905), p. 626.

[62] UNRWA, (as of June 2001).

[63] Report of the Commissioner-General of the United Nations, Relief and Works Agency for Palestine Refugees in the Near East, 1 July 2000-30 June 2001.

[64] Speech to Parliament, April 24, 1950, Abdallah memoirs, p. 13; Aaron Miller, *The Arab States and the Palestine Question*, (DC: Center for Strategic and International Studies, 1986), p. 29.

[65] Leibler, p. 48.

[66] *Prittie in Curtis*, p. 55.

[67] Jerusalem Report, (June 27, 1991).

[68] UNRWA.

[69] Musa Alami, "The Lesson of Palestine," *Middle East Journal*, (October 1949), p. 386.

[70] UNRWA.

[71] *Jerusalem Report*, (July 6, 1998).

[72] Schechtman, p. 220.

[73] *Des Moines Register* editorial, (January 16, 1952).

[74] *New York Times* editorial, (May 14, 1967).

[75] Leibler, p. 45.

[76] UNRWA Annual Reports, (July 1, 1966-June 30, 1967), pp. 11-19; (July 1, 1967-June 30, 1968), pp. 4-10; (July 1, 1968-June 30, 1969), p. 6; (July 1, 1971-June 30, 1972), p. 3.

[77] Maurice Roumani, *The Case of the Jews from Arab Countries: A Neglected Issue*, (Tel Aviv: World Organization of Jews from Arab Countries, 1977), p. 34.

[78] Paul McCann, letter to the editor of *The Weekly Standard*, (May 28, 2002).

[79] Isabel Kershner, "The Refugees' Choice?", *Jerusalem Report*, (August 12, 2002), p. 24.

[80] David Tell, response to McCann, *The Weekly Standard*, (May 28, 2002).

15. The Treatment of Jews in Arab/ Islamic Countries

MYTH

"Arabs cannot possibly be anti-Semitic as they are themselves Semites."

FACT

The term "anti-Semite" was coined in Germany in 1879 by Wilhelm Marrih to refer to the anti-Jewish manifestations of the period and to give Jew-hatred a more scientific sounding name.[1] "Anti-Semitism" has been accepted and understood to mean hatred of the Jewish people. Dictionaries define the term as: "Theory, action, or practice directed against the Jews" and "Hostility towards Jews as a religious or racial minority group, often accompanied by social, economic and political discrimination."[2]

The claim that Arabs as "Semites" cannot possibly be anti-Semitic is a semantic distortion that ignores the reality of Arab discrimination and hostility toward Jews. Arabs, like any other people, can indeed be anti-Semitic.

> *"The Arab world is the last bastion of unbridled, unashamed, unhidden and unbelievable anti-Semitism. Hitlerian myths get published in the popular press as incontrovertible truths. The Holocaust either gets minimized or denied....How the Arab world will ever come to terms with Israel when Israelis are portrayed as the devil incarnate is hard to figure out."*
>
> **— Columnist Richard Cohen[3]**

MYTH

"Modern Arab nations are only anti-Israel and have never been anti-Jewish."

FACT

Arab leaders have repeatedly made clear their animosity toward Jews and Judaism. For example, on November 23, 1937, Saudi Arabia's King Ibn Saud told British Colonel H.R.P. Dickson: "Our hatred for the Jews dates from God's condemnation of them for their persecution and rejection of Isa (Jesus) and their subsequent rejection of His chosen Prophet." He added "that for a Muslim to kill a Jew, or for him to be killed by a Jew ensures him an immediate entry into Heaven and into the august presence of God Almighty."[4]

When Hitler introduced the Nuremberg racial laws in 1935, he received telegrams of congratulation from all corners of the Arab world.[5] Later, during the war, one of his most ardent supporters was the Mufti of Jerusalem.

Jews were never permitted to live in Jordan. Civil Law No. 6, which governed the Jordanian-occupied West Bank, states explicitly: "Any man will be a Jordanian subject if he is not Jewish."[6]

The Arab countries see to it that even young schoolchildren are taught to hate Jews. The Syrian Minister of Education wrote in 1968: "The hatred which we indoctrinate into the minds of our children from their birth is sacred."[7]

After the Six-Day War in 1967, the Israelis found public school textbooks that had been used to educate Arab children in the West Bank. They were replete with racist and hateful portrayals of Jews:

> "The Jews are scattered to the ends of the earth, where they live exiled and despised, since by their nature they are vile, greedy and enemies of mankind, by their nature they were tempted to steal a land as asylum for their disgrace."[8]

> "Analyze the following sentences:

> 1. The merchant himself traveled to the African continent.

> 2. We shall expel all the Jews from the Arab countries."[9]

> "The Jews of our time are the descendants of the Jews who harmed the Prophet Muhammad. They betrayed him, they broke the treaty with him and joined sides with his enemies to fight him..."[10]

> "The Jews in Europe were persecuted and despised because of their corruption, meanness and treachery."[11]

According to a study of Syrian textbooks, "the Syrian educational system expands hatred of Israel and Zionism to anti-Semitism directed at all Jews. That anti-Semitism evokes ancient Islamic motifs to describe the unchangeable and treacherous nature of the Jews. Its inevitable conclusion is that all Jews must be annihilated."[12] To cite one example, an eleventh grade textbook claims that Jews hated Muslims and were driven by envy to incite hostility against them:

> The Jews spare no effort to deceive us, deny our Prophet, incite against us, and distort the holy scriptures.

> The Jews cooperate with the Polytheist and the infidels against the Muslims because they know Islam reveals their crafty ways and abject characteristics.[13]

An Arabic translation of Adolf Hitler's *Mein Kampf* has been distributed in East Jerusalem and territories controlled by the Palestinian Authority (PA) and became a bestseller.[14]

Occasionally, Arab anti-Semitism surfaces at the United Nations. In March 1991, for example, a Syrian delegate to the UN Human Rights Commission read a statement recommending that commission members read "a valuable book" called *The Matzoh of Zion*, written by Syrian Defense Minister Mustafa Tlas. The book justifies ritual murder charges brought against the Jews in the Damascus blood libel of 1840.[15] (The phrase "blood libel" refers to accusations that Jews kill Christian children to use their blood for the ritual of making matzo at Passover.)

King Faisal of Saudi Arabia uttered a similar slander in a 1972 interview:

> Israel has had malicious intentions since ancient times. Its objective is the destruction of all other religions....They regard the other religions as lower than their own and other peoples as inferior to their level. And on the subject of vengeance — they have a certain day on which they mix the blood of non-Jews into their bread and eat it. It happened that two years ago, while I was in Paris on a visit, that the police discovered five murdered children. Their blood had been drained, and it turned out that some Jews had murdered them in order to take their blood and mix it with the bread that they eat on this day. This shows you what is the extent of their hatred and malice toward non-Jewish peoples.[16]

On November 11, 1999, during a Gaza appearance with First Lady Hillary Rodham Clinton, Suha Arafat, wife of Palestinian Authority Chairman Yasser Arafat stated: "Our people have been subjected to the daily and extensive use of poisonous gas by the Israeli forces, which has led to an increase in cancer cases among women and children." Similar specious allegations have been made by other Palestinian officials.[17]

The Arab/Muslim press, which is almost exclusively controlled by the governments in each Middle Eastern nation, regularly publish anti-Semitic articles and cartoons. Today, it remains common to find anti-Semitic publications in Egypt. For example, the establishment *Al-Ahram* newspaper published an article giving the "historical" background of the blood libel tradition while accusing Israel of using the blood of Palestinian children to bake matzos up to the present time.[18] Anti-Semitic articles also regularly appear in the press in Jordan and Syria. Many of the attacks deal with denial of the Holocaust, its "exploitation" by Zionism, and a comparison of Zionism and Israel to Nazism.

In November 2001, a satirical skit aired on the second most popular television station in the Arab world, which depicted a character meant to be Ariel Sharon drinking the blood of Arab children as a grotesque-looking Orthodox Jew looked on. Abu Dhabi Television also aired a skit in which Dracula appears to take a bite out of Sharon, but dies because Sharon's blood is polluted. Protests that these shows were anti-Semitic were ignored by the network.[19]

The Palestinian Authority's media have also contained inflammatory and anti-Semitic material. A Friday sermon in the Zayed bin Sultan Aal Nahyan mosque in Gaza calling for the murder of Jews and Americans was broadcast live on the official Palestinian Authority television:

> Have no mercy on the Jews, no matter where they are, in any country. Fight them, wherever you are. Wherever you meet them, kill them. Wherever you are, kill those Jews and those Americans who are like them and those who stand by them they are all in one trench, against the Arabs and the Muslims because they established Israel here, in the beating heart of the Arab world, in Palestine.... [20]

Even Palestinian crossword puzzles are used to delegitimize Israel and attack Jews, providing clues, for example, suggesting the Jewish trait is "treachery."[21]

> *"Syrian President Bashar Assad on Saturday [May 5] offered a vivid, if vile, demonstration of why he and his government are unworthy of respect or good relations with the United States or any other democratic country. Greeting Pope John Paul II in Damascus, Mr. Assad launched an attack on Jews that may rank as the most ignorant and crude speech delivered before the pope in his two decades of travel around the world. Comparing the suffering of the Palestinians to that of Jesus Christ, Mr. Assad said that the Jews 'tried to kill the principles of all religions with the same mentality in which they betrayed Jesus Christ and the same way they tried to betray and kill the Prophet Muhammad.' With that libel, the Syrian president stained both his country and the pope...."*
>
> — ***Washington Post*** **editorial, (May 8, 2001)**[22]

MYTH

"Jews who lived in Islamic countries were well-treated by the Arabs."

FACT

While Jewish communities in Islamic countries fared better overall than those in Christian lands in Europe, Jews were no strangers to persecution and humiliation among the Arabs. As Princeton University historian Bernard Lewis has written: "The Golden Age of equal rights was a myth, and belief in it was a result, more than a cause, of Jewish sympathy for Islam."[23]

Muhammad, the founder of Islam, traveled to Medina in 622 A.D. to attract followers to his new faith. When the Jews of Medina refused to recognize Muhammad as their Prophet, two of the major Jewish tribes were expelled; in 627, Muhammad's followers killed between 600 and 900 of the men, and divided the surviving Jewish women and children amongst themselves.[24]

The Muslim attitude toward Jews is reflected in various verses throughout the Koran, the holy book of the Islamic faith. "They [the Children of Israel] were consigned to humiliation and wretchedness. They brought the wrath of God upon themselves, and this because they used to deny God's signs and kill His Prophets unjustly and because they disobeyed and were transgressors" (Sura 2:61). According to the Koran, the Jews try to introduce corruption (5: 64), have always been disobedient (5:78), and are enemies of Allah, the Prophet and the angels (2:97-98).

Jews were generally viewed with contempt by their Muslim neighbors; peaceful coexistence between the two groups involved the subordination and degradation of the Jews. In the ninth century, Baghdad's Caliph al-Mutawakkil designated a yellow badge for Jews, setting a precedent that would be followed centuries later in Nazi Germany.[25]

At various times, Jews in Muslim lands lived in relative peace and thrived culturally and economically. The position of the Jews was never secure, however, and changes in the political or social climate would often lead to persecution, violence and death.

When Jews were perceived as having achieved too comfortable a position in Islamic society, anti-Semitism would surface, often with devastating results. On December 30, 1066, Joseph HaNagid, the Jewish vizier of Granada, Spain, was crucified by an Arab mob that proceeded to raze the Jewish quarter of the city and slaughter its 5,000 inhabitants. The riot was incited by Muslim preachers who had angrily objected to what they saw as inordinate Jewish political power.

Similarly, in 1465, Arab mobs in Fez slaughtered thousands of Jews, leaving only 11 alive, after a Jewish deputy vizier treated a Muslim woman in "an offensive manner." The killings touched off a wave of similar massacres throughout Morocco.[26]

Other mass murders of Jews in Arab lands occurred in Morocco in the 8th century, where whole communities were wiped out by the Muslim ruler Idris I; North Africa in the 12th century, where the Almohads either forcibly converted or decimated several communities; Libya in 1785, where Ali Burzi Pasha murdered hundreds of Jews; Algiers, where Jews were massacred in 1805, 1815 and 1830; and Marrakesh, Morocco, where more than 300 Jews were murdered between 1864 and 1880.[27]

Decrees ordering the destruction of synagogues were enacted in Egypt and Syria (1014, 1293-4, 1301-2), Iraq (854-859, 1344) and Yemen (1676). Despite the Koran's prohibition, Jews were forced to convert to Islam or face death in Yemen (1165 and 1678), Morocco (1275, 1465 and 1790-92) and Baghdad (1333 and 1344).[28]

The situation of Jews in Arab lands reached a low point in the 19th century. Jews in most of North Africa (including Algeria, Tunisia, Egypt, Libya and Morocco) were forced to live in ghettos. In Morocco, which contained the largest Jewish community in the Islamic Diaspora, Jews were made to walk barefoot or wear shoes of straw when outside the ghetto. Even Muslim children participated in the degradation of Jews, by throwing stones at them or harassing them in other ways. The frequency of anti-Jewish violence increased, and many Jews were executed on charges of apostasy. Ritual murder accusations against the Jews became commonplace in the Ottoman Empire.[29]

As distinguished Orientalist G.E. von Grunebaum has written:

> It would not be difficult to put together the names of a very size-able number Jewish subjects or citizens of the Islamic area who have attained to high rank, to power, to great financial influence, to significant and recognized intellectual attainment; and the same could be done for Christians. But it would again not be difficult to compile a lengthy list of persecutions, arbitrary confiscations, attempted forced conversions, or pogroms.[30]

The danger for Jews became even greater as a showdown approached in the UN. The Syrian delegate, Faris el-Khouri, warned: "Unless the Palestine problem is settled, we shall have difficulty in protecting and safeguarding the Jews in the Arab world."[31]

More than a thousand Jews were killed in anti-Jewish rioting during the 1940's in Iraq, Libya, Egypt, Syria and Yemen.[32] This helped trigger the mass exodus of Jews from Arab countries.

MYTH

"As 'People of the Book,' Jews and Christians are protected under Islamic law."

FACT

This argument is rooted in the traditional concept of the "*dhimma*" ("writ of protection"), which was extended by Muslim conquerors to Christians and Jews in exchange for their subordination to the Muslims. Yet, as French authority Jacques Ellul has observed: "One must ask: 'protected against whom?' When this 'stranger' lives in Islamic countries, the answer can only be: against the Muslims themselves."[33]

Peoples subjected to Muslim rule usually had a choice between death and conversion, but Jews and Christians, who adhered to the Scriptures, were usually allowed, as *dhimmis* (protected persons), to practice their faith. This "protection" did little, however, to insure that Jews and Christians were treated well by the Muslims. On the contrary, an integral aspect of the *dhimma* was that, being an infidel, he had to acknowledge openly the superiority of the true believer – the Muslim.

In the early years of the Islamic conquest, the "tribute" (or *jizya*), paid as a yearly poll tax, symbolized the subordination of the *dhimmi*.[34]

Later, the inferior status of Jews and Christians was reinforced through a series of regulations that governed the behavior of the *dhimmi*. *Dhimmis*, on pain of death, were forbidden to mock or criticize the Koran, Islam or Muhammad, to proselytize among Muslims, or to touch a Muslim woman (though a Muslim man could take a non-Muslim as a wife).

Dhimmis were excluded from public office and armed service, and were forbidden to bear arms. They were not allowed to ride horses or camels, to build synagogues or churches taller than mosques, to construct houses higher than those of Muslims or to drink wine in public. They were forced to wear distinctive clothing and were not allowed to pray or mourn in loud voices – as that might offend the Muslims. The *dhimmi* also had to show public deference toward Muslims, for example, always yielding them the center of the road. The *dhimmi* was not allowed to give evidence in court against a Muslim, and his oath was unacceptable in an Islamic court. To defend himself, the *dhimmi* would have to purchase Muslim witnesses at great expense. This left the *dhimmi* with little legal recourse when harmed by a Muslim.[35]

By the twentieth century, the status of the *dhimmi* in Muslim lands had not significantly improved. H.E.W. Young, British Vice Consul in Mosul, wrote in 1909:

> The attitude of the Muslims toward the Christians and the Jews is that of a master towards slaves, whom he treats with a certain lordly tolerance so long as they keep their place. Any sign of pretension to equality is promptly repressed.[36]

MYTH
"Muslim schools in the United States teach tolerance of Judaism and other faiths, and promote coexistence with Israel."

FACT
While it is well-known that many Muslim schools in Arab and Islamic countries indoctrinate students with hatred of Jews and Israel, it was only recently revealed that similar teachings are prevalent in the United States. Islamic schools in Virginia, for example, have maps of the Middle East in their classrooms that are missing Israel. On one map, Israel was blackened out and replaced with "Palestine." An 11th grade textbook teaches that one sign of the Day of

Judgment will be that Muslims will fight and kill Jews, who will hide behind trees that say, "Oh Muslim, Oh servant of God, here is a Jew hiding behind me. Come here and kill him."[37]

The attacks are not only against Jews, but also Christians. Students are taught, for example that the Day of Judgment won't come until Jesus Christ returns to Earth, breaks the cross, and converts everyone to Islam.

The private schools are legally allowed to teach whatever they want as long as they meet state requirements.

THE SITUATION TODAY[38]

The Jews of Algeria
1948 Jewish population: 140,000
2001: Less than 100

Jewish settlement in present-day Algeria can be traced back to the first centuries of the Common Era. In the 14th century, with the deterioration of conditions in Spain, many Spanish Jews moved to Algeria. Among them were a number of outstanding scholars, including Rav Yitzchak ben Sheshet Perfet (the Ribash) and Rav Shimon ben Zemah Duran (the Rashbatz). After the French occupation of the country in 1830, Jews gradually adopted French culture and were granted French citizenship.[39]

In 1934, a Nazi-incited pogrom in Constantine left 25 Jews dead and scores injured. After being granted independence in 1962, the Algerian government harassed the Jewish community and deprived Jews of their economic rights. As a result, almost 130,000 Algerian Jews immigrated to France. Since 1948, 25,681 Algerian Jews have immigrated to Israel.

Most of the remaining Jews live in Algiers, but there are individual Jews in Oran and Blida. Jews practice their religion freely, and Jewish community leaders are included in ceremonial state functions. There is no resident rabbi.[40]

In 1994, the terrorist Armed Islamic Group — GIA — declared its intention to eliminate Jews from Algeria, but, so far, no attacks have been reported.[41] Following the announcement, many Jews left Algeria and the single remaining synagogue was abandoned.[42] All other synagogues had previously been taken over for use as mosques.

The Jews of Egypt
1948 Jewish population: 75,000
2001: 100

Between June and November 1948, bombs set off in the Jewish Quarter of Cairo killed more than 70 Jews and wounded nearly 200.[43] In 1956, the Egyptian government used the Sinai Campaign as a pretext for expelling almost 25,000 Egyptian Jews and confiscating their property. Approximately 1,000 more Jews were sent to prisons and detention camps. On November 23, 1956, a proclamation signed by the Minister of Religious Affairs, and read aloud in mosques throughout Egypt, declared that "all Jews are Zionists and enemies of the state," and promised that they would be soon expelled. Thousands of Jews were ordered to leave the country. They were allowed to take only one suitcase and a small sum of cash, and forced to sign declarations "donating" their property to the Egyptian government. Foreign observers reported that members of Jewish families were taken hostage, apparently to insure that those forced to leave did not speak out against the Egyptian government.[44]

When war broke out in 1967, Jewish homes and property were confiscated. Egypt's attitude toward Jews at that time was reflected in its treatment of former Nazis. Hundreds were allowed to take up residence in Egypt and given positions in the government. The head of the Polish Gestapo, Leopold Gleim (who had been sentenced to death in absentia), controlled the Egyptian secret police.

In 1979, the Egyptian Jewish community became the first in the Arab world to establish official contact with Israel. Israel now has an embassy in Cairo and a consulate general in Alexandria. At present, the few remaining Jews are free to practice Judaism without any restrictions or harassment. Shaar Hashamayim is the only functioning synagogue in Cairo. Of the many synagogues in Alexandria only the Eliahu Hanabi is open for worship.[45]

Anti-Semitism in the Egyptian press is found primarily, but not exclusively, in the nonofficial press of the opposition parties. The Government has condemned anti-Semitism and advised journalists and cartoonists to avoid anti-Semitism. There have been no anti-Semitic incidents in recent years directed at the tiny Jewish community.[46]

In September 2000 construction began on a highway-bridge through the ancient Basatin Jewish cemetery in Cairo. Cooperation and funding were provided by the Egyptian Ministry of Housing and an American ultra-Orthodox Jewish Athra Kadisha group. The plans will not harm any tombs and it will honor Jewish law concerning cemeteries.

Anti-Semitism is rampant in the government-controlled press, and increased in late 2000 and 2001 following the outbreak of violence in Israel and the territories. In April 2001, columnist Ahmed Ragheb lamented Hitler's failure to finish the job of annihilating the Jews. In May 2001, an article in *Al-Akhbar* attacked Europeans and Americans for believing in the false Holocaust.[47]

The Jews of Iran

1948 Jewish population: 100,000
2001: 11,500

The Jewish community of Persia, modern-day Iran, is one of the oldest in the Diaspora, and its historical roots reach back to the 6th century B.C.E., the time of the First Temple. Their history in the pre-Islamic period is intertwined with that of the Jews of neighboring Babylon. Cyrus, the first of the Archemid dynasty, conquered Babylon in 539 B.C.E. and permitted the Jewish exiles to return to the Land of Israel, bringing the First Exile to an end. The Jewish colonies were scattered from centers in Babylon to Persian provinces and cities such as Hamadan and Susa. The books of Esther, Ezra, Nehemiah, and Daniel give a favorable description of the relationship of the Jews to the court of the Achaemids at Susa.

Under the Sassanid dynasty (226-642 C.E.), the Jewish population in Persia grew considerably and spread throughout the region; nevertheless, Jews suffered intermittent oppression and persecution. The invasion by Arab Muslims in 642 C.E. terminated the independence of Persia, installed Islam as the state religion, and made a deep impact on the Jews by changing their sociopolitical status.

Throughout the 19th century, Jews were persecuted and discriminated against. Sometimes whole communities were forced to convert. During the 19th century, there was considerable emigration to the Land of Israel, and the Zionist movement spread throughout the community.

Under the Phalevi Dynasty, established in 1925, the country was secularized and oriented toward the West. This greatly benefited the Jews, who were emancipated and played an important role in the economy and in cultural life. On the eve of the Islamic Revolution in 1979, 80,000 Jews lived in Iran. In the wake of the upheaval, tens of thousands of Jews, especially the wealthy, left the country, leaving behind vast amounts of property.

The Council of the Jewish Community, which was established after World War II, is the representative body of the community. The Jews also have a representative in parliament who is obligated by law to support Iranian foreign policy and its anti-Zionist position. Other Jews were eased out of government posts after the revolution.

Despite the official distinction between "Jews," "Zionists," and "Israel," the most common accusation the Jews encounter is that of maintaining contacts with Zionists. The Jewish community does enjoy a measure of religious freedom but is faced with constant suspicion of cooperating with the Zionist state and with "imperialistic America " — both such activities are punishable by death. Jews who apply for a passport to travel abroad must do so in a special bureau and are immediately put under surveillance. The government does not generally allow all members of a family to travel abroad at the same time to prevent Jewish emigration. Again, the Jews live under the status of *dhimmi*, with the restrictions imposed on religious minorities. Jewish leaders fear government reprisals if they draw attention to official mistreatment of their community.

Iran's official government-controlled media often issues anti-Semitic propaganda. A prime example is the government's publishing of the *Protocols of the Elders of Zion*, a notorious Czarist forgery, in 1994 and 1999.[48] Jews also suffer varying degrees of officially sanctioned discrimination, particularly in the areas of employment, education, and public accommodations.[49]

The Islamization of the country has brought about strict control over Jewish educational institutions. Before the revolution, there were some 20 Jewish schools functioning throughout the country. In recent years, most of these have been closed down. In the remaining schools, Jewish principals have been replaced by Muslims. In Teheran there are still three schools in which Jewish pupils constitute a majority. The curriculum is Islamic, and Persian is forbidden as the language of instruction for Jewish studies. Special Hebrew lessons are conducted on Fridays by the Orthodox Otzar ha-Torah organization, which is responsible for Jewish religious education. Saturday is no longer officially recognized as the Jewish sabbath, and Jewish pupils are compelled to attend school on that day. There are three synagogues in Teheran, but since 1994, there has been no rabbi in Iran, and the *bet din* does not function.[50]

Following the overthrow of the shah and the declaration of an Islamic state in 1979, Iran severed relations with Israel. The country has subsequently supported many of the Islamic terrorist organizations that target Jews and Israelis, particularly the Lebanon-based, Hizballah. Nevertheless, Iran's Jewish community is the largest in the Middle East outside Israel.

On the eve of Passover in 1999, 13 Jews from Shiran and Isfahan in southern Iran were arrested and accused of spying for Israel and the United States. Those arrested include a rabbi, a ritual slaughterer and teachers. In September 2000, an Iranian appeals court upheld a decision to imprison ten of the thirteen Jews accused of spying for Israel. In the appeals court, ten of the accused were found guilty of cooperating with Israel and were given prison terms ranging from two to nine years. Three of the accused were found innocent in the first trial.[51] In March 2001, one of the imprisoned Jews was released, a second was freed in January 2002.[52]

At least 13 Jews have been executed in Iran since the Islamic revolution 19 years ago, most of them for either religious reasons or their connection to Israel. For example, in May 1998, Jewish businessman Ruhollah Kakhodah-Zadeh was hanged in prison without a public charge or legal proceeding, apparently for assisting Jews to emigrate.[53]

The Jews of Iraq

1948 Jewish population: 150,000
2001: Approximately 100

The 2,700-year-old Iraqi Jewish community has suffered horrible persecution in modern-day Iraq. In June 1941, the Mufti-inspired, pro-Nazi coup of Rashid Ali sparked rioting and a pogrom in Baghdad. Armed Iraqi mobs, with the complicity of the police and the army, murdered 180 Jews and wounded almost 1,000. Additional outbreaks of anti-Jewish rioting occurred between 1946-49. After the establishment of Israel in 1948, Zionism became a capital crime.

In 1950, Iraqi Jews were permitted to leave the country within a year provided they forfeited their citizenship. A year later, however, the property of Jews who emigrated was frozen and economic restrictions were placed on Jews who chose to remain in the country. From 1949 to 1951, 104,000 Jews were evacuated from Iraq in Operations Ezra & Nechemia; another 20,000 were smuggled out through Iran.[54]

In 1952, Iraq's government barred Jews from emigrating and publicly hanged two Jews after falsely charging them with hurling a bomb at the Baghdad office of the U.S. Information Agency.

With the rise of competing Ba'ath factions in 1963, additional restrictions were placed on the remaining Iraqi Jews. The sale of property was forbidden and all Jews were forced to carry yellow identity cards. After the Six-Day War, more repressive measures were imposed: Jewish property was expropriated; Jewish bank accounts were frozen; Jews were dismissed from public posts; businesses were shut; trading permits were cancelled; telephones were disconnected. Jews were placed under house arrest for long periods of time or restricted to the cities.

Persecution was at its worst at the end of 1968. Scores were jailed upon the discovery of a local "spy ring" composed of Jewish businessmen. Fourteen men — eleven of them Jews — were sentenced to death in staged trials and hanged in the public squares of Baghdad; others died of torture. On January 27, 1969, Baghdad Radio called upon Iraqis to "come and enjoy the feast." Some 500,000 men, women and children paraded and danced past the scaffolds where the bodies of the hanged Jews swung; the mob rhythmically chanted "Death to Israel" and "Death to all traitors." This display brought a world-wide public outcry that Radio Baghdad dismissed by declaring: "We hanged spies, but the Jews crucified Christ."[55] Jews remained under constant surveillance by the Iraqi government. An Iraqi Jew (who later escaped) wrote in his diary in February 1970:

> Ulcers, heart attacks, and breakdowns are increasingly prevalent among the Jews...The dehumanization of the Jewish personality

resulting from continuous humiliation and torment...have dragged us down to the lowest level of our physical and mental faculties, and deprived us of the power to recover.[56]

In response to international pressure, the Baghdad government quietly allowed most of the remaining Jews to emigrate in the early 1970's, even while leaving other restrictions in force. Most of Iraq's remaining Jews are now too old to leave. They have been pressured by the government to turn over title, without compensation, to more than $200 million worth of Jewish community property.[57]

The government also engages in anti-Semitic rhetoric. One statement issued by the government in 2000 referred to Jews as "descendents of monkeys and pigs, and worshippers of the infidel tyrant."[58]

In 1991, prior to the Gulf War, the State Department said "there is no recent evidence of overt persecution of Jews, but the regime restricts travel, (particularly to Israel) and contacts with Jewish groups abroad."

More recently, a *Jerusalem Post* report noted that 75 Jews have fled Iraq in the past five years, mostly relocating to Holland or England. About 20 emigrated to Israel.[59]

At one time, Baghdad was one-fifth Jewish; other communities were first established 2,500 years ago. Today, approximately 100 Jews are left in all Iraq.

Only one synagogue continues to function in Iraq, "a crumbling buff-colored building tucked away in an alleyway" in Batawan, once Baghdad's main Jewish neighborhood. According to the synagogue's administrator, "there are few children to be bar-mitzvahed, or couples to be married. Jews can practice their religion but are not allowed to hold jobs in state enterpizes or join the army."[60] The rabbi died in 1996 and none of the remaining Jews can perform the liturgy and only a couple know Hebrew. The last wedding was held in 1980.[61]

The Jews of Lebanon

1948 Jewish population: 20,000
2001: Fewer than 100

When Christian Arabs ruled Lebanon, Jews enjoyed relative toleration. In the mid-50's, approximately 7,000 Jews lived in Beirut. As Jews in an Arab country, however, their position was never secure, and the majority left in 1967.

Fighting in the 1975-76 Muslim-Christian civil war swirled around the Jewish Quarter in Beirut, damaging many Jewish homes, businesses and synagogues. Most of the remaining 1,800 Lebanese Jews emigrated in 1976, fearing the growing Syrian presence in Lebanon would curtail their freedom of emigration.

In the mid-1980's, Hizballah kidnapped several prominent Jews from Beirut — most were leaders of what remained of the country's tiny Jewish community. Four of the Jews were later found murdered. Nearly all of the remaining Jews are in Beirut, where there is a committee that represents the community.[62] Because of the current political situation, Jews are unable to openly practice Judaism.

The Jews of Libya

1948 Jewish population: 38,000
2001: Probably 0

A savage pogrom in Tripoli on November 5, 1945, killed more than 140 Jews and wounded hundreds more. Almost every synagogue was looted. In June 1948, rioters murdered another 12 Jews and destroyed 280 Jewish homes.[63]

Thousands of Jews fled the country after Libya was granted independence and membership in the Arab League in 1951. After the Six-Day War, the Jewish population of 7,000 was again subjected to pogroms in which 18 were killed, and many more injured, sparking a near-total exodus that left fewer than 100 Jews in Libya.

When Col. Qaddafi came to power in 1969, all Jewish property was confiscated and all debts to Jews cancelled. In 1999, the synagogue in Tripoli was renovated; however, it was not reopened.[64] The last Jew living in Libya, Esmeralda Meghnagi, died in February 2002. This marked the end of one of the world's oldest Jewish communities, which traced its origins to the 3rd century B.C.E.[65]

The Jews of Morocco

1948 Jewish population: 265,000
2001: 5,700

In June 1948, bloody riots in Oujda and Djerada killed 44 Jews and wounded scores more. That same year, an unofficial economic boycott was instigated against Moroccan Jews.

In 1956, Morocco declared its independence, and Jewish immigration to Israel was suspended. In 1963, emigration resumed, allowing more than 100,000 Moroccan Jews to reach Israel.[66]

In 1965, Moroccan writer Said Ghallab described the attitude of his fellow Muslims toward their Jewish neighbors:

> The worst insult that a Moroccan could possibly offer was to treat someone as a Jew....My childhood friends have remained anti-Jewish. They hide their virulent anti-Semitism by contending that

the State of Israel was the creature of Western imperialism....A whole Hitlerite myth is being cultivated among the populace. The massacres of the Jews by Hitler are exalted ecstatically. It is even credited that Hitler is not dead, but alive and well, and his arrival is awaited to deliver the Arabs from Israel.[67]

Nonetheless, before his death in 1999, King Hassan tried to protect the Jewish population, and at present Morocco has one of the most tolerant environments for Jews in the Arab world. Moroccan Jewish emigres, even those with Israeli citizenship, freely visit friends and relatives in Morocco. Moroccan Jews have held leading positions in the business community and government. The major Jewish organization representing the community is the Conseil des Communautes Israelites in Casablanca. Its functions include external relations, general communal affairs, communal heritage, finance, maintenance of holy places, youth activities, and cultural and religious life.[68]

> "The Jews no longer reside in the traditional Jewish mellahs, but intermarriage is almost unknown. The community has always been religious and tolerant....The younger generation prefers to continue its higher education abroad and tends not to return to Morocco. Thus the community is in a process of aging."[69]

There are synagogues, mikvaot, old-age homes, and kosher restaurants in Casablanca, Fez, Marrakesh, Mogador, Rabat, Tetuan and Tangier. In 1992, however, most Jewish schools were closed. Only those in Casablanca – the Chabad, ORT, Alliance, and Otzar Ha-Torah schools – have remained active. All four receive government funding.

> "The Jewish community developed a fascinating tradition of rituals and pilgrimages to the tombs of holy sages. There are 13 such famous sites, centuries old, well kept by Muslims. Every year on special dates, crowds of Moroccan Jews from around the world, including Israel, throng to these graves. A unique Moroccan festival, the Mimunah, is celebrated in Morocco and in Israel."[70]

Morocco is perhaps Israel's closest friend in the Arab world. King Hassan often tried to be a behind-the-scenes catalyst in the Arab-Israeli peace process. In July 1986, he hosted Israeli Prime Minister Shimon Peres in an effort to stimulate progress. Two months later, Hassan met with a delegation of Jews of Moroccan origin, including an Israeli Knesset member. In 1993, after signing the agreement with the PLO, Prime Minister Yitzhak Rabin paid a formal visit to Morocco.

In May 1999, King Hassan organized the first meeting of the World Union of Moroccan Jews, in Marrakech.

In April and May 2000, the Moroccan government sponsored a series of events and lectures promoting respect among religions.[71] Andre Azoulay, royal counselor and a leading Jewish citizen, spoke about the need for interfaith respect and dialogue. In October 2000, two Moroccan youths tried to vandalize a Tangiers synagogue. King Mohamed VI publicly declared in a televised speech on November 6, 2000, that the government would not tolerate mistreatment of Morocco's Jews. The youths were subsequently sentenced to one year in prison.[72]

The Jews of Syria

1948 Jewish population: 30,000
2001: Fewer than 100

In 1944, after Syria gained independence from France, the new government prohibited Jewish immigration to Palestine, and severely restricted the teaching of Hebrew in Jewish schools. Attacks against Jews escalated, and boycotts were called against their businesses.

When partition was declared in 1947, Arab mobs in Aleppo devastated the 2,500-year-old Jewish community. Scores of Jews were killed and more than 200 homes, shops and synagogues were destroyed. Thousands of Jews illegally fled Syria to go to Israel.[73]

Shortly after, the Syrian government intensified its persecution of the Jewish population. Freedom of movement was severely restricted. Jews who attempted to flee faced either the death penalty or imprisonment at hard labor. Jews were not allowed to work for the government or banks, could not acquire telephones or driver's licenses, and were barred from buying property. Jewish bank accounts were frozen. An airport road was paved over the Jewish cemetery in Damascus; Jewish schools were closed and handed over to Muslims.

Syria's attitude toward Jews was reflected in its sheltering of Alois Brunner, one of the most notorious Nazi war criminals. Brunner, a chief aide to Adolf Eichmann, served as an adviser to the Assad regime.[74]

In 1987-88, the Syrian secret police seized 10 Jews on suspicion of violating travel and emigration laws, planning to escape and having taken unauthorized trips abroad. Several who were released reported being tortured while in custody.[75]

In November 1989, the Syrian government promised to facilitate the emigration of more than 500 single Jewish women, who greatly outnumbered eligible men in the Jewish community and could not find suitable husbands. Twenty-four were allowed to emigrate in the fall of 1989 and another 20 in 1991.[76]

For years, the Jews in Syria lived in extreme fear. The Jewish Quarter in Damascus was under the constant surveillance of the secret police, who were present at synagogue services, weddings, bar-mitzvahs and other Jewish gatherings. Contact with foreigners was closely monitored. Travel abroad was permitted in exceptional cases, but only if a bond of $300-$1,000 was left behind, along with family members who served as hostages. U.S. pressure applied during peace negotiations helped convince President Hafez Assad to lift these restrictions, and those prohibiting Jews from buying and selling property, in the early 1990's.

In an undercover operation in late 1994, 1,262 Syrian Jews were brought to Israel. The spiritual leader of the Syrian Jewish community for 25 years, Rabbi Avraham Hamra, was among those who left Syria and went to New York (he now lives in Israel). Syria had granted exit visas on condition that the Jews not go to Israel.[77] The decision to finally free the Jews came about largely as a result of pressure from the United States following the 1991 Madrid peace conference.

By the end of 1994, the Joab Ben Zeruiah Synagogue in Aleppo, in continuous use for more than 1,600 years, was deserted. A year later, approximately 250 Jews remained in Damascus, all apparently staying by choice.[78] By the middle of 2001, Rabbi Huder Shahada Kabariti estimated that 150 Jews were living in Damascus, 30 in Haleb and 20 in Kamashili. Every two or three months, a rabbi visits from Istanbul, Turkey, to oversee preparation of kosher meat, which residents freeze and use until his next visit. Two synagogues remain open in Damascus.[79]

Although Jews are occasionally subjected to violence by Palestinian protesters in Syria, the government has taken strict protective measures, including arresting assailants and guarding the remaining synagogues.[80]

According to the State Department, Jews still have a separate primary school for religious instruction on Judaism and are allowed to teach Hebrew in some schools. About a dozen students still attend the Jewish school, which had 500 students as recently as 1992. Jews and Kurds are the only minorities not allowed to participate in the political system. In addition, "the few remaining Jews are generally barred from government employment and do not have military service obligations. They are the only minority whose passports and identity cards note their religion."[81]

The Jews of Tunisia

1948 Jewish population: 105,000
2001: 1,500

After Tunisia gained independence in 1956, a series of anti-Jewish government decrees were promulgated. In 1958, Tunisia's Jewish Community Council was abolished by the government and ancient synagogues, cemeteries and Jewish quarters were destroyed for "urban renewal."[82]

The increasingly unstable situation caused more than 40,000 Tunisian Jews to immigrate to Israel. By 1967, the country's Jewish population had shrunk to 20,000.

During the Six-Day War, Jews were attacked by rioting Arab mobs, and synagogues and shops were burned. The government denounced the violence, and President Habib Bourguiba apologized to the Chief Rabbi. The government appealed to the Jewish population to stay, but did not bar them from leaving. Subsequently, 7,000 Jews immigrated to France.

In 1982, there were attacks on Jews in the towns of Zarzis and Ben Guardane. According to the State Department, the Tunisian government "acted decisively to provide protection to the Jewish community."[83]

In 1985, a Tunisian guard opened fire on worshipers in a synagogue in Djerba, killing five people, four of them Jewish. Since then, the government has sought to prevent further tragedy by giving Tunisian Jews heavy protection when necessary. Following Israel's October 1, 1985, bombing of the PLO headquarters near Tunis, "the government took extraordinary measures to protect the Jewish community."[84] After the Temple Mount tragedy in October 1990, "the government placed heavy security around the main synagogue in Tunis."[85]

Djerba has one Jewish kindergarten. There are also six Jewish primary schools (three located in Tunis, two in Djerba and one in the coastal city of Zarzis) and four secondary schools (two in Tunis and two in Djerba). There are also yeshivot in Tunis and Djerba. The community has two homes for the aged. The country has several kosher restaurants and five officiating rabbis: the chief rabbi in Tunis, a rabbi in Djerba, and four others in Tunis. The majority of the Jewish community observes the laws of kashrut.

"Many tourists come to visit Djerba's El Ghirba Synagogue in the village of Hara Sghira. Although the present structure was built in 1929, it is believed there has been a continuously used synagogue on the site for the past 1,900 years. Tunisian Jews have many unique and colorful rituals and celebrations, including the annual pilgrimage to Djerba which takes place during Lag BaOmer. The Bardo Museum in Tunis contains an exhibit dealing exclusively with Jewish ritual objects."[86]

Today, the 1,300 Jews comprise the country's largest indigenous religious minority. "The Government assures freedom of worship for the Jewish community and pays the salary of the Grand Rabbi" of the community.[87]

In October 1999, the Jewish community elected a new Board of Directors for the first time since Tunisia's independence in 1956. They also gave the Board a new name: "The Jewish Committee of Tunisia."[88]

On April 11, 2002, a natural gas truck exploded at the outer wall of the Ghriba synagogue on the resort island of Djerba. Tunisian officials at first said the truck accidentally struck the wall of the synagogue, but a group linked to Osama bin Laden's al-Qaeda network claimed responsibility for carrying out what was actually a terrorist attack on the oldest synagogue in Africa. The explosion killed 17 people, including 11 German tourists.[89]

The Jews of Yemen

1948 Jewish population: 55,000 (in Aden: another 8,000)
2001: Fewer than 200

In 1922, the government of Yemen reintroduced an ancient Islamic law requiring that Jewish orphans under age 12 forcibly converted to Islam.

In 1947, after the partition vote, Muslim rioters, joined by the local police force, engaged in a bloody pogrom in Aden that killed 82 Jews and destroyed hundreds of Jewish homes. Aden's Jewish community was economically paralyzed, as most of the Jewish stores and businesses were destroyed. Early in 1948, the false accusation of the ritual murder of two girls led to looting.[90]

This increasingly perilous situation led to the emigration of virtually the entire Yemenite Jewish community — almost 50,000 — between June 1949 and September 1950 in Operation "Magic Carpet." A smaller, continuous migration was allowed to continue into 1962, when a civil war put an abrupt halt to any further Jewish exodus.

Until 1976, when an American diplomat came across a small Jewish community in a remote region of northern Yemen, it was believed the Yemenite Jewish community was extinct. As a result, the plight of Yemenite Jews went unrecognized by the outside world.

It turned out some people stayed behind during Operation "Magic Carpet" because family members did not want to leave sick or elderly relatives behind. These Jews were forbidden from emigrating and not allowed to contact relatives abroad. They were isolated and trapped, scattered throughout the mountainous regions in northern Yemen and lacking food, clothing, medical care and religious articles. As a result, some Yemenite Jews abandoned their faith and converted to Islam.

For a short time, Jewish organizations were allowed to travel openly within Yemen, distributing Hebrew books and materials to the Jewish community.[91]

Today, Jews are the only indigenous religious minority besides a small number of Christians, Hindus and Baha'is. The small community that remains in the northern area of Yemen is tolerated and allowed to practice Judaism. However, its members are still treated as second-class citizens and cannot serve in the army or be elected to political positions. Jews are traditionally restricted to living in one section of a city or village and are often confined to a limited choice of employment, usually farming or handicrafts. Jews may, and do, own property.[92]

The Jews are scattered and a communal structure no longer exists. Yemenite Jews have little social interaction with their Muslim neighbors and are largely prevented from communicating with world Jewry. It is believed that there are two synagogues still functioning in Saiqaya and in Amlah.

Religious life has not changed much in Yemen. Jews are not allowed to eat meals with Muslims. Also, marriage is absolutely forbidden outside of the religion.

During the past few years, about 400 Jews have immigrated to Israel, despite the official ban on emigration.[93]

The State Department reported that in mid-2000, "the Government suspended its policy of allowing Yemeni-origin Israeli passport holders to travel to Yemen on laissez-passer documents. However, Yemeni, Israeli, and other Jews may travel freely to and within Yemen on non-Israeli passports."[94]

In January 2001, the ruling "General People's Party" placed a Yemeni Jewish citizen on the slate for parliamentary elections for the first time. The candidate, Ibrahim Ezer, was reportedly recommended by President Ali Abdallah Salah as a gesture to the incoming Bush administration in a bid to receive economic aid for Yemen. The General Election Committee, subsequently rejected Ezer's application on grounds that a candidate must be the child of two Muslim parents. Political analysts speculated that the true reason was a desire not to establish a precedent of allowing a Jew to run for office.[95]

Notes

[1] Vamberto Morais, *A Short History of Anti-Semitism*, (NY: W.W Norton and Co., 1976), p. 11; Bernard Lewis, *Semites & Anti-Semites*, (NY: WW Norton & Co., 1986), p. 81.

[2] *Oxford English Dictionary*; Webster's Third International Dictionary.

[3] *Washington Post*, (October 30, 2001).

[4] Official British document, Foreign Office File No. 371/20822 E 7201/22/31; Elie Kedourie, *Islam in the Modern World*, (London: Mansell, 1980), pp. 69-72.

[5] Howard Sachar, *A History of Israel: From the Rise of Zionism to Our Time*, (NY: Alfred A. Knopf, 1979), p. 196.

[6] Jordanian Nationality Law, Official Gazette, No. 1171, Article 3(3) of Law No. 6, 1954, (February 16, 1954), p. 105.

[7] From a letter sent to M. Rene Mheu, Director General of UNESCO, and reproduced in *Al-Thawra*, (May 3, 1968).

[8] *The Religious Ordinances Reader*, (Syrian Ministry of Education, 1963-1964), p. 138.

[9] *Basic Syntax and Spelling*, Syrian Ministry of Education, 1963.

[10] Religious Teaching, Egyptian Ministry of Education, 1966.

[11] Modern World History, Jordanian Ministry of Education, 1966, p. 150.

[12] Meyrav Wurmser, *The Schools of Ba'athism: A Study of Syrian Schoolbooks*, (Washington, D.C.: Middle East Media and Research Institute, 2000), p. xiii.

[13] Wurmser, p. 51.

[14] Middle East Media and Research Institute (MEMRI), http://www.memri.org; *Parade*, (June 23, 2002), p. 13.

[15] Jewish Telegraphic Agency, (March 4, 1991).

[16] *Al-Mussawar*, (August 4, 1972).

[17] Middle East Media and Research Institute (MEMRI).

[18] *Al-Ahram*, (October 28, 2000).

[19] *Jerusalem Post*, (November 19, 2001).

[20] Palestinian Authority television, (October 14, 2000).

[21] Palestinian Media Watch, http://www.pmw.org/, (March 15, 2000).

[22] *Washington Post*, (May 8, 2001).

[23] Bernard Lewis, *"The Pro-Islamic Jews,"* *Judaism*, (Fall 1968), p. 401.

[24] Bat Ye'or, *The Dhimmi*, (NJ: Fairleigh Dickinson University Press, 1985), pp. 43-44.

25 Bat Ye'or, pp. 185-86, 191, 194.

26 Norman Stillman, *The Jews of Arab Lands*, (PA: The Jewish Publication Society of America, 1979), p. 84; Maurice Roumani, *The Case of the Jews from Arab Countries: A Neglected Issue*, (Tel Aviv: World Organization of Jews from Arab Countries, 1977), pp. 26-27; Bat Ye'or, p. 72; Bernard Lewis, *The Jews of Islam*, (NJ: Princeton University Press, 1984), p. 158.

27 Stillman, pp. 59, 284.

28 Roumani, pp. 26-27.

29 G.E. Von Grunebaum, "Eastern Jewry Under Islam," Viator, (1971), p. 369.

30 *New York Times*, (February 19, 1947).

31 Roumani, pp. 30-31; Norman Stillman, *The Jews of Arab Lands in Modern Times*, (NY: Jewish Publication Society, 1991), pp. 119-122.

32 Bat Ye'or, p. 61.

33 Bat Ye'or, p. 30

34 Louis Gardet, *La Cite Musulmane: Vie sociale et politique*, (Paris: Etudes musulmanes,1954), p. 348.

35 Bat Ye'or, pp. 56-57.

36 *Middle Eastern Studies*, (1971), p. 232.

37 *Washington Post*, (February 25, 2002).

38 All 2001 population figures from David Singer and Lawrence Grossman, Eds. *American Jewish Year Book 2001*, (NY: American Jewish Committee, 2001), pp. 540-563.

39 World Jewish Congress, Jewish Communities of the World, (http://www.virtual.co.il/communities/wjcbook/index.htm).

40 "Country Reports on Human Rights Practices for 1991," (DC: Department of State, 1992), p. 1339.

41 U.S. State Department Report on Human Rights Practices for 1997.

42 U.S. Department of State, "2000 Annual Report on International Religious Freedom," Released by the Bureau for Democracy, Human Rights, and Labor Washington, DC, (September 5, 2000).

43 Howard Sachar, *A History of Israel*, (NY: Alfred A. Knopf, 1979), p. 401.

44 AP, (November 26, 1956); New York World Telegram, (November 29, 1956).

45 Jewish Communities of the World.

46 U.S. Department of State, "2000 Annual Report on International Religious Freedom," Released by the Bureau for Democracy, Human Rights, and Labor Washington, DC, (September 5, 2000).

47 U.S. Department of State, "2001 Annual Report on International Religious Freedom," Released by the Bureau for Democracy, Human Rights, and Labor Washington, DC, October 26, 2001.

48 U.S. State Department Report on Human Rights Practices for 1997.

49 "Many Jews Choose to Stay in Iran," Associated Press, (Jan. 18, 1998).

50 *Jewish Communities of the World*. Reprinted with permission of the World Jewish Congress (WJC). Copyright 1997; Institute of the World Jewish Congress. U.S. State Department Report on Human Rights Practices for 1997.

51 Schneider, Howard. "Iran Court Reduces Penalties for Jews." *Washington Post*, (September 22, 2000).

52 *Jerusalem Post*, (January 16, 2002).

53 U.S. Department of State, "2001 Annual Report on International Religious Freedom," Released by the Bureau for Democracy, Human Rights, and Labor Washington, DC, (October 26, 2001).

54 *Jerusalem Post*, (Dec. 13, 1997); Arieh Avneri, *The Claim of Dispossession*, (Tel Aviv: Hidekel Press, 1984), p. 274; Maurice Roumani, *The Case of the Jews from Arab Countries: A Neglected Issue*, (Tel Aviv: World Organization of Jews from Arab Countries, 1977), pp. 29-30; Norman Stillman, *The Jews of Arab Lands in Modern Times*, (NY: Jewish Publication Society, 1991), pp. 117-119; Howard Sachar, *A History of Israel*, (NY: Alfred A. Knopf, 1979), p. 399.

55 Judith Miller and Laurie Mylroie, *Saddam Hussein and the Crisis in the Gulf*, (NY: Random House, 1990), p. 34.

56 Max Sawadayee, *All Waiting to be Hanged*, (Tel Aviv: Levanda Press, 1974), p. 115.

57 *New York Times*, (February 18, 1973).

[58] U.S. State Department Report on Human Rights Practices for 1997.

[59] *Jerusalem Post*, (December 13, 1997).

[60] *New York Times Magazine,* (February 3, 1985).

[61] Associated Press, (March 28, 1998).

[62] *Maariv,* (June 21, 1991); Jewish Telegraphic Agency, (July 22, 1993); *Jewish Communities of the World.*

[63] Sachar, p. 400; Stillman, p. 145.

[64] U.S. Department of State, "2000 Annual Report on International Religious Freedom," Released by the Bureau for Democracy, Human Rights, and Labor Washington, DC, (September 5, 2000).

[65] *Jerusalem Report,* (March 11, 2002).

[66] Roumani, pp. 32-33.

[67] Said Ghallab, "Les Juifs sont en enfer," *in Les Temps Modernes,* (April 1965), pp. 2247-2251.

[68] U.S. State Department Report on Human Rights Practices for 1996; *Jewish Communities of the World*; U.S. State Department Report on Human Rights Practices for 1997.

[69] *Jewish Communities of the World.*

[70] *Jewish Communities of the World.*

[71] U.S. Department of State, "2000 Annual Report on International Religious Freedom," Released by the Bureau for Democracy, Human Rights, and Labor Washington, DC, (September 5, 2000).

[72] U.S. Department of State, "2001 Annual Report on International Religious Freedom," Released by the Bureau for Democracy, Human Rights, and Labor Washington, DC, (October 26, 2001).

[73] Sachar, p. 400; Roumani, p. 31; Stillman, p. 146.

[74] Newsday, (November 1, 1987); information provided by Rep. Michael McNulty.

[75] Middle East Watch, *Human Rights in Syria,* (NY: Middle East Watch, 1990), p. 94.

[76] Country Reports on Human Rights Practices for 1991, (DC: Department of State, 1992), p. 1610.

[77] *Jerusalem Post,* (October 18, 1994).

[78] *Jerusalem Post*, (May 27, 1995).

[79] *Associated Press,* (January 27, 2000).

[80] U.S. Department of State, "2000 Annual Report on International Religious Freedom," Released by the Bureau for Democracy, Human Rights, and Labor Washington, DC, (September 5, 2000).

[81] U.S. State Department Report on Human Rights Practices for 2001.

[82] Roumani, pp. 33; Stillman, p. 127.

[83] Country Reports on Human Rights Practices for 1982, (DC: Department of State, 1983), pp. 1290-91.

[84] Country Reports on Human Rights Practices for 1985, (DC: Department of State, 1986), p. 1321.

[85] Country Reports on Human Rights Practices for 1990, (DC: Department of State, 191), pp. 1664-65.

[86] *Jewish Communities of the World.*

[87] U.S. State Department Report on Human Rights Practices for 1997.

[88] U.S. Department of State, "2000 Annual Report on International Religious Freedom," Released by the Bureau for Democracy, Human Rights, and Labor Washington, DC, (September 5, 2000).

[89] *Washington Post,* (April 17 & 23, 2002).

[90] Sachar, pp. 397-98; Roumani, pp. 32-33; Stillman, p. 498.

[91] *Jerusalem Post,* (February 15, 1992); Jewish Telegraphic Agency, (February 26, 1992).

[92] *Jewish Communities of the World;* U.S. State Department Report on Human Rights Practices for 1997.

[93] *Jewish Communities of the World.*

[94] U.S. Department of State, "2000 Annual Report on International Religious Freedom," Released by the Bureau for Democracy, Human Rights, and Labor Washington, DC, (September 5, 2000).

[95] *Jerusalem Post*, (January 30, 2001).

16. Human Rights in Arab Countries

MYTH

*"The governments of Arab states grant
basic human rights to their citizens."*

FACT

While much attention has been focused on alleged Israeli human rights violations in the volatile West Bank and Gaza, the popular press has chosen to virtually ignore violations of fundamental human rights that take place daily in almost every Arab country. According to annual reports compiled by the State Department, most of the Arab states are ruled by oppressive, dictatorial regimes, which deny their citizens basic freedoms of political expression, speech, press and due process. The Arab Human Development Report published by a group of Arab researchers from the UN Development Program concluded that out of the seven regions of the world, Arab countries had the lowest freedom score. They also had the lowest ranking for "voice and accountability," a measure of various aspects of the political process, civil liberties, political rights and independence of the media.[1]

MYTH

"Women's rights are now protected in the Arab world."

FACT

In most Arab countries, the *Shari'a*, or Islamic law, defines the rules of traditional social behavior. Under the law, women are accorded a role inferior to that of men, and are therefore discriminated against with regard to personal rights and freedoms.

As Middle East expert Daniel Pipes explains: "In the Islamic view...female sexuality is thought of as being so powerful that it constitutes a real danger to society." Therefore, unrestrained females constitute "the most dangerous challenge facing males trying to carry out God's commands." In combination, females' "desires and their irresistible attractiveness give women a power over men which rivals God's."[2]

"Left to themselves," Pipes continues, "men might well fall victim to women and abandon God," resulting in civil disorder among believers. In traditional thought, Pipes notes, women pose an internal threat to Islamic society similar to the external one represented by the infidel.

Traditionally, the Arab woman marries at a young age to a man of her father's choice. A husband is entitled to divorce any time, even against his wife's will, by merely declaring verbally that this is his intention.

Although the image of the egalitarian woman is slowly developing within some more secular Arab states, it remains largely confined to urban centers and upper-class circles. Ritual sexual mutilation of females is still common in rural areas of Egypt, Libya, Oman and Yemen.

Furthermore, laws that restrict women's rights remain in force in almost all Arab countries. In Syria, a husband can prevent his wife from leaving the country. In Egypt, Iraq, Libya, Jordan, Morocco, Oman and Yemen, married women must have their husbands' written permission to travel abroad, and they may be prevented from doing so for any reason. In Saudi Arabia, women must obtain written permission from their closest male relative to leave the country or travel on public transportation between different parts of the kingdom.

According to the UN, "utilization of Arab women's capabilities through political and economic participation remains the lowest in the world in quantitative terms….In some countries with elected national assemblies, women are still denied the right to vote or hold office. And one in every two Arab women can neither read nor write."[3]

In a Saudi *Shari'a* court, the testimony of one man equals that of two women. In Kuwait, the male population is allowed to vote, while women are still disenfranchised. Egypt, Morocco, Jordan and Saudi Arabia all have laws stating that a woman's inheritance must be less than that of her male siblings (usually about half the size). Moroccan law excuses the murder or injury of a wife who is caught in the act of committing adultery; yet women are punished for harming their husbands under the same circumstances.

Wife-beating is a relatively common practice in Arab countries, and abused women have little recourse. As the State Department has noted regarding Jordan (and most of the Arab world): "Wife beating is technically grounds for divorce, but the husband may seek to demonstrate that he has authority from the Koran to correct an irreligious or disobedient wife by striking her."[4]

In Saudi Arabia, restrictions against women are among the most extreme in the Arab world. Saudi women may not marry non-Saudis without government permission (which is rarely given); are forbidden to drive motor vehicles or bicycles; may not use public facilities when men are present; and are forced to sit in the backs of public buses, segregated from men. At Riyadh's King Saud University, professors lecture to rooms of men while women watch via closed-circuit television from distant all-female classrooms.[5] "[Islamic] Advice columns" in the Saudi Arabian press recommend strict disciplining of women as part of a proper marriage. Women must cover their entire body and face in public, and those who do not are subject to physical harassment from the Saudi religious police, known as the Mutaaw'in. The Saudis even extend their discriminatory treatment to women abroad. During a visit to the United States by Crown Prince Abdullah, for example, the prince's aides requested that no female air traffic controllers be allowed to control his flight into Texas to meet President Bush. They also requested that no women be allowed on the airport tarmac with the jet.[6]

Arab regimes find different ways to deal with the international pressure to improve women's rights. They often prefer to introduce mild improvements in women's status rather than to enacting radical reforms that might contradict their ideology and antagonize conservative elements in the country.

MYTH

"Freedom for Palestinians in the Palestinian Authority includes the right to sell land to Jews."

FACT

In 1996, the Palestinian Authority (PA) Mufti, Ikremah Sabri, issued a *fatwa* (religious decree), banning the sale of Arab and Muslim property to Jews. Anyone who violated the order was to be killed. At least seven land dealers were killed that year. Six years later, the head of the PA's General Intelligence Service in the West Bank, General Tawfik Tirawi, admitted his men were responsible for the murders.[7]

On May 5, 1997, PA Justice Minister Freih Abu Middein announced that the death penalty would be imposed on anyone convicted of ceding "one inch" to Israel. Later that month, two Arab land dealers were killed. PA officials denied any involvement in the killings. A year later, another Palestinian suspected of selling land to Jews was murdered. The PA has also arrested suspected land dealers for violating the Jordanian law (in force in the West Bank), which prohibits the sale of land to foreigners.[8]

HUMAN RIGHTS BY COUNTRY

(Unless otherwise noted, all information is from U.S. State Department Reports on Human Rights Practices for 2000-2001)

SAUDI ARABIA

Saudi Arabia is a dynastic monarchy, ruled by King Fahd Bin Abd Al-Aziz Al Saud. The country's constitution is the Koran and the Sunna (tradition) of the prophet Muhammad, and the country is thus governed by a strict interpretation of Islamic law. Because there are no democratic institutions, citizens have no role in the government. Security in the country is enforced by both a secular security force, and the Mutawwa'in, the religious police, who comprise the Committee to Promote Virtue and Prevent Vice. Because the traditional Islamic view of human rights does not coincide with the modern view, the government has allowed both the secular and religious security forces to commit serious abuses.

Legal Rights

Torture, beatings, and other abuses of prisoners are committed regularly by both the Mutawwa'in and officials in the Ministry of Interior. Additionally, at least one person was killed recently by the Mutawwa'in for a very minor religious violation. Other executions during the year 2000 were for crimes ranging from "deviant sexual behavior" to sorcery, and were carried out by stoning, beheading, or firing squad; additionally, some prisoners were punished by amputations or the loss of an eye. Prisoners are sometimes held for long periods of time without charge or trial.

Freedom of speech and of the press are severely limited in Saudi Arabia – criticizing Islam or the Royal family is illegal, and can result in prolonged imprisonment without trial. Television, radio, internet and literature are all heavily censored. Freedom of assembly and association are also limited, subject to regulations such as the segregation of men and women at meetings.

Treatment of Women

Women are the victims of systematic discrimination in Saudi Arabia. Domestic violence and rape are widespread problems, and women have no redress for such crimes. Women cannot travel, be admitted to a hospital or drive in a car without their husbands' permission. Buses are segregated, and women must sit in the rear. Those women not wearing an *abaya* (a black garment covering the entire body) and covering their faces and hair are harassed by the Mutawwa'in.

Laws that discriminate against women include those governing property ownership, testimony in court inheritance, and child custody in cases of divorce. Comprising only five percent of the workplace, it is nearly impossible for women to be employed in any but the simplest of tasks. Also, Female Genital Mutilation is legal and is practiced in some parts of Saudi Arabia.

Women from foreign countries also must adhere to the strict laws in Saudi Arabia and the U.S. military has gone so far as to require its female soldiers to wear restrictive clothing, ride in the back seat of cars, and have a male escort when off base. In 2001, the U.S. Air Force's highest ranking female fighter pilot sued the U.S. government to overturn the policy on the grounds that it discriminates against women, violates their religious freedom, and forces them to follow customs required by a religion not their own. The Pentagon no longer requires women to wear the black head-to-toe abayas worn by Saudi women, but the other restrictions still apply.[9]

Workers' Rights

There are no labor laws, unions or collective bargaining in Saudi Arabia. While forced labor is technically illegal, foreign workers and domestic servants are sometimes forced to work up to sixteen hours daily, seven days a week. Pay is often withheld for weeks or months at a time.

Unconfirmed reports indicate that women are sometimes smuggled into Saudi Arabia to work as prostitutes, and children are smuggled in to work in organized begging rings. Officially, trafficking in persons is illegal under Saudi law.

Treatment of Minorities

There is no freedom of religion in Saudi Arabia. All citizens must be Muslims, and only the Sunni branch of Islam can be practiced publicly. There is institutional discrimination against Shi'a Muslims. Religions other than Islam are tolerated if practiced discreetly; a number of Christians were deported in 2000 because they practiced "apostasy" in too public a manner.

Asian and African workers living in Saudi Arabia report widespread discrimination, and difficulty in the redress of grievances.

JORDAN

The Hashemite Kingdom of Jordan is a constitutional monarchy ruled by King Abdullah bin Hussein. While direct elections are used to appoint representatives to the uninfluential lower house of Parliament, the 104-seat Chamber of Deputies, the upper house, the 40-seat senate, is appointed by the king. Virtually all power is concentrated in the king, who can dismiss any representative or disband the parliament altogether, as he did in June 2001. Thus, citizens of Jordan cannot change their government. Many serious human rights violations occur in Jordan and are condoned by the government.

Legal Rights

Jordanian security forces use torture on a regular basis, which has recently resulted in several deaths. Prisoners are often held without charges, are not allowed to meet with lawyers, and are kept in unsanitary conditions; this applies also to journalists charged with "defamation," meaning they criticized the government or the king. Terrorist groups are well represented in Jordan. For example, the Islamic Movement of Jordan ("The Group of Ahmed Al Daganesh") and the Nobles of Jordan claimed responsibility for the August 2001 murder of an Israeli businessman in

Amman. The government denied that the killing was political and has made no arrests in the case.

Freedom of assembly, association, the press and speech are all restricted by the government; authors of articles critical or satirical of the government are often arrested and imprisoned. In August 2002, the Al-Jazeera television network's license was revoked for airing views critical of the government.[10]

Women's Rights

Jordanian women are at a distinct legal disadvantage. Marital rape is legal, wife-beating is rampant, and often allowed by law, and honor crimes (domestic violence against women committed by men who feel the women have undermined their honor by their "immoral behavior") receive minimal sentences. Honor crimes have become so common that they comprise 25% of the total murders committed in Jordan in 2000, according to one study.

Financially, women are at a legal disadvantage as well. Social security, inheritance, divorce and testimony laws all favor men. Women earn less than men for equal work, and are under-represented in the workplace.

Female Genital Mutilation, once practiced widely in Jordan, has largely been discontinued. Some tribes, however, maintain the practice. Much more common is the abuse of female children, especially sexual abuse. While the law calls for strict punishment in such cases, few are ever investigated.

Workers' Rights

Labor laws are generally good; however, there are exceptions. Although forced labor is illegal in Jordan, many foreign servants work under conditions that amount to forced labor. Additionally, child labor is common, although the government has taken steps to curb it.

Treatment of Minorities

Freedom of religion is for the most part respected in Jordan. While only the three "main monotheistic religions" (Islam, Judaism, and Christianity) are officially recognized by the government, all other religions are permitted to practice freely, and are given equal rights. The one exception to this rule is the Baha'i faith, members of which face official, systematic discrimination. They are, however, allowed to practice openly.

Following the 1948 war, and again following the 1967 war, Jordan granted citizenship to Palestinian refugees fleeing from Israel. However, refugees who arrived since then have not been granted citizenship, and are widely discriminated against.

LEBANON

Since ending a 16 year civil war in 1991, Lebanon has been primarily controlled by Syria, which stations 25,000 soldiers in the country. Thus, although Lebanon is technically a parliamentary republic, neither citizens nor government officials have much of a role in changing their government, because Syria makes all policy decisions and heavily influence the elections. The Lebanese government and army do not respect human rights, and the several terrorist organizations that are headquartered in Lebanon commit abuses as well.

Legal Rights

While official governmental killings are unknown in Lebanon, there have been numerous disappearances and deaths of political prisoners in prison awaiting trial. Arbitrary arrests are common, and some prisoners are held for long periods of time without trials or charges. The use of torture is reportedly widespread. In the areas of the country controlled by the Syrian-backed militia Hizballah, only Islamic law is applied; in the independent Palestinian refugee camps in the south, no specific law system is endorsed. In both locations, human rights violations abound.

Freedom of speech and of the press are granted by law, and respected for the most part; however, cases of censorship are common. The right to assembly granted by law is restricted by the government. In August 2001, mostly Christian students staged a non-violent protest against Syria's role in Lebanon and were beaten by security forces. Days earlier, other anti-Syrian activists were arrested.[11]

In August 2001, Lebanese security forces arrested a Christian journalist in a crackdown on anti-Syrian Christian dissidents. The week before, about 200 members of Christian-led opposition groups that oppose Syria's control over Lebanon were arrested.[12]

Inhabitants of Lebanon have suffered from the numerous competing terrorist groups that operate inside Lebanon. These groups either attack targets within the country, or attack Israel to the south; when they do the latter, Lebanon's population is forced to bear the brunt of the reprisals. However, attacks on Israel by Syrian-backed Hizballah and other terrorist groups have significantly decreased since Israel's withdrawal from southern Lebanon in May of 2000.

Women's Rights

Domestic violence and rape are significant social problems, and affect a large segment of the population. Honor crimes are illegal, but reduced sentences are applied in such cases.

While technically women can enter any profession they wish, there is strong societal pressure that prevents most women from doing so. Many other laws in Lebanon are based on Islamic law, and are discriminatory against women and children.

Workers' Rights

Forced labor is not illegal, and many foreign servants, women, and children are compelled to work against their will. Child labor in general is rampant. Children suffer under Lebanese law in other ways as well: child abuse, kidnappings, and even the sale of children to adoption agencies are relatively common, and ignored by the government.

Treatment of Minorities

Freedom of religion is generally respected, although some discrimination is built into the legal system: for example, certain government positions can only be held by certain types of Muslims. Palestinian refugees living in Lebanon have no rights, and cannot become citizens of the state.

SYRIA

Technically, Syria is a parliamentary democracy in which officials are appointed through direct elections; in practice, President Bashar Assad wields virtually absolute power. When his father Hafez Assad, died on June 10, 2000, after a 30-year reign, Bashar ran unopposed for the post, and consequently, the minimum age required by law for a president was lowered from 40 to 34, Bashar's age. Because of an emergency martial law that has been in place since 1963, powerful security services and militias operate independent of each other, and unimpeded by the government. Human rights are significantly restricted by the government, and the security services commit serious abuses as well.

Legal Rights

Because of the power of the security services, the legal rights of citizens of Syria are not enforced. Arbitrary arrests, torture and disappearances of prisoners all occur regularly. Syrian, Lebanese and Jordanian political prisoners have been held incommunicado by the government for long periods of time, as have missing Israeli soldiers captured by Syria, and Hizballah, the terrorist organization it backs in Lebanon. Prisoners captured as many as twenty years ago remain unaccounted for.

Freedom of speech and of the press are granted by law, but severely restricted. Publication of any "false information" that opposes "the goals of the revolution" is punishable by lengthy jail sentences. All press industries are owned and operated by the government. In 2001, ten pro-democracy activists were arrested and convicted of inciting rebellion, disseminating lies and trying to change the constitution by force.[13]

Freedom of association is severely restricted by the government and freedom of assembly does not exist.

Women's Rights

Domestic violence occurs in Syria, though little is known about its extent. Spousal rape is not illegal, and honor crimes occur. Legally, many financial laws, such as inheritance and social security, discriminate against women, and the punishment for adultery for women is twice that of men. Women cannot travel outside the country without their husbands' permission. Women are employed in all areas, but are under-represented in most fields.

Workers' Rights

Child labor is common, despite laws to the contrary. Additionally, the rights to form unions and bargain collectively are restricted.

Treatment of Minorities

Freedom of religion is generally respected, with two exceptions: Jews are systematically excluded from government involvement, and lack many basic rights; and extreme Islamic groups are frequently targeted for attacks and discrimination, due to the numerous Islamic terrorist groups that oppose the government.

Kurds are systematically oppressed by Syria: they cannot become citizens, they have few rights and the teaching of their language and culture is outlawed by the government.

IRAQ

The constitution of Iraq grants rule to the Arab Ba'ath Socialist Party, which is dominated by Saddam Hussein and his relatives. Hussein attempts to legitimate his rule by referring to an October 1995 "referendum," in which he received 99.9 percent of the vote. This election, however, had neither secret ballots nor opposing candidates, and Iraqi citizens reported that they feared reprisals if they cast dissenting votes. Iraq's record on human rights indicates that this fear was warranted – Iraq's government commits serious human rights violations, primarily through the various militias that operate in the state. These militias are instrumental in maintaining an atmosphere of fear and repression.

Legal Rights

The government's police tactics are among the most brutal in the world. Citizens are routinely arrested and executed for such crimes as defecting, criticizing the government and prostitution. Additionally, criminals charged with lesser crimes are routinely killed *en masse* as part of a "prison cleansing" system designed to reduce the prison population. Political or religious figures who are viewed as a threat to Saddam or other higher-ups are killed without compunction, and without being charged with a specific crime. Those who are charged with specific crimes rarely receive fair trials, as any court's decision can be overridden by the President. Sometimes trials are not held at all. Torture is used systematically in Iraqi prisons.

While the government officially respects the rights to freedom of speech, press, assembly, and association, all these rights are restricted in practice. The government owns all the newspapers in the country, and operates them as propaganda sources. Any statements critical of the government are harshly punished, and citizens who assemble peacefully have been repressed and sometimes attacked by government militias.

Allegations of serious war crimes have been frequently directed against Iraq. Atrocities committed during the 1980-1988 Iran-Iraq War, and during the 1991 Persian Gulf War, are mirrored to this day, as Iraqi forces fighting with the Kurdish army that controls the north of Iraq routinely target civilians, and plant mines in civilian areas. UN inspectors who were monitoring Iraq's military and chemical weapons plants were summarily expelled in 1997.

Women's Rights

Domestic violence occurs in Iraq, but no statistics exist to account for its frequency. Honor crimes are legitimate under Iraqi law, and crimes such as prostitution are often punished by beheading. Numerous laws are in place guaranteeing rights for women in the workplace, but it is difficult to determine how successful they have been in producing equality.

Workers' Rights

Workers have virtually no rights in Iraq. Unions are illegal, and while forced labor is technically illegal, resigning from one's job can result in a prison sentence. Child labor is not uncommon, despite government regulations to the contrary.

Treatment of Minorities

Freedom of religion is technically in place, but not respected by the government. While the majority of the population consists of Shi'a Muslims, the Sunni minority controls the Ba'ath Party. Thus, Shi'a religious and lay leaders are frequently assassinated or repressed. The small Christian community has been subjected to abuses as well.

The Kurds that control the north of Iraq have been severely oppressed. Kurds are prohibited from living in Iraq proper, and those in the north have been subjected to atrocities by the Iraqi military, including torture, summary executions and attacks on civilian centers using chemical weapons.

EGYPT

According to its constitution, Egypt is a social democracy in which Islam is the state religion. The President and his National Democratic Party, however, control the political scene to such an extent that citizens do not have a meaningful ability to change their government. There has been an Emergency Law in effect since 1981, allowing the government to arbitrarily detain persons without charge, and to regularly deny legal rights to Egyptian citizens.

Legal Rights

Freedom of speech and of the press are guaranteed by the Constitution, but are often withheld in practice. The government owns and controls the three largest newspapers and holds a monopoly on printing and distribution. Thus, newspapers rarely criticize the government, and the output of opposition parties' newspapers is limited. Scholars and officials who criticize the government are often charged with the crimes of libel, slander, or "disseminating false information about Egypt," and are imprisoned. Freedom of association and assembly are severely restricted.

Physical or psychological torture, while officially outlawed, are nonetheless common, and it is reported that at least eight prisoners were tortured to death in the year 2000. Prison conditions are squalid. The Egyptian police routinely arrest prisoners arbitrarily, often holding them for long periods of time without charge, trial or access to a lawyer.

> *"[Egypt's] autocratic regime, established a half-century ago under the banner of Arab nationalism and socialism, is politically exhausted and morally bankrupt. Mr. Mubarak, who checked Islamic extremists in Egypt only by torture and massacre, has no modern political program or vision of progress to offer his people as an alternative to Osama bin Laden's Muslim victimology. Those Egyptians who have tried to promote such a program...are unjustly imprisoned. Instead, Mr. Mubarak props himself up with $2 billion a year in U.S. aid, while allowing and even encouraging state-controlled clerics and media to promote the anti-Western, anti-modern and anti-Jewish propaganda of the Islamic extremists. The policy serves his purpose by deflecting popular frustration with the lack of political freedom or economic development in Egypt. It also explains why so many of Osama bin Laden's recruits are Egyptian."*
>
> — ***Washington Post*** **editorial, October 11, 2001**[14]

Women's Rights

Domestic violence is a serious social problem in Egypt; one report concluded that one in three married women has been beaten by her husband. Additionally, marital rape is legal. Female Genital Mutilation still occurs, and a majority of women undergo the procedure. In the business world, women are guaranteed pay equal to that of men, but there are strong societal pressures against women being employed. Legally, many laws, particularly inheritance laws, favor males, and men who kill women in honor killings receive significantly lighter sentences than women who kill men under similar circumstances.

Workers' Rights

Labor laws in Egypt do not provide adequately for union members; striking is illegal and punishable by prison terms. Many government mandated labor laws are not enforced, such as minimum wages and maximum hours. While child labor has been a problem in Egypt in the past, there has been marked improvement recently.

Treatment of Minorities

Egypt guarantees freedom of religion, and the Jewish and Christian communities are generally treated well. Nevertheless, the Christian minority has reported that it is sometimes discriminated against, and there have been reports of forced conversions to Islam. Members of the Baha'i faith are categorically banned from practicing or living in Egypt.

PALESTINIAN AUTHORITY

The Palestinian Authority's poor human rights record worsened after the onset of the "al-Aksa intifada." In September 2000, members of the Palestinian security services and Fatah's Tanzim participated in violent attacks against Israeli civilians and soldiers. Because armed Palestinians often launched their attacks near the homes of Palestinian civilians; residents of the homes sometimes found themselves in the line of fire when Israel retaliated. Palestinian security forces also failed to prevent armed Palestinians from opening fire on Israelis in places where bystanders were present.

Legal Rights

On December 2, 2001, Palestinian Authority Chairman Yasser Arafat declared a state of emergency and granted himself broad legal powers.

PA security forces arbitrarily arrest and detain persons, and prolonged detention and lack of due process are prevalent. The courts do not ensure fair and expeditious trials. The PA executive and security services frequently ignore or fail to enforce court decisions.

The PA does not prohibit by law the use of torture or force against detainees, and PA security forces reportedly were responsible for torture and widespread abuse of Palestinian detainees. International human rights monitoring groups have documented widespread arbitrary and abusive conduct by the PA. These organizations state that use of torture is widespread and not restricted to those persons detained on security charges. At least five Palestinians died in PA custody during 2001.

PA security forces infringed on citizens' rights to privacy and restricted freedom of speech and of the press by closing down media outlets, banning publications or broadcasts, and periodically harassing or detaining members of the media. For example, after the brutal killing of two IDF reserve soldiers at a Ramallah police station on October 12, 2000, Palestinian police confiscated film from several journalists who were at the scene. On October 4, a foreign journalist filmed three members of the Palestinian security forces distributing Molotov cocktails to several children. The security forces detained the journalist and his crew for several hours and destroyed the roll of film. PA harassment contributed to the practice of self-censorship by many Palestinian commentators, reporters, and critics.

Violence Against Israelis

Palestinian violence during the "al-Aksa intifada" included violent demonstrations, shootings and incidents in which Palestinians usually threw stones and Molotov cocktails at IDF checkpoints. Israeli civilians and Jews in the territories became frequent targets of drive-by shootings and ambushes, suicide and other bombings, mortar attacks, and armed attacks on settlements and military bases. Palestinians acting individually, or in unorganized or small groups, including some members of Palestinian security services, killed 87 Israelis in the territories in 2001. Off-duty members of PA security forces and members of Chairman Arafat's Fatah faction participated in some of these attacks.

Several Palestinian terrorist groups, including Hamas, Islamic Jihad, the Popular Front for the Liberation of Palestine (PFLP), the Democratic Front for the Liberation of Palestine (DFLP), and Fatah-affiliated groups such as the al-Aqsa Brigades, have also claimed responsibility for attacks specifically targeting civilians within Israel proper. The PA had made few arrests in these killings by year's end.

An estimated 340 suspected collaborators and 180 to 200 political prisoners were held in PA jails at the end of 2001. A number of Palestinians suspected of collaboration with the Israeli government were arrested, tried and executed. Dozens more were simply murdered.[15]

Women's Rights

Spousal abuse, sexual abuse, and honor killings occur, but societal pressures prevent most incidents from being reported and most cases are handled within the families concerned, usually by male family members.

Palestinian women endure various forms of social prejudice and repression within their society. Because of early marriage, girls frequently do not finish the mandatory level of schooling. Cultural restrictions sometimes prevent women from attending colleges and universities. While there is an active women's movement in the West Bank, serious attention has shifted only recently from nationalist aspirations to issues that greatly affect women, such as domestic violence, equal access to education and employment, and laws concerning marriage and inheritance. Women who marry outside of their faith, particularly Christian women who marry Muslim men, often are disowned by their families and sometimes are harassed and threatened with death.

A growing number of Palestinian women work outside the home, where they tend to encounter discrimination. There are no special laws that provide for women's rights in the workplace. Women are underrepresented in most aspects of professional life.

Workers' Rights

Child labor is a problem. Also, there is no minimum wage in the West Bank or Gaza Strip and no laws that protect the rights of striking workers. In practice, such workers have little or no protection from an employer's retribution. In early 2000, West Bank teachers held a strike. On May 5, 2000, PA officials arrested one of the strike leaders for criticizing the PA during a radio interview. The radio station was also shut down. The teachers suspended their strike on May 17, despite the fact that none of their demands were met.

Treatment of Minorities

No PA law protects religious freedom; however, the PA generally respects freedom of religion. In past years, there were allegations that several converts from Islam to Christianity at times are subject to societal discrimination and harassment by PA officials. However, there was no pattern of PA discrimination and harassment against Christians.

Notes

1   Arab Human Development Report 2002, (NY: UN, 2002).

2   Daniel Pipes, *In the Path of God: Islam and Political Power,* (NY: Basic Books, 1983), p. 177.

3   Arab Human Development Report 2002, (NY: UN, 2002).

4   U.S. State Department, Reports on Human Rights Practices for 1999.

5   Martin Peretz, "Remembering Saudi Arabia," *The New Republic,* (January 28, 2002).

6   *USA Today,* (April 29, 2002).

7   *Jerusalem Post,* (August 19, 2002).

8   State Department. Human Rights Report for the Occupied Territories, 1997, 1998.

9   *Washington Post,* (December 4, 2001).

10 Jewish Telegraphic Agency, (August 9, 2002).

11 *Jerusalem Report,* (March 25, 2002).

12 *CNN,* (August 16, 2001).

13 *Jerusalem Post,* (July 1, 2002); BBC News, (August 11, 2002).

14 *Washington Post,* (October 11, 2001).

15 Isabel Kershner, "Below the Law," *Jerusalem Report,* (April 22, 2002), pp. 32-33.

17. Human Rights in Israel and the Territories

MYTH

"Israel discriminates against its Arab citizens."

FACT

Israel is one of the most open societies in the world. Out of a population of 6.3 million, about 1.1 million – 18 percent of the population – are non-Jews (945,000 Muslims, 130,000 Christians and 100,000 Druze).[1]

Arabs in Israel have equal voting rights; in fact, it is one of the few places in the Middle East where Arab women may vote. Arabs currently hold 10 seats in the 120-seat Knesset. Israeli Arabs have also held various government posts, including one who served as Israel's ambassador to Finland. Ariel Sharon's original cabinet included the first Arab minister, Salah Tarif, a Druze who served as a minister without portfolio. An Arab also is a Supreme Court justice. Arabic, like Hebrew, is an official language in Israel. More than 300,000 Arab children attend Israeli schools. At the time of Israel's founding, there was one Arab high school in the country. Today, there are hundreds of Arab schools.[2]

The sole legal distinction between Jewish and Arab citizens of Israel is that the latter are not required to serve in the Israeli army. This is to spare Arab citizens the need to take up arms against their brethren. Nevertheless, Bedouins have served in paratroop units and other Arabs have volunteered for military duty. Compulsory military service is applied to the Druze and Circassian communities at their own request.

Some economic and social gaps between Israeli Jews and Arabs result from the latter not serving in the military. Veterans qualify for many benefits not available to non-veterans. Moreover, the army aids in the socialization process.

On the other hand, Arabs do have an advantage in obtaining some jobs during the years Israelis are in the military. In addition, industries like construction and trucking have come to be dominated by Israeli Arabs.

Although Israeli Arabs have occasionally been involved in terrorist activities, they have generally behaved as loyal citizens. During the 1967, 1973 and 1982 wars, none engaged in any acts of sabotage or disloyalty. Sometimes, in fact, Arabs volunteered to take over civilian functions for reservists. During the outbreak of violence in the territories that began in September 2000, Israeli Arabs for the first time engaged in widespread protests with some violence.

The United States has been independent for 226 years and still has not integrated all of its diverse communities. Even today, nearly 40 years after civil rights legislation was adopted, discrimination has not been eradicated. It should not be surprising that Israel has not solved all of its social problems in only 54 years.

MYTH

"Israel discriminates against Israeli Arabs by barring them from buying land."

FACT

In the early part of the century, the Jewish National Fund was established by the World Zionist Congress to purchase land in Palestine for Jewish settlement. This land, and that acquired after Israel's War of Independence, was taken over by the government. Of the total area of Israel, 92 percent belongs to the State and is managed by the Land Management Authority. It is not for sale to anyone, Jew or Arab. The remaining 8 percent of the territory is privately owned. The Arab Waqf (the Muslim charitable endowment), for example, owns land that is for the express use and benefit of Muslim Arabs. Government land can be leased by anyone, regardless of race, religion or sex. All Arab citizens of Israel are eligible to lease government land.

MYTH

"Israeli Arabs are discriminated against in employment."

FACT

Israeli law prohibits discrimination in employment. According to the State Department, all Israeli workers "may join and establish labor organizations freely." Most unions are part of the Histadrut or the smaller Histadrut Haovdim Haleumit (National Federation of Labor), both of which are independent of the Government.

MYTH

"Arabs held in Israeli jails are tortured, beaten and killed."

FACT

Prison is not a pleasant place for anyone and complaints about the treatment of prisoners in American institutions abound. Israel's prisons are probably among the most closely scrutinized in the world. One reason is the government has allowed representatives of the Red Cross and other groups to inspect them regularly.

Israeli law prohibits arbitrary arrest of citizens, defendants are considered innocent until proven guilty and have the right to writs of habeas corpus and other procedural safeguards. Israel holds no political prisoners and maintains an independent judiciary.

Some prisoners, particularly Arabs suspected of involvement in terrorism, were interrogated using severe methods that have been criticized as excessive. Israel's Supreme Court issued a landmark ruling in 1999 prohibiting the use of a variety of abusive practices.

The death penalty has been applied just once, in the case of Adolf Eichmann, the man largely responsible for the "Final Solution." No Arab has ever been given the death penalty, even after the most heinous acts of terrorism.

MYTH

"Israel uses administrative detention to imprison peaceful Arabs without trial."

FACT

Israel inherited and continued certain laws adopted by the British. One is the use of administrative detention, which is permitted under certain circumstances in security cases. The detainee is entitled to be represented by counsel, and may appeal to the Israeli Supreme Court. The burden is on the prosecution to justify holding closed proceedings. Often, officials believe presenting evidence in open court would compromise its methods of gathering intelligence and endanger the lives of individuals who have provided information about planned terrorist activities.

By contrast, in much of the Arab world, administrative detention is not necessary because the authorities frequently arrest people and throw them in jail without due process. No lawyers, human rights organizations or independent media can protest. Even in the United States, with its exceptionally liberal bail policy, people may be held for extended periods awaiting trial, and special legal standards have been applied to allow the prolonged incarceration of Taliban and al-Qaida members captured in Afghanistan.

"One does not judge a democracy by the way its soldiers immediately react, young men and women under tremendous provocation. One judges a democracy by the way its courts react, in the dispassionate cool of judicial chambers. And the Israeli Supreme Court and other courts have reacted magnificently. For the first time in Mideast history, there is an independent judiciary willing to listen to grievances of Arabs — that judiciary is called the Israeli Supreme Court."

— Alan Dershowitz[3]

MYTH

"Israel has long sought to deny residents of the West Bank and Gaza Strip their political rights."

FACT

While defending its existence against hostile Arab forces, Israel took control of the West Bank and Gaza Strip. Facing a violent insurrection, Israel has been forced to restrict some activities of Palestinians. Israel cannot concede to Palestinians all the rights Americans take for granted in a nation that is not at war, while Arab states maintain a state of belligerency with Israel, and Palestinians engage in terrorism against Israelis.

Given the constraints of Israel's security requirements, efforts were made from the outset to allow Palestinians the greatest possible freedom. After the Six-Day War, the traditional pro-Jordanian leadership continued to hold many civil service positions and was paid by Jordan. Municipal elections were held in 1972 and 1976. For the first time, women and non-landowners were allowed to vote.

The 1976 election brought Arab mayors to power who represented various PLO factions. Muhammad Milhem of Halhoul, Fahd Kawasmeh of Hebron, and Bassam Shaka of Nablus were affiliated with Fatah. Karim Khalaf of Ramallah represented the Popular Front for the Liberation of Palestine, and Ibrahim Tawil of El-Bireh was associated with the Democratic Front for the Liberation of Palestine.[4]

In 1978, these mayors and other radicals formed the National Guidance Committee, which vigorously opposed any accommodation with Israel, attempted to stir up broad allegiance to the PLO on the West Bank and incited rejection of the Egyptian-Israeli peace treaty. In 1981, Israel expelled Milhem and Kawasmeh. They were allowed to return to appeal the expulsion order, but it was upheld by the Israeli Supreme Court.

Two weeks after his expulsion, Milhem said: "There is no room for the existence of the Zionists under a situation of true peace. They are only capable of existing in a situation of tension and war...and that goes for all the parties...[they are] neither doves nor hawks, only pigs."[5]

Kawasmeh was appointed to the PLO Executive Committee in 1984. Later that year, he was assassinated by Palestinian radicals in Amman.

As part of the Camp David negotiations, Israel proposed an autonomy plan to grant the Palestinians greater control over their affairs. The Palestinians rejected autonomy as an option, however, holding out hope for the creation of a Palestinian state.

For the rest of the decade, Israel, nevertheless, attempted to shift increasing responsibilities from the military to civilian administrators and to Palestinians. Efforts to give Palestinians greater responsibility for their affairs were undermined by the intifada. During the uprising, Palestinian Arabs who wished to cooperate with Israel came under attack and were silenced either through intimidation or murder. Israeli government officials sought to maintain a dialogue with many Palestinians, but those whose identities were discovered became targets.

In secret negotiations in Oslo, Norway, in 1993, Israeli and Palestinian negotiators agreed to a plan that would give the latter limited self-government. Subsequent negotiations have resulted in Israeli withdrawal from nearly half the West Bank and most of the Gaza Strip, and increasing Palestinian control over their own affairs. The Palestinian Authority now governs virtually all civil affairs for approximately 98 percent of the Palestinians in the territories. The expectation is that a final political settlement will result in the creation of a Palestinian state in most of the areas once controlled by Israel.

MYTH

"Israel is stealing water from Arabs in the territories. Israel allows Jews to drill wells, but prevents Arabs from doing so."

FACT

In the years immediately following the 1967 war, water resources for the West Bank improved considerably. The water system in the southern Hebron region, for instance, was expanded. New wells were drilled near Jenin, Nablus and Tulkarm. More than 60 towns in the West Bank were given new water supply systems, or had antiquated ones upgraded by the Israeli administration in the territories.

In the late 1970's and early 1980's, however, the Middle East suffered from one of the worst droughts in modern history. Water in the Jordan River and Sea of Galilee dropped to critical levels. The situation deteriorated further at the beginning of the 1990's and has continued to be a problem in the new millennium.

Under these conditions, the Israeli government restricted the drilling of new wells on the West Bank. It had little choice because the West Bank and Israel share the same water table, and the drawing off of fresh water resources could promote saline water seepage.

Arab farmers on the West Bank are served by approximately 100 springs and 300 wells — many dug decades ago and now overutilized. Restrictions on over-exploitation of shallow wells were meant to prevent seepage or total depletion of saline water. Some wells were dug so that Jewish villages could tap new, deep aquifers never before used. These water pools as a rule do not draw from the shallower Arab sources.

At the end of 1991, a conference was scheduled in Turkey to discuss regional water problems. The meeting was torpedoed by Syria. The Syrians, Jordanians and Palestinians all boycotted the multilateral talks in Moscow in January 1992, which included a working group on water issues.

Following the Oslo agreements, Palestinians were more interested in cooperating on water issues. At the meeting of the multilateral working group in Oman in April 1994, an Israeli proposal to rehabilitate and make more efficient water systems in medium-sized communities (in the West Bank/Gaza, Israel and elsewhere in the region) was endorsed. About the same time, a Palestinian Water Authority was created as called for in the Israeli-Palestinian Declaration of Principles.

In November 1994, the working group met in Greece and the Israelis, Jordanians, and Palestinians agreed to begin discussion on principles or guidelines for cooperation on water issues. Further progress was made on a variety of issues during the 1995 meeting in Amman and the 1996 meeting in Tunisia. The working groups have not met since.

Israel has not cut the amount of water allocated to the Palestinian Authority (PA) and is planning to examine the possibility of increasing it despite the cut in water allocations within Israel and the requirement of supplying considerable amounts of water to Jordan as mandated by the peace treaty.

In contrast to claims by the Palestinian side, Israel did not even determine the amount of water to be supplied to the territories. The amount was specified in negotiations between the two sides, with the Americans participating. By the consent of both parties, the amount of water was increased relative to the situation prior to the Interim Agreement. Similarly, a formula was decided upon for increasing the water allocation gradually over the interim period.

The negotiations also led to agreements defining the number of wells that Israel is obligated to dig, and the number the PA and international bodies are obligated to dig. Cooperation on issues of sewage and environment were also defined. It was further decided that jurisdiction over water would be transferred to the Palestinians in the framework of the transfer of civil powers, and that the water situation would be supervised by joint monitoring teams

Israel has fulfilled all of her obligations under the Interim Agreement. The water quota agreed upon, and more, is being supplied. Jurisdiction over water was transferred completely and on time, and Israel approved the additional digging of wells. Israel and the PA carry out joint patrols to locate cases of water theft and other water-related problems.

MYTH

*"Israel's use of deportations violates
the Fourth Geneva Convention."*

FACT

The purpose of the Geneva Convention, approved in 1949, was to prevent a repetition of the Nazis' policy of mass deportations of innocent civilians to slave labor and concentration camps. Israel, of course, does no such thing. What it does, on occasion, is expel a select few individuals who are instigating violence against Jew and Arab alike.

The Geneva Convention itself allows an occupying power to "undertake total or partial evacuation of a given area if the security of the population or imperative military reasons so demand." The Israeli Supreme Court has interpreted this to mean that Israel may expel instigators of violence if necessary to maintain public order or to protect the population from future violence. All deportees have the right to appeal expulsion orders to the Israeli courts, but many Palestinians prefer not to do so.

MYTH

"Israel's treatment of Palestinians is similar to the treatment of blacks in apartheid South Africa."

FACT

Even before the State of Israel was established, Jewish leaders consciously sought to avoid the situation that prevailed in South Africa. As David Ben-Gurion told Palestinian nationalist Musa Alami in 1934:

> We do not want to create a situation like that which exists in South Africa, where the whites are the owners and rulers, and the blacks are the workers. If we do not do all kinds of work, easy and hard, skilled and unskilled, if we become merely landlords, then this will not be our homeland.[6]

Today, within Israel, Jews are a majority, but the Arab minority are full citizens who enjoy equal rights.. Arabs are represented in the Knesset, and have served in the Cabinet, high-level foreign ministry posts (e.g., Ambassador to Finland) and on the Supreme Court. Under apartheid, black South Africans could not vote and were not citizens of the country in which they formed the overwhelming majority of the population. Laws dictated where they could live, work and travel. And, in South Africa, the government killed blacks who protested against its policies. By contrast, Israel allows freedom of movement, assembly and speech. Some of the government's harshest critics are Israeli Arabs who are members of the Knesset.

The situation of Palestinians in the territories is different. The security requirements of the nation, and a violent insurrection in the territories, forced Israel to impose restrictions on Arab residents of the West Bank and Gaza Strip that are not necessary inside Israel's pre-1967 borders. The Palestinians in the territories, typically, dispute Israel's right to exist whereas blacks did not seek the destruction of South Africa, only the apartheid regime.

If Israel were to give Palestinians full citizenship, it would mean the territories had been annexed. No Israeli government has been prepared to take that step. Instead, through negotiations, Israel agreed to give the Palestinians increasing authority over their own affairs. It is likely that a final settlement will allow most Palestinians to become citizens of their own state.

> *"There is still one other question arising out of the disaster of nations which remains unsolved to this day, and whose profound tragedy, only a Jew can comprehend. This is the African question. Just call to mind all those terrible episodes of the slave trade, of human beings who, merely because they were black, were stolen like cattle, taken prisoner, captured and sold. Their children grew up in strange lands, the objects of contempt and hostility because their complexions were different. I am not ashamed to say, though I may expose myself to ridicule for saying so, that once I have witnessed the redemption of the Jews, my people, I wish also to assist in the redemption of the Africans."*
>
> **— Theodor Herzl**[7]

MYTH

"Israel is pursuing a policy of genocide toward the Palestinians that is comparable to the Nazis' treatment of the Jews."

FACT

This is perhaps the most odious claim made by Israel's detractors. The Nazis' objective was the systematic extermination of every Jew in Europe. Israel is seeking peace with its Palestinian neighbors. More than one million Arabs live as free and equal citizens in Israel. Of the Palestinians in the territories, 98 percent live under the civil administration of the Palestinian Authority. While Israel sometimes employs harsh measures against Palestinians in the territories to protect Israeli citizens – Jews and non-Jews – from the incessant campaign of terror waged by the PA and Islamic radicals, there is no plan to persecute, exterminate, or expel the Palestinian people.

Notes

[1] Israeli Central Bureau of Statistics.

[2] Israeli Central Bureau of Statistics.

[3] Speech to AIPAC Policy Conference, (May 23, 1989).

[4] *Newsview,* (March 23, 1982).

[5] *El-Wahda,* (Abu Dhabi).

[6] Shabtai Teveth, *Ben-Gurion and the Palestinian Arabs: From Peace to War,* (London: Oxford University Press, 1985), p. 140.

[7] Golda Meir, *My Life,* (NY: Dell Publishing Co., 1975), pp. 308-309.

18. The Palestinian Uprisings

MYTH

"The intifada was a spontaneous uprising, resulting solely from Arab anger at Israeli atrocities."

FACT

False charges of Israeli atrocities and instigation from the Muslim clergy in the mosques played an important role in starting the intifada (popularly translated as "uprising," but literally means "shaking off"). On December 6, 1987, an Israeli was stabbed to death while shopping in Gaza. One day later, four residents of the Jabalya refugee camp in Gaza were killed in a traffic accident. Rumors that the four had been killed by Israelis as a deliberate act of revenge began to spread among the Palestinians.[1] Mass rioting broke out in Jabalya on the morning of December 9, during which a 17-year-old youth was killed by an Israeli soldier after throwing a Molotov cocktail at an army patrol.[2] This soon sparked a wave of unrest that engulfed the West Bank, Gaza and Jerusalem.

MYTH

"The intifada constituted passive resistance. At its worst, it involved nothing more than children tossing stones at heavily armed soldiers."

FACT

The intifada was violent from the start. During the first four years of the uprising, more than 3,600 Molotov cocktail attacks, 100 hand grenade attacks and 600 assaults with guns or explosives were reported by the Israel Defense Forces. The violence was directed at soldiers and civilians alike. Between December 9, 1987, and the signing of the Oslo accords (September 13, 1993), 160 Israelis were killed, including 100 civilians. Thousands more were injured.[3]

MYTH

"The PLO had no role in fomenting intifada violence."

FACT

Throughout the intifada, the PLO played a lead role in orchestrating the insurrection. The PLO-dominated Unified Leadership of the Intifada (UNLI), for example, frequently issued leaflets dictating which days violence was to be escalated, and who was to be its target.

In 1989, for example, the PLO declared February 13 a day for "escalating attacks on the collaborators" and "traitors" who work for the Civil Administration in the territories. The PLO's Baghdad radio station described methods of arson through which "the orchards and fields of the Zionist enemy can be set ablaze."[4]

The *New York Times* described the discovery of "a cache of detailed secret documents showing that the PLO hired local killers to assassinate other Palestinians and carry out 'military activity' against Israelis." One document described how the PLO wanted the attacks credited to fictional groups so as not to disturb the U.S.-PLO dialogue.[5]

Yasser Arafat defended the killing of Arabs deemed to be "collaborating with Israel." He delegated the authority to carry out executions to the intifada leadership. After the murders, the local PLO death squad sent the file on the case to the PLO. "We have studied the files of those who were executed, and found that only two of the 118 who were executed were innocent," Arafat said. The innocent victims were declared "martyrs of the Palestinian revolution" by the PLO.[6]

Palestinians were stabbed, hacked with axes, shot, clubbed and burned with acid. The justifications offered for the killings varied. Sometimes, being employed by the Civil Administration in the West Bank and Gaza Strip was reason enough. In other cases, contact with Jews warranted a death sentence. In October 1989, a Palestinian father of seven was knifed to death in Jericho after selling floral decorations to Jews who were building a succah. Accusations of "collaboration" with Israel were sometimes used as a pretext for acts of personal vengeance. Women deemed to have behaved "immorally" were also among the victims.[7]

The UNLI's calls for violence escalated after the 1990 Temple Mount riot in which 17 Arabs were killed. Yasser Abd-Rabbo — formerly the PLO's interlocutor in its dialogue with the U.S. — declared that "the war of stabbing with knives against the usurpers of Jerusalem is just beginning."[8]

The PLO continued its efforts to foment violence throughout 1991. On March 3, the UNLI issued a communiqué calling for "increased confrontation" with Israeli forces in the West Bank and Gaza. Another PLO leaflet, issued in September, called for the "execution" of anyone who sells property in Jerusalem to Jews.[9]

According to the Israeli government, the PFLP alone carried out 122 terrorist attacks during 1991, resulting in the murders of 18 residents of Israel and the territories. Crimes committed by Fatah included the July 4 murder of a 61-year-old Arab villager near Jenin; the September killing of Israeli Sgt. Yoram Cohen and the October murder of a man found stabbed to death in a Gaza street, his head covered with a sack. A note bearing the words "Force-17," denoting Arafat's personal bodyguard, was found on the body.[10]

Later in the intifada, Hamas began to vie with the PLO for control of the uprising. In December 1992, for example, Hamas began to target IDF troops, killing four in several daring ambushes.

MYTH

"The Palestinians who died in the intifada were all killed by the Israelis."

FACT

Initially, more Palestinians died in clashes with Israeli troops – battles usually triggered by Arab attacks against soldiers – than were killed by their fellow Palestinians in the *intra*fada. This changed dramatically in early 1990. In that year, the number of Palestinians dying in engagements with Israelis fell by more than half. More Palestinians were murdered by Palestinians in the intrafada during that period. The internecine killings increased in 1991, with 238 Palestinians (up from 156) dying in the intrafada, more than triple the number who died at the hands of Israelis.[11]

Nearly 200 Palestinians were killed by their fellow Palestinians in 1992, more than double the number killed in clashes with Israeli security forces. The methods of murder, Steven Emerson reported, included beheading, mutilation, cutting off ears and limbs and pouring acid on a victim's face.[12]

The reign of terror became so serious that some Palestinians expressed public concern about the disorder. The PLO began to call for an end to the violence, but murders by its members and rivals continued.

When many Palestinians heard a knock at the door late at night, the *New York Times* reported, they were relieved to find an Israeli soldier rather than a masked Palestinian standing outside.[13] Even after the intifada fizzled out following the signing of the Declaration of Principles in 1993, internecine warfare among the Palestinians continued, and persists to this day.

MYTH

"Israel closed West Bank schools during the intifada to deprive Palestinians of an education."

FACT

Educational opportunities in the territories greatly improved under Israeli rule. The number of elementary and secondary schools increased by more than a third from 1967-88. Women were major beneficiaries of the boom. From 1970-86, for example, the percentage of women who had not attended school was slashed by more than half, from 67 percent to 32 percent. Before 1967, no universities existed on the West Bank; six were built under Israel's administration.

Despite the intifada, nursery schools, kindergartens and most West Bank vocational schools remained open because none were used to instigate violence. Gaza schools also stayed open because militant Islamic fundamentalists there used the mosques, not schools, to incite their followers.

The PLO used many schools, however, to stimulate attacks against Israelis. Caches of knives, clubs and iron bars were found hidden in school buildings. "Schools are the natural place for a demonstration to begin," wrote Palestinian journalist Daoud Kuttab. "In school, demonstrations and stone-throwing are part of a tradition....To hit an Israeli car is to become a hero."[14]

In 1988, Israel closed some secondary schools and colleges in the West Bank that were being used to orchestrate the insurrection. After it announced the closures, Israel offered to reopen any school whose principal would guarantee that his school would be used to educate children, not to encourage rioting. But educators, many cowed by the uprising leadership, remained silent. When the violence subsided, Israel reopened all high schools, colleges and universities.

Interestingly, when the U.S.-led coalition attacked Afghanistan in October 2001, the Palestinian Authority reacted to violent protests by Palestinians in the Gaza Strip by closing universities and schools there.[15]

MYTH

"The outbreak of violence in late 2000, dubbed by Arabs the 'al-Aksa intifada,' was provoked by Ariel Sharon's visit to the Temple Mount."

FACT

To believe Palestinian spokesmen, the violence was caused by the desecration of a Muslim holy place – Haram al-Sharif (the Temple Mount) – by Likud leader Ariel Sharon and the "thousands of Israeli soldiers" who accompanied him. The violence was carried out through unprovoked attacks by Israeli forces, which invaded Palestinian-controlled territories and "massacred" defenseless Palestinian civilians, who merely threw stones in self-defense. The only way to stop the violence, then, was for Israel to cease fire and remove its troops from the Palestinian areas.

The truth is dramatically different.

Imad Faluji, the Palestinian Authority Communications Minister, admitted months after Sharon's visit that the violence had been planned in July, far in advance of Sharon's "provocation." "It [the uprising] had been planned since Chairman Arafat's return from Camp David, when he turned the tables on the former U.S. president and rejected the American conditions."[16]

> *"The Sharon visit did not cause the 'Al-Aksa Intifada.'"*
>
> **– Conclusion of the Mitchell Report**[17]

The violence started before Sharon's September 28, 2000, visit to the Temple Mount. The day before, for example, an Israeli soldier was killed at the Netzarim Junction. The next day in the West Bank city of Kalkilya, a Palestinian police officer working with Israeli police on a joint patrol opened fire and killed his Israeli counterpart.

Official Palestinian Authority media exhorted the Palestinians to violence. On September 29, the Voice of Palestine, the PA's official radio station sent out calls "to all Palestinians to come and defend the al-Aksa mosque." The PA closed its schools and bused Palestinian students to the Temple Mount to participate in the organized riots.

Just prior to Rosh Hashanah (September 30), the Jewish New Year, when hundreds of Israelis were worshipping at the Western Wall, thousands of Arabs began throwing bricks and rocks at Israeli police and Jewish worshippers. Rioting then spread to towns and villages throughout Israel, the West Bank and Gaza Strip.

Internal Security Minister Shlomo Ben-Ami permitted Sharon to go to the Temple Mount – Judaism's holiest place — only after calling Palestinian security chief Jabril Rajoub and receiving his assurance that if Sharon did not enter the mosques, no problems would arise. The need to protect Sharon arose when Rajoub later said that the Palestinian police would do nothing to prevent violence during the visit.

> *"It is not a mistake that the Koran warns us of the hatred of the Jews and put them at the top of the list of the enemies of Islam. Today the Jews recruit the world against the Muslims and use all kinds of weapons. They are plundering the dearest place to the Muslims after Mecca and Medina and threaten the place the Muslims have faced at first when they prayed and the third holiest city after Mecca and Medina. They want to erect their temple on that place....The Muslims are ready to sacrifice their lives and blood to protect the Islamic nature of Jerusalem and al-Aksa!"*
>
> **— Sheikh Hian Al-Adrisi, Excerpt of address in the al-Aksa mosque (September 29, 2000)**[18]

Sharon did not attempt to enter any mosques and his 34 minute visit to the Temple Mount was conducted during normal hours when the area is open to tourists. Palestinian youths — eventually numbering around 1,500 — shouted slogans in an attempt to inflame the situation. Some 1,500 Israeli police were present at the scene to forestall violence.

There were limited disturbances during Sharon's visit, mostly involving stone throwing. During the remainder of the day, outbreaks of stone throwing continued on the Temple Mount and in the vicinity, leaving 28 Israeli policemen injured, three of whom were hospitalized. There are no accounts of Palestinian injuries on that day. Significant and orchestrated violence was initiated by Palestinians the following day following Friday prayers.

The real desecration of holy places was perpetrated by Palestinians, not Israelis. In October 2000, Palestinian mobs destroyed a Jewish shrine in Nablus – Joseph's Tomb – tearing up and burning Jewish prayer books. They stoned worshipers at the Western Wall, and attacked Rachel's Tomb in Bethlehem with firebombs and automatic weapons.

None of the violent attacks were initiated by Israeli security forces, which in all cases responded to Palestinian violence that went well beyond stone throwing. It included massive attacks with automatic weapons and the lynching of Israeli soldiers. Most armed attackers were members of the Tanzim – Arafat's own militia.

Since all attacks were initiated by Palestinians under Arafat's orders, only Arafat has the power to end the violence. Israel and the United States have repeatedly called on him to do so and renew the peace process.

MYTH

"A handful of Israelis have been killed in the uprising while thousands of innocent Palestinians have been murdered by Israeli troops."

FACT

During the "al-Aksa intifada," the number of Palestinian casualties has been higher than the figure for Israelis; however, the gap has narrowed as Palestinian suicide bombers have used increasingly powerful bombs to kill larger numbers of Israelis in their terror attacks. As of mid-September 2002, 1,868 Palestinians had been killed and 617 Israelis.[19]

The disproportionate number of Palestinian casualties is primarily a result of the number of Palestinians involved in violence and is the inevitable result of an irregular, ill-trained militia attacking a well-trained regular army. The unfortunate death of noncombatants is largely due to the habit of Palestinian gunmen and terrorists using civilians as shields.

What is more revealing than the tragic totals, however, is the specific breakdown of the casualties. According to one study, Palestinian noncombatants were mostly teenaged boys and young men. "This completely contradicts accusations that Israel has 'indiscriminately targeted women and children,' according to the study. "There appears to be only one reasonable explanation for this pattern: that Palestinian men and boys engaged in behavior that brought them into conflict with Israeli armed forces."

By contrast, the number of women and older people among the noncombatant Israeli casualties illustrates the randomness of Palestinian attacks, and the degree to which terrorists have killed Israelis for the "crime" of being Israeli.[20] Israeli troops do not target innocent Palestinians, but Palestinian terrorists *do* target Israeli civilians.

MYTH

"Violence is an understandable and legitimate reaction to Israel's policies."

FACT

The basis of the peace process is that disputes should be resolved through negotiations. One of the conditions Israel set before agreeing to negotiate with the PLO was that the organization renounce terrorism. It formally did so; however, the PLO and other Palestinian groups and individuals have consistently resorted to violence since the Oslo process began in 1993. Whether or not Israel made concessions, Palestinians have still committed heinous attacks. In some instances atrocities are perpetrated because of alleged mistreatment; in other cases, they are deliberate efforts to sabotage negotiations. Regardless, the Palestinian Authority, which has a nearly 40,000-person police force (larger than allowed under the peace agreements), and multiple intelligence agencies, must be held responsible for keeping the peace.

MYTH

"The al-Aksa uprising has been conducted only in the disputed territories and has had no impact on Israel."

FACT

Palestinian violence in the West Bank and Gaza has taken the lives of numerous civilians and soldiers. In addition, terrorists acting in the name of the uprising have carried out heinous attacks inside Israel. The violence also has collateral impact on the Israeli psyche, military and economy.

Israelis must now be careful traveling through many parts of Israel and the territories that should be safe. Palestinians have also sniped at Jews in cities such as Gilo that are outside the territories. The violence has severely undermined the faith Israelis had that if they made territorial concessions, peace with the Palestinians was possible.

The uprising also affects military readiness because troops must be diverted from training and preparing against threats from hostile nations and instead must focus on quelling riots and fighting terrorism.

Finally, the violence has caused a sharp reduction in tourism and damaged related industries. Tens of thousands of Israelis have lost their jobs because of the Palestinian uprising.

It is not only the Israelis who suffer. The loss of tourism also hurts Palestinians. The number of visitors, for example, who normally visit Bethlehem for Christmas was significantly lower than usual. The same is true in other pilgrimage sites in the Palestinian Authority. Palestinian shopkeepers in places like the Old City are also affected by the drop in tourism. The terror campaign forced Israel to severly restrict the number of Palestinian workers from entering Israel, hurting individuals trying to make a living and provide for their families.

MYTH

"Israel uses excessive force to respond to children who are just throwing stones."

FACT

Palestinians, young and old, attack Israeli civilians and soldiers with a variety of weapons. When they throw stones, they are not pebbles, but large rocks that can and do cause serious injuries.

Typically, Israeli troops under attack have numbered fewer than 20, while their assailants, armed with Molotov cocktails, pistols, assault rifles, machine guns, hand grenades and explosives, have numbered in the hundreds. Moreover, mixed among rock throwers have been Palestinians, often policemen, armed with guns. Faced with an angry, violent mob, Israeli police and soldiers often have no choice but to defend themselves by firing rubber bullets and, in life-threatening situations, live ammunition.

The use of live-fire by the Palestinians has effectively meant that Israeli forces have had to remain at some distance from those initiating the violence. In addition, the threat of force against Israelis has been a threat of lethal force. Both factors have inhibited the use of traditional methods of riot control.

According to the rules of engagement for Israeli troops in the territories, the use of weapons is authorized solely in life-threatening situations or, subject to significant limitations, in the exercise of the arrest of an individual suspected of having committed a grave security offense. In all cases, IDF activities have been governed by an overriding policy of restraint, the requirement of proportionality and the necessity to take all possible measures to prevent harm to innocent civilians.

Meanwhile, the Palestinians escalated their violent attacks against Israelis by using mortars and anti-tank missiles illegally smuggled into the Gaza Strip. Palestinians have fired mortar shells into Jewish communities in Gaza and Israel proper, and IDF reports indicate that anti-tank missiles have been fired at Israeli forces in Gaza. The Palestinian Authority (PA) has also been stockpiling weapons smuggled into Gaza by sea and underground tunnels linked to Egypt.

The possession and use of these weapons and other arms by the Palestinians violates commitments they made in various agreements with Israel. Under the Oslo accords, the only weapons allowed in the Palestinian-controlled areas are handguns, rifles and machine guns, and these are to be held only by PA security officers. The recent violence makes clear that in addition to the police, Palestinian civilians and members of militias, such as the Tanzim, also are in possession of such weapons.[21]

The number of Palestinian casualties in clashes is regrettable, but it is important to remember that no Palestinian would be in any danger or risk injury if they were not waging a terror campaign. If children were in school or at home with their families, rather than throwing rocks in the streets, they would have little to fear. And children throw more than rocks. Abu Mazen, Yasser Arafat's deputy revealed that children are paid to carry out terrorist attacks against Israel. He told a Jordanian newspaper that "at least 40 children in Rafah lost arms from the throwing of Bangalore torpedoes. They received five shekels [approximately $1.00] in order to throw them."[22]

Also, while the number of Palestinians who have died is greater than the number of Israelis, that should not minimize the traumatic loss of life on the Israeli side. From September 29, 2000, through mid-September, 2002, more than 600 Israeli Jews, including 430 civilians, were murdered by Palestinians. Contrary to Palestinian assertions that they are fighting a war against armed forces, fewer than one-third of the Israelis that have been killed were soldiers. In just the first half of 2002, Palestinians carried out 91 suicide attacks.[23]

It is also worth considering how police in the United States and other nations react to mob violence. Abuses do sometimes occur when police are under attack, but no one expects them to stand by and allow their lives to be put in danger to assuage international opinion. In fact, the Palestinian Authority itself does not hesitate to use lethal force against protestors. For example, after the U.S. coalition attacked Afghanistan, Hamas organized a rally in the Gaza Strip in which thousands of Palestinians marched in support of suspected terror mastermind Osama bin Laden. Palestinian police killed two protestors when they tried to break it up.[24]

It is only Israelis who are denied their right to self-defense or see it used as a propaganda weapon against them.

MYTH

"The shooting of a child being protected by his father shown on TV proves Israel does not hesitate to kill innocent Palestinian children."

FACT

Perhaps the most vivid image of the "al-Aksa intifada" was the film of a Palestinian father trying unsuccessfully to shield his son from gunfire. Israel was universally blamed for the death of 12-year-old Mohammed Aldura, but subsequent investigations found that the boy was most likely killed by Palestinian bullets.

The father and son took cover adjacent to a Palestinian shooting position at the Netzarim junction in the Gaza Strip. After Palestinian policemen fired from this position and around it toward an IDF position opposite, IDF soldiers returned fire toward the sources of the shooting. During the exchanges of fire the Palestinian child was hit and killed.

An IDF investigation of the incident released November 27, 2000, found that Aldura was most likely killed by a Palestinian policeman and not by IDF fire. This report was confirmed by an independent investigation by German ARD Television, which said the footage of Aldura's death was censored by the Palestinians to look as if he had been killed by the Israelis when, in fact, his death was caused by Palestinian gunfire.[25]

MYTH

"Israel uses rubber bullets to maim and kill unarmed Palestinians."

FACT

Rubber bullets are an imperfect means of pacifying a violent mob. They are designed to minimize the risk of serious injury but they cannot alleviate it altogether. In the overwhelming majority of cases, rubber bullets do not cause death or serious injury. In many circumstances, they may be the only available option short of live-fire. Children using guns, or intent on causing injury or death to their intended target by some other means, pose a lethal threat, particularly when that threat takes the form of a large-scale attack.

Many police forces around the world use rubber bullets to disperse violent crowds. For example, following the victory of the Los Angeles Lakers in the 2001 National Basketball Association finals, Los Angeles police used rubber bullets to end violent outbursts by rowdy fans.[26] The police felt compelled to use this method of crowd control with a group of overly exuberant basketball fans who turned violent celebrating their team's victory, while Israel uses it against a hostile population with whom it is essentially at war.

MYTH

"The Mitchell Report made clear that Israeli settlement policy is as much to blame for the breakdown of the peace process as Palestinian violence and that a settlement freeze is necessary to end the violence."

FACT

In November 2000, former U.S. Senator George Mitchell was appointed to lead a fact-finding committee to investigate the cause of the "al-Aksa Intifada" and explore how to prevent future violence. The report his committee issued on April 30, 2001, did recommend a settlement freeze — as one of more than 15 different confidence-building measures — but Mitchell and Warren Rudman, another member of the committee, explicitly stated in a letter clarifying their view: "We want to go further and make it clear that we do not in any way equate Palestinian terrorism with Israeli settlement activity, 'seemingly' or otherwise."

Mitchell and Rudman also disputed the idea that the cessation of settlement construction and terrorism were linked. "The immediate aim must be to end the violence....Part of the effort to end the violence must include an immediate resumption of security cooperation between the government of Israel and the Palestinian Authority aimed at preventing violence and combating terrorism." They added, "Regarding terrorism, we call upon the Palestinian Authority, as a confidence-building measure, to make clear through concrete action, to Israelis and Palestinians alike, that terror is reprehensible and unacceptable, and the Palestinian Authority is to make a total effort to prevent terrorist operations and to punish perpetrators acting in its jurisdiction."[27]

MYTH

"Israel's use of F-16 fighter jets typifies the disproportionate use of force applied by Israel against innocent Palestinian civilians."

FACT

How do you determine the proportionate use of military force? When Palestinian terrorists plant bombs at Israeli shopping malls and kill and maim dozens of civilians, would the proportionate response be for Israelis to plant bombs in Palestinian malls? No one in Israel believes this would be a legitimate use of force. Thus, Israel is left with the need to take measured action against specific targets in an effort to either deter Palestinian violence or stop it.

In the specific case of Israel's use of F-16s, Major General Giora Eiland, Head of the IDF Operation Branch, explained Israel's reasoning:

> I know that the F-16 was not designed to attack targets in Palestinian cities. But we have to remember that although we use this

kind of aircraft, it is still very accurate. All the targets were military targets....it was rather a tactical decision, simply because the targets were big enough, were strong enough or solid enough that attack helicopters were considered not effective enough to penetrate or to hit these specific targets. So when we decided or we chose these targets then we were looking for the best ammunition for them and in this specific case it was F-16.[28]

Israel's deployment of the fighters came after 88 Israelis had already lost their lives, including 55 civilians. The civilians were not killed accidentally, they were deliberately targeted. In the previous two-and-a-half months, Palestinians had attempted to place 28 bombs inside Israel. The F-16 attack came in direct response to one that exploded at a Netanya shopping mall May 18, 2001, killing five Israelis.

A month before deploying the F-16s, the U.S. State Department accused Israel of an "excessive and disproportionate" response to Palestinian violence when it launched air strikes against targets in Gaza, even though the spokesman admitted the retaliation was "precipitated by the provocative Palestinian mortar attacks on Israel."[29] The U.S. position is ironic given the so-called Powell Doctrine enunciated by Secretary of State Colin Powell, which holds that "America should enter fights with every bit of force available or not at all."[30] Consider a few examples of the application of this doctrine:

- General Powell insisted on deploying overwhelming force before going to war against Iraq in the Gulf War. The Allied force of more than half a million troops demolished Saddam Hussein's army at a cost of fewer than 200 American lives while approximately 35,000 Iraqis were killed, including many civilians.

- Powell also oversaw the invasion of Panama, which required the deployment of 25,000 troops and the use of F-117 Stealth bombers for the first time. Thousands of Panamanian civilians were injured and displaced and at least 100 killed. He said later, "Use all the force necessary, and do not apologize for going in big if that is what it takes. Decisive force ends wars quickly and in the long run saves lives."[31]

- In reaction to an attempt to assassinate President Bush in 1993, the U.S. launched 23 cruise missiles at Iraq's intelligence headquarters and hit a civilian neighborhood in the process. Powell later said this was an "appropriate, proportional" response.[32]

- The U.S. also deployed massive force in the Balkans and, in 1999, accidentally bombed the Chinese embassy in Belgrade killing three and injuring 20.

- The U.S. has relied heavily on fighter planes and bombers to conduct its post-September 11 war in Afghanistan. A number of incidents have subsequently been reported in which civilians have been killed, including the bombing of a wedding party that killed 48.[33]

The United States has not hesitated to use overwhelming force against its adversaries, even though the threats have been distant and in no way posed a danger to the existence of the nation or the security of its citizens. While U.S. military objectives were accomplished, they also were routinely accompanied by errors and collateral damage that resulted in the loss of civilian lives.

Israel is in a different position. The threat it faces is immediate in time and physical proximity, and poses a direct danger to Israeli citizens. Still, Israel has not used its full might as the Powell Doctrine dictates. The use of force has been judicious and precise. In those instances where mistakes occur — as inevitably happens in war — the incidents are investigated.

The bottom line is that Israel would have no need to respond with military force if the Palestinians were not attacking its citizens and soldiers.

MYTH

"Arafat can't control militant Palestinians."

FACT

The premise of the peace process was that by reaching an agreement with Yasser Arafat, violence could be controlled. If he cannot control the behavior of the people under his authority, then the agreements have little value. On the other hand, if he does have control, then it is clear he is using it to foment violence rather than prevent it.

The evidence suggests that Arafat does have control over most activities by Palestinians in the West Bank and Gaza Strip. Arafat has demonstrated an ability to quickly eliminate Palestinians who challenge his rule by arresting and, in some cases, executing them. When he chooses, he has also arrested members of terrorist groups, but he has routinely released them so they can continue to attack Israel. He has allowed the terrorist organizations to produce explosives, build mortars, train members and recruit youngsters for suicide missions.

MYTH

"Israel has consistently refused to take any steps to calm the situation, and its unrelenting attacks provoked Palestinian violence despite Yasser Arafat's appeals for restraint."

FACT

On May 22, 2001, Prime Minister Ariel Sharon declared a unilateral cease-fire in an effort to calm the situation, and in the hope the Palestinians would reciprocate by ending their violent attacks against Israelis. Instead the Palestinians intensified the level of violence directed at Israeli civilians. Yasser Arafat did nothing to stop or discourage the attacks. More than 70 attacks

were recorded in the next 10 days, during which Israel held its fire and es-
chewed any retaliation. The campaign of Palestinian terror during the Israeli
cease-fire culminated with the suicide bombing at a Tel Aviv disco June 1
that killed 20 people and injured more than 90, mostly teenagers. In the
face of overwhelming international pressure generated by the horrific attack,
and the fear of an Israeli counterattack, Arafat finally declared a cease-fire.
It too didn't last.

> "Israel is at war with an enemy that declines, in its shrewdness
> and its cowardice, to fight Israel's soldiers, but is instead murder-
> ing its civilians, its women and children."
>
> — **Michael Kelly**[34]

MYTH
*"Israel has no justification for withholding tax monies
due to the Palestinian Authority."*

FACT

At the beginning of 2001, Israel decided to withhold more than $50 million
in taxes it owed to the Palestinian Authority (PA) in response to the ongoing
violence. U.S. officials, and others, pressured Israel to transfer the money
because of the PA's dire financial straits and inability to pay many of its bills.
Israel recognized that its action was harsh, but believed it was necessary to
demonstrate to the Palestinians that the unwillingness to stop the violence
had a cost. Israel must use whatever leverage it can to protect its citizens and
this economic sanction was a milder response than a military one.

While Israel's action was blamed for the sorry state of the Palestinian economy,
the truth was the Arab countries suspended the transfer of hundreds of millions of dollars, collected as donations, meant for the PA. The justification for
the Arab states' action was their concern that the funds would be embezzled
and encourage further corruption in the PA. For example, a Kuwaiti newspaper
reported that Yasser Arafat stole more than $5 million in foreign aid intended
for needy Palestinians.[35] In July 2002, Israel agreed to transfer some of the
tax revenues to the Palestinians as a confidence-building measure after
Palestinian violence subsided, and an agreement was reached to set up a
committee of U.S. representatives to oversee the transaction.[36]

Case Study

The speaker of the Palestinian legislative council, Ahmed Karia, suddenly vacated the villa he built for $1.5 million in Jericho after President Bush raised the issue of PA corruption. A sign on the door was posted that said the villa had become a welfare institution for the relatives of Palestinians killed in terror attacks.[37]

MYTH

"The Palestinians have observed the cease-fire negotiated by CIA Director George Tenet."

FACT

In June 2001 CIA Director George Tenet traveled to the Middle East in an effort to solidify a cease-fire between Israel and the Palestinian Authority and lay the groundwork for a resumption of peace talks. The Tenet Plan called for an end to all violent activities. In the six weeks following Tenet's visit, however, Palestinians carried out 850 terrorist attacks resulting in 94 Israeli casualties, 17 of them fatalities.[38]

MYTH

"Israel's policy of assassinating Palestinian terrorists is immoral and counterproductive."

FACT

Israel is faced with a nearly impossible situation in attempting to protect its civilian population from Palestinians who are prepared to blow themselves up to murder innocent Jews. One strategy for dealing with the problem has been the peace process. Since 1993, Israel believed that negotiating was the way to reach peace with the Palestinians, but after Israel gave back much of the West Bank and Gaza Strip, and offered virtually all of the remainder, the Palestinians rejected their concessions and chose to use violence to try to force Israel to capitulate to all their demands.

A second strategy is for Israel to "exercise restraint," that is, not respond to Palestinian violence. The international community lauds Israel when it simply turns the other cheek after heinous attacks. While this restraint might win praise from world leaders, it does nothing to assuage the pain of the victims or to prevent further attacks. Moreover, the same nations that urge restraint to Israel have often reacted forcefully when put in similar situations. For example, the British assassinated Nazis after World War II and targeted IRA terrorists in Northern Ireland. And, in the wake of the murderous attack by terrorists on the World Trade Center and the Pentagon, it was revealed that the Clinton Administration had attempted to assassinate Saudi terrorist Osama bin Laden in 1998 in retaliation for his role in the bombings of the United States embassies in Tanzania and Kenya. The Administration of George W. Bush has said it also would not hesitate to kill bin Laden.[39]

> *"If you've got an organization that has plotted or is plotting some kind of suicide bomber attack, for example, and [the Israelis] have hard evidence of who it is and where they're located, I think there's some justification in their trying to protect themselves by preempting."*
>
> **— U.S. Vice President Dick Cheney**[40]

In April 1986, after the U.S. determined that Libya had directed the terrorist bombing of a West Berlin discotheque that killed one American and injured 200 others, it launched a raid on a series of Libyan targets, including President Muammar Qaddafi's home. This was widely viewed as an assassination attempt. Qaddafi escaped, but his infant daughter was killed and two of his other children were wounded. In addition, a missile went off track and caused fatalities in a civilian neighborhood. Reagan justified the action as self-defense against Libya's state-sponsored terrorism. "As a matter of self-defense, any nation victimized by terrorism has an inherent right to respond with force to deter new acts of terror. I felt we must show Qaddafi that there was a price he would have to pay for that kind of behavior and that we wouldn't let him get away with it."[41]

Israel has chosen a third option – eliminating the masterminds of terror attacks. It is a policy that has caused great debate in Israel, but is supported by a vast majority of the public (70 percent in an August 2001 *Ha'aretz* poll). The policy is also supported by the American public according to an August 2001 poll by the America Middle East Information Network. The survey found that 73 percent of respondents felt Israel was justified in killing terrorists if it had proof they were planning bombings or other attacks that could kill Israelis.[42]

Deputy Chief of Staff Major-General Moshe Ya'alon explained the policy this way:

> There are no executions without a trial. There is no avenging someone who had carried out an attack a month ago. We are acting against those who are waging terror against us. We prefer to arrest them and have detained over 1,000. But if we can't, and the Palestinians won't, then we have no other choice but to defend ourselves.[43]

The Israeli government also went through a legal process before adopting the policy of targeted killings. Israel's attorney general reviewed the policy and determined that it is legal under Israeli and international law.[44]

Targeting the terrorists has a number of benefits. First, it places a price on terror: Israelis can't be attacked with impunity anymore, for terrorists know that if they target others, they will become targets themselves. Second, it is a method of self-defense: pre-emptive strikes eliminate the people who would otherwise murder Jews. While it is true that there are others to take their place, they can do so only with the knowledge they too will become targets. Third, it throws the terrorists off balance. Extremists can no longer nonchalantly plan an operation; rather, they must stay on the move, look over their shoulders at all times, and work much harder to carry out their goals.

> *"I think when you are attacked by a terrorist and you know who the terrorist is and you can fingerprint back to the cause of the terror, you should respond."*
>
> **– U.S. Secretary of State Colin Powell**[45]

Of course, the policy also has costs. Besides international condemnation, Israel risks revealing informers who often provide the information needed to find the terrorists. Soldiers also must engage in sometimes high-risk operations that occasionally cause tragic collateral damage to property and persons.

The most common criticism of "targeted killings" is that they do no good because they perpetuate a cycle of violence whereby the terrorists seek revenge. This is probably the least compelling argument against the policy, because the people who blow themselves up to become martyrs could always find a justification for their actions. They are determined to bomb the Jews out of the Middle East and will not stop until their goal is achieved.

MYTH

"Israel indiscriminately murders terrorists and Palestinian civilians."

FACT

It is always a tragedy when innocent civilians are killed in a counterterrorism operation. Civilians would not be at risk, however, if the Palestinian Authority arrested the terrorists, the murderers did not choose to hide among non-combatants and the civilians refused to protect the killers.

Israel does not attack Palestinian areas indiscriminately. On the contrary, the IDF takes great care to target people who are planning terrorist attacks against Israeli civilians. Israeli forces have a history of accuracy in such assaults, nevertheless, mistakes are sometimes made. Whereas the terrorists make no apology for their attacks on civilians, and purposely target them,

Israel always investigates the reasons for any errors and takes steps to prevent them from reoccurring.

Israel is not alone in using military force against terrorists or in sometimes inadvertently harming people who are not targets. For example, on the same day that American officials were condemning Israel because a number of civilians died when Israel assassinated the leader of the military wing of Hamas, news reports disclosed that the United States bombed a village in Afghanistan in an operation directed at a Taliban leader that instead killed 48 Afghan civilians at a wedding party. In both cases, flawed intelligence played a role in the tragic mistakes.

> *"In Gaza last week, crowds of children reveled and sang while adults showered them with candies. The cause for celebration: the cold-blooded murder of at least seven people — five of them Americans — and the maiming of 80 more by a terrorist bomb on the campus of Jerusalem's Hebrew University."*
>
> **— Israeli scholar Michael Oren**[46]

MYTH

"Israel's use of American-made weapons in retaliatory attacks against the Palestinians is illegal."

FACT

The United States has been closely monitoring Israeli actions. Rep. John Conyers (D-Michigan) wrote a letter to Secretary of State Colin Powell asking whether Israel was violating U.S. law by using American arms in its strikes against Palestinian terrorists. Powell responded in a letter dated August 17, 2001, that Israel's actions did not violate U.S. law.

The law in question is the Arms Export Control Act (AECA) and it states that defense articles will be used only for specified purposes, including internal security and legitimate self-defense. Israel has maintained that it has been acting in self-defense and the Bush Administration concurs.[47]

MYTH

"Israel perpetrated a massacre in the Jenin refugee camp in April 2002."

FACT

Secretary of State Colin Powell concisely refuted Palestinian claims that Israel was guilty of atrocities in Jenin. "I see no evidence that would support a massacre took place."[48] Powell's view was subsequently confirmed by the United Nations, Human Rights Watch and an investigation by the European Union.[49]

The Palestinians repeatedly claimed that a massacre had been committed in the days immediately following the battle. Spokesman Saeb Erekat, for example, told CNN on April 17 that at least 500 people were massacred and 1,600 people, including women and children, were missing. The Palestinians quickly backpedaled when it became clear they could not produce any evidence to support the scurrilous charge; their own review committee reported a death toll of 56, of whom 34 were combatants. No women or children were reported missing.[50]

Israel did not arbitrarily choose to raid the refugee camp in Jenin. It had little choice after a series of suicide bombings had terrorized Israeli civilians for the preceding 18 months. To defend itself and bring about hope for peace, Israeli forces went into Jenin to root out one of the principal terrorist bases.

The Palestinian Authority's own documents call Jenin the "suiciders capital." The camp has a long history as a base for extremists, and no less than 28 suicide attacks were launched from this terror nest during the wave of violence that preceded Israel's action. These terrorists violated the cease-fire agreed to by Israel and undermined Israeli efforts to resume political negotiations toward a final peace agreement.

Palestinian snipers targeted soldiers from a girls' school, a mosque, and an UNRWA building, and, in returning fire and pursuing terrorists, some noncombatants were hit. Any civilian casualty is a tragedy, but some were unavoidable because Palestinian terrorists used civilians as shields. The majority of casualties were gunmen.

While Israel could have chosen to bomb the entire camp, the strategy employed by the U.S. in Afghanistan, the IDF deliberately chose a riskier path to reduce the likelihood of endangering civilians. Soldiers went house to house and 23 were killed in bitter combat with Palestinian terrorists using bombs, grenades, booby-traps and machine guns to turn the camp into a war zone.

Television pictures gave a distorted perspective of the damage in the camp as well. Jenin was not destroyed. The Israeli operation was conducted in a limited area of the refugee camp, which itself comprises a small fraction of the city. The destruction that did occur in the camp was largely caused by Palestinian bombs.

Palestinians have learned from fabricating atrocity stories in the past that a false claim against Israel will get immediate media attention and attract sympathy for their cause. The corrections that inevitably follow these specious charges are rarely seen, read or noticed.

MYTH

"Israel opposed an investigation by the United Nations because it wanted to conceal the crimes it committed in Jenin."

FACT

Israel had nothing to hide and invited an impartial fact-finding team to visit Jenin.[51] The historical animosity of UN bodies toward Israel raised questions, however, about the fairness of its representatives. These doubts were reinforced when the UN refused to include in the proposed team any military or counterterrorism experts who could have assessed the terrorist threat Israel faced from Jenin. One delegate appointed to the UN team previously compared a Star of David with a swastika.[52]

The hypocrisy of the UN and others concerned about Jenin is evident from the fact that they never condemn or investigate the repeated massacres by Palestinian suicide bombers.

MYTH

"Israel prevents Palestinian ambulances from taking sick and injured Palestinians to hospitals."

FACT

One of the unfortunate results of the violence during the "al-Aksa intifada" has been the allegations of Israeli abuse against Palestinian Red Crescent ambulances, which, it is alleged, has resulted in inconveniences, medical complications and even death to the sick passengers on board. These accounts tend to portray the delays as wanton acts of cruelty on the part of Israeli soldiers against Palestinians in need of medical attention.

These allegations are correct in one regard: ambulances are indeed stopped and searched at Israeli checkpoints. They fail, however, to put the facts into a broader context. The reason that ambulances have been held and searched at checkpoints is due to the very real threat that they pose to Israel and its citizens. Ambulances have frequently been used as a means to transport terrorist bombs, and many of the militants who have triggered suicide bombings in Israel gained access by driving or riding in Red Crescent ambulances. For example:

- In October, 2001, Nidal Nazal, a Hamas operative in Kalkilya, was arrested by the IDF. He was an ambulance driver for the Palestinian Red Crescent, and information indicates that he exploited the unrestricted travel to serve as a messenger between the Hamas headquarters in several West Bank towns.[53]

- In January, 2002, Wafa Idris blew herself up on the crowded Jaffa Street in Jerusalem, becoming one of the first female suicide bombers. She was an ambulance driver for the Palestinian Red Crescent, as was Mohammed Hababa, the Tanzim operative who sent her on her mission. She left the West Bank by way of an ambulance.[54]

- On May 17, 2002, an explosive belt was found in a Red Crescent ambulance at a checkpoint near Ramallah. The bomb, the same type generally used in suicide bombings, was hidden under a gurney on which a sick child was lying. The driver, Islam Jibril, was already wanted by the IDF, and admitted that this was not the first time that an ambulance had been used to transport explosives or terrorists.

- The bomb was removed from the ambulance and detonated in the presence of a representative of the International Committee of the Red Cross. In a statement issued the same day, the ICRC said that it "understands the security concerns of the Israeli authorities, and has always acknowledged their right to check ambulances, provided it does not unduly delay medical evacuations." The sick passengers in the ambulance were escorted by soldiers to a nearby hospital.[55]

- On June 30, Israeli troops found 10 suspected Palestinian terrorists hiding in two ambulances in Ramallah. They were caught when soldiers stopped the vehicles for routine checks.[56]

The accusations leveled against Israel by its critics have frequently been based on statements of international law, such as the Fourth Geneva Convention. It is true that the Geneva Convention does place particular emphasis on the immunity and neutrality of ambulances and emergency medical personnel. But the conclusion that Israel must ignore a clear and present danger to its citizens, or else violate international law, is a distortion. It is the Palestinian terrorists, who use ambulances to smuggle explosives into Israel who are compromising the Red Crescent's immunity and neutrality.

Notes

1 *New York Times*, (December 14, 1987).

2 UPI, (December 9, 1987).

3 *Al-Hamishmar*, (December 6, 1991); B'Tselem.

4 *Baghdad Voice of the PLO*, (May 12, 1989).

5 *New York Times*, (October 24, 1989).

6 *Al-Mussawar*, (January 19, 1990).

7 *Wall Street Journal*, (February 21, 1990).

8 Radio Monte Carlo, (October 23, 1990).

9 *Jerusalem Post*, (September 14, 1991).

10 *Jerusalem Post*, (July 6 and October 5, 1991).

11 *Near East Report*, Year End Reports, (1991-1993).

12 *The New Republic*, (November 23, 1992).

13 *New York Times*, (June 12, 1991).

14 Daoud Kuttab, "A Profile of the Stonethrowers," *Journal of Palestine Studies*, (Spring 1988), p. 15.

15 AP, (October 10, 2001).

16 Jerusalem Post, (March 4, 2001).

17 Sharm el-Sheikh Fact-Finding Committee Final Report, (April 30, 2001).

18 Quoted in Sharm El-Sheikh Fact-Finding Committee First Statement of the Government of Israel, Israeli Foreign Ministry, (December 28, 2000).

19 AP, (September 19, 2002).

20 "An Engineered Tragedy: Statistical Analysis of Casualties in the Palestinian-Israeli Conflict, September 2000-June 2002," International Policy Institute for Counter-Terrorism, (June 2002).

21 *Near East Report,* (March 5, 2001).

22 *Almazen* [Kuwait], (June 20, 2002).

23 *Jerusalem Report,* (February 25, 2002); Ma'ariv, (July 31, 2002); Israel Defense Forces.

24 Jewish Telegraphic Agency, (October 8, 2001).

25 CNN, Israel Defense Forces, *Jerusalem Post,* (November 28, 2000); Jewish Telegraphic Agency, (March 21, 2002).

26 *Washington Post,* (June 17, 2001).

27 Letter from George Mitchell and Warren Rudman to ADL Director Abraham Foxman, (May 11, 2001).

28 Briefing by Major General Giora Eiland, Head of the IDF Operation Branch, to the Foreign Press Association, Jerusalem, (May 20, 2001).

29 State Department Briefing, (April 17, 2001).

30 *Time,* (April 19, 2001).

31 Collin Powell, *My American Journey,* (NY: Random House, 1995), p. 434.

32 *Washington Post,* (June 28, 1993).

33 CNN, (July 16, 2002).

34 *Washington Post,* (August 15, 2001).

35 *Al-Watan* (Kuwait), (June 7, 2002).

36 *Jerusalem Post,* (July 21, 2002).

37 Jewish Telegraphic Agency, (June 11, 2002).

38 *Jerusalem Post,* (August 2, 2001).

39 *Washington Post,* (September 14 and 18, 2001).

40 *Fox News,* (August 3, 2001).

41 RonaldReagan.com; *Washington Post* and other news sources.

42 *Jewish Telegraphic Agency,* (August 30, 2001).

43 *Jerusalem Post,* (August 10, 2001).

44 *Jewish Telegraphic Agency,* (November 30, 2001).

45 News Conference, (September 12, 2001).

46 Michael Oren, "Palestinians Cheer Carnage," *Wall Street Journal,* (August 7, 2002).

47 *Jerusalem Post,* (August 24, 2001).

48 *Jerusalem Post,* (April 25, 2002).

49 *Jerusalem Post,* (April 28, 2002); MSNBC, (July 31, 2002).

50 *New York Post,* (May 3, 2002).

51 *New York Times,* (April 20, 2002).

52 *Washington Post,* (April 26, 2002).

53 Israeli Foreign Ministry.

54 *Washington Post,* (January 31, 2002).

55 "Bomb found in Red Crescent Ambulance," *Ha'aretz,* (June 12, 2002).

56 Jewish Telegraphic Agency, (June 30, 2002).

19. Jerusalem

MYTH

"Jerusalem is an Arab City."

FACT

Jews have been living in Jerusalem continuously for nearly two millennia. They have constituted the largest single group of inhabitants there since the 1840's . Jerusalem contains the Western Wall of the Temple Mount, the holiest site in Judaism.

Jerusalem was never the capital of any Arab entity. In fact, it was a backwater for most of Arab history. Jerusalem never served as a provincial capital under Muslim rule nor was it ever a Muslim cultural center. For Jews, the entire city is sacred, but Muslims revere a site — the Dome of the Rock — not the city. "To a Muslim," observed British writer Christopher Sykes, "there is a profound difference between Jerusalem and Mecca or Medina. The latter are holy places containing holy sites." Besides the Dome of the Rock, he noted, Jerusalem has no major Islamic significance.[1]

JERUSALEM'S POPULATION[2]

Year	Jews	Muslims	Christians	Total
1844	7,120	5,000	3,390	15,510
1876	12,000	7,560	5,470	25,030
1896	28,112	8,560	8,748	45,420
1922	33,971	13,411	4,699	52,081
1931	51,222	19,894	19,335	90,451
1948	100,000	40,000	25,000	165,000
1967	195,700	54,963	12,646	263,309
1987	340,000	121,000	14,000	475,000
1990	378,200	131,800	14,400	524,400
2000	530,400	204,100	14,700	758,300

MYTH

"Jerusalem need not be the capital of Israel."

FACT

Ever since King David made Jerusalem the capital of Israel more than 3,000 years ago, the city has played a central role in Jewish existence. The Western

Wall in the Old City — the last remaining wall of the ancient Jewish Temple, the holiest site in Judaism — is the object of Jewish veneration and the focus of Jewish prayer. Three times a day, for thousands of years, Jews have prayed "To Jerusalem, thy city, shall we return with joy," and have repeated the Psalmist's oath: "If I forget thee, O Jerusalem, let my right hand forget her cunning."

Jerusalem "has known only two periods of true greatness, and these have been separated by 2,000 years. Greatness has only happened under Jewish rule," Leon and Jill Uris wrote in *Jerusalem.* "This is so because the Jews have loved her the most, and have remained constant in that love throughout the centuries of their dispersion....It is the longest, deepest love affair in history."[3]

> *For three thousand years, Jerusalem has been the center of Jewish hope and longing. No other city has played such a dominant role in the history, culture, religion and consciousness of a people as has Jerusalem in the life of Jewry and Judaism. Throughout centuries of exile, Jerusalem remained alive in the hearts of Jews everywhere as the focal point of Jewish history, the symbol of ancient glory, spiritual fulfillment and modern renewal. This heart and soul of the Jewish people engenders the thought that if you want one simple word to symbolize all of Jewish history, that word would be "Jerusalem."*
>
> **— Teddy Kollek**[4]

MYTH

"The Arabs were willing to accept the internationalization of Jerusalem. The Jews opposed the idea. Because of their intransigence, Israel illegally occupies the entire city today."

FACT

When the United Nations took up the Palestine question in 1947, it recommended that all of Jerusalem be internationalized. The Vatican and many predominantly Catholic delegations pushed for this status, but a key reason for the UN decision was the Soviet Bloc's desire to embarrass Transjordan's King Abdullah and his British patrons by denying Abdullah control of the city.

The Jewish Agency, after much soul-searching, agreed to accept internationalization in the hope that in the short-run it would protect the city from bloodshed and the new state from conflict. Since the partition resolution called for a referendum on the city's status after 10 years, and Jews comprised a substantial majority, the expectation was that the city would later be incorporated into

Israel. The Arab states were as bitterly opposed to the internationalization of Jerusalem as they were to the rest of the partition plan. [5]

In May 1948, Jordan invaded and occupied East Jerusalem, dividing the city for the first time in its history, and driving thousands of Jews — whose families had lived in the city for centuries — into exile. The UN partition plan, including its proposal that Jerusalem be internationalized, had been overtaken by events.

After the Arab states' rejection of UN Resolution 181 and, on December 11, 1948, UN Resolution 194, establishing the UN Conciliation Commission for Palestine, Prime Minister David Ben-Gurion declared that Israel would no longer accept the internationalization of Jerusalem.

From 1948-67, the city was divided between Israel and Jordan. Israel made western Jerusalem its capital; Jordan occupied the eastern section. Because Jordan — like all the Arab states at the time — maintained a state of war with Israel, the city became, in essence, two armed camps, replete with concrete walls and bunkers, barbed-wire fences, minefields and other military fortifications.

> *"You ought to let the Jews have Jerusalem; it was they who made it famous."*
>
> **— Winston Churchill to diplomat Evelyn Shuckburgh, 1955.**[6]

In 1967, Jordan ignored Israeli pleas to stay out of the Six-Day War and attacked the western part of the city. The Jordanians were routed by Israeli forces and driven out of East Jerusalem, allowing the city's unity to be restored. Teddy Kollek, Jerusalem's mayor for 28 years, called the reunification of the city "the practical realization of the Zionist movement's goals."

Because Israel was defending itself from aggression in the 1948 and 1967 wars, international legal scholar Steven Schwebel wrote, it has a better claim to sovereignty over Jerusalem than its Arab neighbors.[7]

MYTH

"Jordan accepted internationalization."

FACT

Jordan opposed internationalization from the start when it joined the other Arab states in rejecting partition. Jordan's delegate, Fawzi Pasha Malki, bluntly told the UN Ad Hoc Political Committee on December 6, 1949:

> My delegation believes that no form of internationalization...serves any purpose, as the holy places under the protection and control

of my government are safe and secure, without any necessity for a special regime.[8]

When the Trusteeship Council met in Geneva in early 1950 to draw up a new law governing Jerusalem, Jordan refused to permit UN supervision of any kind.[9]

That year, Jordan annexed all the territory it occupied west of the Jordan River, including East Jerusalem. The other Arab countries denied formal recognition of the Jordanian move, and the Arab League considered expelling Jordan from membership. Eventually, a compromise was worked out by which the other Arab governments agreed to view all the West Bank and East Jerusalem as held "in trust" by Jordan for the Palestinians.

MYTH

"From 1948 through 1967, Jordan ensured freedom of worship for all religions in Jerusalem."

FACT

In violation of the 1949 Armistice Agreement, Jordan denied Israelis access to the Western Wall and to the cemetery on the Mount of Olives, where Jews have buried their dead for more than 2,500 years.

Under paragraph eight of the agreement, Jordan and Israel had agreed to establish committees to arrange the resumption of the normal functioning of cultural and humanitarian institutions on Mt. Scopus, and free access to that area; use of the cemetery on the Mount of Olives, and free access to holy places and cultural institutions.

Under Jordanian rule, "Israeli Christians were subjected to various restrictions during their seasonal pilgrimages to their holy places" in Jerusalem, noted Teddy Kollek. "Only limited numbers were grudgingly permitted to briefly visit the Old City and Bethlehem at Christmas and Easter."[10]

In 1955 and 1964, Jordan passed laws imposing strict government control on Christian schools, including restrictions on the opening of new schools, state control over school finances and the appointment of teachers, and the requirement that the Koran be taught. In 1953 and 1965, Jordan adopted laws abrogating the right of Christian religious and charitable institutions to acquire real estate in Jerusalem.

In 1958, police seized the Armenian Patriarch-elect and deported him from Jordan, paving the way for the election of a patriarch supported by King Hussein's government. Because of these repressive policies, many Christians emigrated from Jerusalem. Their numbers declined from 25,000 in 1949 to less than 13,000 in June 1967.[11]

These discriminatory laws were abolished by Israel after the city was reunited in 1967.

MYTH

"Jordan safeguarded Jewish holy places."

FACT

Jordan desecrated Jewish holy places. King Hussein permitted the construction of a road to the Intercontinental Hotel across the Mount of Olives cemetery. Hundreds of Jewish graves were destroyed by a highway that could have easily been built elsewhere. The gravestones, honoring the memory of rabbis and sages, were used by the engineer corps of the Jordanian Arab Legion as pavement and latrines in army camps (inscriptions on the stones were still visible when Israel liberated the city).

The ancient Jewish Quarter of the Old City was ravaged, 58 Jerusalem synagogues — some centuries old — were destroyed or ruined, others were turned into stables and chicken coops. Slum dwellings were built abutting the Western Wall.[12]

MYTH

"Jordan strove to improve conditions in Arab East Jerusalem. By contrast, Israeli authorities bulldozed hundreds of Arab homes in that part of the city, leaving many Arab residents homeless."

FACT

As had been the case under previous Islamic rulers, King Hussein had neglected Jerusalem. After the capture of the Old City in 1967, the scope of his disregard became clear when Israel discovered that much of the city lacked even the most basic municipal services — a steady water supply, plumbing and electricity.[13] As a result of reunification, these and other badly needed municipal services were extended to Arab homes and businesses in East Jerusalem.

Israeli authorities found that hundreds of squatters had made their homes in the Jewish Quarter. Israeli civil engineers cleared the ruins to rebuild the quarter, but only after offering compensation or alternate housing to the squatters.

MYTH

"Under Israeli rule, religious freedom has been curbed in Jerusalem."

FACT

After the 1967 war, Israel abolished all the discriminatory laws promulgated by Jordan and adopted its own tough standard for safeguarding access to religious shrines. "Whoever does anything that is likely to violate the freedom of access of the members of the various religions to the places sacred to them," Israeli law stipulates, is "liable to imprisonment for a term of five years." Israel also entrusted administration of the holy places to their respective religious authorities. Thus, for example, the Muslim Waqf has responsibility for the mosques on the Temple Mount.

Former President Jimmy Carter acknowledged that religious freedom has been enhanced under Israeli rule. There is "no doubt" that Israel did a better job safeguarding access to the city's holy places than did Jordan. "There is unimpeded access today," Carter noted. "There wasn't from 1948-67."[14]

The State Department notes that although Israel has no constitution, the law provides for freedom of worship, and the Government respects this right.[15]

MYTH

"Israel denies Muslims and Christians free access to their holy sites."

FACT

Since 1967, hundreds of thousands of Muslims and Christians — many from Arab countries that remain in a state of war with Israel — have come to Jerusalem to see their holy places. Arab leaders are free to visit Jerusalem to pray if they wish to, just as Egyptian President Anwar Sadat did at the al-Aksa mosque. For security reasons, restrictions are sometimes imposed on the Temple Mount temporarily, but the right to worship is not abridged and other mosques remain accessible even in times of high tension.

According to Islam, the prophet Muhammad was miraculously transported from Mecca to Jerusalem, and it was from there that he made his ascent to heaven. The Dome of the Rock and the al-Aksa Mosque, both built in the seventh century, made definitive the identification of Jerusalem as the "Remote Place" that is mentioned in the Koran, and thus a holy place after Mecca and Medina. Muslim rights on the Temple Mount, the site of the two shrines, have not been infringed. Although it is the holiest site in Judaism, Israel has left the Temple Mount under the control of Muslim religious authorities.

For Christians, Jerusalem is the place where Jesus lived, preached, died and was resurrected. While it is the heavenly rather than the earthly Jerusalem that is emphasized by the Church, places mentioned in the New Testament as the sites of Jesus' ministry have drawn pilgrims and devoted worshipers for centuries. Among these sites are the Church of the Holy Sepulcher, the Garden of Gethsemane, the site of the Last Supper, and the Via Dolorosa with the fourteen Stations of the Cross.

The rights of the various Christian churches to custody of the Christian holy places in Jerusalem were defined in the course of the nineteenth century, when Jerusalem was part of the Ottoman Empire. Known as the "status quo arrangement for the Christian holy places in Jerusalem," these rights remained in force during the period of the British Mandate and are still upheld today in Israel.

MYTH

"Israeli policy encourages attacks by Jewish fanatics against Muslim and Christian residents and their holy sites."

FACT

Israeli authorities have consistently attempted to stop fanatics — of all faiths — from desecrating religious sites or committing acts of violence near them. When it has been unable to stop such acts from occurring, Israel has severely punished the perpetrators. Allen Goodman, a deranged Israeli who in 1982 went on a shooting rampage on the Temple Mount, for example, was sentenced to life imprisonment.

In 1984, Israeli authorities infiltrated a Jewish group that planned acts of violence against non-Jewish sites and civilians. The terrorists were tried and imprisoned.

In 1990, the Temple Mount Faithful, a Jewish extremist group, sought to march to the Temple Mount on Sukkot to lay the cornerstone for the Third Temple. The police, worried that such a march would anger Muslims and exacerbate an already tense situation created by the intifada and events in the Persian Gulf, denied them the right to march. That decision was upheld by the Israeli Supreme Court, a fact communicated immediately to Muslim religious leaders and the Arab press. Despite Israel's preemptive action, "Muslim leaders and intifada activists persisted in inciting their faithful to confrontation."[16] As a result, a tragic riot ensued in which 17 Arabs were killed.

Since that time, Israel has been especially vigilant, and done everything possible to prevent any provocation by groups or individuals that might threaten the sanctity of the holy places of any faith.

MYTH

"Israel has restricted the political rights of Palestinian Arabs in Jerusalem."

FACT

Along with religious freedom, Palestinian Arabs in Jerusalem have unprecedented political rights. Arab residents were given the choice of whether to become Israeli citizens. Most chose to retain their Jordanian citizenship. Moreover, regardless of whether they are citizens, Jerusalem Arabs are permitted to vote in municipal elections and play a role in the administration of the city.

MYTH

"Under UN Resolution 242, East Jerusalem is considered 'occupied territory.' Israel's annexation of Jerusalem therefore violates the UN resolution."

FACT

One drafter of the UN Resolution was then-U.S. Ambassador to the UN Arthur Goldberg. According to Goldberg, "Resolution 242 in no way refers to Jerusalem, and this omission was deliberate....Jerusalem was a discrete matter, not linked to the West Bank." In several speeches at the UN in 1967, Goldberg said: "I repeatedly stated that the armistice lines of 1948 were intended to be temporary. This, of course, was particularly true of Jerusalem. At no time in these many speeches did I refer to East Jerusalem as occupied territory."[17]

After 1948, the UN General Assembly voted on three resolutions calling for the internationalization of Jerusalem. The matter was dropped until Israel gained control of the city. Since 1967, the UN, which for 19 years ignored Jordan's occupation of the city, has adopted numerous resolutions criticizing Israel for altering the status of Jerusalem.

> *"The basis of our position remains that Jerusalem must never again be a divided city. We did not approve of the status quo before 1967; in no way do we advocate a return to it now."*
>
> **— President George Bush**[18]

MYTH

"East Jerusalem should be part of a Palestinian state because all its residents are Palestinian Arabs and no Jews have ever lived there."

FACT

Before 1865, the entire population of Jerusalem lived behind the Old City walls (what today would be considered part of the eastern part of the city). Later, the city began to expand beyond the walls because of population growth, and both Jews and Arabs began to build in new areas of the city.

By the time of partition, a thriving Jewish community was living in the eastern part of Jerusalem, an area that included the Jewish Quarter of the Old City. This area of the city also contains many sites of importance to the Jewish religion, including the City of David, the Temple Mount and the Western Wall. In addition, major institutions like Hebrew University and the original Hadassah Hospital are on Mount Scopus — in eastern Jerusalem.

The only time that the eastern part of Jerusalem was exclusively Arab was between 1949 and 1967, and that was because Jordan occupied the area and forcibly expelled all the Jews.

MYTH

"The United States does not believe Jerusalem should be the united capital of Israel."

FACT

Only two countries have embassies in Jerusalem – Costa Rica and El Salvador. Of the 180 nations with which America has diplomatic relations, Israel is the only one whose capital is not recognized by the U.S. government. The U.S. embassy, like most others, is in Tel Aviv, 40 miles from Jerusalem. The United States does maintain a consulate in East Jerusalem, however, that deals with Palestinians in the territories and works independently of the embassy, reporting directly to Washington. Today, then, we have the anomaly that American diplomats refuse to meet with Israelis in their capital because Jerusalem's status is negotiable, but make their contacts with Palestinians in the city.

In 1990, Congress passed a resolution declaring that "Jerusalem is and should remain the capital of the State of Israel" and "must remain an undivided city in which the rights of every ethnic and religious group are protected." During the 1992 Presidential campaign, Bill Clinton said: "I recognize Jerusalem as an undivided city, the eternal capital of Israel, and I believe in the principle of moving our embassy to Jerusalem." He never reiterated this view as President; consequently, official U.S. policy remained that the status of Jerusalem is a matter for negotiations.

In an effort to change this policy, Congress overwhelmingly passed The Jerusalem Embassy Act of 1995. This landmark bill declared that, as a statement of official U.S. policy, Jerusalem should be recognized as the undivided, eternal capital of Israel and required that the U.S. embassy in Israel be established in Jerusalem no later than May 1999. The law also included a waiver that allowed the President to essentially ignore the legislation if he deemed doing so to be in the best interest of the United States. President Clinton exercised that option.

During the 2000 presidential campaign George W. Bush promised that as President he would immediately "begin the process of moving the United States ambassador to the city Israel has chosen as its capital."[19] In June 2001, however, Bush followed Clinton's precedent and used the presidential waiver to prevent the embassy from being moved.

While critics of Congressional efforts to force the administration to recognize Jerusalem as Israel's capital insist that such a move would harm the peace process, supporters of the legislation argue the opposite is true. By making clear the United States position that Jerusalem should remain unified under Israeli sovereignty, they say, unrealistic Palestinian expectations regarding the city can be moderated and thereby enhance the prospects for a final agreement.

MYTH

"The Temple Mount has always been a Muslim holy place and Judaism has no connection to the site."

FACT

During the 2000 Camp David Summit, Yasser Arafat said that no Jewish Temple ever existed on the Temple Mount.[20] A year later, the Palestinian Authority-appointed Mufti of Jerusalem, Ikrima Sabri, told the German publication *Die Welt*, "There is not [even] the smallest indication of the existence of a Jewish temple on this place in the past. In the whole city, there is not even a single stone indicating Jewish history.

"These views are contradicted by a book entitled *A Brief Guide to al-Haram al-Sharif*, published by the Supreme Moslem Council in 1930. The Council, the supreme Moslem body in Jerusalem during the British Mandate, said in the guide that the Temple Mount site "is one of the oldest in the world. Its sanctity dates from the earliest times. Its identity with the site of Solomon's Temple is beyond dispute. This, too, is the spot, according to universal belief, on which David built there an altar unto the Lord, and offered burnt offerings and peace offerings."

In a description of the area of Solomon's Stables, which Islamic Waqf officials converted into a new mosque in 1996, the guide states: "...little is known for certain about the early history of the chamber itself. It dates probably as far back as the construction of Solomon's Temple... According to Josephus, it was in existence and was used as a place of refuge by the Jews at the time of the conquest of Jerusalem by Titus in the year 70 A.D."[21]

More authoritatively, the Koran – the holy book of Islam – describes Solomon's construction of the First Temple (34:13) and recounts the destruction of the First and Second temples (17:7).

The Jewish connection to the Temple Mount dates back more than 3,000 years and is rooted in tradition and history. When Abraham bound his son Isaac upon an altar as a sacrifice to God, he is believed to have done so atop Mount Moriah, today's Temple Mount. The First Temple's Holy of Holies contained the original Ark of the Covenant, and both the First and Second Temples were the centers of Jewish religious and social life until the Second Temple's destruction by the Romans. After the destruction of the Second Temple, control of the Temple Mount passed through several conquering powers. It was during the early period of Muslim control that the Dome of the Rock was built on the site of the ancient temples.

"I would be blind to disclaim the Jewish connection to Jerusalem."
— Sari Nusseibeh, the PA's representative in Jerusalem[22]

MYTH

"Israel should not be allowed to control the Temple Mount because it denies Muslims access to their holy places."

FACT

Israel has shared the Temple Mount since 1967, when Defense Minister Moshe Dayan, upon reuniting Jerusalem, permitted the Islamic authority, the Waqf, to continue its civil authority on the Temple Mount. The Waqf oversees all day-to-day activity there. An Israeli presence is in place at the entrance to the Temple Mount to ensure access for people of all religions.

The only times Israel has prevented any Muslims from going to the Temple Mount were during periods of high tension when the threat of violence necessitated restrictions on the entrance into the area. These measures were taken to protect worshippers of all faiths and the shrines in the Old City. They usually have lasted only for a day or two.

MYTH

"The Palestinians have been careful to preserve the archaeological relics of the Temple Mount."

FACT

Though it has refused to recognize Israeli sovereignty over the Temple Mount, the Waqf cooperated with Israeli inspectors when conducting work on the holy site. After the 1993 Oslo accords, however, the Jordanian-controlled Waqf was replaced with representatives beholden to the Palestinian Authority. Following the riots that accompanied Israel's decision to open an exit from the Western Wall tunnel, the Waqf ceased cooperating with Israel.

The Waqf has subsequently prevented Israeli inspectors from overseeing work done on the Mount that is believed to be causing irreparable damage to archaeological remains from the First and Second Temple periods. Israeli archaeologists charge that during extensive construction work, thousands of tons of gravel –– which could contain important relics –– have been removed from the Mount and discarded in the trash. Experts say that even if artifacts are not destroyed they will be rendered archaeologically useless because the Palestinian construction workers are mixing finds from diverse periods when they scoop up earth with bulldozers.[23]

Given the sensitivity of the Temple Mount, and the tensions already existing between Israelis and Palestinians over Jerusalem, the Israeli government has not interfered in the Waqf's activities. Meanwhile, the destruction of the past continues.

MYTH

"When Israel excavated the Western Wall tunnel, it threatened the integrity of the Temple Mount and al-Aksa Mosque, and was therefore condemned by the UN Security Council."

FACT

The best known part of the remaining Herodian Temple Mount constructions is the traditional Jewish prayer area of the Western Wall, which has stood exposed, above ground level, for two thousand years. The capture of the Old City in the Six-Day War provided an opportunity to explore along the continuation of the Western Wall from the prayer plaza northwards. Long sections of the southern wall of the Temple Mount and its southwestern corner were exposed during the 1970s, furnishing a comprehensive picture of the monumental Herodian walls surrounding the Temple Mount and the vast, planned areas of public construction outside them.

A tunnel allows pedestrians to walk on 2000-year-old stones along one of the oldest subterranean paths in Jerusalem, beginning at the Western Wall plaza and ending at the Via Dolorosa. For years, Israel kept the exit closed to avoid provoking Palestinians already angered by the excavation. This forced visitors to the tunnel to return the same way they entered, sometimes literally having to turn sideways and squeeze past people moving in the other direction.

In September 1996, Prime Minister Benjamin Netanyahu decided to open the exit. It was done late at night to minimize the prospect for violence, but gave the impression he was doing something underhanded. The Palestinians (and Muslims elsewhere) saw the move as a provocative violation of the peace accords and part of an Israeli campaign to undermine Muslim holy sites. Palestinians rioted in reaction to the Israeli action.

The UN Security Council adopted Resolution 1093 after the Saudi representative complained about Israel opening a tunnel "in the vicinity of al-Aksa mosque." In fact, the tunnel is an archeological site that has nothing to do with the mosque. The restoration of the Western Wall tunnel was undertaken as part of an ongoing effort by Israel to reveal major archeological finds in Jerusalem and to improve the tourism infrastructure in the Old City.

The tunnel was re-excavated under the supervision of archaeologists and engineers. No archeological or religious sites were damaged in its construction. The tunnel does not run underneath the Temple Mount and its restoration did not endanger any buildings or other structures in the Old City. No private property was expropriated, condemned or otherwise confiscated to accomplish this project.

Moreover, the restoration of the tunnel did not violate the Interim Agreement between Israel and the Palestinians as archeological restorations in Jerusalem are not covered by the document.

The controversy eventually died down and today the tunnel may be visited by tourists. By opening the exit, tourists have easier access to the Via Dolorosa from the Western Wall plaza, which, coincidentally, benefits merchants in the Muslim Quarter where the visitors depart.

MYTH

"Internationalization is the best solution to resolve the conflicting claims over Jerusalem."

FACT

The seeming intractability of resolving the conflicting claims to Jerusalem has led some people to resurrect the idea of internationalizing the city. Ironically, the idea had little support during the 19 years Jordan controlled the Old City and barred Jews and Israeli Muslims from their holy sites.

The fact that Jerusalem is disputed, or that it is of importance to people other than Israeli Jews, does not mean the city belongs to others or should be ruled by some international regime. There is no precedent for such a setup. The closest thing to an international city was post-war Berlin when the four powers shared control of the city and that experiment proved to be a disaster.

Even if Israel were amenable to such an idea, what conceivable international group could be entrusted to protect the freedoms Israel already guarantees? Surely not the United Nations, which has shown no understanding of Israeli concerns since partition. Israel can count only on the support of the United States, and it is only in the UN Security Council that an American veto can protect Israel from political mischief by other nations.

MYTH

"Israel tried to burn down the al-Aksa mosque in 1969."

FACT

The readiness of Arab leaders to employ falsehood in their propaganda was demonstrated when Nasser and other leaders called for a Holy War against Israel when an arsonist set fire to the al-Aksa Mosque in August 1969. The guilty party was an Australian Christian tourist, Michael Rohan, who confessed to the crime. The accused was tried and found to be mentally ill.

Notes

1   *Encounter,* (February 1968).

2   John Oesterreicher and Anne Sinai, eds., *Jerusalem,* (NY: John Day, 1974), p. 1; Israel Central Bureau of Statistics; Jerusalem Foundation; Municipality of Jerusalem. The figures for 2000 include 9,000 with no religion classified.

3   Leon and Jill Uris, *Jerusalem,* (New York: Doubleday and Company, 1981), p. 13.

4   Teddy Kollek, *Jerusalem,* (DC: Washington Institute For Near East Policy, 1990), pp. 19-20.

5   Kollek, p. 20-24

6   Sir Eveyln Shuckburgh, *Descent to Suez; Diaries 1951-56,* (London, 1986).

7   *American Journal of International Law,* (April 1970), pp. 346-47.

8   *New York Times,* (December 7, 1949).

9   Special Report of the Trusteeship Council, (June 14, 1950).

10 Kollek, p. 15.

11 Kollek, p. 16.

12 Kollek, p. 15.

13 Meron Benvenisti, *Jerusalem, The Torn City,* (MN: University of Minnesota Press, 1976), pp. 44, 60-61.

14 *Near East Report,* (April 2, 1990).

15 U.S. Department of State, "2001 Annual Report on International Religious Freedom," Released by the Bureau for Democracy, Human Rights, and Labor, (Washington, D.C., December, 2001).

16 Kollek, p. 62.

17 *New York Times,* (March 12, 1980).

18 Letter from President George Bush to Jerusalem Mayor Teddy Kollek, (March 20, 1990).

19 Speech to AIPAC Policy Conference, (May 22, 2000).

20 Interview with Dennis Ross, Fox News Sunday, April 21, 2002.

21 *Jerusalem Post,* (January 26, 2001).

22 *Jerusalem Post,* (November 12, 2001).

23 Jewish Telegraphic Agency, (February 12, 2001).

20. U.S. Middle East Policy

MYTH

"The creation of Israel resulted solely from U.S. pressure."

FACT

When the UN took up the question of Palestine, President Harry Truman explicitly said the United States should not "use threats or improper pressure of any kind on other delegations."[1] Some pressure was nevertheless exerted and the U.S. played a key role in securing support for the partition resolution. U.S. influence was limited, however, as became clear when American dependents like Cuba and Greece voted against partition, and El Salvador and Honduras abstained.

Many members of the Truman Administration opposed partition, including Defense Secretary James Forrestal, who believed Zionist aims posed a threat to American oil supplies and its strategic position in the region. The Joint Chiefs of Staff worried that the Arabs might align themselves with the Soviets if they were alienated by the West. These internal opponents did a great deal to undermine U.S. support for the establishment of a Jewish state.[2]

Although much has been written about the tactics of the supporters of partition, the behavior of the Arab states has been largely ignored. They were, in fact, actively engaged in arm-twisting of their own at the UN trying to scuttle partition.[3]

MYTH

"The United States favored Israel over the Arabs in 1948 because of the pressures of the Jewish lobby."

FACT

Truman supported the Zionist movement because he believed the international community was obligated to fulfill the promise of the Balfour Declaration and because he believed it was the humanitarian thing to do to ameliorate the plight of the Jewish survivors of the Holocaust. He did not believe the rights of the Arabs should or would be compromised. A sense of his attitude can be gleaned from a remark he made with regard to negotiations as to the boundaries of a Jewish state:

> The whole region waits to be developed, and if it were handled the way we developed the Tennessee River basin, it could support from 20 to 30 million people more. To open the door to this kind of future would indeed be the constructive and humanitarian thing to do, and it would also redeem the pledges that were given at the time of World War I.[4]

The American public supported the President's policy. According to public opinion polls, 65 percent of Americans supported the creation of a Jewish state. During the third quarter of 1947 alone, 62,850 postcards, 1,100 letters and 1,400 telegrams flooded the White House, most urging the President to use American influence at the UN.[5]

This public support was reflected in Congress where a resolution approving the Balfour Declaration was adopted in 1922. In 1944, both national parties called for the restoration of the Jewish Commonwealth and, in 1945, a similar resolution was adopted by Congress.

Rather than giving in to pressure, Truman tended to react negatively to the "Jewish lobby." He complained repeatedly about being pressured and talked about putting propaganda from the Jews in a pile and striking a match to it. In a letter to Rep. Claude Pepper, Truman wrote: "Had it not been for the unwarranted interference of the Zionists, we would have had the matter settled a year and a half ago."[6] This was hardly the attitude of a politician overly concerned with Jewish votes.

MYTH

"Most Americans oppose a close U.S. relationship with Israel."

FACT

Support for Israel is not restricted to the Jewish community. Americans of all ages, races and religions sympathize with Israel. This support is also non-partisan, with a majority of Democrats and Republicans consistently favoring Israel by large margins over the Arabs.

The best indication of Americans' attitude toward Israel is found in the response to the most consistently asked question about the Middle East: "In the Middle East situation, are your sympathies more with Israel or with the Arab nations?" The organization that has conducted the most surveys is Gallup. Support for Israel in Gallup Polls has remained consistently around the 50 percent mark since 1967.

In 63 Gallup polls, going back to 1967, Israel has had the support of an average of 46 percent of the American people compared to just over 12 percent for the Arab states/Palestinians. Americans have slightly more sympathy for the Palestinians than for the Arab states, but the results of polls asking respondents to choose between Israel and the Palestinians have not differed significantly from the other surveys.

Some people have the misperception that sympathy for Israel was once much higher, but the truth is that before the Gulf War the peak had been 56 percent, reached just after the Six-Day War. In January 1991, sympathy for Israel reached a record high of 64 percent, according to Gallup. Meanwhile, support for the Arabs dropped to 8 percent and the margin was a record 56 points.

The most recent poll, reported by Gallup in June 2002, found that sympathy for Israel was 49 percent compared to only 14 percent for the Palestinians. Most respondents do not believe the United States should take a side in the conflict, but those who do pick a side choose Israel by a 10 to 1 margin (Gallup, April 2002). More than three-fourths of Americans also believe Palestinian-Israeli peace is somewhat or very important to the United States.

Polls also indicate the public views Israel as a reliable U.S. ally, a feeling that grew stronger during the Gulf crisis. A January 1991 Harris Poll, for example, found that 86 percent of Americans consider Israel a "close ally" or "friendly." This was the highest level ever recorded in a Harris Poll. As recently as May 2002, an ADL poll found that 64 percent of Americans agreed that "Israel can be counted on as a loyal ally."

MYTH

"U.S. policy has always been hostile toward the Arabs."

FACT

Arabs rarely acknowledge the American role in helping the Arab states achieve independence. President Wilson's stand for self-determination for all nations, and the U.S. entry into World War I, helped cause the dissolution of the Ottoman Empire and stimulate the move toward independence in the Arab world.

The Arabs have always asserted that Middle East policy must be a zero-sum game whereby support for their enemy, Israel, necessarily puts them at a disadvantage. Thus, Arab states have tried to force the United States to choose between support for them or Israel. The U.S. has usually refused to fall into this trap. The fact that the U.S. has a close alliance with Israel while maintaining good relations with several Arab states is proof the two are not incompatible.

The U.S. has long sought friendly relations with Arab leaders and has, at one time or another, been on good terms with most Arab states. In the 1930s, the discovery of oil led U.S. companies to become closely involved with the Gulf Arabs. In the 1950s, U.S. strategic objectives stimulated an effort to form an alliance with pro-Western Arab states. Countries like Iraq and Libya were friends of the U.S. before radical leaders took over those governments. Egypt, which was hostile toward the U.S. under Nasser, shifted to the pro-Western camp under Sadat.

Since World War II, the U.S. has poured economic and military assistance into the region and today is the principal backer of nations like Jordan, Saudi Arabia, Morocco, Egypt and the Gulf sheikdoms. Although the Arab states blamed the U.S. for their defeats in wars they initiated with Israel, the truth is most of the belligerents had either been given or offered American assistance at some time.

On occasion, the U.S. has appeared to condone Arab aggression against other Arabs. In 1963, for example, the U.S. recognized the puppet regime set up by the Egyptians in Yemen. In 1991, while rolling back Saddam Hussein's aggression in the Gulf, the Bush Administration looked the other way while Syria completed its virtual annexation of Lebanon.

Whereas Israel has only been able to rely on the United States for assistance, the Arab states could always count on a variety of Western countries as well as the Soviet Union and its allies.

> *"The allied nations with the fullest concurrence of our government and people are agreed that in Palestine shall be laid the foundations of a Jewish Commonwealth."*
>
> **— President Woodrow Wilson, March 3, 1919**[7]

MYTH
"The United States has supported Israel automatically ever since 1948."

FACT

The United States has been Israel's closest ally throughout its history; nevertheless, the U.S. has acted against the Jewish State's wishes many times.

The U.S. effort to balance support for Israel with placating the Arabs began in 1948 when Truman showed signs of wavering on partition and advocating trusteeship. After the surrounding Arab states invaded Israel, the U.S. maintained an arms embargo that severely restricted the Jews' ability to defend themselves.

Ever since the 1948 war, the U.S. has been unwilling to insist on projects to resettle Arab refugees. The U.S. has also been reluctant to challenge Arab violations of the UN Charter and resolutions. Thus, for example, the Arabs were permitted to get away with blockading the Suez Canal, imposing a boycott on Israel and committing acts of terrorism. In fact, the U.S. has taken positions *against* Israel at the UN more often than not, and did not use its Security Council veto to block an anti-Israel resolution until 1972.

Perhaps the most dramatic example of American policy diverging from that of Israel came during the Suez War when President Eisenhower took a strong stand against Britain, France and Israel. After the war, U.S. pressure forced Israel to withdraw from the territory it conquered. David Ben-Gurion relied on dubious American guarantees that sowed the seeds of the 1967 conflict.

At various other times, American Presidents have taken action against Israel. In 1981, for example, Ronald Reagan suspended a strategic cooperation agreement after Israel annexed the Golan Heights. On another occasion, he held up delivery of fighter planes because of unhappiness over an Israeli raid in Lebanon.

In 1991, President Bush held a press conference to ask for a delay in considering Israel's request for loan guarantees to help absorb Soviet and Ethiopian Jews because of his disagreement with Israel's settlement policy. In staking his prestige on the delay, Bush used intemperate language that inflamed passions and provoked concern in the Jewish community that anti-Semitism would be aroused.

Though often described as the most pro-Israel President in history, Bill Clinton also was critical of Israel on numerous occasions. George W. Bush's administration has also shown no reluctance to criticize Israel for actions it deems contrary to U.S. interests, but has generally been more reserved in its public statements.

MYTH
"The U.S. has always given Israel arms to insure it would have a qualitative edge over the Arabs."

FACT
The United States provided only a limited amount of arms to Israel, including ammunition and recoilless rifles, prior to 1962. In that year, President Kennedy sold HAWK anti-aircraft missiles, but only after the Soviet Union provided Egypt with long-range bombers.

By 1965, the U.S. had become Israel's main arms supplier. This was partially necessitated by West Germany's acquiescence to Arab pressure, which led it to stop selling tanks to Israel. Throughout most of the Johnson Administration, however, the sale of arms to Israel was balanced by corresponding transfers to the Arabs. Thus, the first U.S. tank sale to Israel, in 1965, was offset by a similar sale to Jordan.[8]

The U.S. did not provide Israel with aircraft until 1966. Even then, secret agreements were made to provide the same planes to Morocco and Libya, and additional military equipment was sent to Lebanon, Saudi Arabia and Tunisia.[9]

As in 1948, the U.S. imposed an arms embargo on Israel during the Six-Day War, while the Arabs continued to receive Soviet arms. Israel's position was further undermined by the French decision to embargo arms transfers to the Jewish State, effectively ending their role as Israel's only other major supplier.

It was only after it became clear that Israel had no other sources of arms, and that the Soviet Union had no interest in limiting its sales to the region, that President Johnson agreed to sell Israel Phantom jets that gave the Jewish State its first qualitative advantage. "We will henceforth become the principal arms supplier to Israel," Assistant Secretary of Defense Paul Warnke told Israeli Ambassador Yitzhak Rabin, "involving us even more intimately with Israel's security situation and involving more directly the security of the United States."[10]

From that point on, the U.S. began to pursue a policy whereby Israel's qualitative edge was maintained. The U.S. has also remained committed, however, to arming Arab nations, providing sophisticated missiles, tanks and aircraft to Jordan, Morocco, Egypt, Saudi Arabia and the Gulf states. Thus, when Israel received F-15s in 1978, so did Saudi Arabia (Egypt received F-5Es.) In 1981, Saudi Arabia, for the first time, received a weapons system that gave it a qualitative advantage over Israel — AWACS radar planes.

Today, Israel buys near top-of-the-line U.S. equipment, but many Arab states also receive some of America's best tanks, planes and missiles. The qualitative edge may be intact, but it is undoubtedly narrow.

> "Our society is illuminated by the spiritual insights of the Hebrew prophets. America and Israel have a common love of human freedom, and they have a common faith in a democratic way of life.."
>
> **— President Lyndon Johnson**[11]

MYTH
"U.S. aid in the Middle East has always been one-sided, with the Arabs getting practically nothing."

FACT
After Israel's victory in its War of Independence, the U.S. responded to an appeal for economic aid to help absorb immigrants by approving a $135 million Export-Import Bank loan and the sale of surplus commodities. In those early years of Israel's statehood (also today), U.S. aid was seen as a means of promoting peace.

In 1951, Congress voted to help Israel cope with the economic burdens imposed by the influx of Jewish refugees from the displaced persons camps in Europe and from the ghettos of the Arab countries. Arabs then complained the U.S. was neglecting them, though they had no interest in or use for American aid then. In 1951, Syria rejected offers of U.S. aid. Oil-rich Iraq and Saudi Arabia did not need U.S. economic assistance, and Jordan was, until the late 1950s, the ward of Great Britain. After 1957, when the United States assumed responsibility for supporting Jordan and resumed economic aid to Egypt, assistance to the Arab states soared. Also, the United States was by far the biggest contributor of aid to the Palestinians through UNRWA, a status that continues to the present.

Israel has received more direct aid from the United States since World War II than any other country, but the amounts for the first half of this period were relatively small. Between 1949 and 1973, the U.S. provided Israel with an average of about $122 million a year, a total of $3.1 billion (and actually more than $1 billion of that was loans for military equipment in 1971-73) . Prior to 1971, Israel received a total of only $277 million in military aid, all in the form of loans as credit sales. The bulk of the economic aid was also lent to Israel. By comparison, the Arab states received nearly three times as much aid before 1971, $4.4 billion, or $170 million per year. Moreover, unlike Israel, which receives nearly all its aid from the United States, Arab nations have gotten assistance from Asia, Eastern Europe, the Soviet Union and the European Community.

> *"It is my responsibility to see that our policy in Israel fits in with our policy throughout the world; second, it is my desire to help build in Palestine a strong, prosperous, free and independent democratic state. It must be large enough, free enough, and strong enough to make its people self-supporting and secure."*
>
> **— President Truman**[12]

Israel did not begin to receive large amounts of assistance until 1974, following the 1973 war, and the sums increased dramatically after the Camp David agreements. Altogether, since 1949, Israel has received more than $90 billion in assistance. Though the totals are impressive, the value of assistance to Israel has been eroded by inflation.

Arab states that have signed agreements with Israel have also been rewarded. Since signing the peace treaty with Israel, Egypt has been the second largest recipient of U.S. foreign aid ($2 billion in 2002, Israel received $2.8 billion). Jordan has also been the beneficiary of higher levels of aid since it signed a treaty with Israel (increasing from less than $40 million to more than $225 million). The multibillion dollar debts to the U.S. of both Arab nations were also forgiven.

After the Oslo agreements, the United States also began providing funding to the Palestinians. It now provides $80 million in humanitarian assistance via the U.S. Agency for International Development. It provides no direct aid to the Palestinian Authority because it is viewed as corrupt. President Bush specifically warned the Palestinians that they must change their leadership and embrace reform to obtain future assistance. "I can assure you," Bush said, "we won't be putting money into a society which is not transparent and [is] corrupt."[13]

MYTH

"The U.S. has always given Israel billions of dollars without expecting repayment."

FACT

U.S. economic grants to Israel ended in 1959. U.S. aid to Israel from then until 1985 consisted largely of loans, which Israel repaid, and surplus commodities, which Israel bought. Israel began buying arms from the United States in 1962, but did not receive any grant military assistance until after the 1973 Yom Kippur War. As a result, Israel had to go deeply into debt to finance its economic development and arms procurement. The decision to convert military aid to grants that year was based on the prevailing view in Congress that without a strong Israel, war in the Middle East was more likely, and that the U.S. would face higher direct expenditures in such an eventuality.

For several years, most of Israel's economic aid went to pay off old debts. In 1984, foreign aid legislation included the Cranston Amendment (named after its Senate sponsor), which said the U.S. would provide Israel with economic assistance "not less than" the amount Israel owes the United States in annual debt service payments.

MYTH

"Israel continues to demand large amounts of economic aid even though it is now a rich country that no longer needs help."

FACT

Starting with fiscal year 1987, Israel annually received $1.2 billion in all grant economic aid and $1.8 billion in all grant military assistance. In 1998, Israel offered to voluntarily reduce its dependence on U.S. economic aid. According to an agreement reached with the Clinton Administration and Congress, the $1.2 billion economic aid package will be reduced by $120 million each year so that it will be phased out over ten years.

Half of the annual savings in economic assistance each year ($60 million) will be added to Israel's military aid package in recognition of its increased security needs. In 2001, Israel received $840 million in economic aid and $1.98 billion in military aid. In 2002, economic aid was reduced to $720 million and military aid to Israel was budgeted at $2.04 billion.

Israel made the offer because it does not have the same need for assistance it once did. The foundation of Israel's economy today is strong; still, Israel remains saddled with past debts to the U.S., which, unlike those of Jordan and Egypt, were not forgiven. In addition, Israel still can use American help. The country still has the tremendous financial burden of absorbing tens of thousands of immigrants from the former Soviet Union, a very high rate of unemployment and an alarmingly high number of people who fall below the poverty line. The situation was further exacerbated by the violence of the last two years, which has devastated the tourist industry and all related service sectors of the economy. Furthermore, concessions made in peace negotiations have required the dismantling of military bases and the loss of valuable resources that must be replaced.

MYTH

"Israel boasts that it is the fourth strongest nation in the world, so it certainly doesn't need U.S. military assistance."

FACT

Israel has peace treaties with only two of its neighbors. It remains technically at war with the rest of the Arab/Islamic world and several countries, notably Iran and Iraq, are openly hostile. Given the potential threats, it is a necessity that Israel continue to maintain a strong defense. Israel is a powerful country, but as the arms balance chart in the appendix indicates, it is still outmanned and outgunned by its enemies, and therefore must rely on its qualitative advantage to insure it can defeat its enemies, and that can only be guaranteed by the continued purchase of the latest weapons. New tanks, missiles and planes carry high price tags, however, and Israel cannot afford what it needs on its own, so continued aid from the United States is vital to its security. Furthermore, Israel's enemies have numerous suppliers, but Israel must rely almost entirely on the United States for its hardware.

MYTH

"U.S. military aid subsidizes Israeli defense contractors at the expense of American industry."

FACT

Contrary to popular wisdom, the United States does not simply write billion dollar checks and hand them over to Israel to spend as they like. Only about 26 percent of what Israel receives in Foreign Military Financing (FMF) can be spent in Israel for military procurement. The remaining 74 percent is spent in the United States to generate profits and jobs. More than 1,000 companies in 47 states, the District of Columbia and Puerto Rico have signed contracts worth billions of dollars through this program over the last several years. The figures for 2001 are below:

The Value of Foreign Military Financing (FMF) Orders by State[14]

Alabama	$ 15,010,584	Montana	$30,350
Arkansas	$ 496,212	North Carolina	$38, 944,632
Arizona	$ 23,053,020	Nebraska	$3,654
California	$ 155,969,600	New Hampshire	$17,254,145
Colorado	$ 33,864,588	New Jersey	$52,750,873
Connecticut	$ 510,697,156	New Mexico	$55,554
D.C.	$3,609,508	Nevada	$1,043,287
Delaware	$367,011	New York	$110,854,412
Florida	$94,222,258	Ohio	$42,646,748
Georgia	$158,911,735	Oklahoma	$132,572
Iowa	$4,830	Oregon	$5,512,292
Idaho	$151,977	Pennsylvania	$11,478,193
Illinois	$57,492,657	Rhode Island	$841,354
Indiana	$46,200,627	South Carolina	$4,598,444
Kansas	$91,328	South Dakota	$ 4,893,179
Kentucky	$1,539,095	Tennessee	$7,752,077
Louisiana	$145,824	Texas	$62,854,229
Massachusetts	$25,080,078	Utah	$257,378
Maryland	$62,805,516	Virginia	$28,575,976
Maine	$33,201,400	Vermont	$2,062,222
Michigan	$67,447,234	Washington	$3,844,029
Minnesota	$10,886,633	Wisconsin	$6,407,070
Missouri	$1,927,615	West Virginia	$73,746
Mississippi	$2,571,630	Wyoming	$14,500

MYTH

"U.S. loan guarantees provided Israel with billions of dollars from American taxpayers that was used to build settlements in the West Bank and Gaza Strip to house Soviet Jews."

FACT

Since 1989, approximately one million Jews have immigrated to Israel. The majority, roughly 80 percent, has come from the former Soviet Union. Israel must provide these immigrants with food, shelter, employment and training. The task is even more challenging when it comes to absorbing Jews from relatively undeveloped countries such as Ethiopia, who often must be taught everything from using a flush toilet to how to withdraw money from a bank. To meet these challenges, Israel has invested billions of dollars. In addition, the American Jewish community has contributed hundreds of millions of dollars through various philanthropies.

Still, the task was so daunting, Israel turned to the United States for help. To put the challenge in perspective, consider that the United States – a country of 250 million people and a multi-trillion dollar GNP – admits roughly 125,000 refugees a year. In 1990 alone, 185,000 Jews immigrated to Israel.

The United States led the Free World in helping secure the freedom of Soviet Jews. Beginning in 1972, Congress appropriated funds to help resettle Soviet Jews in Israel. Since 1992, $80 million has been earmarked for this purpose.

After the Soviet Union opened its gates, the trickle of immigrants became a flood, skyrocketing from fewer than 13,000 people in 1989 to more than 185,000 in 1990. Israel then asked for a different type of help. The United States responded in 1990 by approving $400 million in loan guarantees to help Israel house its newcomers.

Guarantees are not grants – not one penny of U.S. government funds is transferred to Israel. The U.S. simply cosigns loans for Israel that give bankers confidence to lend Israel money at more favorable terms: lower interest rates and longer repayment periods – as much as 30 years instead of only five to seven. These loan guarantees have no effect on domestic programs or guarantees. Moreover, they have no impact on U.S. taxpayers unless Israel were to default on its loans, something it has never done. In addition, much of the money Israel borrows is spent in the United States to purchase American goods.

When it became clear the flood of refugees was even greater than anticipated, and tens of thousands continued to arrive every month, Israel realized it needed more help and asked the United States for an additional $10 billion in guarantees.

In 1992, Congress authorized the President to provide guarantees of loans to Israel as a result of Israel's extraordinary humanitarian effort to resettle and absorb immigrants. These guarantees were made available in annual increments of $2 billion over five years. While the cost to the U.S. government was zero, Israel paid the United States annual fees amounting to several hundred million dollars to cover administrative and other costs.

Under existing guidelines, no U.S. foreign assistance to Israel can be used beyond Israel's pre-1967 borders. Moreover, to underline dissatisfaction with Israel's settlement policies, the President was authorized to reduce the annual loan guarantees by the amount equal to the estimated value of Israeli activities in the West Bank and Gaza Strip undertaken the previous year.

Thus, as the table indicates, the State Department determined that Israel spent just under $1.4 billion for settlement activity from 1993-1996. The President was authorized, however, to rescind deductions when making the funds available to Israel was in the security interests of the United States. President Clinton used this authority in the last three years of the program, so the actual reduction in the amount of guarantees available to Israel was $773.8 million.

The money related to settlements also had nothing to do with the new immigrants, none of whom were forced to live in the territories. In fact, only a tiny percentage *voluntarily* chose to do so.

By all measures, the U.S. loan guarantee program was a huge success. Israel used the borrowed funds primarily to increase the amount of foreign currency available to the country's business sector and to support infrastructure projects, such as roads, bridges, sewage and electrical plants. The guarantees also helped Israel to provide housing and jobs for virtually all of the new immigrants

MYTH

"Israel was never believed to have any strategic value to the United States."

FACT

In 1952, Gen. Omar Bradley, head of the Joint Chiefs of Staff, believed the West required 19 divisions to defend the Middle East and that Israel could supply two. He also expected only three states to provide the West air power in Middle Eastern defense by 1955: Great Britain, Turkey and Israel. Bradley's analysis was rejected because the political echelon decided it was more important for the United States to work with Egypt, and later Iraq. It was feared that integration of Israeli forces in Western strategy would alienate the Arabs.[15]

Israel's crushing victory over the combined Arab forces in 1967 caused this view to be revised. The following year, the United States sold Israel sophisticated planes (Phantom jets) for the first time. Washington shifted its Middle East policy from seeking a balance of forces to ensuring that Israel enjoyed a qualitative edge over its enemies.

Israel proved its value in 1970 when the United States asked for help in bolstering King Hussein's regime. Israel's willingness to aid Amman, and movement of troops to the Jordanian border, persuaded Syria to withdraw the tanks it had sent into Jordan to support PLO forces challenging the King during "Black September."[16]

By the early 1970s it had become clear that no Arab state could or would contribute to Western defense in the Middle East. The Baghdad Pact had long ago expired, and the regimes friendly to the United States were weak compared to the anti-Western forces in Egypt, Syria and Iraq. Even after Egypt's reorientation following the signing of its peace treaty with Israel, the United States did not count on any Arab government for military assistance.

The Carter Administration began to implement a form of strategic cooperation (it was not referred to as such) by making Israel eligible to sell military equipment to the United States. The willingness to engage in limited, joint military endeavors was viewed by President Carter as a means of rewarding Israel for "good behavior" in peace talks with Egypt.

Though still reluctant to formalize the relationship, strategic cooperation became a major focus of the U.S.-Israel relationship when Ronald Reagan entered office. Before his election, Reagan had written: "Only by full appreciation of the critical role the State of Israel plays in our strategic calculus can we build the foundation for thwarting Moscow's designs on territories and resources vital to our security and our national well-being."[17]

> *"Since the rebirth of the State of Israel, there has been an ironclad bond between that democracy and this one."*
>
> **— President Reagan, September 3, 1980, address to B'nai B'rith**[18]

Reagan's view culminated in the November 30, 1981, signing of a Memorandum of Understanding on "strategic cooperation." On November 29, 1983, a new agreement was signed creating the Joint Political-Military Group (JPMG) and a group to oversee security assistance, the Joint Security Assistance Planning Group (JSAP).

The JPMG was originally designed to discuss means of countering threats posed by increased Soviet involvement in the Middle East. It has placed increasing emphasis, however, on bilateral concerns about the proliferation of chemical weapons and ballistic missiles.

The JSAP was formed in response to Israel's economic crisis in the mid-1980s. It is a binational group that meets annually in Washington to examine Israel's current and future military procurement requirements. It also formulates plans for the allocation of U.S. Foreign Military Sales credits in light of current threat assessments and U.S. budgetary capabilities.

In 1987, Congress designated Israel as a major non-NATO ally. This law formally established Israel as an ally, and allowed its industries to compete equally with NATO countries and other close U.S. allies for contracts to produce a significant number of defense items.

In April 1988, President Reagan signed another MOU encompassing all prior agreements. This agreement institutionalized the strategic relationship.

By the end of Reagan's term, the U.S. had prepositioned equipment in Israel, regularly held joint training exercises, began co-development of the Arrow Anti-Tactical Ballistic Missile and was engaged in a host of other cooperative military endeavors.

Since then, U.S.-Israel strategic cooperation has continued to evolve. Today, these strategic ties are stronger than ever. Israel is now a de facto ally of the United States.

MYTH

"Israelis are able to live comfortably because of American aid, and they see no reason to reform their country's economic system."

FACT

Israelis are among the most highly taxed people in the world with income taxes ranging up to 50 percent. This in a country where the average Israeli earns $18,000.

For years Israelis saw their standard of living decline in large part due to the government's extraordinary defense burden, which comprised roughly one-fifth to one-fourth of the budget. The situation has improved in recent years, thanks largely to the peace process, so defense spending has been reduced to 16% of the budget.

When Israel gave up the oil fields it developed in the Sinai as part of the peace agreement with Egypt, it sacrificed the opportunity to become energy-independent. Consequently, its economy suffers from oil price swings.

Most recently, with the influx of hundreds of thousands of immigrants from the former Soviet Union and Ethiopia, Israelis have voluntarily accepted even greater sacrifices to facilitate the absorption of the newcomers.

Israelis have long recognized the need to dramatically reform their economy. In 1985, Israel implemented a stabilization program that included several major features: a large cut in subsidies on basic products and services; a large currency devaluation followed by a stable exchange rate against the dollar; wage and price controls and the cessation of direct indexing of wages and savings to inflation; and a monetary policy that would control the growth of credit, thus driving interest rates upward.

The *New York Times* later described the sacrifices of the Israeli people, and the message of the stabilization program, as "Everybody takes a step backward — together."[19]

Israel's stabilization program worked like "a mini-miracle." Inflation fell sharply, from triple digits to zero in 2000. The exchange rate of the shekel stabilized, foreign-currency reserves recovered, exports increased and the budget deficit contracted.

Today, Israel is striving to go beyond stabilization, to make the underlying structural changes required for sustained economic growth. The government has continued to slash subsidies on food and public services, including health care and education, remove price controls and reform its tax structure. The government has moved to privatize state-run companies. Such steps are painful, but Israelis recognize the need for such difficult measures.

Israel has welcomed the U.S. as an involved partner, and has proved to be one of the few U.S. foreign aid recipients that has responded positively to U.S. overtures to make major reforms in its economy.

MYTH

"Israel takes protectionist measures that create impediments to American trade."

FACT

Israel has one of the most open markets for U.S. goods. Much of the growth in U.S.-Israel trade is a result of the 1985 Free Trade Agreement (FTA). The FTA affords U.S. products the opportunity to compete equally with European goods, which also have free access to Israel's domestic markets. This was the first such agreement signed by the United States with any foreign government.

Since signing the FTA, U.S. exports to Israel have grown by 234 percent, while the total volume of trade between the two countries has risen 317 percent to nearly $20 billion. This growth has resulted in more sales and profits for American exporters.

MYTH

"The employment of Jonathan Pollard to spy on the United States is proof that Israel works against American interests."

FACT

In November 1985, the FBI arrested Jonathan Pollard, a U.S. Navy intelligence analyst, on charges of selling classified material to Israel. Pollard was subsequently sentenced to life imprisonment. His wife, Anne, got five years in jail for assisting her husband.

Immediately upon Pollard's arrest, Israel apologized and explained that the operation was unauthorized. "It is Israel's policy to refrain from any intelligence activity related to the United States," an official government statement declared, "in view of the close and special relationship of friendship" between the two countries. Prime Minister Shimon Peres stated: "Spying on the United States stands in total contradiction to our policy."[20]

The United States and Israel worked together to investigate the Pollard affair. The Israeli inquiry revealed that Pollard was not working for Israeli military intelligence or the Mossad. He was directed by a small, independent scientific intelligence unit. Pollard initiated the contact with the Israelis.

A subcommittee of the Knesset's Defense and Foreign Affairs Committee on Intelligence and Security Services concluded: "Beyond all doubt...the operational echelons (namely: the Scientific Liaison Unit headed by Rafael Eitan) decided to recruit and handle Pollard without any check or consultation with the political echelon or receiving its direct or indirect approval." The Knesset committee took the government to task for not properly supervising the scientific unit.

As promised to the U.S. government, the spy unit that directed Pollard was disbanded, his handlers punished and the stolen documents returned.[21] The last point was crucial to the U.S. Department of Justice's case against Pollard.

Pollard denied spying "against" the United States. He said he provided only information he believed was vital to Israeli security and was being withheld by the Pentagon. This included data on Soviet arms shipments to Syria, Iraqi and Syrian chemical weapons, the Pakistani atomic bomb project and Libyan air defense systems.[22]

Pollard was convicted of espionage. His life sentence was the most severe prison term ever given for spying for an ally. It also was far greater than the average term imposed for spying for the Soviet Union and other enemies of the United States.[23]

Though initially shunned by Israel, the government of Benjamin Netanyahu admitted that Pollard had worked for Israeli intelligence and granted him citizenship. Netanyahu requested clemency for Pollard during Middle East peace talks at the Wye Plantation in Maryland in 1998. Since then, Israeli officials have made additional entreaties on Pollard's behalf.

Pollard's supporters in the United States also routinely request that he be pardoned. President Clinton reportedly considered a pardon, but defense and intelligence agency officials vigorously opposed the idea. At the end of Clinton's term, the issue was again raised and Sen. Richard Shelby (R-AL), chairman of the Senate's Select Committee on Intelligence, along with a majority of senators argued against a pardon. "Mr. Pollard is a convicted spy who put our national security at risk and endangered the lives of our intelligence officers," Shelby said. "There not terms strong enough to express my belief that Mr. Pollard should serve every minute of his sentence...."[24]

MYTH

"Israel tricked the United States into selling arms to Iran in exchange for hostages, and helped divert the profits to the Contras."

FACT

According to the Report of the Congressional Committees Investigating the Iran-Contra Affair issued in November 1987, the sale of U.S. arms to Iran through Israel began in the summer of 1985, after receiving the approval of President Reagan. The report shows that Israel's involvement was stimulated by separate overtures in 1985 from Iranian arms merchant Manucher Ghorbanifar and National Security Council (NSC) consultant Michael Ledeen, the latter working for National Security Adviser Robert McFarlane. When Ledeen asked Prime Minister Shimon Peres for assistance, the Israeli leader agreed to sell weapons to Iran at America's behest, providing the sale had high-level U.S. approval.[25]

Before the Israelis would participate, says the report, they demanded "a clear, express and binding consent by the U.S. Government." McFarlane told the Congressional committee he first received President Reagan's approval in July 1985. In August, Reagan again orally authorized the first sale of weapons to Iran, over the objections of Defense Secretary Caspar Weinberger and Secretary of State George Shultz.[26] Because of that deal, Rev. Benjamin Weir, held captive in Lebanon for 16 months, was released.

When a shipment of HAWK missiles was proposed in November of that year, Israeli Defense Minister Yitzhak Rabin again demanded specific U.S. approval. According to McFarlane, the President agreed.

By December 1985, the President had decided future sales to the Iranians would come directly from U.S. supplies.

According to the committees' report, NSC aide Lt. Col. Oliver North first used money from the Iran operation to fund the Nicaraguan resistance in November 1985. He later testified, however, that the diversion of funds to the Contras was proposed to him by Ghorbanifar during a meeting in January 1986.

The Joint House-Senate Committee praised the Israeli government for providing detailed chronologies of events based on relevant documents and interviews with key participants in the operation. Its report also corroborated the conclusion of the Tower Commission: "U.S. decisionmakers made their own decisions and must bear responsibility for the consequences."[27]

MYTH

"U.S. dependence on Arab oil has decreased over the years."

FACT

In 1973, the Arab oil embargo dealt the U.S. economy a major blow. This, combined with OPEC's subsequent price hikes and a growing American dependence on foreign oil, triggered the recession in the early seventies.

In 1973, foreign oil accounted for 35 percent of total U.S. oil demand. By 2001, the figure had risen to 53 percent, and OPEC accounted for 45 percent of U.S. imports. Saudi Arabia ranked number three and Iraq (#6) and Kuwait (#12) were among the top 20 suppliers of petroleum products to the United States in 2001. The Persian Gulf states alone supply 29 percent of U.S. petroleum imports.[28]

The growing reliance on imported oil has also made the U.S. economy even more vulnerable to price jumps, as occurred in 1979, 1981, 1982 and 1990 and 2000. Oil price increases have also allowed Arab oil-producers to generate tremendous revenues at the expense of American consumers. These profits have subsidized large weapons purchases and nonconventional weapons programs such as Iraq's.

America's dependence on Arab oil has occasionally raised the specter of a renewed attempt to blackmail the United States to abandon its support for Israel. In April 2002, for example, Iraq suspended oil shipments for a month to protest Israel's operation to root out terrorists in the West Bank. No other Arab oil producers follow suit and the Iraqi action had little impact on oil markets and no effect on policy.

The good news for Americans is that three of the top four suppliers of U.S. oil today – Canada, Venezuela and Mexico – are more reliable and better allies than the Persian Gulf nations.

MYTH

"The major American oil companies never take positions on the Arab-Israeli conflict."

FACT

Egypt's President Sadat persuaded the late Saudi King Faisal to threaten to withhold oil from the West to exploit for political advantage the growing dependence of the industrialized West on Arab oil. The tactic was effective: Soon the major American oil companies backed the Arab cause in public and privately worked to weaken U.S. support for Israel.[29]

According to a 1974 report of the Senate Foreign Relations subcommittee on Multinational Corporations, the ARAMCO consortium — Exxon, Mobil, Texaco and SOCAL — attempted to block America's emergency airlift to Israel during the 1973 war. The companies also cooperated closely with Saudi Arabia to deny oil and fuel to the U.S. Navy.[30]

On other occasions, the major oil firms have advocated the positions of the Arab countries, particularly Saudi Arabia. The major oil companies vigorously lobbied Congress on behalf of the sale of F-15s in 1978 and AWACS aircraft in 1981. Together with Saudi foreign agents, these corporations enlisted many other American firms to lobby on the Saudis' behalf.[31] Saudi Arabia has a powerful lobby in the United States because hundreds of America's largest corporations do billions of dollars worth of business with the Kingdom. "And each of these corporations," Hoag Levins noted, "had hundreds of subcontractors and vendors equally dependent on maintaining the good graces of Muslim leaders whose countries now collectively represent the single richest market in the world."[32]

The Saudis often attack what they claim is the excessive influence of Israel's supporters in the United States, but investigative journalist Steve Emerson turned that claim upside down. After detailing many of the ties between Saudi Arabia and U.S. businesses, universities, lobbyists and former high-ranking government officials, he concluded:

> The breadth and scope of the petrodollar impact is beyond any legal remedy. With so many corporations, institutions, and individuals thirsting after-and receiving-oil money, petrodollar influence is ubiquitous in American society. The result is the appearance of widespread, spontaneous support for the policies of Saudi Arabia and other Arab oil producers by American institutions ranging from universities to the Congress. The proliferation of vested ties has allowed special interests to be confused with national interests.
>
> Never before in American history has any foreign economic power been as successful as Saudi Arabia in reaching and cultivating powerful supporters all across the country. The Saudis have discovered that one quintessential American weakness, the love of money, and the petrodollar connection has become diffused throughout the United States.[33]

MYTH
"The United States and Israel have nothing in common."

FACT
The U.S.-Israel relationship is based on the twin pillars of shared values and mutual interests. Given this commonality of interests and beliefs, it should not be surprising that support for Israel is one of the most pronounced and consistent foreign policy values of the American people.

Although Israel is geographically located in a region that is relatively unde-veloped and closer to the Third World than the West, Israel has emerged in less than half a century as an advanced nation with the characteristics of Western society. This is partially attributable to the fact that a high percent-age of the population came from Europe or North America and brought with them Western political and cultural norms. It is also a function of the common Judeo-Christian heritage.

Simultaneously, Israel is a multicultural society with people from more than 100 nations. Today, nearly half of all Israelis are Eastern or Oriental Jews who trace their origins to the ancient Jewish communities of the Islamic countries of North Africa and the Middle East.

While they live in a region characterized by autocracies, Israelis have a com-mitment to democracy no less passionate than that of Americans. All citizens of Israel, regardless of race, religion or sex, are guaranteed equality before the law and full democratic rights. Freedom of speech, assembly and press is embodied in the country's laws and traditions. Israel's independent judiciary vigorously upholds these rights.

The political system does differ from America's — Israel's is a parliamentary democracy — but it is still based on free elections with divergent parties. And though Israel does not have a formal "constitution," it has adopted "Basic Laws" that establish similar legal guarantees.

Americans have long viewed Israelis with admiration, at least partly because they see much of themselves in their pioneering spirit and struggle for in-dependence. Like the United States, Israel is also a nation of immigrants. Despite the burden of spending nearly one-fifth of its budget on defense, it has had an extraordinary rate of economic growth for most of its history. It has also succeeded in putting most of the newcomers to work. As in America, immigrants to Israel have tried to make better lives for themselves and their children. Some have come from relatively undeveloped societies like Ethiopia or Yemen and arrived with virtually no possessions, education or training and become productive contributors to Israeli society.

Israelis also share Americans' passion for education. Israelis are among the most highly educated people in the world.

From the beginning, Israel had a mixed economy, combining capitalism with socialism along the British model. The economic difficulties Israel has experienced — created largely in the aftermath of the 1973 Yom Kippur War by increased oil prices and the need to spend a disproportionate share of its Gross National Product on defense — have led to a gradual movement toward a free market system analogous to that of the United States. America has been a partner in this evolution.

In the 1980's, attention increasingly focused on one pillar of the relationship — shared interests. This was done because of the threats to the region and because the means for strategic cooperation are more easily addressed with legislative initiatives. Despite the end of the Cold War, Israel continues to have a role to play in joint efforts to protect American interests, including close cooperation in the war on terror. Strategic cooperation has progressed to the point where a de facto alliance now exists. The hallmark of the relationship is consistency and trust: The United States knows it can count on Israel.

It is more difficult to devise programs that capitalize on the two nations' shared values than their security interests; nevertheless, such programs do exist. In fact, these *Shared Value Initiatives* cover a broad range of areas such as the environment, energy, space, education, occupational safety and health. Nearly 400 American institutions in 47 states, the District of Columbia and Puerto Rico have received funds from binational programs with Israel. Little-known relationships like the Free Trade Agreement, the Cooperative Development Research Program, the Middle East Regional Cooperation Program and various memoranda of understanding with virtually every U.S. governmental agency demonstrate the depth of the special relationship. Even more important may be the broad ties between Israel and each of the individual 50 states and the District of Columbia.

MYTH

"America's support of Israel is the reason that terrorists attacked the World Trade Center and Pentagon on September 11."

FACT

The heinous attacks against the United States were committed by Muslim fanatics who had a variety of motivations for these and other terrorist attacks. These Muslims have a perverted interpretation of Islam and believe they must attack infidels, particularly Americans and Jews, who do not share their beliefs. They oppose Western culture and democracy and object to any U.S. presence in Muslim nations. They are particularly angered by the existence of American military bases in Saudi Arabia and other areas of the Persian Gulf. This would be true regardless of U.S. policy toward the Israeli-Palestinian conflict. Nevertheless, an added excuse for their fanaticism is the fact that the United States is allied with Israel. Previous attacks on American targets, such as the *USS Cole* and U.S. embassies in Kenya and Tanzania, were perpetrated by suicide bombers whose anger at the United States had little or nothing to do with Israel.

> *"Osama bin Laden made his explosions and then started talking about the Palestinians. He never talked about them before."*
>
> **— Egyptian President Hosni Mubarak**[34]

Osama bin Laden claimed he was acting on behalf of the Palestinians, and that his anger toward the United States was shaped by American support for Israel. This was a new invention by bin Laden clearly intended to attract support from the Arab public and justify his terrorist acts. The fact is bin Laden's antipathy toward the United States has never been related to the Arab-Israeli conflict. Though many Arabs were taken in by bin Laden's transparent effort to drag Israel into his war, Dr. Abd Al-Hamid Al-Ansari, dean of Shar'ia and Law at Qatar University was critical, "In their hypocrisy, many of the [Arab] intellectuals linked September 11 with the Palestinian problem — something that completely contradicts seven years of Al-Qaida literature. Al-Qaida never linked anything to Palestine."[35]

MYTH

"The hijacking of four airliners in one day, on September 11, was an unprecedented act of terror."

FACT

The scale of the massacre and destruction on September 11 was indeed unprecedented, as was the use of civilian aircraft as bombs. The coordinated hijackings, however, were not new.

On September 6, 1970, members of the Popular Front for the Liberation of Palestine (PFLP) hijacked three jets (Swissair, TWA and Pan Am) with more than 400 passengers on flights to New York. A fourth plane, an El Al flight, was also targeted, but Israeli security agents foiled the hijacking in mid-air and killed one of the two terrorists when they tried to storm the cockpit. On the 9th, a British BOAC jet was also hijacked by the PFLP.[36]

The UN could not muster a condemnation of the hijackings. A Security Council Resolution only went so far as to express grave concern, and did not even bring the issue to a vote.

Instead of flying their planes into buildings, they landed them on airfields (three in Jordan, one in Cairo). All four hijacked planes were blown up on the ground – after the passengers were taken off the planes — on September 12.

More than three dozen Americans were among the passengers who were then held hostage in Jordan as the terrorists attempted to blackmail the Western governments and Israel to swap the hostages for Palestinian terrorists held in their jails. On Sept. 14, after releasing all but 55 hostages, the terrorists said all American hostages would be treated as Israelis.

A tense standoff ensued. Seven terrorists were ultimately set free by Britain, Germany and Switzerland in exchange for the hostages.[37]

After the hijackings, shocked members of congress called for immediate and forceful action by the United States and international community. They insisted on quick adoption of measures aimed at preventing air piracy, punishing the perpetrators and recognizing the responsibility of nations that harbor them.[38] Virtually nothing was done until 31 years later.

MYTH

"Groups like Hizballah, Islamic Jihad, Hamas and the PFLP should be excluded from the U.S. war on terrorism because they are 'freedom fighters' and not terrorists."

FACT

When the United States declared a war on terrorists and the nations that harbor them after September 11, Arab states and their sympathizers argued that many of the organizations that engage in violent actions against Americans and Israelis should not be targets of the new American war because they are "freedom fighters" rather than terrorists. This has been the mantra of the terrorists themselves, who claim that their actions are legitimate forms of resistance to Israeli occupation.

> *"You can't say there are good terrorists and there are bad terrorists."*
> **— U.S. National Security Adviser Condoleezza Rice**[39]

This argument is deeply flawed. First, the enemies of Israel rationalize any attacks as legitimate because of real and imagined sins committed by Jews since the beginning of the 20th century. Consequently, the Arab bloc and its supporters at the United Nations have succeeded in blocking any condemnation of any terrorist attacks against Israel. Instead, they routinely sponsor resolutions criticizing Israel when it retaliates.

Second, nowhere else in the world is the murder of innocent men, women and children considered a "legitimate form of resistance." The long list of heinous crimes includes snipers shooting infants, suicide bombers blowing up pizzerias and discos, hijackers taking and killing hostages, and infiltrators murdering Olympic athletes. Hizballah, Islamic Jihad, Hamas, the PFLP, and a number of other groups, mostly Palestinian, have engaged in these activities for decades and rarely been condemned or brought to justice. All of them qualify as terrorist groups according to the U.S. government's own definition — "Terrorism is the unlawful use of force or violence against persons or property to intimidate or coerce a government, the civilian population, or any segment thereof, in furtherance of political or social objectives"[40] — and therefore should be targets of U.S. efforts to cut off their funding, to root out their leaders and to bring them to justice.

In the case of the Palestinian groups, there is no mystery as to who the leaders are, where their funding comes from and which nations harbor them. American charitable organizations have been linked to funding some of these groups and Saudi Arabia, Syria, Lebanon, Iraq, Iran and the Palestinian Authority all shelter and/or financially and logistically support them.

MYTH

"Israel's Mossad carried out the bombing of the World Trade Center to provoke American hatred of Arabs."

FACT

Syrian Defense Minister Mustafa Tlas told a delegation from Great Britain that Israel was responsible for the September 11 attacks on the United States. He claimed the Mossad had warned thousands of Jewish employees not to go to work that day at the World Trade Center. He was the highest-ranking Arab public official to publicly voice a view that was reportedly widespread in the Arab world that the attacks were part of a Jewish conspiracy to provoke U.S. retaliation against the Arab world and to turn American public opinion against Muslims. One poll published in the Lebanese newspaper *An Nahar*, for example, found that 31 percent of the respondents believed Israel was responsible for the hijackings while only 27 percent blamed Osama bin Laden. A *Newsweek* poll found that a plurality of Egyptians believed the Jews were responsible for the Trade Center bombings.[41]

The conspiracy theory is also being circulated by American Muslim leaders. Imam Mohammed Asi of the Islamic Center of Washington said Israeli officials decided to launch the attack after the United States refused their request to put down the Palestinian intifada. "If we're not going to be secure, neither are you," was the Israelis' thinking following the U.S. response, according to Asi.[42]

No U.S. authority has suggested, nor has any evidence been produced, to suggest any Israeli or Jew had any role in the terrorist attacks. These conspiracy theories are complete nonsense and reflect the degree to which many people in the Arab world are prepared to accept anti-Semitic fabrications and the mythology of Jewish power. They may also reflect a refusal to believe that Muslims could be responsible for the atrocities and the hope that they could be blamed on the Jews.

MYTH

"American universities should divest from companies that do business in Israel to force an end to Israeli 'occupation' and human rights abuses."

FACT

The word "peace" does not appear in divestment petitions, which makes clear the intent is not to resolve the conflict but to delegitimize Israel. Petitioners blame Israel for the lack of peace and demand that it make unilateral concessions without requiring anything of the Palestinians, not even the cessation of terrorism. Divestment advocates also ignore Israel's efforts during the Oslo peace process, and at the summit meetings with President Clinton, to reach historic compromises with the Palestinians that would have created a Palestinian state.

The divestment campaign against South Africa was specifically directed at companies that were using that country's racist laws to their advantage. In Israel no such racist laws exist; moreover, companies doing business there adhere to the same standards of equal working rights that are applied in the United States.

Harvard University President Lawrence Summers observed that the divestment efforts are anti-Semitic. "Profoundly anti-Israel views are increasingly finding support in progressive intellectual communities," said Summers. "Serious and thoughtful people are advocating and taking actions that are anti-Semitic in their effect, if not their intent."[43]

Peace in the Middle East will come only from direct negotiations between the parties, and only after the Arab states recognize Israel's right to exist, and the Palestinians and other Arabs cease their support of terror. American universities cannot help through misguided divestment campaigns that unfairly single out Israel as the source of conflict in the region. Divestment proponents hope to tar Israel with an association with apartheid South Africa, an offensive comparison that ignores the fact that all Israeli citizens are equal under the law.

MYTH

"Advocates for Israel try to silence critics by labeling them anti-Semitic."

FACT

Criticizing Israel does not necessarily make someone anti-Semitic. The determining factor is the intent of the commentator. Legitimate critics accept Israel's right to exist, whereas anti-Semites do not. Anti-Semites use double standards when they criticize Israel, for example, denying Israelis the right to pursue their legitimate claims while encouraging the Palestinians to do so. Anti-Semites deny Israel the right to defend itself, and ignore Jewish victims, while blaming Israel for pursuing their murderers.

No campaign exists to prevent people from expressing negative opinions about Israeli policy. In fact, the most vociferous critics of Israel are Israelis themselves who use their freedom of speech to express their concerns every day. A glance at any Israeli newspaper will reveal a surfeit of articles questioning particular government policies. Anti-Semites, however, do not share Israelis' interest in improving the society; their goal is to delegitimize the state in the short-run, and destroy it in the long-run. There is nothing Israel could do to satisfy these critics.

Notes

[1] *Foreign Relations of the United States 1947,* (DC: GPO, 1948), pp. 1173-4, 1198-9, 1248, 1284. [Henceforth FRUS 1947.]

[2] Mitchell Bard, *The Water's Edge And Beyond,* (NJ: Transaction Publishers, 1991), p. 132.

[3] FRUS 1947, p. 1313.

[4] Harry Truman, *Years of Trial and Hope,* Vol. 2, (NY: Doubleday, 1956), p. 156.

[5] John Snetsinger, Truman, *The Jewish Vote and the Creation of Israel,* (CA: Hoover Institution Press, 1974), pp. 9-10; David Schoenbaum, "The United States and the Birth of Israel," *Wiener Library Bulletin,* (1978), p. 144n.

[6] Peter Grose, Israel in the Mind of America, (NY: Alfred A. Knopf, 1983), p. 217; Michael Cohen, "Truman, The Holocaust and the Establishment of the State of Israel," *Jerusalem Quarterly,* (Spring 1982), p. 85.

[7] Mitchell Bard, *U.S.-Israel Relations: Looking to the Year 2000, AIPAC Papers on U.S.-Israel Relations*: 17, (DC: American Israel Public Affairs Committee, 1991), p. 3.

[8] Memorandum of conversation regarding Harriman-Eshkol talks, (February 25, 1965); Memorandum of conversation between Ambassador Avraham Harman and W. Averill Harriman, Ambassador-at-Large, (March 15, 1965), LBJ Library; Yitzhak Rabin, *The Rabin Memoirs,* (MA: Little Brown and Company, 1979), pp. 65-66..

[9] Robert Trice, "Domestic Political Interests and American Policy in the Middle East: Pro-Israel, Pro-Arab and Corporate Non-Governmental Actors and the Making of American Foreign Policy, 1966-1971," (Unpublished Ph.D. Dissertation, University of Wisconsin-Madison, 1974), pp. 226-230.

[10] Memorandum of conversation between Yitzhak Rabin et al., and Paul Warnke et al., (November 4, 1968), LBJ Library.

[11] President Lyndon Johnson, speech to B'nai B'rith, (September 10, 1968).

[12] President Harry Truman, campaign speech at Madison Square Garden, (October 28, 1948).

[13] *Jerusalem Post,* (June 27, 2002).

[14] Israeli Ministry of Defense, (http://www.idf.il).

[15] Dore Gold, *America, the Gulf, and Israel,* (CO: Westview Press, 1988), p. 84.

[16] Yitzhak Rabin, address to conference on "Strategy and Defense in the Eastern Mediterranean," sponsored by the Washington Institute for Near East Policy and Israel Military Correspondents Association, Jerusalem, (July 9-11, 1986).

[17] Ronald Reagan, "Recognizing the Israeli Asset," *Washington Post,* (August 15, 1979).

[18] President Ronald Reagan, address to B'nai B'rith, (September 3, 1980).

[19] *New York Times*, (August 9, 1987).

[20] Wolf Blitzer, *Territory of Lies,* (NY: Harper & Row, 1989), p. 201.

[21] *New York Times,* (December 2 and 21, 1985).

[22] Blitzer, pp. 166-171.

[23] Alan Dershowitz, *Chutzpah,* (MA: Little Brown, & Co., 1991), pp. 289-312.

[24] *Washington Post,* (December 23, 2000).

[25] Much of this information was verified by the disclosure of tapes of conversations involving key figures in the scandal, "Nightline," (October 2, 1991).

[26] Report of the Congressional Committees Investigating the Iran-Contra Affair, (DC: GPO, 1987), pp. 164-76.

[27] *The Tower Commission Report,* (NY: Bantam Books and Time Books, 1987), p. 84.

[28] Energy Information Administration, (http://www.eia.doe.gov/).

[29] See Steven Emerson, "The ARAMCO Connection," *The New Republic,* (May 19, 1982), pp. 11-16; Russell Howe and Sarah Trott, *The Power Peddlers,* (NY: Doubleday, 1977), pp. 342-343; Anti-Defamation League, *The U.S.-Saudi Relationship,* (NY: ADL, 1980), p. 6.

[30] Steven Emerson, *The American House of Saud,* (NY: Franklin Watts, 1985), pp. 36-37; Steven Spiegel, *The Other Arab-Israeli Conflict: Making America's Middle East Policy from Truman to Reagan,* (IL: University of Chicago Press, 1985), pp. 258-59; Anthony Sampson, *The Seven Sisters,* (NY: Viking Press, 1975), pp. 248-50; Hoag Levins, *Arab Reach: The Secret War Against Israel,* (NY: Doubleday, 1983), p. 51.

[31] Steven Emerson, "The Petrodollar Connection," *The New Republic,* (February 17, 1982), pp. 18-25; also Emerson, (85), pp. 177-213.

[32] Levins, p. 19.

[33] Emerson (85), p. 413.

[34] *Newsweek,* (October 29, 2001).

[35] *Al-Raya* (Qatar), (January 6, 2002).

[36] Henry Kissinger, *The White House Years,* (MA: Little Brown & Co., 1979), pp. 600-617.

[37] *Guardian Unlimited,* (January 1, 2001).

[38] *Near East Report,* (September 16, 1970).

[39] *Jerusalem Post,* (October 17, 2001).

[40] *Washington Post,* (September 13, 2001).

[41] *Jerusalem Post,* (October 19, 2001); *Newsweek* poll quoted in "Protocols," *The New Republic Online,* (October 30, 2001).

[42] Jewish Telegraphic Agency, (November 2, 2001).

[43] Jewish Telegraphic Agency, (September 22, 2002).

21. The Peace Process

MYTH

*"Anwar Sadat deserves all of the credit
for the Egyptian-Israeli peace treaty."*

FACT

The peace drive did not begin with President Anwar Sadat's November 1977 visit to Jerusalem. Sadat's visit was unquestionably a courageous act of statesmanship. But it came only after more than a half-century of efforts by early Zionist and Israeli leaders to negotiate peace with the Arabs.

"For Israel to equal the drama," said former Israeli Ambassador to the U.S. Simcha Dinitz, "we would have had to declare war on Egypt, maintain belligerent relations for years, refuse to talk to them, call for their annihilation, suggest throwing them into the sea, conduct military operations and terrorism against them, declare economic boycotts, close the Strait of Tiran to their ships, close the Suez Canal to their traffic, and say they are outcasts of humanity. Then Mr. Begin would go to Cairo, and his trip would be equally dramatic. Obviously, we could not do this, because it has been our policy to negotiate all along."[1]

Nonetheless, Israeli Prime Minister Menachem Begin proved that, like Sadat, he was willing to go the extra mile to achieve peace. Although he faced intense opposition from within his Likud Party, Begin froze Israeli settlements in the West Bank to facilitate the progress of negotiations. Despite the Carter Administration's tilt toward Egypt during the talks, Begin remained determined to continue the peace process. In the end, he agreed to give the strategically critical Sinai — 90 percent of the territory won by Israel during the Six-Day War — back to Egypt in exchange for Sadat's promise to make peace.

In recognition of his willingness to join Sadat in making compromises for peace, Begin shared the 1978 Nobel Peace Prize with the Egyptian leader.

MYTH

"Egypt made all the concessions for peace."

FACT

Israel made tangible concessions to Egypt in exchange only for promises.

Israel — which had repeatedly been the target of shipping blockades, military assaults and terrorist attacks staged from the area — made far greater economic and strategic sacrifices in giving up the Sinai than Egypt did in normalizing relations with Israel.

While it received additional U.S. aid for withdrawing, Israel gave up much of its strategic depth in the Sinai, returning the area to a neighbor that had repeatedly used it as a launching point for attacks. Israel also relinquished direct control of its shipping lanes to and from Eilat, 1,000 miles of roadways, homes, factories, hotels, health facilities and agricultural villages.

Because Egypt insisted that Jewish civilians leave the Sinai, 7,000 Israelis were uprooted from their homes and businesses, which they had spent years building in the desert. This was a physically and emotionally wrenching experience, particularly for the residents of Yamit, who had to be forcibly removed from their homes by soldiers.

Israel also lost electronic early-warning stations situated on Sinai mountain-tops that provided data on military movement on the western side of the Suez Canal, as well as the areas near the Gulf of Suez and the Gulf of Eilat, which were vital to defending against an attack from the east. Israel was forced to relocate more than 170 military installations, airfields and army bases after it withdrew.

> *"Israel is a malignant tumor in the region. It must be cut off. It must be eradicated."*
>
> **— Iranian Ayatollah Ali Khamenei,**
> statement to armed forces staff, July 31, 1991

By turning over the Sinai to Egypt, Israel may have given up its only chance to become energy-independent. The Alma oil field in the southern Sinai, discovered and developed by Israel, was transferred to Egypt in November 1979. When Israel gave up this field, it had become the country's largest single source of energy, supplying half the country's energy needs. Israel, which estimated the value of untapped reserves in the Alma field at $100 billion, had projected that continued development there would make the country self-sufficient in energy by 1990.

Israel also agreed to end military rule in the West Bank and Gaza, withdraw its troops from certain parts of the territories and work toward Palestinian autonomy. The Begin government did this though no Palestinian Arab willing to recognize Israel came forward to speak on behalf of residents of the territories.

In 1988, the Jewish State relinquished Taba — a resort built by Israel in what had been a barren desert area near Eilat — to Egypt. Taba's status had not been resolved by the Camp David Accords. When an international arbitration panel ruled in Cairo's favor on September 29, 1988, Israel turned the town over to Egypt.

MYTH

"If the Palestinian problem was solved, the Middle East would be at peace."

FACT

The Palestinian problem is but one of many simmering ethnic, religious and nationalistic feuds plaguing the region. Here is but a partial list of other conflicts from the end of the 20th century: the 1991 Gulf War; the Iran-Iraq War; the Lebanese Civil War; Libya's interference in Chad; the Sudanese Civil War; the Syria-Iraq conflict and the war between the Polisario Front and Morocco.

"Almost every border in that part of the world, from Libya to Pakistan, from Turkey to Yemen, is either ill-defined or in dispute," scholar Daniel Pipes noted. "But Americans tend to know only about Israel's border problems, and do not realize that these fit into a pattern that recurs across the Middle East."[2]

If the Palestinian problem was solved, it would have negligible impact on the many inter-Arab rivalries that have spawned numerous wars in the region. Nor would it eliminate Arab opposition to Israel. Syria, for example, has a territorial dispute with Israel unrelated to the Palestinians. Other countries, such as Iran and Iraq, maintain a state of war with Israel despite having no territorial disputes.

> *"Israel wants to give the Palestinians what no one else gave them — a state. Not the Turks, the British, the Egyptians, or the Jordanians gave them this possibility...All Israel asks is that Arafat commit himself to stopping the terror, to live in peace."*
>
> **— Prime Minister Ariel Sharon**[3]

MYTH

"A Palestinian state will pose no danger to Israel."

FACT

Though reconciled to the creation of a Palestinian state, and hopeful that it will coexist peacefully, Israelis still see such an entity as a threat to their security. Even after returning much of the West Bank and Gaza and allowing the Palestinians to govern themselves, terrorism against Israelis has continued. So far, no amount of concessions by Israel has been sufficient to prompt Arafat to end the violence. This has not reassured Israelis; on the contrary, it has made them more reluctant to give up additional territory for a Palestinian state.

Israelis also fear that a Palestinian state will become dominated by Islamic extremists and serve as a staging area for terrorists. The greatest danger, however, would be that a Palestinian state could serve as a forward base in a future war for Arab nations that have refused to make peace with Israel.

"In Israeli hands, the West Bank represents a tremendous defensive asset whose possession by Israel deters Arab foes from even considering attack along an 'eastern front,'" a report by the Institute for Advanced Strategic and Political Studies notes. Today, an Arab coalition attacking from east of the Jordan "would face very difficult fighting conditions" because "it would be fighting uphill from the lowest point on the face of the earth: the Dead Sea and the Rift Valley that runs below it." The mountain ranges in the West Bank constitute "Israel's main line of defense against Arab armies from the east."[4]

MYTH

"Israel has not acknowledged Palestinian claims to Jerusalem.

FACT

Jerusalem was never the capital of any Arab entity. Palestinians have no special claim to the city, they simply demand it as their capital. Israel has recognized that the city has a large Palestinian population, that the city is important to Muslims and that making concessions on the sovereignty of the city might help resolve the conflict with the Palestinians. The problem has been that Palestinians have shown no reciprocal appreciation for the Jewish majority in the city, the significance of Jerusalem to the Jewish people or the fact that it is already the nation's capital.

The Israeli-Palestinian Declaration of Principles (DoP) signed in 1993 leaves open the status of Jerusalem. Article V says only that Jerusalem is one of the issues to be discussed in the permanent status negotiations. The agreed minutes also mention Jerusalem, stipulating that the Palestinian Council's jurisdiction does not extend to the city. Prime Minister Yitzhak Rabin said that Jerusalem will "not be included in any sphere of the prerogatives of whatever body will conduct Palestinian affairs in the territories. Jerusalem will remain under Israeli sovereignty."

The agreement also says that the final status will be based on UN Security Council Resolutions 242 and 338, neither of which mentions Jerusalem.

Other than agreeing to discuss Jerusalem during the final negotiating period, Israel conceded nothing else regarding the status of the city during the interim period. Israel retains the right to build anywhere it chooses in Jerusalem and continues to exercise sovereignty over the undivided city. Nothing in the agreements that Israel and the Palestinian Authority have concluded so far changes those conditions.

The two sides agreed on interim autonomy for the Palestinians, the creation of a Palestinian Authority, the election of a Palestinian Council and the redeployment of Israeli military forces in the West Bank and Gaza. Jerusalem, however, was specifically excluded from all these arrangements. It was also decided that during the interim period, the Palestinian Council would have no jurisdiction over issues to be determined in the final status negotiations, including Jerusalem. It was explicitly agreed that the authority of the Palestinian Authority would extend only over those parts of the West Bank and Gaza that were transferred to its jurisdiction, to the exclusion of those areas to be discussed in the permanent status negotiations, including Jerusalem and Israeli settlements.

> *"Anyone who relinquishes a single inch of Jerusalem is neither an Arab nor a Muslim."*
>
> **— Yasser Arafat**[5]

The overwhelming majority of Israelis oppose any division of Jerusalem. Still, efforts have been made to find some compromise that could satisfy Palestinian interests. For example, while the Labor Party was in power under Yitzhak Rabin and Shimon Peres, Knesset Member Yossi Beilin reportedly reached a tentative agreement that would allow the Palestinians to claim the city as their capital without Israel sacrificing sovereignty over its capital. Beilin's idea was to allow the Palestinians to set up their capital in a West Bank suburb of Jerusalem — Abu Dis.

Prime Minister Ehud Barak offered dramatic concessions that would have allowed the Arab neighborhoods of East Jerusalem to become the capital of a Palestinian state, and given the Palestinians control over the Muslim holy places on the Temple Mount. These ideas were discussed at the White House Summit in December 2000, but were rejected by Yasser Arafat.

Barak's proposals were controversial. Giving up sovereignty over the Temple Mount would place potentially hostile Arabs literally over the heads of Jews praying at their holiest site. Other suggested compromises involving a division of sovereignty over the Old City run into practical complications created by the labyrinthine nature of the city, and the intertwining of the Muslim, Christian, Jewish and Armenian quarters.

In February 2001, Ariel Sharon ran for Prime Minister against Barak — and was overwhelmingly elected — on a platform specifically repudiating the concessions Barak offered on Jerusalem. The prospect for a compromise now depends in large measure on whether the Palestinians will recognize Jewish claims to Jerusalem and offer their own concessions.

"I'll urge the Muslims to launch jihad and to use all their capabilities to restore Muslim Palestine and the holy al-Aqsa mosque from the Zionist usurpers and aggressors. The Muslims must be united in the confrontation of the Jews and those who support them."

— **Saudi King Fahd**[6]

MYTH
"All the Palestinian refugees have the right to return to their homes; this is a prerequisite for a final settlement."

FACT
After the 1948 war, no more than 650,000 Palestinians (and probably considerably fewer) were refugees. Today, the number has swelled to 3.9 million. Does Israel have any obligation to accept all of those? Where would they live?

The current Israeli population is 6 million. If every Palestinian was allowed to move to Israel, the population would be nearly 10 million and more than 40 percent Arab. Given the Arabs' significantly higher birth rate, the Jews would soon be a minority in their own country, the very situation they fought to avoid in 1948, and which the UN expressly ruled out in deciding on a partition of Palestine.

Israel has consistently sought a solution to the refugee problem. David Ben-Gurion said as early as August 1, 1948, that the refugee issue would be part of the general settlement "when the Arab states are ready to conclude a peace treaty."[7]

The Arabs, however, have consistently rejected all Israeli compromises.

Furthermore, most Palestinians now live in historic Palestine, which is an area including the Palestinian Authority and Jordan. When Palestinians speak of the right to return, however, they don't mean just to Palestine, but to the exact houses they lived in prior to 1948. These homes are either gone or inhabited now.

Even respected Palestinian leaders have begun to acknowledge that it is a mistake to insist that millions of refugees return to Israel. The Palestinian representative in Jerusalem, Sari Nusseibeh, for example, said the refugees should be resettled in a future Palestinian state, "not in a way that would undermine the existence of the State of Israel as a predominantly Jewish state. Otherwise, what does a two-state solution mean?"[8]

In the context of a peace settlement, Israel could be expected to accept some refugees, as Ben-Gurion said he would do more than 50 years ago. If and when a Palestinian state is created, many of the refugees should be allowed to move there, though it is hard to imagine how the territory envisioned for that state could accommodate so many people, and the Palestinian leadership has expressed no great interest in absorbing these people.

> *"...if there were a Palestinian state, why would its leaders want their potential citizens to be repatriated to another state? From a nation-building perspective it makes no sense. In fact, the original discussions about repatriation took place at a time that there was no hope of a Palestinian state. With the possibility of that state emerging, the Palestinians must decide if they want to view themselves as a legitimate state or if it is more important for them to keep their self-defined status as oppressed, stateless refugees. They really can't be both."*
>
> **— Fredelle Spiegel**[9]

Paradoxically, just as PA negotiators are demanding the right of refugees to return, tens of thousands of Palestinians are bolting the West Bank and Gaza Strip. In the first part of 2002, an estimated 80,000 Palestinians left and another 50,000 were trying to enter Jordan. This time the Palestinians cannot repeat their old charges that they are being expelled. These Palestinians are fleeing, much as the majority did in 1947-1948, because they do not want to be in the middle of a conflict, and because their ties to the land are tenuous.

The Jordanians are only reluctantly accepting a handful of these new "refugees," and only after they deposit 1,000 dinars ($1,400) to ensure they will not stay in the kingdom. "We have a national duty to Jordan, first, and to Palestine, second, to block gradual transfer and prevent the Palestinian state from being relocated outside Palestine, specifically to Jordan," wrote Jordanian columnist Fahed Fanek.[10]

MYTH

"Peace with Syria has been prevented only by Israel's obstinate refusal to withdraw from the Golan Heights."

FACT

For Israel, relinquishing the Golan to a hostile Syria could jeopardize its early-warning system against surprise attack. Israel has built radar systems on Mt. Hermon, the highest point in the region. If Israel withdrew from the Golan and had to relocate these facilities to the lowlands of the Galilee, they would lose much of their strategic effectiveness.

One possible compromise might be a partial Israeli withdrawal, along the lines of its 1974 disengagement agreement with Syria. Another would be a complete withdrawal, with the Golan becoming a demilitarized zone.

After losing the 1999 election, Benjamin Netanyahu confirmed reports that he had engaged in secret talks with Syrian President Hafez Assad to withdraw from the Golan and maintain a strategic early-warning station on Mount Hermon. Publicly, Assad continued to insist on a total withdrawal with no compromises and indicated no willingness to go beyond agreeing to a far more limited "non-belligerency" deal with Israel than the full peace treaty Israel has demanded.

The election of Ehud Barak stimulated new movement in the peace process, with intensive negotiations held in the United States in January 2000 between Barak and Syrian Foreign Minister Farouk al-Sharaa. These talks raised new hope for the conclusion of a peace treaty, but the discussions did not bear fruit. Hafez Assad died in June 2000 and no further talks have been held as Assad's son and successor, Bashar has moved to consolidate his power. Rhetorically, Bashar has not indicated any shift in Syria's position on the Golan.

Israel has made clear it is prepared to compromise on the Golan and make significant territorial concessions. The only obstacle is Assad's unwillingness to say yes to peace with Israel.

> *"Palestine is not only a part of our Arab homeland, but a basic part of southern Syria."*
>
> **— Syrian President Hafez Assad**[11]

MYTH

"Israel's continued occupation of Lebanese territory is the only impediment to the conclusion of a peace treaty."

FACT

Israel has never had any hostile intentions toward Lebanon, but has been forced to fight as a result of the chaotic conditions in southern Lebanon that have allowed terrorists, first the PLO, and now Hizballah, to menace citizens living in northern Israel. In 1983, Israel did sign a peace treaty with Lebanon, but Syria forced President Amin Gemayel to renege on the agreement.

Israel pulled all its troops out of southern Lebanon on May 24, 2000. The Israeli withdrawal was conducted in coordination with the UN, and according to the UN, constituted an Israeli fulfillment of its obligations under Security Council Resolution 425. Still, Hizballah and the Lebanese government insist that Israel holds Lebanese territory in a largely uninhabited patch called Shebaa Farms. This claim provides Hizballah with a pretext to continue its attacks against Israel. The Israelis maintain, however, that the land was captured from Syria.

Given Syria's de facto control over Lebanon, Syria will not allow the Lebanese government to negotiate peace with Israel until its claims on the Golan Heights are resolved. Once Israel and Syria reach an agreement, the expectation is that Lebanon would quickly do so afterward.

MYTH

"Following the Oslo accords, the Palestinians have been educating their children about Israel and a future of coexistence with Israeli Jews."

FACT

Rather than use education to promote peace with their Jewish neighbors, the Palestinians have persistently indoctrinated their children with anti-Semitic stereotypes, anti-Israel propaganda and other materials designed more to promote hostility and intolerance than coexistence.

For example, a Palestinian children's television show called the "Children's Club" uses a "Sesame Street" formula involving interaction between children, puppets and fictional characters to encourage a hatred for Jews and the perpetration of violence against them in a *jihad* (holy war). In one song, young children are shown singing about wanting to become "suicide warriors" and taking up machine guns against Israelis. Another song features young children singing a refrain, "When I wander into Jerusalem, I will become a suicide bomber." Children on the show also say, "We will settle our claims with stones and bullets," and call for a "*jihad* against Israel."

> *"We have found books with passages that are so anti-Semitic, that if they were published in Europe, their publishers would be brought up on anti-racism charges."*
>
> **— French lawyer and European Parliament member Francois Zimeray**[12]

Palestinians are also calling on their youth to join the battle against Israel in commercials on Palestinian TV that tell children to drop their toys, pick up rocks, and do battle with Israel. In one commercial, actors recreate the incident where a child was killed in the crossfire of a confrontation between Israelis and Palestinians. The commercial shows the child in paradise urging other children to "follow him."[13]

Similar messages are conveyed in Palestinian textbooks, many of which were prepared by the Palestinian Ministry of Education. The 5th grade textbook *Muqarar al-Tilawa Wa'ahkam Al-Tajwid* describes Jews as cowards for whom Allah has prepared fires of hell. In a text for 8th graders, *Al-Mutala'ah Wa'alnussus al-Adabia*, Israelis are referred to as the butchers in Jerusalem. Stories glorifying those who throw stones at soldiers are found in various texts. A 9th grade text, *Al-Mutala'ah Wa'alnussus al-Adabia*, refers to the bacteria of Zionism that has to be uprooted out of the Arab nation.

Newer textbooks are less strident, but still problematic. For example, they describe the Palestinian nation as one comprised of Muslims and Christians. No mention is made of Jews or the centuries-old Jewish communities of Palestine that predated Zionism. The State of Israel also is not mentioned, though many problems of Palestinian society are attributed to the Arab-Israeli conflict. References to Jews are usually stereotypical and are often related in a negative way to their opposition to Muhammad and refusal to convert to Islam. A lesson on architecture describes prominent mosques and churches, but makes no mention of Jewish holy places.[14] A recent study concludes:

> Despite the evident reduction in anti-Semitic references, compared to the old textbooks, the history of the relationship between Muslims, Christians and Jews in the new textbooks strengthen classical stereotypes of Jews in both Islamic and Christian cultures. The linkage of present conflicts with ancient disputes of the time of Jesus or Muhammad implies that nothing has really changed.[15]

The lessons don't end in school. Summer camp teaches Palestinian children how to resist the Israelis and that the greatest glory is to be a martyr. Campers stage mock kidnappings and learning how to slit the throats of Israelis. Four "Paradise Camps" run by Islamic Jihad in the Gaza Strip offer 8-12 year-olds military training and encourage them to become suicide bombers. The BBC filmed children marching in formation and practicing martial arts.[16]

The Palestinian authorities also try to convince children that Israel is out to kill them by all sort of devious methods. For example, the Palestinian daily newspaper, *Al Hayat Jadida,* reported that Israeli aircraft were dropping poisonous candy over elementary and junior high schools in the Gaza Strip.[17]

These teachings violate the letter and spirit of the peace agreements.

> *"We are teaching the children that suicide bombs make Israeli people frightened and we are allowed to do it....We teach them that after a person becomes a suicide bomber he reaches the highest level of paradise."*
>
> **– Palestinian "Paradise Camp" counselor speaking to BBC interviewer**[18]

MYTH

*"Israeli textbooks are no better than those of the Palestinians.
Jewish children are not taught tolerance toward Arabs
and Muslims and they are told Palestinians do not exist."*

FACT

The best hope for the future is that Israeli and Arab children will grow up with a greater understanding and tolerance of one another. Unfortunately, the textbooks in Arab countries, and the Palestinian Authority, in particular, do not promote coexistence. By contrast, Israeli textbooks are oriented toward peace and tolerance. The Palestinians are accepted as Palestinians. Islam and Arab culture are referred to with respect. Islamic holy places are discussed along with Jewish ones. Stereotypes are avoided to educate against prejudice.

In addition, the Arab-Israeli conflict is factually described as an ongoing conflict between two national entities over the same territory. Both the Arab and Israeli sides are presented. The content of the peace treaties between Israel and Egypt and Jordan is detailed, along with the implications of those agreements. Agreements with the Palestinians are discussed as well, and the atlas used in Israeli schools shows the Palestinian Authority.[19]

MYTH

*"The Interim Agreement called for the creation
of a Palestinian police force and that is precisely
what the Palestinian Authority created."*

FACT

Israel was wary of allowing the Palestinian Authority to create a police force because of the threat to Israeli security armed Palestinians might create. Israel understood, however, that the Palestinians required a means of keeping order and the Interim Agreement therefore allowed for up to 12,000 police officers to be deployed in the West Bank and up to 18,000 in the Gaza Strip.

Contrary to the agreement, however, the Palestinians have not only created a much larger police force (the Palestinian Authority submitted a list of 39,899 names), but also a variety of other security organizations, most of which are designed less for maintenance of public order than the guarantee of Yasser Arafat's political control.

Israel would probably overlook the violation of the agreed limit on the number of police officers if they were carrying out their responsibility to maintain order. It is clear from the violence that has persisted in 2000-2002, however, that the police are not doing their jobs. Worse, in many instances the police have participated in attacks against Israelis.

President Bush observed that the "Palestinian authorities are encouraging, not opposing terrorism" and made clear "the United States will not support the establishment of a Palestinian state until its leaders engage in a sustained fight against the terrorists and dismantle their infrastructure." He added that this necessitated "an externally supervised effort to rebuild and reform the Palestinian security services. The security system must have clear lines of authority and accountability, and a unified chain of command."[20]

> *"We will not arrest the sons of our people in order to appease Israel. Let our people rest assured that this won't happen."*
>
> **— Chief of the PA Preventive Security in the West Bank, Jebril Rajoub**[21]

MYTH
"The Palestinians have fulfilled their commitment to arrest and prosecute terrorists."

FACT

Israel viewed the Palestinian obligation to prevent terror as crucial to providing the security its citizens needed to make territorial concessions. The Palestinians have arrested suspected terrorists from time to time; however, they have had a revolving door whereby most of them are subsequently released. In the period following the breakdown of the Camp David negotiations on July 25, 2000, and the start of the violence in late September 2000, more than 50 members of Hamas, Islamic Jihad and the Popular Front for the Liberation of Palestine were released from prison.

To give one example of the failure to act against the terrorists, the head of Hamas, Sheikh Ahmed Yassin, was not arrested until the end of June 2002, and then he was only placed under house arrest. Shortly thereafter he attended a rally in the Gaza Strip.[22] Despite leading the organization most responsible for the suicide bombing campaign against Israeli civilians, Yassin is still not in jail.

The Palestinian Authority's treatment of Palestinians suspected of terrorism against Israel is in stark contrast to how it handles Palestinians accused of collaborating with Israel or threatening the political domination of Yasser Arafat. Palestinians who commit "crimes" against the Palestinian people are usually arrested and, in several instances, quickly executed.[23]

The unwarranted release of those accused of violence against Israel sends the message to the Palestinian public that terrorism is acceptable. It also allows the terrorists themselves to continue their campaign of violence against Israel.

MYTH

"Palestinians are justified in using violence because the peace process has not allowed them to achieve their national aspirations."

FACT

The premise from the beginning of the Oslo peace process was that disputes would be resolved by talking, not shooting. The Palestinians have never accepted this most basic of principles for coexistence. The answer to complaints that Israel is not withdrawing far enough or fast enough should be more negotiations, more confidence-building measures and more demonstrations of a desire to live together without using violence.

To understand why the Oslo process has not succeeded, and why Palestinians and Israelis are not living peacefully beside each other, it is useful to look at the first Arab-Israeli peace process that did work, the Egyptian-Israeli negotiations. Though the peace agreement was hammered out in intensive negotiations at Camp David, the route to peace was a long, tortuous one that took years to navigate. What made it possible, however, was the commitment both nations made to peace and the actions they took to insure it.

Egypt maintained a state of war with Israel for more than 25 years before Anwar Sadat seriously talked about peace. Bloody conflicts were fought in 1948, 1956, 1967, 1968-70 and 1973. The anger, heartache and distrust of a quarter century did not dissipate overnight. The process began after the 1973 war when Henry Kissinger facilitated the negotiation of a disengagement agreement in which both sides made significant concessions.

Egypt had demanded that Israel make a substantial withdrawal from Sinai and commit to abandon all its territorial gains from 1967, but Israel gave up only a tiny area of the Sinai. Rather than resort to violence, the Egyptians engaged in more negotiations.

The first agreement was signed in January 1974. It took about a year and a half before a second agreement was reached. It wasn't easy. Israel was criticized for "inflexibility," and the Egyptians were no less difficult. Anwar Sadat agreed to limit anti-Israel propaganda in the Egyptian press and to end his country's participation in the Arab boycott. Yitzhak Rabin also made difficult territorial concessions, giving up oil fields and two critical Sinai passes.

After "Sinai II," Egypt still had not recovered all of its territory. Sadat was dissatisfied and was pilloried by the other Arabs for going as far as he did toward peace with Israel. Nevertheless, he did not resort to violence. There was no unleashing of *fedayeen*, as Nasser had done in the 1950s. Instead, he continued talking.

It took three more years before the Camp David Accords were signed and another six months after that before the final peace treaty was negotiated. It took five years to work out issues that were as complex as those in the current impasse.

In return for its tangible concessions, Israel received a promise of a new future of peaceful relations. Israel could take this risk because Egypt had demonstrated over the previous five years that it would resolve disputes with Israel peacefully, and that it no longer wished to destroy its neighbor.

Egypt still wasn't completely satisfied. Sadat demanded a small sliver of land that Israel retained in the Sinai. It took another nine years before international arbitration led Israel to give up Taba. Rather than using this dispute as a pretext for violating the peace treaty, Egypt negotiated.

> *"If the Israelis can make compromises and you can't, I should go home. You have been here 14 days and said no to everything. These things will have consequences. Failure will end the peace process....."*
>
> **— President Clinton to Yasser Arafat**[24]

MYTH

"Israel has a surplus of water and its refusal to share with its neighbors could provoke the next war."

FACT

The supply of water is a matter of life and death, war and peace for the peoples of the Middle East. A *Jerusalem Post* headline concisely stated the security threat for Israel, "The hand that controls the faucet rules the country."[25]

King Hussein said in 1990 the one issue that could bring Jordan to war again is water, so it is not surprising that an agreement on water supplies was critical to the negotiation of the peace treaty with Israel. Jordan now receives an annual allotment of water from Israel.[26]

Israel has had an ongoing water deficit for a number of years. Simply put, the amount of water consumed is greater than the amount of water collected from rainfall. In a drought year, the situation worsens, because the amount of water in reservoirs and the amount of water flowing in rivers and streams is significantly decreased.

The situation is growing more dangerous each year as the population of the region continues to grow exponentially, tens of thousands of immigrants arrive in Israel, political disputes over existing water supplies become more pronounced and Israel and the Palestinians negotiate rights to the water in the West Bank and Gaza Strip.

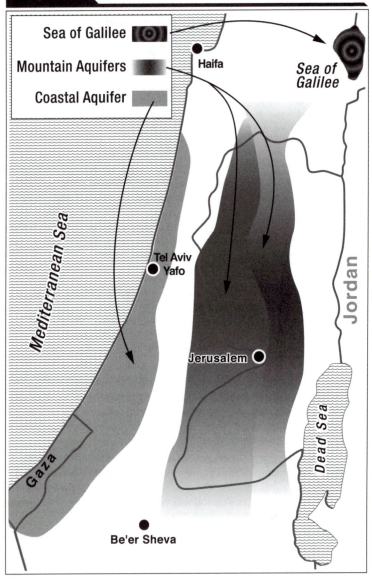

Map 22 Water Resources

Israel has three main water sources: the coastal and mountain aquifers and Lake Kinneret (Sea of Galilee). Each supply approximately 25 percent of the total consumed. Roughly 20 percent is derived from smaller aquifers. The remaining 5 percent comes from the Shafdan project that recycles sewage in metropolitan Tel Aviv.

The coastal aquifer's water quality is deteriorating because of over-pumping and contamination from sewage. Lake Kinneret requires a delicate water level balance. If the level is too low, salty water from neighboring springs seeps in. If the level rises too high, it can flood. The mountain aquifer is in the best condition.

The mountain aquifer is also the most politically contentious. Prior to 1967, Israel used 95 percent of this water, the Arabs only 5 percent. Since then, the Arab share has more than tripled, but the Palestinians are still demanding that these proportions be reversed. They argue that since the aquifer lies under the West Bank, it should come under the control of the Palestinian Authority (PA). The Palestinians maintain that Israel is "stealing" their water, but Israel wants to retain control over the lion's share of the water.

The water issue clearly affects Israel's economy and security. One danger, for example, is that pumping of water in Judea and Samaria by Palestinians could increase to a degree that would completely eliminate pumping in Israel. The Palestinians have also demanded the right to expand their agricultural sector, using the same limited water resources that Israel's State Comptroller said were inadequate to expand Israel's agricultural production. Meanwhile, Palestinian water authorities have said as much as 50 percent of domestic water is lost because of old, inefficient supply systems. The PA's dilemma is even worse in Gaza, where the sole aquifer is already virtually unusable because of contamination and salinity.

The amount of water to be supplied to the territories by Israel was determined in negotiations between the two sides, and Israel has fulfilled all of its obligations under the Interim Agreement.

In response to the threat to water supplies posed by the "al-Aksa Intifada," Palestinian and Israeli water officials issued a joint statement in January 2001 opposing any damage to water and wastewater infrastructure and expressing the intent to ensure the water supply to the Palestinian and Israeli cities, towns and villages in the West Bank and Gaza Strip.[27]

Israel could secure its water future by maintaining control over three West Bank regions comprising 20 percent of the land; however, pressure from the international community and the momentum of the peace process may force Israel to give up some or all of these territories.

"Israel has no right even to a single drop of water in this region."

— Syrian Foreign Minister Farouq al-Sharaa[28]

Water is also an issue in negotiations with the Syrians. Syria demands the full return of the Golan Heights in return for peace with Israel. According to water expert Joyce Starr, an Israeli government that concedes territory on the Golan without a guaranteed supply of Yarmuk waters, or some alternative source of water, would be putting the nation in "grave jeopardy."[29]

Israel is taking steps to ameliorate the water issue by beginning construction of major desalination plants that are scheduled to provide, by 2006, nearly one-fourth of Israel's needs. An agreement has also been reached that will allow Israel to import water from Turkey. Israel has offered to build a desalination plant in Hadera for the Palestinians in the West Bank, but they have rejected the idea.

MYTH

"The Islamic Resistance Movement (Hamas) is a force for moderation in the territories. It advocates Muslim-Jewish harmony and reconciliation."

FACT

Hamas is opposed to Israel's existence in any form. Its platform states that "there is no solution for the Palestinian question except through *jihad* (holy war)." The group warns that any Muslim who leaves "the circle of struggle with Zionism" is guilty of "high treason." Hamas' platform calls for the creation of an Islamic republic in Palestine that would replace Israel. Muslims should "raise the banner of Allah over every inch of Palestine," it says.[30]

MYTH

"Israel withdrew from all of the Sinai to achieve peace with Egypt, withdrew to the international border with Lebanon and has offered to withdraw from the entire Golan Heights in a peace agreement with Syria; therefore, Israel should withdraw from 100 percent of the West Bank and Gaza Strip to make peace with the Palestinians."

FACT

Israel has no obligation, legal or otherwise, to withdraw from the entire West Bank and Gaza Strip. Moreover, those territories are very different than the others that were the subject of negotiations. Israel did not have a claim to either the Sinai or the security zone in Lebanon. Those territories were held as defensive measures to protect Israel after hostile forces had used them to stage attacks. In the case of Sinai, even after the withdrawal, a series of security measures were put into place, including the introduction of U.S. observers to monitor compliance with the peace treaty terms. Israel has not formally offered to withdraw from the entire Golan though it has hinted at a willingness to give up much or all of that territory in exchange for peace with Syria. Such an agreement would also include terms for monitoring compliance and maintaining Israeli security.

The situation in the West Bank and Gaza Strip is very different. Unlike the Sinai, for example, no buffer zone would exist to separate hostile Palestinian forces from Israel if it were to withdraw completely from the territories. Every Israeli government, and most nonpartisan observers, agree that Israel's security requires a presence in the Jordan Valley. Furthermore, Israel has a historic connection to Judea and Samaria, which have been home to Jews for centuries and have important religious significance to the Jewish people. Finally, Egypt, Lebanon and Syria could legitimately argue the territories in dispute belonged to them; this is not true of the Palestinians. The West Bank was never part of any country and the Palestinian claim to the territory is no better than that of Israel.

Israel has acknowledged that it will be necessary to withdraw from parts of the West Bank and Gaza Strip to reach a peace agreement with the Palestinians, and has already withdrawn from large swaths of both, but its security needs are such that it cannot withdraw from 100 percent of those lands.

MYTH

"The Palestinians have never been offered a state of their own."

FACT

The Palestinians have actually had numerous opportunities to create an independent state, but have repeatedly rejected the offers:

- In 1937, the Peel Commission proposed the partition of Palestine and the creation of an Arab state.

- In 1939, the British White Paper proposed the creation of an Arab state alone, but the Arabs rejected the plan.

- In 1947, the UN would have created an even larger Arab state as part of its partition plan.

- From 1948 to 1967, Israel did not control the West Bank. The Palestinians could have demanded an independent state from the Jordanians.

- The 1979 Egypt-Israel peace negotiations offered the Palestinians autonomy, which would almost certainly have led to full independence.

- The Oslo process that began in 1993 was leading toward the creation of a Palestinian state before the Palestinians violated their commitments and scuttled the agreements.

■ In 2000, Prime Minister Barak offered to create a Palestinian state, but Arafat rejected the deal.

A variety of reasons have been given for why the Palestinians have in Abba Eban's words, "never missed an opportunity to miss an opportunity." Historian Benny Morris has suggested that the Palestinians have religious, historical, and practical reasons for opposing an agreement with Israel. He says that "Arafat and his generation cannot give up the vision of the greater land of Israel for the Arabs. [This is true because] this is a holy land, Dar al-Islam [the world of Islam]. It was once in the hands of the Muslims, and it is inconceivable [to them] that infidels like us [the Israelis] would receive it." The Palestinians also believe that time is on their side. "They feel that demographics will defeat the Jews in one hundred or two hundred years, just like the Crusaders." The Palestinians also hope the Arabs will acquire nuclear weapons in the future that will allow them to defeat Israel. "Why should they accept a compromise that is perceived by them as unjust today?"[31]

MYTH

"Yasser Arafat rejected Ehud Barak's proposals at Camp David and the White House in 2000 because they did not offer the Palestinians a viable state. Palestine would have been denied water, control of its holy places, and would have been divided into cantons surrounded by Israelis. Israel would have also retained control of Jerusalem and denied refugees the right to return."

FACT

Israeli Prime Minister Ehud Barak offered to withdraw from 95 percent of the West Bank and 100 percent of the Gaza Strip. In addition, he agreed to dismantle 63 isolated settlements. In exchange for the 5 percent annexation of the West Bank, Israel would increase the size of the Gaza territory by roughly a third.

Barak also made previously unthinkable concessions on Jerusalem, agreeing that Arab neighborhoods of East Jerusalem would become the capital of the new state. The Palestinians would maintain control over their holy places and have "religious sovereignty" over the Temple Mount.

According to U.S. peace negotiator Dennis Ross, Israel offered to create a Palestinian state that was contiguous, and not a series of cantons. Even in the case of the Gaza Strip, which must be physically separate from the West Bank unless Israel were to be cut into non-contiguous pieces, a solution was devised whereby an overland highway would connect the two parts of the Palestinian state without any Israeli checkpoints or interference.

The proposal also addressed the refugee issue, guaranteeing them the right of return to the Palestinian state and reparations from a $30 billion international fund that would be collected to compensate them.

Israel also agreed to give the Palestinians access to water desalinated in its territory to ensure them adequate water.

Arafat was asked to agree to Israeli sovereignty over the parts of the Western Wall religiously significant to Jews (i.e., *not* the entire Temple Mount), and three early warning stations in the Jordan valley, which Israel would withdraw from after six years. Most important, however, Arafat was expected to agree that the conflict was over at the end of the negotiations. This was the true deal breaker. Arafat was not willing to end the conflict. "For him to end the conflict is to end himself," said Ross.[32]

The prevailing view of the Camp David/White House negotiations – that Israel offered generous concessions, and that Yasser Arafat rejected them to pursue the intifada that began in September 2000 – prevailed for more than a year. To counter the perception that Arafat was the obstacle to peace, the Palestinians and their supporters then began to suggest a variety of excuses for why Arafat failed to say "yes" to a proposal that would have established a Palestinian state. The truth is that if the Palestinians were dissatisfied with any part of the Israeli proposal, all they had to do was offer a counterproposal. They never did.

> *In his last conversation with President Clinton, Arafat told the President that he was "a great man." Clinton responded, "The hell I am. I'm a colossal failure, and you made me one."*[33]

MYTH

"The members of the Arab League signed an antiterrorism pact and oppose any form of terrorism."

FACT

The Arab League, a moribund institution that usually convenes only when it feels the need to publicly flay Israel, made headlines on April 22, 1998, for adopting the first Arab antiterrorism agreement. The agreement calls on Arab countries to deny refuge, training and financial or military support to groups that launch attacks on other Arab nations. It says attacks on ruling Arab regimes or the families of rulers should be considered terrorism and that Islam rejects "all forms of violence and terror." The signatories also promised to exchange information on terrorist groups.

Arab countries and organizations have typically defined terrorism in such a way that groups attacking Israel are excluded. The agreement does the same thing by exempting "resistance movements" because efforts to secure "liberation and self-determination" are not considered terrorism by the League (unless it is a liberation effort directed at an Arab government). Not surprisingly, Syria and Lebanon were the countries maintaining that individuals "resisting occupation" in Southern Lebanon, the Golan Heights and the West Bank should not be labeled as terrorists. For the members of the Arab League, the objective of "national liberation" justifies attacks against civilians, including women and children.

The agreement did not signal a change in Arab morality or a newfound concern over terrorism. It was merely an act of self-preservation taken by autocrats who recognized that Israel was not as great a threat to them as their own disaffected citizens.

Meanwhile, the Palestinian Authority, Lebanon, Syria, Libya, Iraq and Iran all have continued to fund, organize and harbor terrorist organizations, and heinous acts have been perpetrated by Arab terrorists against innocent men, women and children in Israel and elsewhere around the world.

MYTH

"Israel illegally took over the District Governor's Compound and the Palestinians' offices in Orient House, and has reoccupied territory in Jerusalem that was given to the Palestinians."

FACT

Following a series of terrorist attacks, including the bombing of a Jerusalem pizza restaurant that killed 15 and injured more than 130, children, men, and women, Israel took a series of defensive measures in the Jerusalem area. One of these steps was to take over the District Governor's Compound and several adjacent buildings that were being used by Palestinian security forces to organize and instigate terrorist activities. A second measure was to close Palestinian Authority offices in the Orient House in Jerusalem. This latter move was especially controversial because Orient House had become a popular place for foreign journalists to meet Palestinians, and was viewed by Palestinians as their unofficial capital, where they frequently scheduled meetings with foreign dignitaries.

Under the Israel-Palestinian agreements, security responsibilities in Jerusalem are the exclusive province of Israel (Interim Agreement). In addition to acting according to the well established principal of self-defense under international law, Israel's actions have been consistent with the terms of the Israel-Palestinian agreements. By using these areas as bases to instigate terror, the Palestinians violated their commitment to combat terrorism and violence (Interim Agreement Annex I, Article IV.1.f) and to implement a policy of zero tolerance for terror and violence (Wye River Memorandum II.A.1). Moreover, they have violated the promise to "renounce the use of terrorism and other acts of violence" (letter from Yasser Arafat to Yitzhak Rabin) that was the basis for the entire Oslo process. Finally, the decision of the Palestinian leadership to reject negotiations and to adopt a strategy of terrorism, flouts the first recommendation of the Mitchell Commission Report, calling on the parties to "immediately implement an unconditional cessation of violence."

The Palestinians may be angry that they can no longer carry out their political activities at Orient House, but the truth is the agreements with Israel barred them from doing so in the first place. The Interim Agreement states that all PA offices can only be located in areas under Palestinian territorial jurisdiction in the West Bank and Gaza Strip (Interim Agreement Article I.7). Furthermore, the frequent meetings held at the Orient House between Palestinian officials and foreign diplomats violated the general prohibition on the exercise of foreign relations contained in Article IX of the Interim Agreement.

Israel has agreed to allow the Palestinians to set up economic, social, educational, and cultural institutions to serve the needs of the population in Jerusalem; however, no political activity is permitted under any of the agreements signed by the two sides. And, of course, Israel cannot be expected to permit terrorist operations in its capital.

MYTH
"The Palestinians joined the rest of the world in condemning the September 11 terrorist attacks on the United States."

FACT
Having learned his lesson from allying himself and the Palestinian people with Saddam Hussein during the Gulf War, Yasser Arafat did condemn the attack against the United States. Palestinians throughout the West Bank, Gaza Strip and refugee camps in Lebanon, however, celebrated the attacks. In one rally in Gaza, for example, demonstrators carried posters supporting Saudi terrorist Osama bin Laden. After the U.S. coalition attacked Afghanistan, Hamas organized another rally in the Gaza Strip in which thousands of Palestinians marched in support of bin Laden Among those celebrating at these events were members of the Palestinian Authority police force, who fired their guns in the air. Others chanted, "God is Great," and handed out sweets.

MYTH
"The Palestinian Authority has seized illegal weapons and fulfilled its other obligations under the Oslo agreements to restrict the possession of arms to the authorized police force."

FACT
According to the Interim Agreement signed by Israel and the Palestinians, "no organization, group or individual in the West Bank and the Gaza Strip shall manufacture, sell, acquire, possess, import or otherwise introduce into the West Bank or the Gaza Strip any firearms, ammunition, weapons, explo-

sives, gunpowder or any related equipment" except the Palestinian police. The agreement's annex further specifies that the police are only permitted a limited number of pistols, rifles and machine guns and that all weapons must be registered.

During the "al-Aksa intifada" it has become clear that the Palestinians have abandoned all pretense of fulfilling what Israel viewed as a crucial security requirement in the Oslo accords. A number of militias have formed that are not allowed to exist or possess weapons according to the peace agreements. They have used rifles, machine guns, mortars, grenades and other explosive to carry out terrorist attacks against Israel. Every time a photo is shown of a Palestinian holding a weapon – and they appear in the press all the time – it is evidence the Palestinians have broken their promises.

In June, when they agreed to the Tenet Cease-Fire Plan, the Palestinians committed themselves, again, to "make a concerted effort to locate and confiscate illegal weapons, including mortars, rockets, and explosives" and "to prevent smuggling and illegal production of weapons." They have failed to do either. This is a serious violation of the agreement signed by the Palestinians, one that provokes mistrust and threatens Israeli security.

MYTH
"Palestinian terrorists only attack Israelis; they never assault Americans."

FACT
The PLO has a long history of brutal violence against innocent civilians of many nations, including the United States. Palestinian Muslim terrorist groups are a more recent phenomenon, but they have not spared Americans either. Here are a few examples of Palestinian terrorist incidents involving American citizens:

■ More than three dozen Americans were among the passengers who were held hostage when the Popular Front for the Liberation of Palestine hijacked four jets in September 1970.

■ In 1972, the PLO attempted to mail letter bombs to President Nixon, former Secretary of State William Rogers and Secretary of Defense Melvin Laird.

■ On March 2, 1973, members of the PLO murdered U.S. Ambassador to the Sudan Cleo Noel and chargé d'affaires George Moore. The killers were captured by Sudan and admitted they had gotten orders directly from the PLO. U.S. intelligence officials were believed to also have evidence directly tying Yasser Arafat to the killings, but for unknown reasons suppressed it. All the terrorists were released.[34]

■ On March 11, 1978, PLO terrorists landed on Israel's coast and murdered an American photographer walking along the beach. The terrorists then commandeered a bus along the coastal road, shooting and lobbing grenades from the bus window at passersby. When Israeli troops stopped their deadly ride, 34 civilians were dead and another 82 wounded.

■ In October 1985, a PLF terror squad commanded by Abul Abbas hijacked the ocean liner *Achille Lauro*. Leon Klinghoffer, a wheelchair-bound American passenger was murdered.

■ In March 1988, Arafat's Fatah declared it had attempted to murder Secretary of State George Shultz by planting a car bomb near his Jerusalem hotel.[35]

■ On April 9, 1995, a Hamas suicide bomber blew up an Israeli bus killing eight people, including 20-year-old Brandeis University student Alisa Flatow.

■ August 9, 2001, Shoshana Yehudit Greenbaum, 31, was among 15 people killed in a suicide bombing at the Sbarro pizzeria in downtown Jerusalem. Hamas and the Islamic Jihad claimed responsibility for the attack.

■ July 31, 2002, a bomb exploded at the Hebrew University cafeteria killing seven and wounding 80. Five Americans were among the dead.

MYTH

"Israel's opposition to the creation of a Palestinian state is the cause of the present conflict."

FACT

For many years, the consensus in Israel was that the creation of a Palestinian state would present a grave risk to Israeli security. These fears were well founded given the longstanding Palestinian commitment to the destruction of Israel and the later adoption of the phased plan whereby the Palestinians expressed a reluctant willingness to start with a small state in the short-term and use it as a base from which to pursue the longer-term goal of replacing Israel.

Israelis still believe a Palestinian state will present a threat, especially given the Palestinians' illegal smuggling of weapons into the Palestinian Authority; nevertheless, a radical shift in opinion has occurred and even most "right-wing" Israelis are now reconciled to the likelihood that the Palestinians will establish a state and are prepared to accept the risks involved in exchange for peace.

> *"If we agree to declare our state over what is now 22 percent of Palestine, meaning the West Bank and Gaza, our ultimate goal is the liberation of all historic Palestine from the River to the Sea...We distinguish the strategic, long-term goals from the political phased goals, which we are compelled to temporarily accept due to international pressure."*
> **— Faisal al-Husseini**[36]

MYTH

"The Palestinian Authority is abiding by its commitments and preventing illegal arms from being smuggled into areas under its control."

FACT

On January 3, 2002, IDF commandos captured the *Karine-A*, a 4,000-ton freighter carrying 50 tons of Iranian and Russian-made weapons, including long-range Katyusha rockets, LAW anti-tank missiles, Sagger anti-tank missiles, long-range mortar bombs, mines, sniper rifles, ammunition and more than two tons of high explosives.

Despite denials by Yasser Arafat, Omar Akawi, a Palestinian Authority naval officer who captained the Palestinian-owned and operated ship, admitted the smuggling operation was ordered by the PA: "I am an officer in the navy. I am an employee of the Palestinian Authority. I take my salary from them. I have to obey orders."[37]

The Bush Administration also found Arafat's denials unconvincing. "The information we are receiving and developing on our own," said" Secretary of State Colin Powell, "makes it clear that there are linkages to the Palestinian Authority."[38]

Akawi said the weapons were intended for Palestinians in the Gaza Strip. The plan had been to take the boat through the Suez Canal and then transfer the arms to three smaller boats near the Egyptian port of Alexandria. The small boats would then carry the weapons to a spot off the Gaza coast, where they would be dropped into the sea packed in special waterproof containers enabling the arsenal to float undamaged until it could be picked up by Palestinian navy officers disguised as fisherman.[39]

The smuggling operation violated the terms of the Oslo agreements signed by the Palestinians and represented a serious escalation of the already tense situation. The quantity and quality of the arms in the shipment, which exceeded what the Palestinians had already smuggled in through tunnels in the Gaza Strip and elsewhere, also reinforced Israeli concerns about Palestinian intentions, and the threat that a future Palestinian state might pose.

MYTH

"Hundreds of Israeli soldiers are refusing to serve in the territories. This proves that Israel's policies are unjust."

FACT

As of now, about 400 Israelis who serve in the reserves (out of 445,000 - 0.08 percent) have signed a petition saying they will no longer serve in the territories. They received a lot of publicity because it is so unusual for Israeli soldiers to refuse to serve their country. What attracted no media attention was the reaction of most Israelis to the call to serve in Operation Defensive

Shield. The response was more than 100 percent. Israelis who were not obligated to report because they were too old, had disabilities, or were otherwise excused from service volunteered to go to the territories.

In a democracy, such as Israel, people may protest their government's policies, but the voices of a minority do not carry more weight than the majority. In fact, a poll from Tel Aviv University showed that 61.5 percent of Israelis were very much opposed to the activists' refusal to serve and another 17.6 percent considerably opposed it. That's nearly 80 percent of the public that rejected the refuseniks' argument. Total support for their point of view was 15 percent. In addition, a counter-petition was published in Israeli newspapers signed by more than 1,000 other reservists who said they were "amazed and ashamed" by the original letter written by a group of what they called "draft dodgers."[40] Also, more than 4,500 reservists volunteered for additional duty.[41]

The soldiers raised important issues about the treatment of Palestinians by the military that are being taken seriously by the Israeli public and government, but their actions were also politically motivated and not mere acts of conscience. Shlomo Gazit, a former head of Israeli military intelligence, and someone who sympathizes with the political goals of the refusenik soldiers, wrote an impassioned plea for them to give up their protest. He pointed out that Israeli security depends on soldiers' absolute loyalty to the elected officials of the nation and the apolitical nature of the security system. Gazit points out that soldiers can't decide which orders they wish to carry out and said that if the refuseniks' principles were adopted they could find that many other soldiers would take the exact opposite views and, say, refuse to carry out orders to evacuate settlements or withdraw from the territories. As he points out, the soldiers can carry out their missions without losing their humanity and can refuse *illegal* orders.[42] In addition, Israel's democratic society gives them other outlets to pursue their political agenda, namely creating a new political movement or using an existing one to change Israeli policy.

MYTH

"A fence is being constructed to separate Israel from the Palestinian Authority. This will not solve any problems and will lead to the racist creation of a Palestinian ghetto."

FACT

A growing number of Israelis have come to the conclusion that the best solution to the conflict with the Palestinians is separation. They propose that a fence or wall be built to demarcate a new border between Israel and the Palestinians. Even Israelis who are not enthusiastic about the establishment of a Palestinian state argue the fence is needed to reduce the number of terror attacks. The head of the Shin Bet, Avi Dichter, for example, has said that a physical barrier can be a deterrent and cites the example of the fence that was built to separate Israel from the Gaza Strip.[43]

Many people, including Israelis, have raised a great hue and cry over the idea of a fence, but it is not unusual to separate peoples and borders with barriers. A fence already has been built between Israel and the Gaza Strip, and the frontiers between Israel and Lebanon, Jordan and Syria all have fences.

The difficult political questions are where the fence should be built and whether the barrier should demarcate a final border with a future Palestinian state. These questions are now being debated. In the meantime, construction of the fence has begun, and the expectation is that a wall extending the length of the "Green Line" (the unofficial boundary after 1967) can be completed by mid-2003.

Palestinian charges that a fence would have the effect of creating a ghetto are nonsense. On the contrary, most proponents of the idea advocate the creation of a Palestinian state on their side of the barrier. The Palestinians would have the independent state in the West Bank and Gaza Strip they say they want. The longer term issue would be how open the fence would be. If the Palestinians decided to live in peace with Israel, people and goods could flow freely back and forth; however, if the Palestinians remained committed to violence and unwilling to coexist with their Israeli neighbors, the barrier could be sealed to prevent any infiltration by Palestinian terrorists.

In addition, the position of the fence need not be permanent. Should the Palestinians decide to return to the bargaining table, it is possible that negotiations could lead to the fence being moved or torn down.

MYTH

"The demolition of Palestinian homes is an example of the barbaric policies of Israeli oppression."

FACT

Israel does not arbitrarily decide to demolish the homes of Palestinians. The army usually decides to take this drastic measure only after extreme provocation, and to insure the security of soldiers and civilians. In the case of Palestinian homes in the Gaza Strip, in particular, they have been used as bomb factories, to provide cover for snipers, and to conceal tunnels used to smuggle weapons from Egypt. By demolishing homes, the objective is also to demonstrate that terrorists bring destruction not only to their victims, but to their own families and communities. The hope is that before engaging in terrorism, a Palestinian might think twice about the consequences.

Homes are also sometimes demolished when they are built illegally, without government approval or the proper permits. This practice is not applied only to Palestinians; however, Jewish homes have also been torn down when they were built illegally. Efforts by Jewish settlers, for example, to create new outposts or illegally expand existing settlements often result in the new structures being demolished.[44]

MYTH

*"The Palestinians have given up their maximalist dream
of destroying Israel and reconciled themselves
to the establishment of a state in part of the West Bank
and Gaza Strip that will peacefully coexist with Israel."*

FACT

The Palestinian Authority has made clear its territorial objective in its school textbooks, the way Yasser Arafat wears his kaffiyeh (i.e., shaped like Palestine), and the emblems of its organizations (see that of the PLO, for example). The most dramatic expression of the goal is in the following map of Palestine that was published on the PA web site, which shows Palestine encompassing not only the West Bank and Gaza Strip, but all of Israel as well.[45]

Israelis have expressed a willingness to live in peace with a Palestinian state beside Israel. As the map vividly indicates, however, the Palestinians continue to dream of a Palestinian state that replaces Israel.

MYTH

"The Arab League peace plan of 2002 represents a dramatic new vision in which the Arabs are, for the first time, giving up their maximalist demands."

FACT

Saudi Crown Prince Abdullah presented a vision of peace that was subsequently revised and adopted by the Arab League as a peace initiative that offered Israel "normal relations" in exchange for a withdrawal to the 1967 borders and resolution of the Palestinian refugee issue.

> *"There are some who have urged, as a single, simple solution, an immediate return to the situation as it was on June 4….this is not a prescription for peace but for renewed hostilities."*
>
> **– President Lyndon Johnson**[46]

In fact, the "new" initiative is nothing more than a restatement of the Arab interpretation of UN Resolution 242. The problem is that 242 does not say what the peace plan calls on Israel to do. The resolution calls on Israel to withdraw from territories occupied during the war, not "all" the territories in exchange for peace. In fact, the Arab delegates lobbied to have the word "all" included in the resolution and this idea was rejected.

Map 23
The Palestinian Authority's Map of Palestine

LEBANON

SYRIA

Mediterranean Sea

PALESTINE

JORDAN

EGYPT

State Information Service

N

In addition, Resolution 242 also says that every state has the right to live within "secure and recognizable boundaries," which all military analysts have understood to mean the 1967 borders *with modifications* to guarantee Israel's security. Incidentally, the resolution does not say that one comes before the other; rather, they are equal principles. Israel is under no obligation to withdraw before the Arabs agree to live in peace.

The Arab plan calls for Israel to withdraw from the Golan Heights. The Israeli government has offered to do withdraw from most, if not all the Golan in exchange for a peace agreement; however, Syrian President Bashar Assad has so far been unwilling to negotiate at all with Israel.

The demand that Israel withdraw from "the remaining occupied Lebanese territories in the south of Lebanon" is not only ingenuous, but at odds with the UN conclusion that Israel has completely fulfilled its obligation to withdraw from Lebanese territory.

The Arab initiative also calls for a just solution to the Palestinian Refugee problem based on the non-binding UN General Assembly Resolution 194. Today, the UNRWA says that 3.9 million Palestinians are refugees. The current population of Israel is approximately 6 million, 5 million of whom are Jews. If the Palestinians all returned, the population would be nearly 10 million, and the proportion of Jews and Palestinian Arabs would be nearly 50-50. Given the higher Arab birth rate, Israel would soon cease to be a Jewish state and would de facto become a second Palestinian state (along with the one expected to be created on the West Bank and Gaza Strip). This suicidal formula has been rejected by Israel since the end of the 1948 war and is totally unacceptable to all Israelis today.

Israel has agreed to allow some Palestinian refugees to return on a humanitarian basis and as part of family reunification. Thousands have returned already this way. In the past, Israel has repeatedly expressed a willingness to accept as many as 100,000 refugees as part of a resolution of the issue. In fact, Israel accepted 140,000 refugees just since the Oslo agreement of 1993.[47]

The Arab demand that Israel accept the establishment of a Palestinian state in the West Bank and Gaza with East Jerusalem as its capital has been part of the negotiations since Oslo. Israel's leaders, including Sharon, have accepted the idea of creating a Palestinian state in part of those territories, and Israel has even offered compromises on the status of Jerusalem, but the Palestinians have rejected them all.

It is also worth noting that most of the Arab League nations have no reason not to be at peace with Israel now. Israel holds none of their territory and is more than willing to make peace with the members of the League. Several members of the League had already begun to normalize relations with Israel before the latest outbreak of violence, and their principle critic was Saudi Arabia.

For the plan to have any chance of serving as a starting point for negotiations, the Saudis and other Arab League members would have to be prepared to negotiate directly with Israel. Israeli Prime Minister Ariel Sharon even said he would go the Arab League summit to discuss the plan, but he was not invited. The Saudis have also been invited to Jerusalem to discuss their proposal, but they have rejected this idea as well.

MYTH

"Arab leaders have condemned suicide bombers and other acts of terrorism since September 11, and responded to President Bush's call to take steps to fight terrorism."

FACT

In April 2002, President Bush called on the Arab states to "do everything possible to stop terrorist activities, to disrupt terrorist financing and stop incitement of violence in state-owned media." He also urged them to publicly denounce suicide bombings, and to use their influence with the Palestinian Authority and other groups to stop the violence.[48] Not only did the Arab leaders reject the President's request, they did the exact opposite. For example, Iraqi President Saddam Hussein publicly promised to pay $25,000 to the families of suicide bombers. Saudi Arabia held a terrerthon to raise millions of dollars for "martyrs," with the two biggest contributors being King Fahd and Crown Prince Abdullah, the latter hailed as the architect of the latest Arab League peace initiative.[49] So both radicals, such as Iraq, and "moderates" such as Saudi Arabia, are underwriting terrorism. This is in addition to the broader sponsorship of terror of these and other countries, including Iran.

On April 2, the 57-member Organization of the Islamic Conference meeting in Malaysia rejected any linkage between Palestinian attacks and terrorism and refused to even define terrorism. Malaysian Prime Minister Mahathir Mohamad called on the group to classify all attacks on civilians, including those by Palestinian suicide bombers, as terrorism, but the Conference would not do so.[50]

> *"You cannot negotiate with terrorists because the single response of terrorists for fulfilling their demands is blackmail....[Israel] cannot negotiate with people who kill civilians for political purpose....Any political leader who tolerates political terrorism as a legitimate tool for his political campaign – is a terrorist."*
>
> **— Czech Prime Minister Milos Zeman**[51]

Perhaps the best example of the Arab refusal to condemn terrorism came from King Abdullah of Jordan, generally regarded as the most moderate Arab leader and America's closest Arab ally. In an interview with CNN, Christiane Amanpour asked Abdullah in a variety of ways if he would make a simple declarative statement condemning suicide bombings against Israel and he repeatedly evaded the question.[52]

So long as the Arab states continue to support terrorism, Israel will remain at risk, and there is little hope for regional peace or stability. Furthermore, the Arab policy legitimates the use of terror not only against Israel, but other nations as well, including the United States.

MYTH

"Israel is making specious comparisons between Palestinian resistance and the September 11 attacks on the United States in the hope of generating sympathy for its policies."

FACT

Israel and the United States are allies in the war on terrorism. Both face a common threat from radical Islamic and ideological groups that want to destroy them because of what they represent — freedom, democracy, modernity and Judeo-Christian values. The Palestinians are not engaged in resistance, but cold-blooded murder. No excuse justifies the killing of innocents. That is terrorism.

It is true that the terror attacks in Israel and the United States are not completely analogous. September 11 was a terrible day, but just one of only a handful where Americans have been victimized by terror. Israelis face threats to their lives on a daily basis. Americans have had to learn to live with new precautions at airports, a relatively mild inconvenience. Israelis must be wary of people and packages everywhere. Thankfully, Americans do not yet have to think twice before they send their kids out to play, go shopping at a mall, or enjoy an evening out at a restaurant. Israelis now must worry constantly about the safety of their children, and risk their lives going to discos, pizzerias and grocery stores. For most Americans the Sabbath is a time of prayer, reflection, leisure and enjoyment. For Israelis, the Sabbath has often been marked by murder and mayhem from Palestinian suicide bombers. After the March 2002 Passover massacre in which 29 people were murdered during their Seder, Israelis cannot even enjoy their religious festivals.

It is sometimes difficult for Americans to appreciate the magnitude of the impact of a terror attack that "only" kills 29 people, but in a country as small as Israel that number is devastating, and it is likely that many Israelis will personally know the victims. In fact, one study found that one-third of Israelis between 14 and 18 know someone killed or wounded in a terrorist attack.

On a proportional basis, the death of 20 Israelis is roughly equivalent to 1,000 Americans, so from the perspective of Israelis, they've been experiencing September 11 almost weekly. And this does not count all the foiled attacks.

Dozens of attempts have been stopped by the police and courageous men and women who have sometimes literally put their bodies between the suicide bombers and their intended victims. And it is also important to note that while most of America's enemies are thousands of miles away, the terrorists who threaten Israel are literally on its doorstep.

> "...any culture that takes pride in having the next generation as a ready supply of cheap weapons has already lost its future. Any leader who cultivates or condones suicide as its war plan has lost all moral standing. What do we say about societies that practice human sacrifice?"
>
> — **Columnist Ellen Goodman**[53]

MYTH
"Palestinians are driven to terror by desperation."

FACT

The situation many Palestinians find themselves in is unfortunate and often quite severe. Many live in poverty, see the future as hopeless, and are unhappy with the way they are treated by Israelis. None of these are excuses for engaging in terrorism. In fact, many of the terrorists are not poor, desperate people at all. The world's most wanted terrorist, Osama bin Laden, for example, is a Saudi millionaire. When asked about two Palestinian suicide bombers who blew themselves up on a pedestrian mall in Jerusalem, killing 10 people between the ages of 14 and 21, the cousin of one of the men said, "These two were not deprived of anything."[54]

A report by the National Bureau of Economic Research concluded that "economic conditions and education are largely unrelated to participation in, and support for, terrorism." The researchers said the latest outbreak of violence in the region cannot be blamed on deteriorating economic conditions because there is no connection between terrorism and economic depression. Furthermore, the authors found that support for violent action against Israel, including suicide bombing, does not vary much according to social background.[55]

Amnesty International published a study that condemned all attacks by Palestinians against Israeli civilians and said that no Israeli action justified them. According to the report, "The attacks against civilians by Palestinian armed groups are widespread, systematic and in pursuit of an explicit policy to attack civilians. They therefore constitute crimes against humanity under international law." [56]

Terrorism is not Israel's fault. It is not the result of "occupation." And it certainly is not the only response available to the Palestinians' discontentment. Palestinians have an option for improving their situation, it is called negotiations. And that is not the only option either. The Palestinians could also choose the nonviolent path taken by Martin Luther King or Gandhi. Unfortunately, they have chosen to pursue a war of terror instead of a process for peace. Israel has proven time and again a willingness to trade land for peace, but it can never concede land for terror.

MYTH

"Palestinian attacks on Israeli civilians are part of a legitimate armed struggle; they are not terrorism."

FACT

Amnesty International succinctly disposed of this fallacious argument in its report on Palestinian terrorism:

> … attacks on civilians are not permitted under any internationally recognized standard of law, whether they are committed in the context of a struggle against military occupation or any other context. Not only are they considered murder under general principles of law in every national legal system, they are contrary to fundamental principles of humanity which are reflected in international humanitarian law. In the manner in which they are being committed in Israel and the Occupied Territories, they also amount to crimes against humanity.[57]

MYTH

"Ariel Sharon has made clear that he does not want peace and no deal is possible as long as he is Prime Minister."

FACT

Ariel Sharon has been demonized by the Arabs and caricatured by the media, which often insists on referring to him as the "right-wing" or "hard-line" Prime Minister, appellations rarely affixed to any other foreign leaders. Sharon has spent most of his life as a soldier and public servant trying to bring peace to his nation.

It was Ariel Sharon who gave then Prime Minister Menachem Begin the critical backing that made the Israel-Egypt Peace Treaty possible. At a crucial moment at Camp David, the negotiations were on the verge of collapse over Egyptian President Anwar Sadat's insistence that all Israeli settlements in the Sinai be dismantled. Begin called Sharon and asked if he should give up the settlements; Sharon not only advised him to do so, but ultimately was the one who implemented the decision to remove the settlers, some by force.[58]

Sharon's views have also evolved over time. While he was once fiercely opposed to the creation of a Palestinian state, as Prime Minister he has endorsed the idea, in opposition to members of his own party. Since taking office, Sharon has repeatedly offered to negotiate with the Palestinians on condition only that they end the violence. He asked for only seven days of peace — a demand some found onerous despite the fact that the Palestinians had promised at Oslo *eight years* of peace — and later even dropped that demand. When he did, the Palestinians answered his gesture with the Passover massacre, the suicide bombing of a religious observance in a Netanya hotel in which 29 people were killed.

Sharon subsequently proposed a peace conference, an idea the Bush Administration endorsed. Even when Saudi Crown Prince Abdullah proposed a peace initiative that was filled with provisions the Saudi knew Israel could never accept, Sharon did not reject the plan, and called for direct negotiations to discuss it.

If the Arabs doubt Sharon's commitment to peace, all they need do is put him to the test – end the violence and begin negotiations. So long as the Palestinians keep up their terrorist attacks, no Israeli Prime Minister can offer them concessions.

> *"In the end we [Israel and the Palestinians] will reach a solution in which there will be a Palestinian state, but it has to be a Palestinian state by agreement and it has to be a demilitarized Palestinian state."*
>
> — **Ariel Sharon**[59]

MYTH

"Israel's presence in the West Bank is the cause of terrorism."

FACT

If Israel were to withdraw completely from the West Bank tomorrow it would not end terrorism. Radical Islamic groups such as Hamas and Islamic Jihad are opposed to the existence of a Jewish state anywhere in what they consider the Islamic heartland. These and other terrorist groups have never said they were prepared to live in peace with Israel if it were to withdraw anywhere short of the border of the Mediterranean Sea.

Long before 1967, when Israel captured the West Bank, Arabs used violence to try to first prevent the establishment of a Jewish state and then to destroy Israel. Anti-Jewish riots began in 1920 and were instigated repeatedly over the years of the British mandate in an effort to either drive out the Jews or convince the British to renege on the promise to create a Jewish homeland. These were the first "intifadas" and were characterized by the cold-blooded murder of innocents.

After Israel fended off the invading Arab nations in 1948, Egyptian President Gamal Nasser turned Palestinian terrorists against Israel and provoked the Six-Day War. In 1964, while Jordan controlled the West Bank, the Arab League created the Palestine Liberation Organization as a terrorist tool to fight against Israel. History has shown that Arab radicals are prepared to use terror to destroy Israel regardless of its borders.

MYTH

"Palestinians are living under the oppressive control of Israeli military authorities."

FACT

Israel engaged in negotiations with the Palestinians at Oslo and afterward because Israelis desperately crave peace and because they do not want to control the lives of Palestinians. After withdrawing from most of the Gaza Strip and more than 40 percent of the West Bank, approximately 98 percent of the Palestinian population came under the jurisdiction of the Palestinian Authority. Most of their affairs are now controlled by Yasser Arafat's regime, and if Israel has its way, negotiations will lead to the Palestinian Authority assuming full control over the lives of all the Palestinians living in what will eventually be a Palestinian state.

In the meantime, Israelis still intrude on Palestinian lives. Because the Palestinians' leaders have chosen the path of violence rather than negotiations, Israel still controls part of the disputed territories, and must use checkpoints, occasional curfews and other security measures to protect Israel's civilian population from terrorists. These steps certainly cause hardship and frustration, but they will not be necessary if the Palestinian Authority stops the terror.

MYTH

"Yasser Arafat condemns terrorism and leading Palestinian moderates signed a public statement saying terrorist attacks against Israel are immoral."

FACT

It is a sad commentary that praise is now heaped on Palestinians when they condemn heinous terrorist attacks against innocent Jews. Still, Palestinians cannot bring themselves to make unequivocal statements against terrorism. Yasser Arafat has come up with masterful formulations that he automatically issues after each terrorist outrage in which he condemns the attack on Israelis but always balances the statement with some criticism of

Israel. Thus, for example, the Palestinian Authority condemned the July 31, 2002, terrorist bombing of the Hebrew University cafeteria that killed seven people, including five Americans, but said Ariel Sharon was responsible for the "cycle of terror."[60]

After a similar equivocal statement following the bombing of an Israeli pizzeria, the *Washington Post* editorialized that the Palestinian leadership should have had no difficulty condemning unequivocally the bombing, but their response "was worse than equivocal....This celebration of murder, along with the perverse attempt to shift responsibility for the attack onto Mr. Sharon, adds a measure of insult to the grave injury the bombing itself inflicted."[61]

After the United States began to pressure the Palestinians to depose Arafat and do more to stop terror, a group of Palestinian intellectuals, including well-known spokespeople such as Sari Nusseibeh and Hanan Ashrawi, received publicity for signing the first public complaint about Palestinian "military operations." On June 19, 2002, the day after a suicide bus bombing killed 19 Israeli civilians, 55 Palestinians signed a full-page ad in the *Al-Quds* newspaper that called on the people who attack civilians *inside* Israel to reconsider their strategy.

The signatories did not condemn attacks against Jews in the territories. Apparently a woman or child becomes fair game if they are a foot beyond the 1967 border. Even in this statement, the courageous intellectuals suggested the problem was that the terrorist attacks give Sharon an excuse to continue his "war of aggression." As *Jerusalem Report* columnist Stuart Schoffman noted, they could not bring themselves to say that "blowing up buses is immoral, not merely counterproductive."[62]

Incidentally, the intellectuals didn't feel strongly enough about the issue to pay for the ad themselves. It was financed by sources from within the European Union.

MYTH

"Saudi Arabia is a force for peace and moderation that does not sponsor terror."

FACT

"The Saudis are active at every level of the terror chain, from planners to financiers, from cadre to foot-soldier, from ideologist to cheerleader," said Laurent Murawiec, a Rand Corporation analyst in a secret briefing to a top Pentagon advisory board. "Saudi Arabia," he added, "supports our enemies and attacks our allies."[63]

The most dramatic evidence of Saudi involvement in terror is the fact that 15 of the 19 September 11 terrorists were from Saudi Arabia. Despite this, the Saudi government refused to cooperate with the U.S. investigation of the attacks and rejected American requests to stop the flow of money through charitable organizations to terrorist groups. Many such charities are based in the United States and are being investigated by the Treasury Department.

Saudi support for terrorism and al-Qaida, in particular, is not restricted to extremists in the kingdom. A classified American intelligence report revealed that an October 2001 survey of educated Saudis between the ages of 25 and 41 found that 95 percent of the respondents supported Osama bin Laden's cause.[64]

The Saudis have been heavily involved in supporting Palestinian terror. They were the largest financial backer of Hamas during the 1990s, providing perhaps as much as $10 million annually. In a letter from a top Arafat aide to the governor of Riyadh, Abu Mazen even complained that Saudi money wasn't reaching the "martyrs," but was going directly to Hamas.[65]

The Saudis held a terror telethon on April 11, 2002, which raised $150 for families of Palestinian "martyrs," including the families of suicide bombers,[66] and during Operation Defensive Shield, the Israelis found numerous documents linking the Saudis to terror. One, for example, itemized their allocations line by line, detailing the circumstances of the death of Palestinians whose families received assistance, and making clear the allocation was for suicide attacks. The information came from the Saudi Committee for Aid to the Al-Quds Intifada, which is headed by Saudi Minister of the Interior, Prince Nayef bin 'Abd al-Aziz.

MYTH

"Yasser Arafat is the democratically elected leader of the Palestinian people and Israel must negotiate with him."

FACT

Palestinians have the right to select their own leaders, but both Israel and the United States also have the right to decide which leaders they are prepared to recognize and negotiate with. Israel cannot be expected to negotiate with someone who conducts a terror campaign against its citizens. Every Arab leader who has recognized Israel and been prepared to make peace has gotten both land and peace.

The Palestinian Authority is a corrupt dictatorship run by a terrorist who was "elected" in a sham election in 1996, and whose term was supposed to be over long ago. He clings to power through intimidation and violence. Only true democratic elections monitored by international observers, with multiple candidates, can bring representative leadership to the Palestinians.

When the Palestinians democratically elect a leader who is prepared to recognize Israel's right to exist, end violence, and negotiate peace, they will find a willing and eager partner in Israel.

As the only democracy in the region, one which allows women to vote and even pro-PLO Israeli Arabs to serve in its parliament, Israel respects democratically elected leaders. Israelis, like Americans, believe that democracies do not make war on each other, so it is in Israel's interest to see that the Palestinians develop democratic institutions. To date, however, the history of the Palestinians is one in which leaders are determined by bullets, not ballots.

Notes

[1] Speech to AIPAC Policy Conference, (May 8, 1978).

[2] Daniel Pipes, *The Long Shadow: Culture and Politics in the Middle East*, (NJ: Transaction Publishers, 1989), pp. 273-74.

[3] Reuters, (September 24, 2001).

[4] Michael Widlanski, *Can Israel Survive A Palestinian State?*, (Jerusalem: Institute for Advanced Strategic and Political Studies, 1990), pp. 10, 35.

[5] *Voice of Palestine*, Algiers, (September 2, 1993).

[6] Saudi Press Agency, (July 15, 1986).

[7] Howard Sachar, *A History of Israel: From the Rise of Zionism to Our Time*, (NY: Alfred A. Knopf, 1979), p. 335.

[8] AP, (October 22, 2001).

[9] Jerusalem Report, (March 26, 2001).

[10] *Jerusalem Post*, (August 26, 2002).

[11] Radio Damascus, (March 8, 1974).

[12] *Jerusalem Post*, (October 16, 2001).

[13] NBC News and MSNBC, (May 8, 2001).

[14] Lee Hockstader, "At Arab, Israeli Schools, Hatred Is Common Bond," *Washington Post*, (September 5, 2001).

[15] Goetz Norbruch, *Narrating Palestinian Nationalism: A Study of the New Palestinian Textbooks*, (DC: MEMRI, 2002).

[16] *Near East Report*, (June 25, 2001); *Jerusalem Post*, (July 20, 2001).

[17] *Jerusalem Post*, (May 23, 2001).

[18] Quoted in *Jerusalem Post*, (July 20, 2001).

[19] Lecture by Dr. Yohanan Manor, March 7, 2002.

[20] *Washington Post*, (June 25, 2002).

[21] Islamic Association for Palestine, (June 9, 2001).

[22] *Jerusalem Post*, (June 29, 2002).

[23] See, for example, CNN, (January 13, 2001); AP, (July 31, 2001).

[24] *Washington Post*, (July 18, 2001), citing an article by Robert Malley and Hussein Agha in the *New York Review of Books* in which they quote the President at the Camp David summit in July 2000.

[25] *Jerusalem Post*, (July 16, 1994).

[26] *Washington Times*, (July 30, 1990).

[27] Israeli-Palestinian Joint Water Committee, "Joint Declaration for Keeping the Water Infrastructure out of the Cycle of Violence," (January 31, 2001).

[28] *Mideast Mirror*, (October 7, 1991).

[29] *Washington Post*, (September 10, 1995).

[30] Hamas Covenant, The Avalon Project, (http://www.yale.edu/lawweb/avalon/avalon.htm).

[31] *Yediot Aharonot*, (November 23, 2001).

[32] *Ma'ariv,* (April 6, 2001); Interview with Dennis Ross, Fox News Sunday, (April 21, 2002); President Clinton, Press Conference, (July 25, 2000); *"Camp David: An Exchange." The New York Review of Books,* (September 20, 2001); Fred Barnes, "Myths of the Intifada," *The Daily Standard,* (April 25, 2002).

[33] MSNBC, (March 26, 2002).

[34] Neil Livingstone and David Halevy, *Inside the PLO,* (Readers Digest Press, 1990), pp. 276-288.

[35] *Chicago Tribune,* (May 5, 1988).

[36] *Al-Arabi,* (June 24, 2001).

[37] Fox News, (January 8, 2002).

[38] *USA Today,* (January 10, 2002).

[39] Associated Press, (January 8, 2002), and Michael Kelly, "Red-Handed and unrepentant," MSNBC, (January 10, 2002).

[40] *The Jewish Week* (NY), (February 8, 2002).

[41] *Jerusalem Post,* (April 5, 2002).

[42] *Washington Jewish Week,* (February 14, 2002).

[43] *Ha'aretz,* (February 13, 2002).

[44] *Jerusalem Post,* (November 23, 2001, and June 30, 2002).

[45] Palestinian Authority.

[46] President Lyndon Johnson speech, (June 19, 1967).

[47] Jewish Telegraphic Agency, (February 6, 2002).

[48] White House Press Briefing, (April 11, 2002).

[49] *Washington Post,* (April 2 and 12, 2002).

[50] AP, (April 2, 2002).

[51] *Jerusalem Post,* (February 18, 2002).

[52] CNN, (April 11, 2002).

[53] *Washington Post,* (April 6, 2002).

[54] *Washington Post,* (December 5, 2001).

[55] Jitka Maleckova and Alan Kreuger, "Education, Poverty, Political Violence and Terrorism: Is There a Causal Connection?" (July 2002), quoted in the *Daily Star* [Lebanon], (August 6, 2002).

[56] "Without Distinction: Attacks on Civilians by Palestinian Armed Groups," Amnesty International, (July 11, 2002).

[57] "Without Distinction: Attacks on Civilians by Palestinian Armed Groups," Amnesty International, (July 11, 2002).

[58] Steven Spiegel, *The Other Arab-Israeli Conflict: Making America's Middle East Policy from Truman to Reagan,* (IL: University of Chicago Press, 1986), p. 358; Ariel Sharon, *Warrior,* (NY: Touchstone Books, 2001), pp. 400-401.

[59] Reuters, (November 11, 2001).

[60] *New York Times,* (August 1, 2002).

[61] *Washington Post,* (August 10, 2001).

[62] *Jerusalem Report,* (July 15, 2002), p. 51.

[63] *Washington Post,* (August 6, 2002).

[64] *New York Times,* (January 27, 2002).

[65] Kenneth Timmerman, "Hamas' Friends," *Australia/Israel Review,* (June 2002), p. 13.

[66] *Washington Post,* (August 2 and 12, 2002).

22. Settlements

MYTH

"Israel has no right to be in the West Bank.
Israeli settlements are illegal."

FACT

Jews have lived in Judea and Samaria – the West Bank – since ancient times. The only time Jews have been prohibited from living in the territories in recent decades was during Jordan's rule from 1948 to 1967. This prohibition was contrary to the Mandate for Palestine adopted by the League of Nations, which provided for the establishment of a Jewish state, and specifically encouraged "close settlement by Jews on the land."

Numerous legal authorities dispute the charge that settlements are "illegal." International law scholar Stephen Schwebel notes that a country acting in self-defense may seize and occupy territory when necessary to protect itself. Schwebel also observes that a state may require, as a condition for its withdrawal, security measures designed to ensure its citizens are not menaced again from that territory.[1]

According to Eugene Rostow, a former Undersecretary of State for Political Affairs in the Johnson Administration, Resolution 242 gives Israel a legal right to be in the West Bank. The resolution, Rostow noted, "allows Israel to administer the territories" it won in 1967 "until 'a just and lasting peace in the Middle East' is achieved."[2]

MYTH

"Settlements are an obstacle to peace."

FACT

Settlements have never been an obstacle to peace.

- From 1949-67, when Jews were forbidden to live on the West Bank, the Arabs refused to make peace with Israel.

- From 1967-77, the Labor Party established only a few strategic settlements in the territories, yet the Arabs were unwilling to negotiate peace with Israel.

- In 1977, months after a Likud government committed to greater settlement activity took power, Egyptian President Sadat went to Jerusalem and later signed a peace treaty with Israel. Incidentally, Israeli settlements existed in the Sinai and those were removed as part of the agreement with Egypt.

- One year later, Israel froze settlement building for three months, hoping the gesture would entice other Arabs to join the Camp David peace process. But none would.

- In 1994, Jordan signed a peace agreement with Israel and settlements were not an issue. If anything, the number of Jews living in the territories was growing.

- Between June 1992 and June 1996, under Labor-led governments, the Jewish population in the territories grew by approximately 50 percent. This rapid growth did not prevent the Palestinians from signing the Oslo accords in September 1993 or the Oslo 2 agreement in September 1995.

- In 2000, Prime Minister Barak offered to dismantle dozens of settlement, but the Palestinians still would not agree to end the conflict.

Settlement activity may be a stimulus to peace because it forced the Palestinians and other Arabs to reconsider the view that time is on their side. References are frequently made in Arabic writings to how long it took to expel the Crusaders and how it might take a similar length of time to do the same to the Zionists. The growth in the Jewish population in the territories forced the Arabs to question this tenet. "The Palestinians now realize," said Bethlehem Mayor Elias Freij, "that time is now on the side of Israel, which can build settlements and create facts, and that the only way out of this dilemma is face-to-face negotiations."[3]

Many Israelis nevertheless have concerns about the expansion of settlements. Some consider them provocative, others worry that the settlers are particularly vulnerable, and have been targets of repeated Palestinian terrorist attacks. To defend them, large numbers of soldiers are deployed who would otherwise be training and preparing for a possible future conflict with an Arab army. Some Israelis also object to the amount of money that goes to communities beyond the Green Line and special subsidies that have been provided to make housing there more affordable. Still others feel the settlers are providing a first line of defense and developing land that rightfully belongs to Israel.

The disposition of settlements is a matter for the final status negotiations. The question of where the final border will be between Israel and a Palestinian entity will likely be influenced by the distribution of these Jewish towns. Israel wants to incorporate as many settlers as possible within its borders while the Palestinians want to expel all Jews from the territory they control.

If Israel withdraws toward the 1967 border unilaterally, or as part of a political settlement, many settlers will face one or more options: remain in the territories, expulsion from their homes, or voluntary resettlement in Israel. The impediment to peace is not the existence of those settlements; it is the Palestinians' unwillingness to accept a state next to Israel instead of one replacing Israel.

MYTH

"The Geneva Convention probibits the construction of Jewish settlements in occupied territories."

FACT

The Fourth Geneva Convention prohibits the *forcible* transfer of people of one state to the territory of another state that it has occupied as a result of a war. The intention was to insure that local populations who came under occupation would not be forced to move. This is in no way relevant to the settlement issue. Jews are not being forced to go to the West Bank and Gaza Strip; on the contrary, they are voluntarily moving back to places where they, or their ancestors, once lived before being expelled by others. In addition, those territories never legally belonged to either Jordan or Egypt, and certainly not to the Palestinians, who were never the sovereign authority in any part of Palestine. "The Jewish right of settlement in the area is equivalent in every way to the right of the local population to live there," according to Professor Eugene Rostow, former Undersecretary of State for Political Affairs.[4]

As a matter of policy, moreover, Israel does not requisition private land for the establishment of settlements. Housing construction is allowed on private land only after determining that no private rights will be violated. The settlements also do not displace Arabs living in the territories. The media sometimes gives the impression that for every Jew who moves to the West Bank, several hundred Palestinians are forced to leave. The truth is that the vast majority of settlements have been built in uninhabited areas and even the handful established in or near Arab towns did not force any Palestinians to leave.

> *"Settlements in various parts of the so-called occupied area... [were] the result of a war which they [the Israelis] won."*
>
> **U.S. Defense Secretary, Donald Rumsfeld**[5]

MYTH

"Israel is provocatively settling Jews in predominantly Arab towns, and has established so many facts on the ground territorial compromise is no longer possible."

FACT

Altogether, built-up settlement area is less than two percent of the disputed territories. An estimated 80 percent of the settlers live in what are in effect suburbs of major Israeli cities such as Jerusalem and Tel Aviv. These are areas that virtually the entire Jewish population believes Israel must retain to ensure its security, and even President Clinton indicated in December 2000 should remain under permanent Israeli sovereignty.[6]

Strategic concerns have led both Labor and Likud governments to establish settlements. The objective is to secure a Jewish majority in key strategic regions of the West Bank, such as the Tel Aviv-Jerusalem corridor, the scene of heavy fighting in several Arab-Israeli wars. Still, when Arab-Israeli peace talks began in late 1991, more than 80 percent of the West Bank contained no settlements or only sparsely populated ones.[7]

Today, approximately 200,000 Jews live in roughly 150 communities in the West Bank. The overwhelming majority of these settlements have fewer than 1,000 citizens. Analysts have noted that 80 percent of the Jews could be brought within Israel's borders with minor modifications of the "Green Line."

MYTH

"Israel must evacuate all Jewish settlements before a final peace agreement can be achieved with the Palestinians."

FACT

The implication of many settlement critics is that it would be better for peace if the West Bank were *Judenrein* (empty of Jews). This idea would be called anti-Semitic if Jews were barred from living in New York, Paris or London; barring them from living in the West Bank, the cradle of Jewish civilization, would be no less objectionable.

Any peace settlement would inevitably permit Jews who preferred to live outside the State of Israel under Palestinian authority to live in the West Bank — just as Arabs today live in Israel. No Israeli government would be expected to enforce the kind of policies instituted by the British by which large areas of Palestine were declared off-limits to Jews.

MYTH

"At Camp David, during Jimmy Carter's presidency, Israel agreed to halt the construction of settlements for five years. Within months, Israel had violated the accords by establishing new settlements on the West Bank."

FACT

The five-year period agreed to at Camp David was the time allotted to Palestinian self-government in the territories. The Israeli moratorium on West Bank settlements agreed to by Prime Minister Menachem Begin was only for three months. Begin kept this agreement.

Israel's position on the matter received support from an unexpected source: Egyptian President Anwar Sadat, who said: "We agreed to put a freeze on the establishment of settlements for the coming three months, the time necessary in our estimation for signing the peace treaty."[8]

The Palestinians rejected the Camp David Accords and therefore the provisions related to them were never implemented. Had they accepted the terms offered by Begin, it is very likely the self-governing authority would have developed long before now into the state the Palestinians say they desire.

MYTH

"Anyone who defends settlements is rationalizing the perpetual occupation of the Palestinian people and their land."

FACT

While making a strong case for its right to the territories, the Israeli government also acknowledges that Palestinians have legitimate claims to the area and that a compromise can be reached through negotiations:

> Politically, the West Bank and Gaza Strip is best regarded as territory over which there are competing claims which should be resolved in peace process negotiations. Israel has valid claims to title in this territory based not only on its historic and religious connection to the land, and its recognized security needs, but also on the fact that the territory was not under the sovereignty of any state and came under Israeli control in a war of self-defense, imposed upon Israel. At the same time, Israel recognizes that the Palestinians also entertain legitimate claims to the area. Indeed, the very fact that the parties have agreed to conduct negotiations on settlements indicated that they envisage a compromise on this issue.[9]

In fact, in the 2000 negotiations at Camp David and the White House, Prime Minister Barak reportedly offered to dismantle at least 63 settlements.[10] The Palestinians rejected the proposal.

> *"If settlement-building is now concentrated in areas that the Palestinians themselves acknowledge will remain part of Israel in any future peace agreement, why the obsessive focus on settlements as an 'obstacle to peace?'"*
>
> **— Yossi Klein Halevi**[11]

MYTH

"The peace agreements Israel signed with the Palestinians pro-hibit settlement activity."

FACT

Neither the Declaration of Principles of September 13, 1993, nor the Interim Agreement contains any provisions prohibiting or restricting the establishment or expansion of Jewish communities in the West Bank or Gaza Strip. While a clause in the accords prohibits changing the status of the territories, it was intended to ensure only that neither side would take unilateral measures to alter the legal status of the areas (such as annexation or declaration of statehood).

MYTH

"The Red Cross has declared that Israeli settlements are a war crime."

FACT

The Jerusalem representative of the International Committee of the Red Cross (ICRC), Rene Kosimik, on May 17, 2001, said, "The installation of a population of the occupying power in occupied territory is considered an illegal move, it is a grave breach. In principal it is a war crime." Rep. Eliot Engel protested to the President of the ICRC, Jakob Kellenberger, who replied, "The expression 'war crime' has not been used by the ICRC in relation to Israeli settlements in the occupied territories in the past and will not be used anymore in the present context." He added, "The reference made to it on May 17 was inappropriate and will not be repeated."[12]

Notes

[1] *American Journal of International Law,* (April, 1970), pp. 345-46.

[2] *New Republic,* (October 21, 1991), p. 14.

[3] *Washington Post,* (November 1, 1991).

[4] American Journal of International Law, (1990, Vol. 84), p. 72.

[5] *USA Today,* (August 7, 2002).

[6] *Ha'aretz,* (September 13, 2001).

[7] *Jerusalem Post,* (October 22, 1991).

[8] Middle East News Agency, (September 20, 1978).

[9] Israeli Foreign Ministry, "Israeli Settlements and International Law," (May 2001).

[10] Temporary International Presence in Hebron, (http://www.tiph.org/).

[11] *Los Angeles Times,* (June 20, 2001).

[12] *Jerusalem Post,* (May 24, 2001).

23. The Arms Balance

MYTH

"The threat from Israel and the withdrawal of the United States' offer to build the Aswan Dam drove Egypt to seek arms from the Soviet Union in 1955. This started the Middle East arms race."

FACT

In 1955, Nasser turned to the Soviet Union in anger because the United States had armed Iraq, Egypt's hated rival, and promoted the Baghdad Pact. Nasser opposed that agreement, as he did any defense alliance with the West.

Egypt began to receive Soviet Bloc arms in 1955. The United States, hoping to maintain a degree of influence in Egypt and to induce Nasser to reduce his arms acquisitions, offered to build the Aswan Dam. But Nasser increased his arms orders and spurned a U.S. peace initiative. Egypt had embarked on a policy of "neutralism," which meant that Nasser intended to get aid from both East and West if he could, while maintaining his freedom to attack the West and assist Soviet efforts to gain influence in the Arab and Afro-Asian worlds. As a result of these actions, and Nasser's increasing hostility to the West, the United States withdrew the Aswan offer. Egypt then nationalized the Suez Canal.

Immediately after Nasser made his 1955 arms deal, Israel appealed to the United States — not for a gift of arms, but for the right to purchase them. The U.S. recognized the need to maintain an arms balance, but it referred Israel to France and other European suppliers. It was not until 1962 that the United States agreed to sell Israel its first significant American system, the HAWK anti-aircraft missile.

MYTH

"The Arab states have had to keep pace with an Israeli-led arms race."

FACT

In most cases, the reverse was true. Egypt received the Soviet IL-28 bomber in 1955. It was not until 1958 that France provided Israel with a squadron of comparable Sud Vautour twin-jet tactical bombers. In 1957, Egypt obtained MiG-17 fighter planes. Israel received the comparable Super Mystere in 1959. Egypt had submarines in 1957, Israel in 1959. After the Egyptians obtained the MiG-21, the Israelis ordered the Dassault Mirage III supersonic interceptor and fighter-bomber.

Egypt received ground-to-air missiles — the SA-2 — two years before Israel obtained HAWK missiles from the United States. Later, Washington reluctantly agreed to sell Israel Patton tanks.

Despite being supplied arms at bargain prices in exchange for cotton, and with long-term, cheap-money credits, Egypt's debt to the USSR was estimated to be $11 billion by 1977.[1] Israel had to pay much more, plus interest, for comparable weapons.

Even when the United States began selling arms to Israel in the 1960s, it maintained a policy of balance whereby similar sales were made to Arab states. In 1965, for example, the first major tank sale to Israel was matched by one to Jordan. A year later, when Israel received Skyhawks, the U.S. provided planes to Morocco and Libya, as well as additional military equipment to Lebanon, Saudi Arabia and Tunisia.[2]

It was not until 1968, when the Johnson Administration sold Israel Phantom jets, that America's arms transfer policy shifted to emphasize maintaining the Jewish State's qualitative advantage. Since then, however, the U.S. has frequently sold sophisticated arms (e.g., F-15s, AWACS and Stinger missiles) to Israel's adversaries, which have eroded the Jewish State's qualitative edge.

MYTH

"Israel is militarily superior to its Arab neighbors in every area and has the means to maintain its qualitative edge without outside help."

FACT

Israel's qualitative military edge has declined as Arab and Muslim states acquire increasingly sophisticated conventional and unconventional arms. In fact, despite its pledges to the contrary, the United States is allowing Israel's qualitative edge to dissipate. In some cases, U.S. arms transfers to the Arabs are the reason for this erosion.

Israel's standing army is smaller than those of Egypt, Iraq, Iran and Syria. Even with its reserves, Israel is outmanned by each of the first three. In addition, Israel is likely to have to face a combination of enemies, as it has in each of its previous wars; together, virtually any combination of likely opponents would be superior in manpower, tanks and aircraft.

During the 1990's, the Arab states and Iran imported more than $180 billion worth of the most sophisticated weapons and military infrastructure available from both the Western and Eastern blocs. They continue to spend approximately $30 billion annually on their armed forces. Several of the world's largest arms-importing countries have been Arab nations in a state of war with Israel: Iraq, Syria, Saudi Arabia and Libya. While Israel spends approximately $9 billion on defense, Saudi Arabia alone spends more than $20 billion.[3]

In addition to the sheer quantity of arms, these states are also buying and producing increasing numbers of nonconventional weapons. The buildup of chemical and biological weapons, combined with the pursuit of a nuclear capability, makes Israel's strategic position more precarious.

Beyond the security threat, this massive arms build-up also requires Israel to spend a sixth of its GNP on defense. Even this high level of spending is insufficient, however, to meet the Arab threat, as budgetary restrictions have forced Israel to make substantial cuts in its defense allocations. Arab arms sales have significantly raised the cost to Israel of maintaining its own defense, exacerbating the strain on Israel's economy.

MYTH

"Iraq's defeat in the Gulf War ensures that Israel will be facing only Syria in any future conflict. Other Arab involvement is of little importance."

FACT

Israel has no choice but to base its defense planning on actual Arab capabilities. If history is any lesson, a future Arab-Israeli conflict will be the result of an alliance of Arab states joining, if only temporarily, to launch a strike at Israel. The Arabs have traditionally put aside their differences at times of conflict with Israel.

Even alone, Syria would pose a serious threat to Israel. Damascus received more than $2 billion from the Gulf states because of the Gulf crisis. Much of this was spent on new modern weaponry to advance Hafez Assad's quest for "strategic parity" with Israel. Today, Syria has more tanks than Israel, and nearly as many troops and aircraft. Syria has also acquired long-range missiles from North Korea and acquired biological and chemical weapons. Syria has first-strike capabilities against key Israeli installations, including air bases and troop mobilization points.

Iraq remains a long-term concern for Israel's security. Saddam still has some 2,400 tanks and 300 combat aircraft. Some of Iraq's chemical arsenal, nuclear materials, facilities and mobile ballistic missile launchers survived the Gulf War intact and went undetected by United Nations inspectors. The German Federal Intelligence Service issued a report that said Iraq could have a bomb within three years and was developing a long-range ballistic missile that could threaten Europe by 2005. The German report also indicated that Iraq is putting a great deal of effort into producing chemical weapons and may have resumed production of biological weapons.[4]

Despite its massive arsenal of Soviet-supplied weaponry, Libya until recently had only limited capability to directly attack Israel. Libya has now acquired the capacity for aerial refueling of its bombers, giving them the means to reach

Israel. U.S. intelligence also discovered the construction of a second Libyan chemical plant being built underground, in addition to the now-operational Rabta facility. The latter is estimated to have produced as much as 100 tons of chemical agents. Libya is also a state sponsor of terrorism. It is responsible for the Pan Am 103 bombing in 1988, which resulted in the deaths of more than 200 Americans.

Saudi Arabia and the Gulf states continue to order weapons on a grand scale, seeking to acquire military capabilities far beyond their own defense needs. Though these countries are unlikely to attack Israel, they could supply arms, as they have in the past, to a future Arab coalition fighting Israel.

While Egypt remains formally at peace with Israel and honors its Camp David commitments, Cairo has nevertheless amassed a substantial offensive military capability in recent years. Prudent Israeli military planners have no choice but to carefully monitor Egypt's buildup, should regional events take a dramatic turn for the worse. If the present regime in Cairo should be overthrown, the prospect for continued stable relations with Israel would diminish substantially. Despite its status as a U.S. ally, Egypt has purchased Scud missiles from North Korea and is thought to possess chemical weapons. Its army, air force and navy now field a wide range of the most sophisticated Western arms, many identical to Israel's own weapons.

MYTH

"The sale of U.S. arms to Saudi Arabia has reduced the need for American troops to defend the Persian Gulf. These weapons pose no threat to Israel."

FACT

The Saudi armed forces are structurally incapable of defending their country. They were helpless in the face of the Iraqi threat despite the Saudi acquisition of more than $50 billion in U.S. arms and military services in the decade preceding the Gulf War.[5] If Saddam Hussein had continued his blitzkrieg into Saudi Arabia before American forces arrived in August 1990, much of the weaponry the United States sold Riyadh over the years might now be in Iraqi hands.

Even if all past U.S. arms sales to the Saudis had sailed through Congress without question or modification, it is doubtful whether the military equation on the ground, or the decision-making process in Riyadh would have been different. The Saudis' small armed forces cannot unilaterally withstand an assault by a force three to four times its size.

Administration officials frequently argue the Saudis need advanced weapons to counter threats to their security from countries as powerful as the old Soviet Union, but maintain these same weapons would pose no danger to Israel.

The U.S. cannot hand over vast quantities of aircraft and missiles to the Saudi armed forces when it cannot ensure these weapons will not be used against Israel. The "Iran scenario" — that is, the monarchy is overthrown and a more hostile regime takes control of the Saudi arsenal — cannot be ruled out either.

In past Arab-Israeli wars, the Saudis never had a modern arsenal of sufficient size to make their participation in an Arab coalition against Israel a serious concern. The Saudi buildup since the 1973 War changes this equation. The Kingdom could be pressured into offensive action against Israel by other eastern front partners precisely because of this buildup.

> *"I wish Israel did not need defensive weapons of mass destruction or the region's most powerful defense forces. I wish the world had not driven the Jewish State into allocating its limited resources away from its universities and toward its military, but survival must come first, and Israel's military strength is the key to its survival. Anyone who believes that survival can be assured by moral superiority alone must remember the Warsaw Ghetto and the Treblinka gas chambers."*
>
> **— Alan Dershowitz**[6]

MYTH

"Israel refuses to sign the Nuclear Non-Proliferation Treaty to conceal its nuclear arsenal, and therefore threatens its neighbors."

FACT

Though Israel does not formally acknowledge that it has a nuclear capability, it has been widely reported that Israel has been a member of the nuclear club for a number of years.

Israel's decision not to be bound by the Non-Proliferation Treaty (NPT) is based largely on the grounds that the treaty has done little to stem nuclear proliferation in the region. Iraq is a signatory to the NPT, and yet was able to amass a large amount of nuclear material without the knowledge of the International Atomic Energy Agency.

Israel has called for the creation of a nuclear-free zone in the Middle East and has stated many times that it will not be the first state to introduce nuclear weapons into the region. Simultaneously, numerous Middle Eastern countries have been trying to build their own nonconventional capabilities.

In addition to Iraq, which is believed to possess the materials to produce a bomb, Algeria, Syria, Egypt and Iran all reportedly have ongoing covert programs to develop an atomic weapon.

MYTH

"Arms control in the Middle East is impossible so long as Israel refuses to give up its nuclear weapons."

FACT

Israel's assumed nuclear deterrent is an option of last resort, needed to offset the large imbalance in conventional arms, chemical weapons and ballistic missiles possessed by the Arab states. Israel has no incentive to unilaterally attack its neighbors with nuclear weapons whereas the Arabs — as history has shown — have both the capability and motivation to join in a war against Israel. Arms control must therefore begin with a reduction in Arab military offensive capability. Arab "arms control" proposals in essence have only called for Israel to give up nuclear arms without offering anything substantive in return.

Notes

[1] Adeed Dawisha and Karen Dawisha, Eds., *The Soviet Union in the Middle East, Policies and perspectives,* (NY: Holmes and Meier, 1982), pp. 8, 11, 15.

[2] Mitchell Bard, *The Water's Edge And Beyond,* (NJ: Transaction Publishers, 1991), p. 194-209.

[3] Adapted by Anthony Cordesman from the U.S. Arms Control and Disarmament Agency, *World Military Expenditures and Arms Transfers,* (DC: GPO); Cordesman for the International Institute for Strategic Studies, *Military Balance*; Shai Feldman and Yiftah Shapir, Eds., *The Middle East Military Balance,* (Cambridge: MIT Press, 2001).

[4] *Jerusalem Post,* (February 25, 2001).

[5] Arms Control and Disarmament Agency; Defense Security Assistance Agency Report; World Military Expenditures and Arms Transfers.

[6] Alan Dershowitz, *Chutzpah,* (MA: Little Brown, and Co., 1991), p. 249.

24. The Media

MYTH

*"Press coverage of Israel is proportional
to its importance in world affairs."*

FACT

It is hard to justify the amount of news coverage given to Israel based on the nation's importance in world affairs or American national interests. How is it that a country the size of New Jersey routinely merits top billing over seemingly more newsworthy nations like Russia, China and Great Britain?

Israel probably has the highest per capita fame quotient in the world. Americans know more about Israeli politics than that of any other foreign country. Most of Israel's leaders, for example, are more familiar in the United States than those of America's neighbors in Canada or Mexico. In addition, a high percentage of Americans are conversant on the Arab-Israeli conflict.

One reason Americans are so knowledgeable about Israel is the extent of coverage. American news organizations usually have more correspondents in Israel than in any country except Great Britain.

MYTH

*"Israel receives so much attention because it is the only country
in the Middle East that affects U.S. interests."*

FACT

The Middle East is important to the United States (and the Western world) primarily because of its oil resources. Events that might threaten the production and supply of oil affect vital U.S. interests. The United States also has an interest in supporting friendly regimes in the region. Attention is warranted because the Middle East is the scene of repeated conflagrations that directly or indirectly affect American interests. Events in countries like Jordan, Lebanon and Iran have required the intervention of U.S. troops, and nothing focuses the attention of the public like American lives being endangered abroad. The United States has been deeply involved in each of the Arab-Israeli wars, but has also had its own independent battles, most notably the Gulf War with Iraq.

On the other hand, Americans are not typically interested in the fratricidal wars of people in distant lands when the fighting does not appear to have any bearing on U.S. interests. This is true in Africa, Latin America and even the Balkans. Similarly, inter-Arab wars have not generated the kind of interest that Israel's problems have. However, the Israeli-Palestinian dispute — two people fighting over one land — is a particularly compelling story. It is made all the more so by the fact that it is centered in the Holy Land.

Another explanation for the disproportionate coverage Israel receives relative to Arab countries is that few correspondents have a background in Middle East history or speak the regional languages. Journalists are more familiar with the largely Western culture in Israel than the more alien Muslim societies.

MYTH
"Western media coverage of the Arab world is equal to that of Israel."

FACT
The journalistic community regards the Arab/Islamic world as the "arc of silence."[1] The media in those countries is strictly controlled by totalitarian governments. By contrast, Israel is a democracy with one of the most free-wheeling press corps in the world.

The limited access is often used as an excuse for the media's failure to cover news in the region. This was the case, for example, during the Iran-Iraq war — one of the bloodiest conflicts in the last four decades. Still, given the resourcefulness of American journalists, it is shocking that so little coverage is given to even the most authoritarian of regimes.

MYTH
"Media coverage of the Arab world is objective."

FACT
When journalists are allowed to pierce the veil of secrecy, the price of access to dictators and terrorists is often steep. Reporters are sometimes intimidated or blackmailed. In Lebanon during the 1980s, for example, the Palestine Liberation Organization (PLO) had reporters doing their bidding as the price for obtaining interviews and protection. During the "al-Aksa intifada," Israeli journalists were warned against going to the Palestinian Authority (PA) and some received telephone threats after publishing articles critical of the PA leadership.[2]

When asked to comment on what many viewers regard as CNN's bias against Israel, Reese Schonfeld, the network's first president explained, "When I see them on the air I see them being very careful about Arab sensibilities." Schonfeld suggested the coverage is slanted because CNN doesn't want to risk the special access it has in the Arab world.[3]

In Arab countries, journalists are usually escorted to see what the dictator wants them to see or they are followed. Citizens are warned by security agencies, sometimes directly, sometimes more subtly, that they should be careful what they say to visitors.

In the case of coverage of the PA, the Western media relies heavily on Palestinian assistants to escort correspondents in the territories. In addition, Palestinians often provide the news that is sent out around the world. "By my own estimate," journalist Ehud Ya'ari wrote, "over 95 percent of the TV pictures going out on satellite every evening to the various foreign and Israeli channels are supplied by Palestinian film crews. The two principle agencies in the video news market, APTN and Reuters TV, run a whole network of Palestinian stringers, freelancers and fixers all over the territories to provide instant footage of the events. These crews obviously identify emotionally and politically with the intifada and, in the 'best' case, they simply don't dare film anything that could embarrass the Palestinian Authority. So the cameras are angled to show a tainted view of the Israeli army's actions, never focus on the Palestinian gunmen and diligently produce a very specific kind of close-up of the situation on the ground."[4]

A particularly egregious incident occurred in October 2000 when two non-combatant Israeli reservists were lynched in Ramallah by a Palestinian mob. According to reporters on the scene, the Palestinian police tried to prevent foreign journalists from filming the incident. One Italian television crew managed to film parts of the attack and these shocking images ultimately made headlines around the world. A competing Italian news agency took a different tack, placing an advertisement in the PA's main newspaper, *Al Hayat-Al-Jadidah*, explaining that it had nothing to do with filming the incident:

> My dear friends in Palestine. We congratulate you and think that it is our duty to put you in the picture (of the events) of what happened on October 12 in Ramallah. One of the private television stations which competes with us (and not the official Italian television station RTI) filmed the events; *that* station filmed the events. Afterwards Israeli Television broadcast the pictures, as taken from one of the Italian stations, and thus the public impression was created as if we (RTI) took these pictures.

> We emphasize to all of you that the events did not happen this way, because we always respect (will continue to respect) the journalistic procedures with the Palestinian Authority for (journalistic) work in Palestine and we are credible in our precise work.

> We thank you for your trust, and you can be sure that this is not our way of acting (note: meaning we do not work like the other television stations). We do not (and will not) do such a thing.

> Please accept our blessings.

> Signed
> **Ricardo Christiano**
> Representative of the official Italian
> station in Palestine[5]

If a news organization strays from the pro-Palestinian line, it comes under immediate attack. In November 2000, for example, the Palestinian Journalist's Union complained that the Associated Press was presenting a false impression of the "al-Aksa intifada." The Union called AP's coverage a conscious crime against the Palestinian people and said it served the Israeli position. The Union threatened to adopt all necessary measures against AP staffers as well as against AP bureaus located in the PA if the agency continued to harm Palestinian interests.[6]

MYTH

"Journalists covering the Middle East are driven by the search for the truth."

FACT

It will come as no surprise to learn that journalists in the Middle East share an interest in sensationalism with their colleagues covering domestic issues. The most egregious examples come from television reporters whose emphasis on visuals over substance encourages facile treatment of the issues. For example, when NBC's correspondent in Israel was asked why reporters turned up at Palestinian demonstrations in the West Bank they knew were being staged, he said, "We play along because we need the pictures."[7] The networks can't get newsworthy pictures from closed societies such as Syria, Saudi Arabia, Iran or Libya.

Israel often faces an impossible situation of trying to counter images with words. "When a tank goes into Ramallah, it does not look good on TV," explains Gideon Meir of the Israeli Foreign Ministry. "Sure we can explain why we are there, and that's what we do. But it's words. We have to fight pictures with words."[8]

> "We were filming the beginning of the demonstration. Suddenly, a van pulled in hurriedly. Inside, there were Fatah militants. They gave their orders and even distributed Molotov cocktails. We were filming. But these images, you will never see. In a few seconds, all those youngsters surrounded us, threatened us, and then took us away to the police station. There, we identified ourselves but we were compelled to delete the controversial pictures. The Palestinian Police calmed the situation but censored our pictures. We now have the proof that those riots are no longer spontaneous. All the orders came from the Palestinian hierarchy."
>
> — **Jean Pierre Martin**[9]

The magnitude of the problem Israel confronts is clear from Tami Allen-Frost, deputy chairman of the Foreign Press Association and a producer for Britain's ITN news, who says "the strongest picture that stays in the mind is of a tank in a city" and that "there are more incidents all together in the West Bank than there are suicide bombings. In the end, it's quantity that stays with you."[10]

MYTH

"The media lets Israel get away with more because of its alliance with the U.S."

FACT

Americans tend to have a double-standard about the Jews, expecting more from them than other peoples. This is in part due to the Jews' own high expectations and goal of being a "light unto the nations." Thus, when Israelis do something bad, it often attracts attention, whereas Arabs are usually held to a lower standard. For example, when Israel expelled four Palestinians, it generated banner headlines, but when Kuwait deported hundreds of thousands, it was a nonevent. Similarly, the death of one Palestinian in the West Bank received far more coverage than thousands of Arabs killed in Algeria. On a day when Israel got a banner headline for killing four terrorists, a story on page 19 of the *Washington Post* buried in the 12th paragraph the news that more than 80 people were killed in violence during a summit between Pakistan and India.[11] Rightly or wrongly, the attitude of the public and press is that Jews should behave differently.

MYTH

"Israel gets favorable coverage because American Jews control the media and have disproportionate political influence."

FACT

If Jews controlled the media, it's not likely you'd hear Jews complaining so much about the anti-Israel bias of the press. It is true that the amount of attention Israel receives is related to the fact that the largest Jewish population in the world is in the United States and that Israel greatly concerns American Jews. Large numbers of Jews do hold significant positions in the media (though they by no means "control" the press as anti-Semites maintain), and the Jewish population is concentrated in major media markets like New York and Los Angeles, so it is not surprising the spotlight would be directed at Israel.

Politically, Jews wield disproportionate power in the United States and use it to advocate policies that strengthen the U.S.-Israel relationship; however, there is no evidence this has translated into favorable press coverage for

Israel. It is possible to argue that pro-Arab forces, such as the petrochemical industry, have as much or more influence on the media and encourage an anti-Israel bias.

MYTH

"Arab officials tell Western journalists the same thing they tell their own people."

FACT

Arab officials often express their views differently in English than they do in Arabic. They express their true feelings and positions to their constituents in their native language. For external consumption, however, Arab officials have learned to speak in moderate tones and often relate very different views when speaking in English to Western audiences. Long ago, Arab propagandists became more sophisticated about how to make their case. They now routinely appear on American television news broadcasts and are quoted in the print media and come across as reasonable people with legitimate grievances. What many of these same people say in Arabic, however, is often far less moderate and reasonable. Since Israelis can readily translate what is said in Arabic they are well aware of the views of their enemies. Americans and other English-speakers, however, can easily be fooled by the slick presentation of an Arab propagandist.

To give just one example, Palestinian peace negotiator Saeb Erekat is frequently quoted by the Western media. After the brutal murder of two Israeli teenagers on May 9, 2001, he was asked for a reaction. The *Washington Post* reported his response:

> Saeb Erekat, a Palestinian official, said in English at a news conference that "killing civilians is a crime, whether on the Palestinian or the Israeli side." The comment was not reported in Arabic-language Palestinian media.[12]

The unusual aspect of this story was that the *Post* reported the fact that Erekat's comment was ignored by the Palestinian press.

Over the years Yasser Arafat has consistently said one thing in English to the Western media and something completely different to the Arabic press in his native tongue. This is why the Bush Administration insisted that he repeat in Arabic what he says in English, in particular condemnations of terrorist attacks and calls to end violence.

MYTH

"Journalists are well-versed in Middle East history and therefore can place current events in proper context."

FACT

One cause of misunderstanding about the Middle East and bias in media reporting is the ignorance of journalists about the region. Few reporters speak Hebrew or Arabic, so they have little or no access to primary resources. They frequently regurgitate stories they read in English language publications from the region rather than report independently. When they do attempt to place events in historical context, they often get the facts wrong and create an inaccurate or misleading impression. To cite one example, during a recitation of the history of the holy sites in Jerusalem, CNN's Garrick Utley reported that Jews could pray at the Western Wall during Jordan's rule from 1948 to 1967.[13] In fact, Jews were prevented from visiting their holiest shrine. This is a critical historical point that helps explain Israel's position toward Jerusalem.

MYTH

"The media effectively captures the danger average Israelis face from Palestinians."

FACT

During the intifada it was common for the media to portray the battle in David versus Goliath terms, an image reinforced by pictures of children tossing stones at heavily armed soldiers. The situation was actually quite different, as U.S. journalist Sidney Zion discovered during an August 1988 visit to Bethlehem. Zion was nearly struck by a rock while riding in a taxicab. "It's a good thing the rock missed me," he said. "I didn't see it coming, and wouldn't have lived to see the next second had the driver been going a kilometer faster. Fortunately, nobody was in that seat, but it was clear that the Arabs weren't aiming at dead air."

Zion — who had been writing about the Middle East for more than 20 years — said that American media reports had led him to believe that "the rock-throwers were aiming at the Israeli Army, not at taxicabs. Did you ever see anything else on TV? Did you read anything to the contrary in the newspapers? Kids were tossing stones at soldiers, that's all."

"It simply didn't occur to me that American journalists would suppress news of a life-and-death danger. It was only later that I discovered that what happened to us was hardly uncommon," Zion wrote. "On any given day in the West Bank, Israeli civilians are getting brain-damaged from these nice little Arab youngsters and their pebbles."[14]

The "al-Aksa intifada" has featured many of the same images as the first uprising, and the media has continued to distort the impact on Israelis in the way Zion described.

MYTH

"Media coverage of the intifada was fair and balanced."

FACT

Candid members of the media admitted that coverage of the intifada was skewed. According to Steven Emerson, then a CNN correspondent, U.S. reporters acquiesced to Palestinian control over what was filmed. An Israeli cameraman who worked for several U.S. networks told Emerson that "if we aim the camera at the wrong scene, we'll be dead." In other instances, the networks handed out dozens of video cameras to Palestinians so that they could provide footage of strikes, riots and funerals. "There is absolutely no way to ensure the authenticity of what is filmed, nor is there any way to stop the cameras from being used as a tool to mobilize a demonstration," Emerson wrote.[15]

Although nearly one-third of all Palestinians murdered in 1989 were killed by their Arab brethren, only 12 of the more than 150 stories filed by U.S. networks from the West Bank that year dealt with the internecine warfare. "While Palestinian political terror on the West Bank fails to make the news," Emerson observed, "utter fabrications about Israeli brutality are reported uncritically."

For example, in early 1988, reporters were called to el-Mokassed Hospital in Jerusalem to film a dying Palestinian boy. His Palestinian doctor showed him hooked to life-support tubes, and claimed the child had been savagely beaten by Israeli troops. On February 8, 1988, ABC's Peter Jennings introduced the report by saying UN officials "say that the Israelis have beaten another Palestinian to death in the territories." NBC and CBS also gave the claims wide publicity.

But the story wasn't true. According to the child's autopsy and medical records, he died of a cerebral hemorrhage. He had been sick for more than a year. Overall, the U.S. networks, Emerson wrote, "have been complicit in a massive deception about the West Bank conflict."

NBC's Tel Aviv bureau chief Martin Fletcher acknowledged that the intifada posed a fairness problem. He noted the Palestinians manipulated the Western media by casting themselves as "David" against the Israeli "Goliath," a metaphor used by Fletcher himself in a 1988 report.

"The whole uprising was media-oriented, and, without a doubt, kept going because of the media," he said. Fletcher openly admitted accepting invitations from young Palestinians to film violent attacks against Jewish residents of the West Bank.

"It's really a matter of manipulation of the media. And the question is: How much do we play that game? [We do it] in the same way that we turn up at all those Bush or Reagan photo opportunities. We play along because we need the pictures."[16]

Case Study

A *Washington Post* story about the "cycle of death" in the West Bank included an interview with Raed Karmi, an official in Fatah, the dominant faction in Yasser Arafat's Palestine Liberation Organization. The report begins with the observation that Karmi is running out to join a battle against Israeli soldiers and grabs an M-16 assault rifle. What the story fails to mention is that only Palestinian police are supposed to be armed. The report implies that Israeli and Palestinian violence is equivalent in this "cycle" because Karmi said he was acting to avenge the death of a Palestinian who the Israelis assassinated for organizing terrorist attacks. Karmi admits that he participated in the kidnapping and execution-style murder of two Israelis who had been eating lunch in a Tulkarm restaurant. Karmi was jailed by the Palestinian Authority, but he was released after just four months and subsequently killed four more Israelis, including a man buying groceries and a driver who he ambushed. "I will continue attacking Israelis," he told the *Post*.[17]

MYTH

"Israelis cannot deny the truth of pictures showing their abuses."

FACT

A picture may be worth thousand words, but sometimes the picture and the words used to describe it are distorted and misleading. There is no question that photographers and television camera crews seek the most dramatic pictures they can find, most often showing brutal Israeli Goliaths mistreating the suffering Palestinian Davids, but the context is often missing.

In one classic example, the Associated Press circulated a dramatic photo of an angry Israeli soldier standing over a bloody young man pointing his baton. It appeared the soldier had just beaten the youth. The picture was in the *New York Times*[18] and spurred international outrage because the caption, supplied by AP, said, "An Israeli policeman and a Palestinian on the Temple Mount." Taken at a time when Palestinians were rioting following Ariel Sharon's controversial visit to the al-Aksa mosque, the picture appeared to be a vivid case of Israeli brutality. It turned out, however, the caption was inaccurate and the photo actually showed an incident that might have conveyed almost the exact opposite impression had it been reported correctly.

The victim was not a Palestinian beaten by an Israeli soldier, it was a policeman protecting an American Jewish student, Tuvia Grossman, who had been riding in a taxi when it was stoned by Palestinians. Grossman was pulled out of the taxi, beaten and stabbed. He broke free and fled toward the Israeli policeman. At that point a photographer snapped the picture.

Besides getting the victim wrong, AP also inaccurately reported that the photograph was taken on the Temple Mount. When AP was alerted to the errors, it issued a series of corrections, several of which still did not get the story straight. As is usually the case when the media makes a mistake, the damage was already done. Many outlets that had used the photo did not print clarifications. Others issued corrections that did not receive anywhere near the prominence of the initial story.

Another example of how photos can be both dramatic and misleading was a Reuters photo showing a young Palestinian being arrested by Israeli police on April 6, 2001. The boy is obviously frightened and has wet his pants. Once again the photo attracted worldwide publicity and reinforced the media image of Israelis as brutal occupiers who abuse innocent children.

In this instance it is the context that is misleading. Another Reuters photographer snapped a picture just before the first one was taken. It shows the same boy participating in a riot against Israeli soldiers. Few media outlets published this photo.

MYTH

"The press makes no apologies for terrorists."

FACT

On the contrary, the media routinely accepts and repeats the platitudes of terrorists and their spokespersons with regard to their agendas. The press gullibly treats claims that attacks against innocent civilians are acts of "freedom fighters." In recent years some news organizations have developed a resistance to the term "terrorist" and replaced it with euphemisms like "militant" because they don't want to be seen as taking sides or making judgments about the perpetrators.

For example, after a Palestinian suicide bomber blew up a pizza restaurant in downtown Jerusalem on August 9, 2001, killing 15 people, the attacker was described as a "militant" *(Los Angeles Times, Chicago Tribune,* NBC Nightly News) and "suicide bomber" *(New York Times, USA Today)*. ABC News did not use the word "terrorist." By contrast, every media outlet called the September 11 attack on the United States a terrorist attack.

Clifford May of the Middle East Information Network pointed out the absurdity of the media coverage: "No newspaper would write, 'Militants struck the World Trade Center yesterday,' or say, 'They may think of themselves as freedom fighters, and who are we to judge, we're newspeople.'"[19]

Rather than apologize for terrorists, the media sometimes portrays the victims of terror as equivalent to the terrorists themselves. For example, photos are sometimes shown of Israeli victims on the same page with photos of Israelis capturing terrorists, giving the sense, for example, that the Palestinian held in handcuffs and blindfolded by a soldier is as much a victim as the woman in shock being helped from the scene of a suicide bombing.

In one of the most egregious examples, after a suicide bombing in Petah Tikva on May 27, 2002, CNN interviewed the mother of the bomber, Jihad Titi. The parents of a 15-month-old girl killed in the attack, Chen and Lior Keinan, were also interviewed. The interviews with the Keinans were not shown on CNN international in Israel or elsewhere around the world until hours after the interview with Titi's mother had been broadcast several times.

This was even too much for CNN, which subsequently announced a policy change whereby it would no longer "report on statements made by suicide bombers or their families unless there seemingly is an extraordinarily compelling reason to do so."[20]

MYTH
"The Palestinian Authority places no restrictions on foreign reporters."

FACT

A case study of the Palestinian Authority's idea of freedom of the press occurred following the September 11 terrorist attacks against the United States. An Associated Press cameraman filmed Palestinians at a rally in Nablus celebrating the terror attacks and was subsequently summoned to a Palestinian Authority security office and told that the material must not be aired. Yasser Arafat's Tanzim also called to threaten his life if he aired the film. An AP still photographer was also at the site of the rally. He was warned not to take pictures and complied.

Several Palestinian Authority officials told AP in Jerusalem not to broadcast the videotape. Ahmed Abdel Rahman, Arafat's Cabinet secretary, said the Palestinian Authority "cannot guarantee the life" of the cameraman if the footage was broadcast.[21]

The cameraman requested that the material not be aired and, AP caved in to the blackmail and refused to release the footage.

More than a week later, the Palestinian Authority returned a videotape it confiscated from AP showing a Palestinian rally in the Gaza Strip in which some demonstrators carried posters supporting Saudi terrorist Osama bin Laden. Two separate parts of the six-minute tape involving "key elements" were erased by the Palestinians, according to an AP official.[22]

The Foreign Press Association (FPA) in Israel expressed "deep concern over the harassment of journalists by the Palestinian Authority as police forces and armed gunmen tried to prevent photo and video coverage of Tuesday's rally in Nablus where hundreds of Palestinians celebrated the terror attacks in New York and Washington." The FPA also condemned the threats against videographers and "the attitude of Palestinian officials who made no effort to counter the threats, control the situation, or to guarantee the safety of the journalists and the freedom of the press."

Israel Radio reported September 14, 2001, that the Palestinian Authority seized the footage filmed that day by cameramen from various international (including Arab) news agencies covering celebrations of the attacks against America held in cities across the West Bank and Gaza by Hamas. The celebrants waived photographs of wanted terrorist Osama bin Laden.[23] The very same news programs and networks that broadcast the photo opportunities produced by the Palestinian Authority (Arafat donating blood, Palestinian students in a moment of silence, posters supporting America) failed to broadcast the news that the PA is using terror and intimidation to discourage the airing of unfavorable reports.[24]

In October 2001, after the United States launched attacks against Afghanistan, Palestinians supporting Osama bin Laden staged rallies in the Gaza Strip that were ruthlessly suppressed by Palestinian police. The PA took measures to prevent any media coverage of the rallies or the subsequent riots. The Paris-based Reporters Without Frontiers issued a scathing protest to the PA. "We fear the Palestinian Authority takes advantage of the focus of international media on the American riposte to restrain more and more the right to free information," said Robert Menard, general secretary of the journalists' organization. The group also protested Palestinian orders not to broadcast calls for general strikes, nationalistic activities, demonstrations or other news without permission from the PA. The aim of the press blackout was expressed by an anonymous Palestinian official, "We don't want anything which could undermine our image."[25]

In August 2002, the Palestinian journalists union banned journalists from photographing Palestinian children carrying weapons or taking part in activities by terrorist organizations because the pictures were hurting the Palestinians' image. The ban came after numerous photographs were published showing children carrying weapons and dressing up like suicide bombers. Shortly before the union acted, six children were photographed carrying M16 rifles and Kalashnikovs during a pro-Iraq rally in the Gaza Strip. Another group, the Palestinian Journalists Syndicate, issued a similar ban that included photographing masked men. The Foreign Press Association expressed "deep concern" over the effort to censor coverage, and the threats of sanctions against journalists who disregarded the ban.[26]

MYTH

"Al-Jazeera is the 'Arabic CNN' providing the Arab world with an objective source of news."

FACT

Al-Jazeera is an Arabic-language television network based in Qatar that is widely viewed throughout the Arab world. The channel began in 1996 as a pet project of Qatar's emir, Sheik Hamad bin-Khalifa al-Thani and gained prominence during the U.S. war in Afghanistan because of its longstanding contacts with the Taliban rulers and Osama bin Laden. By airing a variety of viewpoints, including those of Bush Administration officials, the network sought to create the impression that it is an objective news source for the Arab world. In fact, Al-Jazeera has a long history as a propaganda outlet for extremist views in the Arab world. One Muslim scholar blamed the network for inciting the Arab masses against the West and for making bin Laden and his aides celebrities. "There is a difference between giving different opinions an opportunity [to be heard] and leaving the screen open to armed murderers to spread their ideas," said Dr. Abd Al-Hamid Al-Ansari, dean of Shar'ia and Law at Qatar University.[27]

In an interview on *60 Minutes*, one Al-Jazeera correspondent was asked about coverage of the Palestinian issue. He refers to Palestinians who are killed as martyrs. When Ed Bradley pointed out that the Israelis would call them terrorists, he replied, "This is a problem for the Israelis. It's a point of view." When asked what he calls Israelis who are killed by Palestinians, the reporter answered, "We call it that: the Israeli is killed by Palestinians." Bradley added that Al-Jazeera's coverage of the Intifada was "credited with igniting pro-Palestinian demonstrations all over the Middle East."[28]

Notes

1 Daniel Pipes, *The Long Shadow: Culture and Politics in the Middle East,* (NJ: Transaction Publishers, 1990), p. 278.

2 *Jerusalem Report,* (May 7, 1991).

3 *New York Jewish Week,* (August 31, 2001).

4 *Jerusalem Report,* (May 7, 1991).

5 *Al Hayat-Al-Jadidah,* (October 16, 2001).

6 *Al Hayat-Al-Jadidah,* (November 2, 2001).

7 *Near East Report,* (August 5, 1991).

8 *Jerusalem Report,* (April 22, 2002).

9 Report filed by Jean Pierre Martin on October 5, 2000, a day after his Belgian television team from RTL-TV1 was filming in the area of Ramallah.

10 *Jerusalem Report,* (April 22, 2002).

11 *Washington Post,* (July 18, 2001).

12 *Washington Post,* (May 10, 2001).

13 CNN, (October 10, 2000).

14 Sidney Zion, "Intifada Blues," *Penthouse,* (March 1990), pp. 56, 63.

15 *Wall Street Journal,* (February 21, 1990).

16 *Near East Report,* (August 5, 1991).

17 *Washington Post,* (September 7, 2001).

18 *New York Times,* (September 30, 2000).

19 *Washington Post,* (September 13, 2001).

20 *Forward,* (June 28, 2002).

21 AP, (September 12, 2001).

22 Jewish Telegraphic Agency, (September 20, 2001).

23 Associated Press and *Jerusalem Post,* (September 13, 2001); IMRA, (September 13-14, 2001); Jewish Telegraphic Agency, (September 20, 2001).

24 Associated Press and *Jerusalem Post,* (September 13, 2001); Jewish Telegraphic Agency, (September 20, 2001); Israel Radio, (September 14, 2001).

25 *Jerusalem Post,* (October 10, 2001).

26 *Jerusalem Post,* (August 26, 2002).

27 *Al-Raya* (Qatar), (January 6, 2002).

28 *60 Minutes,* "Inside Al Jazeera," (October 10, 2001).

25. Arab/Muslim Attitudes Toward Israel

The desire for peaceful relations between Jews and Arabs sometimes leads people to overlook public comments by Arab officials and media publications that are often incendiary and sometimes outright anti-Semitic. Frequently, more moderate tones are adopted when speaking to Western audiences, but more accurate and heartfelt views are expressed in Arabic to the speaker's constituents. The following is just a tiny sample of some of the remarks that have been made regarding Israel and the Jews. They are included here because they demonstrate the level of hostility and true beliefs of many Arabs and Muslims. Of course, *not all* Arabs and Muslims subscribe to these views, but the examples are not random, they are beliefs held by important officials and disseminated by major media. They are also included because one of the lessons of the Holocaust was that people of good will are often unwilling to believe that people who threaten evil will in fact carry out their malevolent intentions.

Anti-Semitism

"They [the Jews] try to kill the principle of religions with the same mentality that they betrayed Jesus Christ and the same way they tried to betray and kill the Prophet Mohammed."

— Syrian President Bashar Assad at May 5 welcoming ceremony for the Pope, Canadian Broadcasting Corporation, May 6, 2001.

"It is not a mistake that the Koran warns us of the hatred of the Jews and put them at the top of the list of the enemies of Islam. Today the Jews recruit the world against the Muslims and use all kinds of weapons. They are plundering the dearest place to the Muslims, after Mecca and Medina and threaten the place the Muslims have faced at first when they prayed and the third holiest city after Mecca and Medina. They want to erect their temple on that place....The Muslims are ready to sacrifice their lives and blood to protect the Islamic nature of Jerusalem and al-Aksa!"

— Sheikh Hian Al-Adrisi, Excerpt of address in the al-Aksa mosque, September 29, 2000.

"The Jews are Jews, whether Labor or Likud, the Jews are Jews. They do not have any moderates or any advocates of peace. They are all liars. They are the ones who must be butchered and killed. As Allah the Almighty said: 'Fight them.'

Allah will torture them by your hands and will humiliate them and will help you to overcome them, and will relieve the minds of the believers. ... Our people must unite in one trench, and receive armaments from the Palestinian leadership to confront the Jews. ... Have no mercy on the Jews, no matter where they are, in any country. Fight them, wherever you are. Whenever you meet them, kill them. Wherever you are, kill those Jews and those Americans who are like them – and those who stand with them – they are all in one trench, against the Arabs and the Muslims – because they established Israel here, in the beating heart of the Arab world, in Palestine. They created it in order that it be the outpost of their civilization – and the vanguard of their army, and to be the sword of the West and the Crusaders, hanging over the necks of the Muslim monotheists, the Muslims in this land. They wanted the Jews to be the spearhead for them..."

— Dr Ahmad Abu-Halabia, a member of the "Fatwa Council" appointed by the Palestinian Authority, and the former acting Rector of the Islamic University in Gaza, delivered in the Zayd bin Sultan Nahyan mosque in Gaza, on October 13, 2000, the day after the lynching of the Israeli reservists in Ramallah, and carried live on Palestinian television.

"Thanks to Hitler, blessed memory, who on behalf of the Palestinians, revenged in advance, against the most vile criminals on the face of the earth. Although we do have a complaint against him for his revenge on them was not enough."

— Columnist Ahmad Ragab, Al-Akhbar (Egypt), April 18, 2001.

"All weapons must be aimed at the Jews, at the enemies of Allah...whom the Koran describes as monkeys and pigs, worshippers of the calf and idol worshippers. Allah shall make the Moslem rule over the Jew, we will blow them up in Hadera, we will blow them up in Tel Aviv and in Netanya in the righteousness of Allah against this rif-raff.....We will enter Jerusalem as conquerors, and Jaffa as conquerors, and Haifa as conquerors and Ashkelon as conquerors...we bless all those who educate their children to jihad and to Martyrdom, blessing be he who shot a bullet into the head of a Jew."

— Sermon broadcast on Palestinian Authority television, August 3, 2001.

"O God, the Jews have transgressed all limits in their tyranny. O God, shake the ground under their feet, pour torture on them, and destroy all of them."

— Sheikh Abd-al-Bari al-Thubayt, June 7, 2002, sermon at the Holy Mosque of Medina, broadcast on official Saudi television.

"All signs unequivocally prove that the conflict between the Jews and the Muslims is an eternal on-going conflict, even if it stops for short intervals.... This conflict resembles the conflict between man and Satan.... This is the fate of the Muslim nation, and beyond that the fate of all the nations of the world, to be tormented by this nation [the Jews]. The fate of the Palestinian people is to struggle against the Jews on behalf of the Arab peoples, the Islamic peoples and the peoples of the entire world."

— Al-Hayat Al-Jadeeda quoted in The *New Republic Online*, October 30, 2001.

Blood Libel

"The Talmud says that if a Jew does not drink every year the blood of a non-Jewish man, he will be damned for eternity."

— Saudi Arabian delegate Marouf al-Dawalibi, before the UN Human Rights Commission, conference on religious tolerance, December 5, 1984.

"During this holiday [Purim], the Jew must prepare very special pastries, the filling of which is not only costly and rare –– it cannot be found at all on the local and international markets....For this holiday, the Jewish people must obtain human blood so that their clerics can prepare the holiday pastries....Before I go into the details, I would like to clarify that the Jews' spilling human blood to prepare pastry for their holidays is a well-established fact, historically and legally, all throughout history. This was one of the main reasons for the persecution and exile that were their lot in Europe and Asia at various times....during the holiday, the Jews wear carnival-style masks and costumes and overindulge in drinking alcohol, prostitution, and adultery....."

— Dr. Umayma Ahmad Al-Jalahma of King Faysal University, Saudi government daily *Al-Riyadh*, March 10, 2002.

"Christian Europe showed enmity toward the Jews when it transpired that their rabbis craftily hunt anyone walking alone, [tempting] him to enter their house of worship. Then they take his blood to use for baked goods for their holidays, as part of their ritual."

— **Columnist Dr. Muhammad bin S'ad Al-Shwey'ir, *Al-Jazirah* (Saudi Arabia), September 6, 2002.**

Fabrications of Abuses

"[Israeli doctors] use Palestinian patients... for experimental medicines and training new doctors."

— **PA Health Minister, Riyadh Al-Za'anoon, *Al-Ayam*, July 25, 1998.**

"Israel carries out a clear policy of annihilating our people and destroying our national economy by smuggling spoiled foodstuff... not fit for human consumption, into PA territories.... Israel did not change its strategy, which aims to kill and destroy our people, rather it began counting on means other than bombs, missiles and planes. These measures are distributing and smuggling spoiled foodstuffs... into the PA territories."

— **PA Deputy Minister of Supplies, Abd Al-Hamid Al-Qudsi, *Al-Hayat Al-Jadida*, August 22, 1998.**

"Our people have been subjected to the daily and extensive use of poisonous gas by the Israeli forces, which has led to an increase in cancer cases among women and children."

— **Suha Arafat, wife of Yasser Arafat, November 11, 1999, during a Gaza appearance with First Lady Hillary Rodham Clinton.**

Holocaust Denial

"...Lies surfaced about Jews being murdered here and there, and the Holocaust. And, of course, they are all lies and unfounded claims. No Chelmno, no Dachau, no Auschwitz! [They] were disinfection sites... They began to publicize in their propaganda that they were persecuted, murdered and exterminated... Committees acted here and there to establish this entity [Israel-Ed.], *this foreign entity, implanted as a cancer in our country, where our fathers lived, where we live, and where our children after us will live. They always portrayed themselves as victims, and they made a Center for Heroism and Holocaust. Whose heroism? Whose Holocaust? Heroism is our nation's, the holocaust was against our people... We were the victims, but we shall not remain victims forever..."*

**— Dr. Issam Sissalem, history lecturer, Islamic University Gaza,
PA TV broadcast, November 29, 2000.**

"The issue of the holocaust rises again. It defies disappearing over its half-century because the Zionist propaganda has converted it into a means to produce political and economic benefit, besides exploiting it for the advancement of occupation and settlement..."

"A recently published book by an American researcher, discusses the holocaust. Employing scientific and chemical evidence, it proves that the figure of six million Jews cremated in the Nazi Auschwitz camps is a lie for propaganda, as the most spacious of the vaults in the camp could not have held even one percent of that number."

**— Hiri Manzour in the official Palestinian Authority daily,
Al-Hayat Al-Jadida, April 13, 2001.**

"One of the Jews' evil deeds is what has come to be called 'the Holocaust,' that is, the slaughter of the Jews by Nazism. However, revisionist [historians] have proven that this crime, carried out against some of the Jews, was planned by the Jews' leaders, and was part of their policy...These are the Jews against whom we fight, oh beloved of Allah."

**— Sermon broadcast on Palestinian Authority television,
September 21, 2001.**

Peace

"Unless the Palestine problem is settled, we shall have difficulty in protecting and safeguarding the Jews in the Arab world."

**— Syrian delegate, Faris el-Khouri, *New York Times,*
February 19, 1947.**

"The Arab world is not in a compromising mood. It's likely, Mr. Horowitz, that your plan is rational and logical, but the fate of nations is not decided by rational logic. Nations never concede; they fight. You won't get anything by peaceful means or compromise. You can, perhaps, get something, but only by the force of your arms. We shall try to defeat you. I am not sure we'll succeed, but we'll try. We were able to drive out the Crusaders, but on the other hand we lost Spain and Persia. It may be that we shall lose Palestine. But it's too late to talk of peaceful solutions."

— Arab League Secretary Azzam Pasha, September 16, 1947.

"[A]ll our efforts to find a peaceful solution to the Palestine problem have failed. The only way left for us is war. I will have the pleasure and honor to save Palestine."

— Transjordan's King Abdullah, April 26, 1948.

"The representative of the Jewish Agency told us yesterday that they were not the attackers, that the Arabs had begun the fighting. We did not deny this. We told the whole world that we were going to fight."

— Jamal Husseini before the Security Council, April 16, 1948,

"This will be a war of extermination and a momentous massacre which will be spoken of like the Mongolian massacres and the Crusades."

**— Azzam Pasha, Secretary-General of the Arab League
May 15, 1948.**

"I am not solely fighting against Israel itself. My task is to deliver the Arab world from destruction through Israel's intrigue, which has its roots abroad. Our hatred is very strong. There is no sense in talking about peace with Israel. There is not even the smallest place for negotiations."

— Egyptian President Nasser, October 14, 1956.

"Our forces are now entirely ready not only to repulse the aggression, but to initiate the act of liberation itself, and to explode the Zionist presence in the Arab homeland. The Syrian army, with its

finger on the trigger, is united....I, as a military man, believe that the time has come to enter into a battle of annihilation."

— Syrian Defense Minister Hafez Assad, May 20, 1967,

"Arab policy at this stage has but two objectives. The first, the elimination of the traces of the 1967 aggression through an Israeli withdrawal from all the territories it occupied that year. The second objective is the elimination of the traces of the 1948 aggression, by the means of the elimination of the State of Israel itself. This is, however, as yet an abstract, undefined objective, and some of us have erred in commencing the latter step before the former."

— Mohammed Heikal, a Sadat confidant and editor of the semi-official *Al-Ahram*, February 25, 1971,

"Let us work together until we achieve victory and regain liberated Jerusalem."

— Yasser Arafat, Baghdad Republic of Iraq Radio Network, November 16, 1991.

"I have always rejected normalizing relations with (Israeli) women....They always invite me to their functions and I categorically refuse because I hate Israel."

— Suha Arafat, wife of Yasser Arafat, Saudi Arabian women's magazine, *Sayidaty*, quoted by AP, May 3, 2001.

"We will not give up a single grain of soil in Palestine, from Haifa, and Jaffa, and Acre, and Mulabbas [Petah Tikvah] and Salamah, and Majdal [Ashkelon], and all the land, and Gaza, and the West Bank...."

— Dr Ahmad Abu-Halabia, a member of the "Fatwa Council" appointed by the Palestinian Authority and the former acting Rector of the Islamic University in Gaza, delivered in the Zayd bin Sultan Nahyan mosque in Gaza on October 13, 2000, the day after the lynching of the Israeli reservists in Ramallah, and carried live on Palestinian television.

"...Allah willing, this unjust state...Israel will be erased; this unjust state, the United States will be erased; this unjust state, Britain will be erased...Blessings to whoever waged Jihad for the sake of Allah...Blessings to whoever put a belt of explosives on his body or on his sons' and plunged into the midst of the Jews..."

— **Sermon by Sheikh Ibrahim Madhi a few days after Yasser Arafat's cease-fire declaration, PA Television, June 8, 2001.**

"We said from the beginning that there is no ceasefire for the settlers."

— **Fatah leader, Ziad ibu-Aid,** *International Herald Tribune,* **June 20, 2001.**

Phased Plan & the Destruction of Israel

"The Palestinian people accepted the Oslo agreements as a first step and not as a permanent arrangement, based on the premise that the war and struggle on the ground [i.e., locally against Israeli territory] is more efficient than a struggle from a distant land... for the Palestinian people will continue the revolution until they achieve the goals of the '65 revolution..."

— **PA Minister of Supply Abd El Aziz Shahian,** *Al Ayaam,* **May 30, 2000. [The "65 Revolution" is the founding of the PLO and the publication of the Palestinian covenant that calls for the destruction of Israel via an armed struggle.]**

"Our people have hope for the future, that the Occupation State ceases to exist, and that it makes no difference [how great] its power and arrogance...".

— **PA Minister of Communications, Amad Alfalugi,** *Al-Hayat Al-Jadida,* **November 18, 1999.**

"When we picked up the gun in '65 and the modern Palestinian Revolution began, it had a goal. This goal has not changed and it is the liberation of Palestine."

— **Salim Alwadia Abu Salem, Supervisor of Palestinian Political Affairs,** *Al-Hayat Al-Jadida,* **January 20, 2000.**

"I want to say that this is our Palestine, from Metulla [Israel's northernmost city] to Rafiah [Southern border] and to Aqaba [Israel's southernmost point], from the [Jordan] River to the [Mediterranean] Sea; whether they want it or not."

— Dr. Jareer Al-Kidwah, advisor to President Arafat, PA TV broadcast, November 29, 2000.

"Israel is much smaller than Iran in land mass, and therefore far more vulnerable to nuclear attack."

— Former Iranian President Ali Rafsanjani, quoted in Jerusalem Report, March 11, 2002.

"We defeated the Crusaders 800 years ago and we will defeat the enemies of Islam today."

— Nazareth Deputy Mayor Salman Abu Ahmed, quoted in Jerusalem Report, March 4, 2002.

Sanctioning Violence

"The ruling to kill the Americans and their allies — civilians and military — is an individual duty for every Muslim who can do it in any country in which it is possible to do it, in order to liberate the al-Aksa Mosque and the holy mosque [Mecca] from their grip, and in order for their armies to move out of all the lands of Islam, defeated and unable to threaten any Muslim."

— The fatwa (religious edict) issued by Osama bin Laden in 1998.

"We decided to liberate our homeland step by step... this is the strategy... we say: 'should Israel continue – no problem. And so we honor the peace treaties and non-violence, so long as the agreements are fulfilled step-by-step. [But] if and when Israel says 'enough,' namely, 'we will not discuss Jerusalem, we will not return refugees, we will not dismantle settlements, we will not withdraw to the borders,' in that case it is saying that we will return to violence. But this time it will be with 30,000 armed Palestinian soldiers and in a land with elements of freedom. I am the first to call for it. If we reach a dead end we will go back to our war and struggle like we did forty years ago."

— PA Minister of Planning and International Cooperation Nabil Sha'ath, Interview with ANN television, London, October 7, 2000.

"Violence is around the corner, and the Palestinians are willing to sacrifice even 5,000 casualties."

— PA Justice Minister Freih Abu Middein,
Al-Hayat Al-Jadida, **(PA) August 24, 2000.**

"The Intifada will continue until the achievement of our national goals."

— PA Finance Minister Muhammad Al-Nashashibi,
Al-Ayyam, **October 10, 2000.**

"The Intifada is a means of popular struggle in which all parts of the people take part in order to realize the internationally recognized legitimate rights of the Palestinian people... This is the goal of the Intifada... The use of violence, the struggle and martyrdom... used by people to achieve their rights."

— PLO representative in Washington, Hassan Abd Al-Rahman,
TV MBC, October 10, 2000.

"The Intifada should be continued and escalated."

— The head of the Fatah organization in the West Bank, Marwan Al-Barghuthi, Al-Jazeera TV (Qatar), October 11, 2000.

"The issues of Jerusalem, the refugees and sovereignty are one and will be finalized on the ground and not in negotiations. At this point it is important to prepare Palestinian society for the challenge of the next step because we will inevitably find ourselves in a violent confrontation with Israel in order to create new facts on the ground. ... I believe that the situation in the future will be more violent than the Intifada."

— Abu-Ali Mustafa of the Palestinian Authority, July 23, 2000.

"Hamas has tens of martyrs who are willing to carry out attacks against Israeli targets. An operation of such martyrs exceeds that of the Arab armies who fought the Hebrew state. The importance of the weapons of such martyrs is no less than the importance of nuclear weapons."

— Khaled Mash'al, head of the Hamas Politbureau,
Al-Hayat Al-Jadida **(PA), June 24, 2001.**

"We are teaching the children that suicide bombs make Israeli people frightened and we are allowed to do it....We teach them that after a person becomes a suicide bomber he reaches the highest level of paradise."

— Palestinian "Paradise Camp" counselor speaking to BBC interviewer, quoted in *Jerusalem Post,* July 20, 2001.

"I promise that the number of shootings at the occupation will increase to 500 to 1,000 shooting [incidents] per day....The Palestinians have trained themselves to attack the Israeli tanks and explode their bodies that will be loaded with a belt of explosives, as part of the preparations for a possible Israeli attack in the Palestinian territories....The current intifada differs from the previous one because it is armed and the Palestinians are fighting inside their territory and from it."

— Deputy Commander of Force-17, Muhammad Dhamrah (a.k.a., Abu Awdh), *Al-Hayat,* August 17, 2001.

"The suicide bombers of today are the noble successors of their noble predecessors...the Lebanese suicide bombers, who taught the U.S. Marines a tough lesson in [Lebanon]....These suicide bombers are the salt of the earth, the engines of history....They are the most honorable [people] among us....."

— *Al-Hayat Al-Jadida* (PA), June 24, 2001.

"I do not think that a Muslim would let an Islamic homeland like Palestine, and Jerusalem, remain in the hands of the Zionists, who plunder it and damage its holy sites, without the owners of the land having the right to defend themselves. All I said is that this oppressed people that was expelled from its home has the right to become a human bomb and blow himself up inside this military society."

— Sheikh Yussef Al-Qaradhawi, a leader of the Muslim Brotherhood. Al-Jazeera TV (Qatar), September 16, 2001.

"Our efforts to continue the Intifada and resistance will persist until we achieve our right of return, and our independence, with Jerusalem as the capital."

— Ahmad Sa'adat speaking at a press conference after becoming leader of the PFLP, *Jerusalem Post*, October 4, 2001.

"Resistance is legitimate and those who give up their lives do not require permission from anyone....We must not stand in the way of the intifada and jihad [holy war]. Rather, we must stand at their side and encourage them."

— Mufti of Jerusalem, Sheikh Ikrima Sabri,
***Al-Hayat*, December 7, 2001.**

"With God's help, next time we will meet in Jerusalem, because we are fighting to bring victory to our prophets, every baby, every kid, every man, every woman and every old person and all the young people, we will all sacrifice ourselves for our holy places and we will strengthen our hold of them and we are willing to give 70 of our martyrs for every one of theirs in this campaign, because this is our holy land. We will continue to fight for this blessed land and I call on you to stand strong.."

— Palestinian Authority Chairman Yasser Arafat, Speech at a rally in Ramallah, December 18, 2001.

"We have examined our options and our path, and we have chosen the path of slaughter, by acts of Jihad, Istshahad (suicide) and resistance of every form, side-by-side with our brothers in the Hamas, the Islamic Jihad and all the other Palestinian resistance groups, until the liberation of Palestine and the return of the refugees."

— Part of a warning posted on the web site of the al-Aqsa Martyrs Brigades, the military arm of Yasser Arafat's Fatah organization, August 7, 2002.

Sources:

Foreign Broadcast Information Service
Ha'aretz
Israeli Foreign Ministry
Jerusalem Post
MEMRI
Near East Report
Palestinian Media Watch
Various news sources

APPENDICES

The Military Balance in the Middle East

Country	Regular Troops	Reserve Troops	Tanks	Aircraft*
Israel	186,500	445,000	3,930	800
Egypt	450,000	254,000	3,505	494
Jordan	94,200	60,000	1,200	100
Iraq	432,500	650,000	2,400	333
Iran	350,000	350,000	1,460	333
Syria	380,000	132,500	4,800	520
Saudi Arabia	171,500	20,000	1,015	355

* Refers to total number of combat aircraft.

Source: Shai Feldman and Yiftah Shapir, Eds., The Middle East Military Balance, (Cambridge: MIT Press, 2001).

United Nations Security Council Resolution 242

(November 22, 1967)

The Security Council,

Expressing its continuing concern with the grave situation in the Middle East,

Emphasizing the inadmissibility of the acquisition of territory by war and the need to work for a just and lasting peace in which every State in the area can live in security,

Emphasizing *further* that all Member States in their acceptance of the Charter of the United Nations have undertaken a commitment to act in accordance with Article 2 of the Charter.

1. *Affirms* that the fulfillment of Charter principles requires the establishment of a just and lasting peace in the Middle East which should include the application of both the following principles:

    (i) Withdrawal of Israeli armed forces from territories occupied in the recent conflict;

    (ii) Termination of all claims or states of belligerency and respect for and acknowledgement of the sovereignty, territorial integrity and political independence of every State in the area and their right to live in peace within secure and recognized boundaries free from threats or acts of force;

2. *Affirms further* the necessity:

    (a) For guaranteeing freedom of navigation-through international waterways in the area;

    (b) For achieving a just settlement of the refugee problem;

    (c) For guaranteeing the territorial inviolability and political independence of every State in the area, through measures including the establishment of demilitarized zones;

3. *Requests* the Secretary General to designate a Special Representative to proceed to the Middle East to establish and maintain contacts with the States concerned in order to promote agreement and assist efforts to achieve a peaceful and accepted settlement in accordance with the provisions and principles in this resolution;

4. *Requests* the Secretary General to report to the Security Council on the progress of the efforts of the Special Representative as soon as possible.

Israel-PLO Recognition

(September 9, 1993)

1. LETTER FROM
YASSER ARAFAT TO PRIME MINISTER RABIN:

September 9, 1993

Yitzhak Rabin
Prime Minister of Israel

Mr. Prime Minister,

The signing of the Declaration of Principles marks a new era in the history of the Middle East. In firm conviction thereof, I would like to confirm the following PLO commitments:

The PLO recognizes the right of the State of Israel to exist in peace and security.

The PLO accepts United Nations Security Council Resolutions 242 and 338.

The PLO commits itself to the Middle East peace process, and to a peaceful resolution of the conflict between the two sides and declares that all outstanding issues relating to permanent status will be resolved through negotiations.

The PLO considers that the signing of the Declaration of Principles constitutes a historic event, inaugurating a new epoch of peaceful coexistence, free from violence and all other acts which endanger peace and stability. Accordingly, the PLO renounces the use of terrorism and other acts of violence and will assume responsibility over all PLO elements and personnel in order to assure their compliance, prevent violations and discipline violators

In view of the promise of a new era and the signing of the Declaration of Principles and based on Palestinian acceptance of Security Council Resolutions 242 and 338, the PLO affirms that those articles of the Palestinian Covenant which deny Israel's right to exist, and the provisions of the Covenant which are inconsistent with the commitments of this letter are now inoperative and no longer valid. Consequently, the PLO undertakes to submit to the Palestinian National Council for formal approval the necessary changes in regard to the Palestinian Covenant.

Sincerely,
Yasser Arafat
Chairman
The Palestine Liberation Organization

2. LETTER FROM
YASSER ARAFAT TO NORWEGIAN FOREIGN MINISTER:
September 9, 1993

His Excellency
Johan Jorgen Holst
Foreign Minister of Norway

Dear Minister Holst,

I would like to confirm to you that, upon the signing of the Declaration of Principles, the PLO encourages and calls upon the Palestinian people in the West Bank and Gaza Strip to take part in the steps leading to the normalization of life, rejecting violence and terrorism, contributing to peace and stability and participating actively in shaping reconstruction, economic development and cooperation.

Sincerely,

Yasser Arafat
Chairman
The Palestine Liberation Organization

3. LETTER FROM
PRIME MINISTER RABIN TO YASSER ARAFAT:
September 9, 1993

Yasser Arafat
Chairman
The Palestinian Liberation Organization

Mr. Chairman,

In response to your letter of September 9, 1993, I wish to confirm to you that, in light of the PLO commitments included in your letter, the Government of Israel has decided to recognize the PLO as the representative of the Palestinian people and commence negotiations with the PLO within the Middle East peace process.

Yitzhak Rabin

Prime Minister of Israel

The Covenant of the Islamic Resistance Movement (HAMAS)

The following is excerpted from the covenant of the Islamic Resistance Movement (HAMAS). The full text is available in the Jewish Virtual Library (http://www.jewishvirtuallibrary.org/jsource/Terrorism/Hamas_covenant_complete.html).

Our struggle against the Jews is very great and very serious. It needs all sincere efforts. The Islamic Resistance Movement is but one squadron that should be supported...until the enemy is vanquished and Allah's victory is realized. It strives to raise the banner of Allah over every inch of Palestine...It is one of the links in the chain of the struggle against the Zionist invaders...

The Prophet, Allah bless him and grant him salvation, has said: "The Day of Judgement will not come about until Moslems fight the Jews (killing the Jews), when the Jew will hide behind stones and trees. The stones and trees will say 'there is a Jew behind me, come and kill him'"....There is no solution for the Palestine question except through *Jihad*. Initiatives, proposals and international conferences are all a waste of time and vain endeavors. Palestine is an Islamic land.

Zionist organizations under various names and shapes, such as Freemasons, Rotary Clubs, espionage groups and others...are all nothing more than cells of subversion and saboteurs. The Islamic peoples should perform their role in confronting the conspiracies of these saboteurs.

Moslem society confronts a vicious enemy which acts in a way similar to Nazism. He has deprived people of their homeland. In their Nazi treatment, the Jews made no exception for women or children.

Our enemies took control of the world media. They were behind the French Revolution and the Communist Revolution....They were behind World War I, when they were able to destroy the Islamic Caliphate, making financial gains and controlling resources. They obtained the Balfour Declaration, formed the League of Nations through which they could rule the world. They were behind World War II, through which they made huge financial gains by trading in armaments, and paved the way for the establishment of their state. It was they that instigated the replacement of the League of Nations with the United Nations and the Security Council to enable them to rule the world through them. There is no war going on any where, without [them] having their finger in it.

The Palestinian Liberation Organization adopted the idea of the secular state, which completely contradicts the idea of religious ideology. The day the PLO adopts Islam as its way of life, we will become its soldiers, and fuel for its fire that will burn the enemies. Until that day, the Islamic Resistance Movement's stand towards the PLO is that of the son towards his father, the brother towards his brother and the relative to relative, who suffers his pain and supports him in confronting the enemies, wishing him to be wise and well-guided....

The Zionist invasion is a vicious invasion. It does not refrain from resorting to all methods, using all evil and contemptible ways to achieve its end. It relies greatly on the secret organizations it gave rise to, such as the Freemasons, the Rotary and Lions Club, other sabotage groups. All these organizations work in the interest of Zionism... They aim at undermining societies, destroying values, corrupting consciences, deteriorating character and annihilating Islam. It is behind the drug trade and alcoholism in all its kinds so as to facilitate its control and expansion.

Writers, intellectuals, media people, orators, educators and teachers, and all the various sectors in the Arab and Islamic world – all of them are called upon to perform their role, and to fulfill their duty, because of the ferocity of the Zionist offensive and the Zionist influence in many countries exercised through financial and media control.

The Zionist plan is limitless. After Palestine, the Zionists aspire to expand from the Nile to the Euphrates. When they will have digested the region they overtook they will aspire to further expansion, and so on. Their plan is embodied in the Protocols of the *Elders of Zion*, and their present conduct is the best proof of what we are saying. Leaving the circle of struggle with Zionism is high treason, and cursed be he who does that.

Recommended Internet Resources

For the most comprehensive coverage of topics related to this book, as well as a regularly updated version of **Myths & Facts**, visit our *Jewish Virtual Library* **(http://www.JewishVirtualLibrary.org)**. The Library contains an extensive bibliography of more than 1,000 web sites. The following are selected from that list:

American Israel Public Affairs Committee (AIPAC)
http://www.aipac.org

American Jewish Committee
http://www.ajc.org

American Jewish Press Association
http://www.ajpa.org

Anti-Defamation League (ADL)
http://www.adl.org

Arutz Sheva Israel National Radio
http://www.a7.org

Begin-Sadat Center for Strategic Studies
http://www.biu.ac.il/SOC/besa/

birthright Israel
http://www.birthrightisrael.com

CAMERA
http://www.camera.org

Central Zionist Archives
http://www.wzo.org.il/cza/index.htm

Dinur Center for the Study of Jewish History
http://www.hum.huji.ac.il/dinur

Embassy of Israel (US)
http://www.israelemb.org

Golan Heights Information Server
http://english.golan.org.il

Ha'aretz
http://www.haaretz.co.il

Hillel
http://www.hillel.org

HonestReporting.com
http://www.honestreporting.com

Information Regarding Israel's Security (IRIS)
http://www.iris.org.il

International Christian Embassy Jerusalem
http://www.intournet.co.il/icej

International Policy Institute for Counter-Terrorism
http://www.ict.org.il

Internet Jewish History Sourcebook
http://www.fordham.edu/halsall/jewish/jewishsbook.html

Institute for Advanced Strategic and Political Studies
http://www.iasps.org.il/

Israel Defense Forces (IDF)
http://www.idf.il

Israel Government Gateway
http://info.gov.il/eng/mainpage.asp

Israel Radio
http://www.israelradio.org

Israeli Central Bureau of Statistics
http://www.cbs.gov.il/engindex.htm

Israeli Ministry of Foreign Affairs
http://www.israel-mfa.gov.il/mfa/home.asp

Israeli Prime Minister's Office
http://www.pmo.gov.il/english

Jaffee Center for Strategic Studies
http://www.tau.ac.il/jcss

Jerusalem Capital of Israel
http://www.jerusalem-archives.org

Jerusalem Center for Public Affairs
http://www.jcpa.org

Jerusalem Post
http://www.jpost.com

Jerusalem Report
http://www.jrep.com

Jewish Telegraphic Agency (JTA)
http://www.jta.org

Knesset The Israeli Parliament
http://www.knesset.gov.il

Maps of the Middle East
ttp://www.lib.utexas.edu/Libs/PCL/Map_collection/middle_east.html

Maven
http://www.maven.co.il

Middle East Insight
http://www.mideastinsight.org

Middle East Media & Research Institute
http://www.memri.org

Middle East Review of International Affairs
http://www.biu.ac.il/SOC/besa/meria/index.html

Palestinian Media Watch
http://www.pmw.org.il

Peace Now
http://www.peacenow.org.il/English.asp

Pedagogic Center, The Department for Jewish Zionist Education, The Jewish Agency for Israel
http://www.jajz-ed.org.il

Terrorism Research Center
http://www.terrorism.com

U.S. State Department
http://www.state.gov

United Jewish Communities UJC
http://www.ujc.org

Virtual Jerusalem
http://www.virtualjerusalem.com

Washington Institute for Near East Policy
http://www.washingtoninstitute.org

World Zionist Organization Student and Academics Department
http://www.wzo.org.il

Suggested Reading

Aumann Moshe. *Land Ownership in Palestine 1880-1948.* Jerusalem: Academic Committee on the Middle East, 1976.

Avineri Shlomo. *The Making of Modern Zionism: Intellectual Origins of the Jewish State.* NY Basic Books, 1981.

Avneri Arieh. *The Claim of Dispossession.* NJ: Transaction Books, 1984.

Bard, Mitchell G. and Moshe Schwartz. *1001 Facts Everyone Should Know About Israel.* NJ: Jason Aronson, 2002.

Bard, Mitchell G. *From Tragedy to Triumph: The Politics behind the Rescue of Ethiopian Jewry.* CT: Greenwood, 2002.

Bard, Mitchell G. *The Complete Idiot's Guide to Middle East Conflict.* NY: Alpha Books, 2002.

Bard, Mitchell. *The Water's Edge And Beyond.* NJ: Transaction Publishers, 1991.

Becker, Jillian. *The PLO.* NY: St. Martin's Press, 1985.

Begin, Menachem. *The Revolt.* NY: EP Dutton, 1978.

Bell, J. Bowyer. *Terror Out Of Zion.* NJ: Transaction, 1996.

Ben Gurion, David. *Rebirth and Destiny of Israel.* NY: Philosophical Library, 1954.

Benvenisti, Meron. *Intimate Enemies: Jews and Arabs in a Shared Land.* CA.: University of California Press, 1995.

Collins, Larry and Dominique Lapierre. *O Jerusalem!.* NY: Simon and Schuster, 1972.

Eban, Abba. *Heritage: Civilization and the Jews.* NY: Summit Books, 1984.

Eban Abba. *My Country: The Story of Modern Israel.* NY: Random House, 1972.

Gilbert, Martin. *Israel: A History.* NY: William Morrow & Co., 1998.

Hazony, Yoram. *The Jewish State: The Struggle for Israel's Soul.* NY: Basic Books, 2001.

Hertzberg Arthur. *The Zionist Idea.* PA: Jewish Publications Society, 1997.

Herzl, Theodore. *The Diaries of Theodore Herzl.* NY: Peter Smith Publishers, 1987.

Herzl, Theodore. *The Jewish State.* Dover Publications, 1989.

Herzog, Chaim. *The Arab-Israeli Wars.* NY: Random House, 1984.

Johnson, Paul. *A History of the Jews.* NY: HarperCollins, 1988.

Katz, Samuel. *Battleground-Fact and Fantasy in Palestine.* SPI Books, 1986.

Kollek, Teddy. *Jerusalem.* Washington, D.C.: Washington Institute For Near East Policy, 1990.

Lacquer, Walter and Barry Rubin. *The Israel-Arab Reader.* NY: Penguin, 2001.

Lewis, Bernard. *The Jews of Islam.* NJ: Princeton University Press, 1984.

Lewis, Bernard. *The Middle East: A Brief History of the Last 2000 Years.* NY: Touchstone Books, 1997.

Livingstone, Neil C., and David Halevy. *Inside the PLO*. NY: William Morrow and Co., 1990.

Lorch Netanel. *One Long War*. NY: Herzl Press, 1976.

Meir, Golda. *My Life.* NY: Dell, 1975.

Netanyahu, Benjamin. *A Place Among Nations: Israel and the World.* NY: Warner Books, 1998.

Oren, Michael. *Six Days of War: June 1967 and the Making of the Modern Middle East.* NY: Oxford University Press, 2002.

Pipes, Daniel. *The Hidden Hand: Middle East Fears of Conspiracy.* Griffin Trade Paperback, 1998.

Pipes, Daniel. *The Long Shadow: Culture and Politics in the Middle East.* NJ: Transaction Publishers, 1990.

Porath Yehoshua. *The Emergence of the Palestinian-Arab National Movement, 1918-1929*. London: Frank Cass, 1996.

Porath Yehoshua. *In Search of Arab Unity 1930-1945*. London: Frank Cass and Co., Ltd., 1986.

Porath Yehoshua. *Palestinian Arab National Movement: From Riots to Rebellion: 1929-1939*. vol. 2. London: Frank Cass and Co., Ltd., 1977.

Quandt, William B. Camp David: *Peacemaking and Politics.* DC: Brookings Institution, 1986.

Rabin, Yitzhak. *The Rabin Memoirs.* CA: University of California Press, 1996.

Sachar Howard. *A History of Israel: From the Rise of Zionism to Our Time*. NY: Alfred A. Knopf, 1998.

Safran Nadav. *Israel The Embattled Ally*. MA: Harvard University Press, 1981.

Schiff Ze'ev and Ehud Ya'ari. *Intifada.* NY: Simon & Schuster, 1990.

Schiff Zeev and Ehud Yaari. *Israel's Lebanon War*. NY: Simon and Schuster, 1984.

Schoenberg, Harris. *Mandate For Terror: The United Nations and the PLO*. NY: Shapolsky 1989.

Stillman Norman. *The Jews of Arab Lands.* PA: The Jewish Publication Society of America 1989.

Stillman Norman. *The Jews of Arab Lands in Modern Times*. NY: Jewish Publication Society, 1991.

Weizmann Chaim. *Trial and Error*. NY: Greenwood Press, 1972.

Wigoder, Geoffrey, ed. *New Encyclopedia of Zionism and Israel.* NJ: Fairleigh Dickinson University Press, 1994.

Ye'or, Bat. *The Dhimmi.* NJ: Associated University Press, 1985.

Index of Myths

Alphabetical Index

American-Israeli Cooperative Enterprise (AICE)

The AMERICAN-ISRAELI COOPERATIVE ENTERPRISE (AICE) was established in 1993 as a nonprofit 501(c)(3), nonpartisan organization to strengthen the U.S.-Israel relationship by emphasizing the fundamentals of the alliance and the values our nations share. Tangibly, this means developing social and educational programs in the U.S. based on innovative, successful Israeli models that address similar domestic problems, and bringing novel U.S. programs to Israel. These cooperative activities, which stem from our common values, are called *Shared Value Initiatives*.

The objectives and purposes of AICE include:

- To provide a vehicle for the research, study, discussion and exchange of views concerning nonmilitary cooperation (*Shared Value Initiatives*) between the peoples and governments of the United States and Israel.

- To facilitate the formation of partnerships between Israelis and Americans.

- To publicize joint activities, and the benefits accruing to America and Israel from them.

- To explore issues of common historical interest to the peoples and governments of the United States and Israel.

- To sponsor research, conferences and documentaries.

- To serve as a clearinghouse on joint U.S.-Israeli activities.

- To provide educational materials on Jewish history and culture.

AICE also runs the Jewish Virtual Library, a comprehensive online Jewish encyclopedia covering everything from anti-Semitism to Zionism (www.JewishVirtualLibrary.org).

BOARD OF DIRECTORS

Howard Rosenbloom President/Treasurer
Dr. Arthur Bard Vice President/Secretary
Mitchell G. Bard Executive Director

ADVISORY BOARD

Dorothy Bard
Newton Becker
Martin Block
Renee Comet
Henry Everett
Howard Friedman
Jerry Gottesman
Paula Gottesman
Eugene M. Grant
Andy Lappin
Dr. Brad Levinson
Stephen J. Lovell

Bernice Manocherian
J. George Mitnick
Sy Opper
Terry M. Rubinstein
Charles Schusterman z"l
Lynn Schusterman
Irving Shuman
Alan Slifka
Louis S. Sorell
Mark Vogel
Arnold Wagner
Jane Weitzman

About the Author

Mitchell Bard is the Executive Director of the nonprofit *American-Israeli Cooperative Enterprise (AICE)* and a foreign policy analyst who lectures frequently on U.S.-Middle East policy. Dr. Bard is also the director of the *Jewish Virtual Library (www.Jewis hVirtualLibrary.org)*, one of the world's most comprehensive online encyclopedias of Jewish history and culture.

Dr. Bard is a member of the *United Jewish Communities Speakers Bureau* and a member of *Hillel's Israel Speakers Program.*

For three years he was the editor of the *Near East Report*, the *American Israel Public Affairs Committee's (AIPAC)* weekly newsletter on U.S. Middle East policy.

Prior to working at AIPAC, Dr. Bard served as a senior analyst in the polling division of the 1988 Bush campaign.

Dr. Bard has appeared on Fox News, MSNBC and other local and national television and radio outlets. His work has been published in academic journals, magazines and major newspapers. He is the author of:

The Water's Edge And Beyond:
Defining the Limits to Domestic Influence on U.S. Middle East Policy

Partners for Change: How U.S.-Israel Cooperation
Can Benefit America U.S.-Israel Relations: Looking to the Year 2000

Building Bridges: Lessons For America From
Novel Israeli Approaches To Promote Coexistence

Myths And Facts: A Concise Record of the Arab-Israeli Conflict

Forgotten Victims: The Abandonment of Americans in Hitler's Camps

The Complete Idiot's Guide to World War II

The Complete Idiot's Guide to Middle East Conflict

The Complete History of the Holocaust

The Holocaust (Turning Points in World History)

The Nuremberg Trials (At Issue in History)

The Nuremberg Trials (Eyewitness to History)

From Tragedy to Triumph: The Politics Behind the Rescue of Ethiopian Jews

The Complete Idiot's Guide to Understanding the Brain

Forthcoming books include: *1001 Facts Everyone Should Know About Israel, and The Founding of Israel.*

Bard holds a Ph.D. in political science from UCLA and a master's degree in public policy from Berkeley. He received his B.A. in economics from the University of California at Santa Barbara.